GUITAR

A COMPLETE GUIDE FOR THE PLAYER

GUITAR
A COMPLETE GUIDE FOR THE PLAYER

A QUANTUM BOOK

This book is produced by
Quantum Publishing Ltd.
6 Blundell Street
London N7 9BH

ISBN 978-1-84573-380-3

QUMGACG

Printed in Singapore by
Star Standard Industries Pte Ltd.

ART DIRECTOR Nigel Osborne
DESIGN Paul Cooper
EDITORIAL DIRECTOR Tony Bacon
EDITOR Dave Hunter
PRODUCTION Phil Richardson

Origination by Global Graphics (Czech Republic)
Printed by Colorprint Offset Ltd. (Hong Kong)

GUITAR

A COMPLETE GUIDE FOR THE PLAYER

Quantum Books

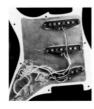

contents

GUITAR
INTRODUCTION

In this age of increasing specialization, it's encouraging to know that some disciplines still require you to be an all-arounder. To fulfil his or her potential, a guitarist today needs to be receptive to every element of the craft – from equipment technology to playing techniques. This book offers you that total awareness, and helps you hang on to it.

Learn what goes *into* your gear and you'll be able to get the most *out* of it: if you understand why different types of guitars, amps and pedals respond the way they do, it's easier to achieve that elusive objective – 'your sound' – or recreate the timeless tones of your guitar heroes.

Rather than dwelling on familiar histories of classic makes and models, *Guitar* concentrates on the basic specifications, components, and construction of the instruments – in short, the ingredients that make them sound and play as they do. This knowledge will help you choose the equipment that's right for you. Once the ideal instrument is in your hands, our thorough primer on care and maintenance will equip you to keep it in top playing condition – saving you years of set-up fees.

With the hardware covered, we move on to the central issue – the music. Most of today's popular playing styles are hectic brews of earlier genres; by grounding yourself in the skills behind each of these you can discover your potential as a fully-rounded, eclectically-minded guitarist, ready to specialize in any chosen genre. Immerse yourself in *Guitar*'s comprehensive tasters on ten seminal styles – and possibly discover a new love along the way – or just dip in as the mood suits, picking up fresh new licks, tricks and techniques as you go.

Finally, you need to talk the talk. It's hard to keep up if you don't speak the language. This book's illustrated glossary is the most comprehensive compendium of guitar-related terminology ever assembled – a priceless reference resource in itself. Fluency starts here.

Guitar: the more you understand it, the better you can play it.

"Unlike rosewood, maple accentuates the higher frequencies to produce a crisp, cutting sound. In the hands of a country star, the maple-bodied J-200 could double as a snare drum in the days when the Grand Ole Opry would not permit drums on stage."

"Gretsch, Guild and Harmony were among the many U.S. manufacturers who opted to champion the twin-cutaway cause, usually adding their own touches. Surprisingly, none initially perceived the benefit of adding a solid center block as Gibson did."

chapter 1

GUITAR
SOUND & CONSTRUCTION

Any good instrument is far more than the sum of its individual parts, but the design and materials used for each component – and the way they all come together – determine the sound and playability of your guitar. From the bright twang of a Tele to the warm wail of a Les Paul, this chapter tells how great guitars are built, and what factors shape their voices.

Excelling in moods that are mellow, mysterious, romantic and enchanting, yet able to exhibit startling aggression and impressive dynamic range in the hands of the right performer, the classical guitar manages simultaneously to be both the six-string world's highest achiever and its most undersung instrument. Whatever its generally accepted refinement, it is also often widely misunderstood by those who fail to probe the subtleties of its performance and construction – but is capable of an addictive allure for both player and listener.

Thanks to its obvious associations with classical music, we tend to think of the classical guitar as the somehow more noble and ancient member of the six-string family. In fact, although differently built and strung "guitars" were in existence since the end of the 15th century, the template for the classical guitar as we know it today goes back no further than that of the steel-strung flat-top, and is just a few generations senior to the modern archtop. Indeed, pioneering flat-top builder C.F. Martin was born a full 21 years before the father of the modern classical guitar, Antonio de Torres. By the 1850s both were making instruments which set molds for their type that are still referred to today.

As a musical instrument the guitar was traditionally a humble beast, even an outcast at times, more at home in the campsites and cornfields of the working classes than in the parlors and concert halls of the gentry. Its slow acceptance into the upper strata of the arts influenced its status as a late-bloomer among concert instruments, with far fewer virtuoso builders applying

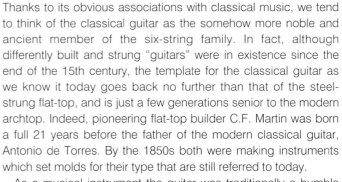

Among the most-prized woods used for soundboards today are (top, l-r): European spruce, Hokkaido spruce, and western red cedar (seen in a matt finish far right). For backs (bottom row): cypress, Brazilian rosewood (in both center photos) and Indian rosewood are highly valued.

A look inside this guitar from contemporary British luthier Paul Fischer reveals many of the most-used materials of the classical builder today: spruce top (here with "fan strutting"), rosewood back and sides, mahogany neck and ebony fingerboard.

their talents to the evolving six-string (then generally a four or five-string) than to violins or cellos – although there do exist two five-course guitars built by the great Antonio Stradivari of Cremona, Italy, and rare examples by other known master builders. From its earliest incarnations, however, the guitar proved its abilities both to express the emotions of players and win the hearts of listeners – whatever their social status. Louis XIV of France employed his own court guitarists, while Charles II of

1

American virtuoso Alice Artzt recorded her 1979 album of music by Tárrega (above left) on a guitar once thought to have been a Torres, but now considered to be from another maker. Andrés Segovia was an important endorser for builders from Ramírez III to German luthier Hermann Hauser; Brazilian duo Sergio and Eduardo Abreu also played Hausers.

England was so enamored of the instrument he took it up both as player and patron. Yet among concert musicians the guitarist long remained an underdog – in part, it has widely been acknowledged, due to the primitive form of the instrument prior to the 19th century. Yet, as with any means of expression that is passionately embraced, the enthusiasm of a growing rank of virtuoso musicians dragged the guitar from the peasantry to the performance stage, and inspired builders to design better and better instruments.

Prior to Torres, guitars were generally smaller, of shorter scale and had fewer frets than instruments we would recognise today. The Spanish luthier standardized the modern six-string by enlarging the body, increasing the scale length to the now-familiar 25½" (650mm), developing the internal "fan" bracing system that supports and strengthens the top, and refining the now-ubiquitous bridge/string anchor with its structurally integral but functionally separate saddle. Torres's approach proved so timeless that the raw materials which continue to comprise the majority of quality hand-built classical guitars today – spruce top, rosewood back and sides, cedar neck, ebony fingerboard (with some notable alterations in each case) – are little changed from the ingredients selected as best by Torres some 150 years ago.

With this template in mind, the primary constructional elements of the modern classical guitar include:

1. A top (known in the classical world as a "table") light enough and thin enough to resonate tonefully, but strong enough

British virtuoso Nicola Hall played a Smallman on her debut release, above…

… Which she borrowed from John Williams, the best known classical guitarist today.

1. 1882 TORRES
Materials: *solid two-piece spruce top; solid three-piece Brazilian rosewood back and rosewood sides; cedar neck with rosewood fingerboard.*
Features: *rosewood bridge with then-revolutionary separate saddle.*
Historical note: *this rare Torres was discovered in South America in 1989.*

2. 1992 SMALLMAN
Materials: *solid western red cedar top; laminated Brazilian rosewood back and sides; mahogany neck with ebony fingerboard.*
Features: *this builder from New South Wales, Australia, uses unusually thin tops on his guitars, supported with a unique latticework-style balsa and carbon fiber bracing.*

3. 1994 GILBERT
Materials: *solid western red cedar top; solid Indian rosewood back and sides; mahogany neck with rosewood fingerboard.*
Features: *Gilbert's ebony bridge is of an unconventional design, using individual 'pin' saddles for each string rather than the more common one-piece saddle.*

4. 1956 RAMÎREZ II
Materials: *solid two-piece spruce top; solid Brazilian rosewood back and sides (note inset photos); mahogany neck with ebony fingerboard.*
Historical note: *son of famed Spanish builder José Ramirez I, José Ramirez II built his guitars in his adopted home of Buenos Aires. His son Ramirez III carried on the tradition.*

2   3   4

classical guitars

11

While X bracing is almost universal on steel-string flat-top acoustics (below left), classical builders generally select between a Torres-inspired "fan-strut" system (bottom right) or a more modern technique of choice, such as Paul Fischer's "TAUT" latticework bracing system.

the ingredients selected as best by Torres some 150 years ago.

With this template in mind, the primary constructional elements of the modern classical guitar include:

1. A top (known in the classical world as a "table") light enough and thin enough to resonate tonefully, but strong enough to withstand the string tension of a full-scale neck.

2. Back and sides strong enough for structural rigidity but, like the top, light enough to be musically responsive.

3. A neck made of wood strong enough to withstand string tension but not so heavy as to impair the guitar's resonance.

4. A wide, flat fingerboard – often approaching or exceeding 2" (51mm) at the nut, versus a standard 1¾" for steel-string flat-tops – to aid fingering in the thumb-behind-neck playing position.

For many players today, the terms "classical guitar" and "nylon string guitar" are interchangeable but, while they both do bear the same types of strings, they can be greatly different instruments.

Built roughly along the lines of the proper classical guitar but without its refinement, the mere nylon-strung "folk" guitar is an instrument associated with the first lessons of the fledgling musician and pain-free playability for tender fingertips. Its tonality and build quality, however, are often indifferent at best. Ironically, cheap instruments aping the scale and dimensions of genuine classical models can turn off as many new players as they attract. Despite callus-friendly nylon strings, the wide neck and flat fingerboard of the design makes chording extremely difficult for unfamiliar hands, and the mellow tones that ultimately result may in no way resemble the bright, steely jangle of Bob Dylan or the bluesy wail of Stevie Ray Vaughan that first inspired the student to learn to play – before he or she was sold a "classical" guitar because it would be "easier to play."

Approached for what it is, however, the classical guitar yields some of the sweetest, subtlest tonalities in the instrument world. Whether plumbing classic compositions in the hands of John Williams, oozing mellow jazz melodies at the fingertips of Earl Klugh, or thrumming out pop-fusion arpeggios strapped around

Frédéric Zigante plays his 1987 Kohno on this recording of Giuliani's Le Rossiniane.

classical guitars

Even in the modern Alhambra factory in Muro de Alcoy, Spain, much of the more detailed work on classical guitars is still done by hand. Left, one craftsman shapes a headstock, while another makes final adjustments to the sides before gluing.

art of the classical guitar builder is a form which resolutely refuses to stagnate.

Meanwhile, other instruments offering affordable quality or revolutionary performance-aiding elements extend the feel and vibe of the nylon-stringed guitar through the jazz and pop worlds. An attainable excellence is championed, for example, in Japanese builder Kohno's distillation of master-grade luthiery into well-priced midrange guitars, while US giant Gibson's development of the easily amplified semi-solid thinline Chet Atkins models with piezo-pickup-loaded bridge saddles helps to further demolish the boundaries between musical genres.

form has been adapted and updated in workshops around the world, and continues to evolve as craftsmen seek the ultimate in acoustic tone and playability. Whether it's being refreshed and renewed in the "TAUT" bracing system of English luthier Paul Fischer, the "double body" construction of Spaniard Manuel Contreras, or Australian Greg Smallman's ultra-thin tops and supporting balsawood and carbon fiber latticework bracing, the

1. 1992 BERNABÉ
Materials: *solid European spruce top; solid European maple back and sides; mahogany neck with ebony fingerboard.*
Features: *back, sides and headstock facing of beautifully 'flamed' maple (less often seen in classical construction), with intricately detailed inlay work at soundhole rosette and delicate purfling.*

2. 1974 KOHNO
Materials: *solid Hokkaido spruce top; solid Brazilian rosewood back and sides; mahogany neck with ebony fingerboard.*
Features: *this high-end model from the Japanese builder (whose company also builds student-priced Sakurai guitars) features unusual dual ebony inlays at the back of the neck for strengthening purposes.*

3. 1990 GIBSON CHET ATKINS CEC
Materials: *semi-solid spruce-topped body with two 'tone chambers' for improved acoustic sound with low feedback; mahogany neck with ebony fingerboard.*
Features: *electro-acoustic bridge carries six under-saddle piezo pickups, each individually adjustable for volume; onboard preamp/EQ.*

4. 1934 ESTESO
Materials: *solid European spruce topped flamenco guitar; solid Spanish cypress back and sides; mahogany neck with ebony fingerboard.*
Features: *flamenco models such as this are generally more lightly constructed than their classical brethren; traditionally, they also feature wooden 'friction peg' tuners rather than geared machineheads.*

Virtuoso Pepe Romero (far left, above) plays a Rodriguez guitar on this 1970s recording.

5. 1976 RODRIGUEZ
Materials: *solid western red cedar top; solid Brazilian rosewood back and sides; mahogany neck with ebony fingerboard.*
Features: *as the inset photos demonstrate, this instrument features highly figured rosewood with distinctive stripes, which the builder supposedly salvaged from a church door.*

Manitas de Plata (left), whose name means "hands of silver," popularized flamenco guitar in the 1960s, while Paco de Lucia (center) revolutionized the art in the late '60s and '70s, taking it to an even wider audience. In the early '90s, pop-flamenco became a world craze at the hands of the Gipsy Kings (right).

4

5

classical guitars

The steel-string flat-top guitar can't scream with the intensity of an electric guitar, and it can't purr with the serenity of a nylon-string classical, but it can do everything in between – and otherwise offers plenty of voices unique to its breed.

Utter the word "guitar" and the flat-top acoustic is probably the instrument that comes to mind more than any other. It can lay down a steady rhythm, whether it's an easy strum on a country record such as The Eagles' *Lyin' Eyes* or the heavy strumming

that kicked off the rock'n'roll era on Elvis's *That's All Right*. It can sing out as a lead instrument on a melodic, finger-picked statement by James Taylor or a blazing, flat-picked run by Doc Watson. It can even serve up rhythm and melody at the same time. And all this versatility is accomplished by surprisingly few variations in design and materials.

Generally speaking, the bigger the body, the bigger the sound is going to be. Since the 1850s, when C.F. Martin developed the flat-top guitar that we know today, acoustic guitars have grown progressively larger as guitar-makers have tried to meet players' needs for louder instruments. Martin's largest size in 1854, designated by the numeral 0, was only 13" wide (measured across the widest part of the body). By 1916 Martin bodies had grown over two inches, to the 15⅝" D or dreadnought size (although it wouldn't appear with the Martin brand until 1932).

Gibson started small, too, with a 13" flat-top in 1926, but by 1938 the company was making a 17" Super Jumbo model. Other makers pushed on to the extreme, such as a 21" guitar made by the Larson Brothers of Chicago, but such behemoths went beyond the limits of practicality. Dreadnoughts and "jumbos" (Gibson's term for a 16" body) still dominate, although the advent of high-quality acoustic amplification has brought new popularity to the smaller, more comfortable sizes.

Martin and Gibson body shapes are the reference points for almost all steel-string flat-top bodies. Traditionally the most popular shape is the dreadnought, named after a British battleship that was the largest of its kind. A dreadnought guitar, such as a Martin D-18 or a Gibson J-45, is identifiable by its thick waist which makes it more box-like than other styles and contributes to a big, booming sound.

Gibson's jumbo body shape is identifiable by a circular lower bout. Although Gibson used the term jumbo as a size designation for any 16" guitar, most guitar people use it to describe the shape rather than the size. The shape is found on Gibsons ranging from the original 13" L-1 used by Robert Johnson to the 17" J-200 that is a badge of identification for many country stars.

Of the smaller body styles, Martin's 000, 15" wide with a pinched waist that gives it an hourglass look, has became one of

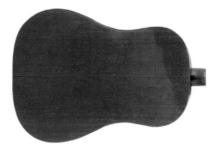

The exploded view of this steel-string flat-top displays the major constructional characteristics of the contemporary design. Note, in particular, the X bracing pattern underneath the thin spruce top, established as standard by Martin as long ago as 1850 and a major contributing factor to the breed's lively yet powerful sound.

The archaic-looking Martin & Coupa below, built in 1840, pre-dates the X-braced guitars Martin built just a decade later that would point the way forward for steel-string guitars. C.F. Martin had arrived in the United States just seven years prior to this. Far right, a Martin price list, probably circa 1870s.

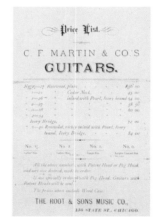

the most popular, due in no small part to Eric Clapton's use of a 000-42 on his MTV *Unplugged* appearance in the mid 1990s. In Clapton's wake, Gibson's 1930s L-00 style (14" wide with a slightly more elongated look than the Martin 000) has also made a comeback.

Woods that are suitable for the back and sides of a guitar are referred to as tone woods, and with good reason. More than any other factor they shape the tone of the instrument.

When practically all guitars had gut strings, Brazilian rosewood was the preferred wood for back and sides. It delivered a warm, rich tone that suited the guitarists' repertoire of semi-classical music. The changeover to steel strings in the 1920s, along with the move to larger guitars, only accentuated the sonic qualities of rosewood. Martin's rosewood dreadnought D-28, for example, has a booming bass sound as its calling card, and it is still the favorite of bluegrass players. Due to Brazil's restriction on

exporting unsawn rosewood logs in 1969, the great majority of rosewood guitars are now Indian rosewood.

Gibson approached the steel-string flat-top from a different direction than the classical tradition of Martin. Gibson's earliest guitars had been carved-top models conceived as members of the mandolin family. Gibson started with walnut backs and sides but soon settled on maple (or in some cases birch as a cheaper substitute) as the ideal tone wood. Although the company would make flat-tops in the years prior to World War II out of rosewood and mahogany as well as maple, their top model, the J-200, emerged after the war with maple back and sides. Unlike rosewood, maple accentuates the higher frequencies to produce a crisp, cutting sound. In the hands of a country star, the maple-bodied J-200 could double as a snare drum in the days when the Grand Ole Opry would not permit drums on stage.

Mahogany stands in the middle of the spectrum, offering some

Edna Leeper clutches a Martin D-28 with The Oklahoma Sweethearts in 1941.

1. '24 DITSON DREADNOUGHT STYLE
Materials: *two-piece solid spruce top; solid mahogany back and sides; slot-head mahogany neck with unbound ebony fingerboard (12 frets to the body); ebony bridge.*
Historical note: *built by Martin for the Ditson music stores in Boston and New York, who first suggested the design as far back as 1916.*

2. '38 GIBSON J-200 SUPER JUMBO
Materials: *solid spruce top; solid rosewood back and sides; mahogany neck with bound ebony fingerboard.*
Features: *rosewood 'mustache' bridge; Grover Imperial tuners.*
Historical note: *post-WWII, Gibson's biggest flat-top featured maple back and sides rather than rosewood.*

3. '41 MARTIN D-28
Materials: *solid spruce top; solid rosewood back and sides; mahogany neck (14 frets to the body) with ebony fingerboard.*
Features: *ebony bridge; herringbone trim.*
Historical note: *herringbone inlay (purfling) featured on pre-1947 D-28s; post-1969 Martins used Indian rosewood after Brazil embargoed exportation of its own highly-figured variety.*

In the early days, Elvis Presley thranged out his own rhythms on a Martin D-18.

Richard Thompson put his 000-18 to more eclectic use, as on this early '70s album.

1   2   3

of the low-end "warmth" of rosewood without sacrificing the high-end "brilliance" of maple. Mahogany is also cheaper than rosewood or maple, giving mahogany-bodied guitars an extra economic attraction.

Many other woods have been used for guitar bodies, such as koa, ash, walnut and cocobola, and each adds its own subtle differences to sound and tone.

The soundboard of a good flat-top has different requirements from its back and sides. Spruce has the best combination of strength and flexibility – the qualities required by the vibrating top of a guitar. There is an art to finding the right combination, however. The more the top can vibrate, the louder the sound will be, but the top must be a certain thickness to withstand the pull of the strings, which is about 175 pounds on a standard steel-string flat-top. Unfortunately, a top that thick won't do much

vibrating, so guitar makers have little choice but to use braces under the top in order to strengthen it without dampening the vibrations, which in turn allows them to use thinner and more toneful wood in the soundboard.

Most steel-string makers use some variation of an X-pattern of bracing developed by C.F. Martin by 1850. Cheaper guitars have used simple cross braces, known as "ladder" bracing, and this – more than any other element of flat-top construction – can be the difference between a good sounding guitar and a dud.

Even before ecological concerns prompted the search for alternatives to wood, guitar-makers experimented with new materials. Wood laminates made from thin veneers, for example, are cheaper and stronger than solid pieces. However, all things being equal, laminated wood doesn't perform as well as solid wood. Predictably, the earliest examples – particularly those with a laminated top – were inferior. Ovation pioneered the use of fiberglass for the back and sides of a guitar, utilizing sensitive aeronautical vibration-measuring devices in an attempt to quantify "good sound" and replicate it with the new designs and materials. In recent years, manufacturers have redesigned bracing systems and construction techniques specifically for laminates and man-made materials, and the quality of these guitars has risen.

Most guitars have a neck made from the same wood as the back and sides, except for rosewood-body guitars, which usually have a mahogany neck. Virtually all makers reinforce the neck with a metal rod (truss rod) that can be adjusted to change its curvature. Fingerboards are typically rosewood or, on more expensive models, ebony. The traditional manner of fastening the neck to the body is with glue by way of a large dovetail joint, although many contemporary makers now use some form of a

The wood used for the back and sides of a flat-top has a significant impact on its voice, and wise players choose accordingly. Maple (above, left) is bright and precise; rosewood (second from left) is warm and rich with a pronounced low end; mahogany (third from left) retains fair low-end presence with good high-end sparkle; the lesser-seen koa (far right) offers brightness blended with decent warmth.

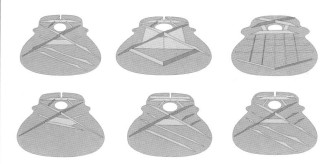

BRACING PATTERNS

The bracing pattern – that is, the configuration of struts glued to the underside of a guitar's top – plays an enormous part in shaping an instrument's tone. The six illustrations above come from C.F. Martin, and like them, most steel-string acoustic builders today use some derivation of the X-brace pattern. Variations (aside from extremes like the latticework system, top right) are found in the number of support struts and the precise position of the X in relation to the soundhole.

bolt-on neck. The critical factor regarding a guitar neck is rigidity. Although some woods are stronger than others, the reinforcing rod makes up for the difference. A neck that is not rigid enough will vibrate – not enough to make any noise, but enough to diminish the tone and sustaining quality that the guitar would

otherwise have.

In the early 1930s guitar-makers began offering musicians more playing room on the neck, putting 14 frets clear of the body rather than the 12 which is still the standard for classical guitars. However, a 14-fret neck requires either a smaller body length or different placement of the soundhole and bridge, and some musicians believe that the larger body of a 12-fret guitar (a Martin dreadnought 12-fret, for example) gives it a more desirable sound. Other players want even more accessibility in the higher registers of the neck, and they are willing to sacrifice or "cut away" part of the body to get it. Cutaway flat-tops began appearing shortly after World War II and have become more and more popular with advances in amplification.

The term "steel-string" covers a variety of string alloys and gauges. Different alloys – the metal content of the string wrappings – such as "80/20" (the ratio of copper to zinc) or "phosphor bronze" (a combination of copper, tin and phosphor), make for subtle differences in tone. Different gauges, however, make for great differences in performance. Heavier-gauge strings will be louder because they require more tension to reach

Martin body sizes form the most commonly used standards of flat-top size designation for many builders today. Shown below, left to right in ascending order of size, are the five most popular shapes.

1. '27 MARTIN 0-45
Materials: *solid spruce top and Brazilian rosewood back and sides on 13½"-wide body. Bound slot-head mahogany neck (12 frets to the body, 24⁹⁄₁₀" scale) with ebony fingerboard.*
Features: *ebony bridge; deluxe Style 45 abalone inlay.*

2. '38 MARTIN 00-21
Materials: *solid spruce top and Brazilian rosewood back and sides on 14½"-wide body. Unbound slot-head mahogany neck (12 frets to the body, 24⁹⁄₁₀" scale) with ebony fingerboard.*
Features: *ebony bridge; herringbone soundhole trim and back stripe.*

3. '36 MARTIN 000-28
Materials: *solid spruce top and Brazilian rosewood back and sides on 15"-wide body. Unbound mahogany neck (14 frets to the body, 24⁹⁄₁₀" scale) with ebony fingerboard.*
Features: *ebony bridge; herringbone body trim; snowflake fingerboard inlays.*

4. '33 MARTIN OM-45
Materials: *solid spruce top and Brazilian rosewood back and sides on 15"-wide body. Bound mahogany neck (14 frets to the body, larger 25⁶⁄₁₀" scale length) with bound ebony fingerboard.*
Features: *ebony bridge; deluxe Style 45 abalone inlay.*

5. '37 MARTIN D-18
Materials: *solid spruce top and solid mahogany back and sides on 15½"-wide body. Mahogany neck (14 frets to the body, larger 25⁶⁄₁₀" scale length) with unbound ebony fingerboard.*
Features: *rosewood bridge; rare sunburst finish on this example.*

Bryan Sutton applies a dread to some stunning flat-picking on this Ricky Skaggs release.

4

5

This 1990 Martin HD-28P is the 500,000th instrument built by C.F. Martin & Co and has been signed on the top by the entire workforce. At the time of printing – thanks to heavy production in the '90s – Martin is already closing in on its 800,000th instrument.

pitch (about 12 extra pounds) and exert more tension on the top of the guitar. The downside is that heavier strings make a guitar harder to play, especially if the added tension causes the neck to bow, raising the "action" or string height and adversely affecting intonation (although this can usually be compensated for by careful adjustment of the truss rod).

In the early 1900s, probably in response to the popularity of the mandolin (whose eight strings are arranged in pairs), the 12-string guitar appeared. Typically the four lower-pitched pairs are tuned in octaves and the higher two pairs are tuned in unison, which accentuates single-string-style picking and creates a powerful ensemble effect when the 12-string is strummed. However, the extra tension creates significant problems for the player, who has to develop extra hand-strength, as well as for the maker, who must strengthen the top bracing and the neck joint.

Guitar builders in the Martin factory display how hand-craftsmanship is still used in flat-top manufacture today – even by a company producing tens of thousands of guitars each year. Below, one for the road: the Martin Backpacker.

1. '90 TAKAMINE LTD-90
Materials: *solid bookmatched koa top with solid koa back and sides on cutaway dreadnought-shaped body; mahogany neck with bound ebony fingerboard.*
Features: *ebony bridge; gold-plated hardware; slotted diamond fingerboard inlays.*
Historical Note: *A specially designed Takamine 'Limited' series guitar made of different woods is offered every year.*

2. 1976 OVATION CUSTOM LEGEND
Materials: *solid spruce top with molded Lyrachord fiberglass bowl-back. Bound mahogany neck (14 frets to the body, 25.27" scale length) with ebony fingerboard.*
Electrics: *under-saddle piezo pickup and onboard preamp.*
Features: *abalone neck and binding inlays; deluxe rosette; 'pinless' rosewood bridge.*

3. 1987 MANSON SLIDESLAMMER
Materials: *two-piece solid spruce top; solid rosewood back and sides; mahogany neck (14 frets to the body) with unbound ebony fingerboard.*
Features: *Manson's 'Slideslammer' device to instantly raise nut for slide playing; acoustic B-string bender at bridge; ebony bridge; abalone inlay.*

4. 2000 TAYLOR PALLET GUITAR
Materials: *solid 'pallet-grade' oak for top, sides and neck. Ebony fingerboard and bridge.*
Features: *Abalone 'forklift' neck inlay; abalone rosette.*
Historical Note: *The first Pallet Guitar was made from scrap wood by Bob Taylor in 1995 to prove that it's the luthier's skill rather than the wood that determines a toneful guitar.*

5. '99 SANTA CRUZ MODEL D
Materials: *solid bookmatched spruce top with solid rosewood back and sides on a dreadnought-shaped design; mahogany neck (14 frets to the body, 25.34" scale length) with bound ebony fingerboard and ebony bridge.*
Features: *Schaller mini-tuner machineheads; mock tortoiseshell pickguard.*

6. '01 COLLINGS D-2H
Materials: *solid bookmatched spruce top with solid rosewood back and sides on a dreadnought-shaped design; mahogany neck (14 frets to the body, 25.5" scale length) with bound ebony fingerboard and ebony bridge.*
Features: *abalone snowflake position markers; herringbone purfling; mock tortoiseshell pickguard.*

1

2

3

Although there have been virtuosos on the 12-string – from Leadbelly to Leo Kottke – it is still considered a specialty instrument rather than a mainstream flat-top model.

The quest for true-sounding amplification of acoustic guitars began in earnest in the 1970s with the development of piezo-electric pickups and various specialized microphones (some mounted directly onto the instrument, others fitted inside). Amplifiers and, by the late 1990s, digital processors designed specifically for steel-string flat-tops advanced the cause and at the same time undermined the traditional demands on the guitar itself for exceptional volume and tone. Today a guitar with virtually no unamplified volume at all such as the "solidbody acoustic" (a solidbody, amplified guitar meant to sound like an acoustic) can be more desirable to some players in a concert or recording setting than the finest traditional acoustic, thanks to the instrument's ease of amplification and lack of feedback.

As a result of advances in amplification, guitar-makers can now design instruments that would not have been practical in earlier years, with smaller or oddly-shaped bodies and even solid bodies. Although there will always be a demand for guitars with outstanding natural acoustic qualities, the range of instruments that can be categorized as steel-string flat-top guitars is today wider than ever.

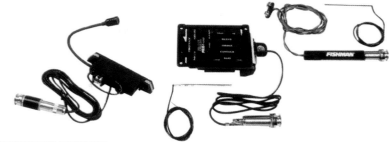

ACOUSTIC PICKUPS

The increasing popularity of using acoustic guitars in all forms of live performance has led to a boom in pickup development, and more makes and styles of acoustic pickups are available today than ever before. This selection from Fishman displays a good cross-section of the market, with something to cover most requirements.

The unit above-left is a blender-style system which includes the familiar soundhole-fitted magnetic pickup plus a miniature electret microphone on a small gooseneck to be positioned inside the guitar. Center is a Prefex Pro Blend system, which includes a piezo pickup strip, built-in mic, plus preamp unit with volume and EQ for onboard mounting. An even simpler system, the final unit consists of Fishman's under-saddle piezo strip plus a battery-powered preamp mounted in the end-pin jack housing, with no volume or EQ controls attached.

Steve Earle used a Santa Cruz Tim Rice model to belt out the rhythm on this bluegrass album.

4

5

6

flat-top acoustics

The acoustic archtop guitar is still very much rooted in tradition, with its strong violin design influences, and has been enchanting musicians since its inception 100 years ago. Played to create some of the most advanced music today, as well as some of the most traditional, the acoustic archtop – in its highest form – represents the epitome of the luthier's art.

Funk & Wagner ought to define the acoustic archtop guitar as "the consummate fretted instrument." That would be a somewhat biased view, but the archtop guitar is certainly enjoying a renaissance in the marketplace, and the influence of particular makers on others is quite obvious. D'Angelico's earliest guitars were direct descendants of Gibson's groundbreaking L-5, yet the

very popular Gibson Johnny Smith model was designed after a D'Angelico. Epiphone also followed Gibson's lead, as did Gretsch and Guild.

Other individual makers, too, have had an influence – and have been influenced by others in turn: Albanus's blend of D'Angelico's designs and Stromberg's single diagonal tonebar (the latter perpetuated by Bill Barker); the evolution of the ebony/brass-hinged tailpiece through Albanus, then Phil Petillo, then Jimmy D'Aquisto; D'Aquisto's development of segmented sound openings as used by German maker Artur Lang some 25 years before, and so on. This ebb and flow of ideas is not always the result of friendly sharing, but it's the way that the builder's art progresses – an evolution equally indebted to the collaboration of the player, who is after all the builder's most reliable and consistent link to reality.

Through all of these contributions, the archtop guitar continues to evolve at a slow but steady and energized pace. It is still primarily a jazz instrument and, to date, has not been truly embraced by other genres.

The voice of the archtop is of course a direct result of the acoustical design and materials used. It should be balanced so that the high notes are as "fat" and clear as the mid-range, blending with a rich bass – not at all typical of its flat-top cousin.

For the laboriously carved arched top plate (often known as the "top" or "face" of the guitar), spruce is most preferred. Redwood, cedar, pine or any other conifer will function equally as well. Spruce is an industry standard. It is readily available, affordable and easily marketable. From that point of view, there's not much incentive to use alternative woods.

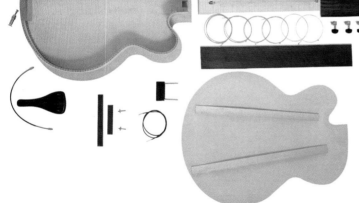

This disassembled jazz box reveals the key components of a carved-top acoustic archtop guitar. Note the parallel braces – making it a strong projector for rhythm playing – and the one-piece ebony tailpiece and two-piece bridge. Neck, back and sides are all of maple.

2

1

D'Angelico fan Johnny Smith captures the archtop's smooth tones for posterity.

Quarter-sawn, close and straight-grained stock is most desirable. Is there a difference in sound between close-grained and wide-grained spruce? Contrary to popular consensus, no – but close-grained cuts continue to get the nod.

The back plate (or simply, back) and matching ribs (sides) are traditionally made from flamed maple. Maple has two categories: soft and hard. The soft varieties are most desirable for carving the back, not necessarily because soft maple is easier to carve than hard, but because it's more acoustically responsive. It is one of many components which contribute to the rich, warm timbre of a well-made archtop guitar.

The wood used to make the neck can be either matching flamed maple or, by extreme aesthetic contrast, mahogany. Traditionalists will invariably prefer flamed maple. The hard American maples, with the obvious advantage of having stiffness and strength over and above that of the soft varieties, have long been the mainstay for neck construction. Ideally, the back, ribs and neck should have matching grain, flame and color.

Because of its many attributes, however, it's likely we will begin to see more use of mahogany. Unfortunately, mahogany has often been used for necks on less expensive guitars, while maple has enjoyed its regal status on the most expensive and prized instruments. Thus with mahogany comes a stigma rendering it a less desirable choice for necks – a "cheaper look." Interestingly, mahogany is far more stable than maple and lighter in weight, which, setting tradition aside, qualifies it as a better choice, especially on high priced instruments. Its lighter weight does certainly qualify its marriage to today's more lightly constructed modern bodies. Nevertheless, maple's beautiful flaming and luster helps to keep it the top choice for many builders and players alike.

Many great makers in the past have used what would be considered by today's standards to be inferior tone woods. Great notables, like Stradivari, Guarnieri, D'Angelico, Lloyd Loar and others have had great success using woods with irregular grain patterns, knots, and a variety of cosmetic blemishes.

1. '50 D'ANGELICO EXCEL
Materials: *solid carved spruce top on 17"-wide body with cutaway; maple back and sides; maple neck with ebony fingerboard.*
Features: *deluxe metal stairstep tailpiece; two-piece ebony bridge; abalone block fingerboard inlays; Grover Imperial tuners.*

2. '28 GIBSON L-5
Materials: *solid carved spruce top on 16"-wide non-cutaway body; maple back and sides; maple neck with ebony fingerboard.*
Features: *basic metal trapeze tailpiece; two-piece ebony bridge; dot fingerboard inlays; pearloid button tuners*
Historical note: *model conceived mainly by influential Gibson designer Lloyd Loar.*

3. '51 STROMBERG DELUXE CUTAWAY
Materials: *solid carved spruce top on 17¼"-wide body with cutaway; maple back and sides; maple neck with ebony fingerboard.*
Features: *deluxe engraved metal tailpiece; two-piece ebony bridge; abalone block fingerboard inlays; tulip-button tuners.*

4. '45 GRETSCH SYNCROMATIC
Materials: *solid carved spruce top on 18"-wide non-cutaway body; maple back and sides; maple neck with ebony fingerboard.*
Features: *metal stairstep tailpiece; two-piece stairstep ebony bridge; abalone 'hump-top' fingerboard inlays; 'cat's eye' f-holes; Grover Imperial tuners.*

Joe Pass – accompanying Ella Fitzgerald here – at one time played an Epiphone Emperor.

5. '54 EPIPHONE EMPEROR CUTAWAY
Materials: *solid carved spruce top on 18½"-wide cutaway body; maple back and sides; maple neck with ebony fingerboard.*
Features: *metal 'Frequensator' tailpiece; two-piece ebony bridge; abalone 'V-top' fingerboard inlays; deluxe multiple binding.*

Freddie Green cooked up a swingin' rhythm on his Gretsch Syncromatic for Count Basie.

Grant Green offers another take on the Epiphone archtop's sonic splendor.

3   4   5

In addition to tone woods, there are many other components and design factors which affect the outcome, one of which is bracing. Of the many possible bracing configurations, the "X" brace is most desirable, fitted to a top plate with a thickness of slightly less than ¼" under the bridge, and tapering toward both f-holes to a final thickness of approximately ³⁄₃₂" in the recurve. Conversely, the parallel bracing pattern fitted to a thinner top plate is better suited for acoustic rhythm guitar.

If we keep in mind that a lighter instrument produces a more responsive sound, then it is relatively easy to understand that a smaller Schaller mini tuning machine with ebony buttons will certainly have an advantage over the massive and considerably heavier Grover Imperial tuners that appeared on many high-end vintage guitars.

The ebony tailpiece, lighter in weight and acoustically superior to its metal counterpart, is now widely accepted among individual makers as an integral component of the acoustic archtop guitar. Nevertheless, at the time of this writing, there are – strangely – no production guitars fitted with a solid ebony tailpiece. Smaller headstocks, although not as fashionable to some, are another means of reducing weight from the

BUILDING AN ARCHTOP

The creation of a high quality, hand-built archtop guitar is one of the finest expressions of the luthier's art, requiring levels of skill that can be traced back to the classic violin makers. In the photos below Robert Benedetto, the author of this chapter and one of the world's most respected makers of acoustic jazz guitars, takes us inside his workshop for a look at some of the major steps in the construction process.

While the building of any high-end guitar – whether a flat-top, classical or solidbody electric – undoubtedly requires great craftsmanship, the touch, eye and "ear" needed to carve a well-tuned arched top and back are arguably unparalleled in the guitar-building world. While such labor-intensive construction methods translate to high purchase prices for the player, they also yield some of the sweetest, subtlest tonalities in acoustic guitar music. The finished guitar above, with a top of rough-sawn construction-grade pine, was built to prove the importance of craftsmanship over wood selection.

The quest for tone starts here: using a palm plane to shape the rough top arch.

Applying thumb pressure to the top arch as part of the tuning process.

Gluing the side braces. These will help hold the top and back in place.

Robert Benedetto hand-shaping the fingerboard radius with a belt sander.

Fitting neck to body – the guitar is finally starting to come together.

Buffing the finished guitar: the result will be a resonant, high-gloss finish.

1

2

archtop acoustics

instrument. Likewise, eliminating inlays and bindings also results in a more acoustical outcome. The soundholes of an archtop guitar can be of traditional "f" design or any number of variations. For the best acoustical balance, the traditional f-hole locations are optimal. Several new bridge designs have appeared in recent years, but none are real improvements as the small, lightweight , traditionally-shaped two-piece adjustable type has yet to be improved upon.

The most popular neck width has evolved to 1¾" at the nut. Although with no advantage in sound or intonation, the 25" fingerboard scale now overshadows the older, more traditional, 25½". A round shaped neck has always been, and remains, the preferred "feel" for the jazz artist.

String selection is of course a matter of personal preference, although pure nickel roundwound gauges .012–.052 are today's most popular choice. The preferred finish – and still the industry standard – is nitro-cellulose lacquer. Tried and true options are of course oil varnish and spirit varnish, the latter of which can be French polished. All of these variations yield great results. The intended result for the maker is a clear, thin protective coating with enough elasticity to allow the wood to vibrate freely, yet hard enough to buff or rub to a high gloss. Most modern hard poly or epoxy finishes are not at all suitable and will only serve to impair an otherwise good guitar's sound.

Amplifying the acoustic archtop requires more thought and planning than simply fitting it with an "electric guitar" pickup. Generally, a suspended mini-humbucker is preferred. It should be engineered to produce a sound similar to that of the guitar's natural voice: well-balanced, fat, and warm. It should blend with – and enhance – the guitar's acoustic voice.

---

1. '55 MACCAFERRI G-40
Materials: *plastic top, back and sides on 13¼"-wide flat-cutaway body; bolt-on steel-reinforced plastic neck.*
Features: *rosewood bridge.*
Historical note: *builder Mario Maccaferri had earlier designed the flat-topped Selmer Maccaferri Jazz model guitar, as used by the legendary Django Reinhardt.*

2. '42 GIBSON SUPER 400
Materials: *solid carved spruce top on 18"-wide non-cutaway body; maple back and sides; maple neck with ebony fingerboard.*
Features: *deluxe metal tailpiece; two-piece ebony bridge.*
Historical note: *this example exhibits Gibson's post-'40 shift from X-bracing to parallel.*

Accomplished jazzer Jimmy Bruno is a long-time player of Benedetto archtops.

3. BENEDETTO LA CREMONA AZZURRA
Materials: *solid carved spruce top on 18"-wide body; solid maple back and sides; maple neck with ebony fingerboard.*
Features: *ebony bridge, tailpiece and pickguard; floral design upper and lower bout soundholes.*
Historical note: *this guitar is a feature piece of the famous Chinery Blue Guitar Collection.*

4. '92 D'AQUISTO SOLO
Materials: *solid carved spruce top on 17"-wide non-cutaway body; flamed solid maple back and sides (see inset photo); bound maple neck with ebony fingerboard.*
Features: *ebony bridge, Brazilian rosewood tailpiece; ebony pickguard; minimalistic segmented soundholes and modernistic slotted headstock (but with rear-loaded tuners).*

5. '96 FENDER D'AQUISTO CUSTOM ULTRA
Materials: *solid carved spruce top on 17¾"-wide body; solid maple back and sides; bound maple neck with ebony fingerboard.*
Features: *ebony bridge and tailpiece; abalone block inlays. (This model was also built for the Chinery Blue Guitar Collection, by Stephen Stern in the Fender Custom Shop.)*

Seemingly anathema today to anything pertaining to heavy music, the electrified archtop acoustic gave birth to rock'n'roll. Even before Fender's "plank" and Gibson's "canoe paddle" were invented, the acoustic-electric was bringing jazz, blues and country swing guitarists out of the shadows – and before the fledgling solidbodies were fully accepted, it was still on hand to usher in a whole new way of playing.

Occasionally rather muddy of tone, lacking in sustain, prone to howls of feedback, the "electric Spanish" guitar, as it was generally first known, was nevertheless nothing short of a miracle in its day, and built the bridge to modern guitar music as we now know it. In the hands of a player like Charlie Christian – known for taking up Gibson's first electric model, the ES-150, almost from

its arrival in 1936 – it gave the guitarist a means of competing with the horn player as a soloist… and finally being heard doing so. We have never looked back.

The first electrified archtop models were essentially standard acoustic archtops with slightly adapted lap steel pickups bolted on to them. They retained the full-sized body and elaborate hand-carved spruce top, even though when amplified at the back of an orchestra in a large, crowded dancehall the tonal subtleties of the luthier's art weren't likely to be appreciated. Early production electrics from big makers like Gibson and Epiphone were still fully hand-built, but were generally somewhat low-end models compared to their upscale archtop-acoustic brethren. The makers saw no particular problem with this right from the start, because they still saw the electric guitarist as a fringe market, and even something of a novelty.

---

1. '37 GIBSON ES-150
Materials: *solid carved spruce top, maple back and sides on 16¼"-wide non-cutaway hollow body; mahogany neck with rosewood fingerboard.*
Electrics: *one single-coil Charlie Christian (blade) pickup; single tone and volume controls.*
Features: *basic trapeze tailpiece; two-piece floating rosewood bridge.*

2. '41 EPIPHONE ZEPHYR
Materials: *solid carved maple top, maple back and sides on 16⅜"-wide non-cutaway hollow body; maple neck with rosewood fingerboard.*
Electrics: *one single-coil Master pickup and Mastervoicer control system.*
Features: *basic trapeze tailpiece; two-piece floating maple/ebony bridge.*

3. '69 GIBSON SUPER 400CN
Materials: *solid carved parallel-braced spruce top, maple back and sides on 18"-wide cutaway body; maple neck with triple-bound ebony fingerboard (25½" scale).*
Electrics: *floating DeArmond pickup; pickguard-mounted tone and volume controls.*
Features: *deluxe engraved tailpiece; split-block inlays.*

4. '53 GIBSON ES-175D
Materials: *laminated maple top, back and sides on 16¼"-wide cutaway hollow body; maple neck, bound rosewood fingerboard (24⅜" scale).*
Electrics: *dual P-90 pickups with individual volume and tone controls; three-way switch.*
Features: *trapeze-shape tailpiece; floating two-piece rosewood bridge.*

5. '58 KAY BARNEY KESSEL ARTIST
Materials: *pressed spruce top and laminated back and sides on 16"-wide cutaway hollow body; maple neck with rosewood fingerboard.*
Electrics: *dual single-coil pickups with individual tone and volume controls; three-way toggle switch.*
Features: *Melita bridge; Grover Imperial tuners.*

6. '58 GUILD STUART X-550
Materials: *carved solid spruce top; maple back and sides; maple neck with bound ebony fingerboard.*
Electrics: *dual single-coil pickups with individual tone and volume controls; three-way toggle switch.*
Features: *engraved lyre-shape tailpiece; floating two-piece ebony bridge; abalone inlays.*

The first electric guitar hero, Charlie Christian, still impresses with his virtuosity.

A young George Benson puts a Gibson Super 400 through its paces.

1

2

3

acoustic-electrics

Gibson bosses gather round a gold-finish cousin of the company's ES-175, their first archtop with a laminated top. On its debut in 1949 the ES-175 had a P-90 pickup, developed just years before. Never as highly lauded as the humbucker, Gibson's single-coil P-90 is nevertheless the oldest pickup design still in popular use today. Known for a hot, raw sound with gritty highs and aggressive mids, if first appeared on Gibson acoustic-electrics in 1946, and in 1952 graduated – in its "soapbar" guise – to the new solidbody Les Paul model.

Robert Benedetto in the previous chapter, and as still preferred by many traditional jazz guitarists today.)

The burgeoning awareness that the electric guitar was indeed a breed apart, with different requirements and capabilities alike, led naturally to the notion that acoustic-electrics could be designed to accentuate their electric qualities – while making welcome cost savings through compromises in the acoustic department. Why go to the trouble and expense of hand-carving a spruce or maple top when you couldn't tell it from plywood after the body-mounted magnetic pickup and tube amp had dealt with the tone? In 1949 Gibson introduced its first electric with a pressed, laminated top in the form of the ES-175, which has since proved good enough for the likes of Joe Pass, Jim Hall, Pat Metheny and many others.

Of course, the cheaper production techniques were not widely publicized at the time. But as well as these savings at the factory, the use of laminated woods also gave the guitars a brighter, snappier edge than their predecessors, which suited amplification even better for many purposes. A number of rival manufacturers followed suit with laminated construction and it quickly became the standard for acoustic-electric archtops.

Still thought of first and foremost as a jazz box, and a rare breed in the rock arena – despite the efforts of noisemongers like Ted Nugent and Billy Duffy, or prog whiz Steve Howe – it behoves us to remember what a revolution-in-the-making the acoustic-electric was half a century ago or more in the hands of Scotty Moore, Chuck Berry, or T-Bone Walker.

Even top-of-the-line electric models like Gibson's ES-300 or Epiphone's Zephyr lacked such niceties as bound f-holes, deluxe trim and upgraded hardware found on the acoustic-only L-5 and Emperor that were their respective contemporaries. Of course, as players of these and other high-end models decided they wanted to be heard too, Gibson Super 400s, Gretsch Syncromatics and even D'Angelicos soon appeared with retro-fit pickups mounted to them. (At first these were generally of the less intrusive, "floating" neck- or pickguard-mounted variety, as described by

Jim Hall is a long-standing proponent of the 'plywood' topped Gibson ES-175..

4

5

6

It's difficult to conceive of rock without the solidbody electric guitar, even though the instrument was developed before that radical musical genre even existed. Plenty of early rock'n'roll was played on big-bodied archtops with pickups mounted on top (as discussed in the previous chapter), but their limitations were always clear. For real power with volume and attack, enough brightness to cut through the clutter, and a sound free from the severe restraints of feedback, solidbodys proved the only way forward.

They were scorned, jeered at, derided and generally shown little respect by the traditional guitar-playing masses of the day. But the introduction of early solidbody designs in the '30s and '40s and the arrival of the first mass-produced solidbody electric in 1950, the Fender Broadcaster, nevertheless represented a revolution in the making. The sound and the look and the sheer volume of popular music would never be the same again.

As with all of his early successes in the manufacture of electric instruments and amplification, Leo Fender arrived at the first mass-production solidbody guitar by a combination of careful R&D, clever artist liaison, and happy accident. A mere stylized rendering of the existing guitar, the Broadcaster (which by mid-1951 and forever after was known as the Telecaster) took the concept of the instrument back to the drawing board, preserving little more than its six strings, scale length and standardized tuning.

The essentially acoustic "electrics" by Gibson, Epiphone, Gretsch and others were great instruments but had inherent limitations that were still making it difficult for guitarists to step front-of-stage and seriously compete as soloists. The relatively dark, often muddy sound of these guitars could get lost amid the brass sections of large western swing orchestras and smaller jazz combos alike, and they were prone to howls of feedback when turned up loud enough to be heard in larger halls.

Leo Fender's Telecaster had improved pickups, a treble-enhancing, sustain-encouraging and highly adjustable bridge design, and resonant through-body stringing in a solid ash body. It combated all the limitations of the acoustic-electric and gave guitarists the chance to be heard on a grand scale. (Similar models followed from most of Fender's major competitors.) Furthermore, the rugged construction and the screw-off, screw-on repairability of nearly every part on the Telecaster made it a workhorse able to withstand the knocks of the road and be easily serviced when the need arose. Coupled with that, the instrument's slim, fast neck and easy action introduced exciting new levels of playability.

What could be simpler? As this view of a disassembled Tele-style guitar shows, the ingredients of a standard bolt-on solidbody instrument require significantly less craftsmanship and sheer workshop sweat to whip into shape than, for example, a hand-carved archtop or quality flat-top acoustic. The results, nevertheless, have fueled rock history.

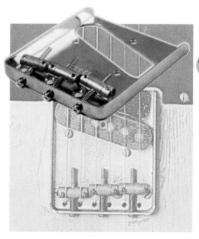

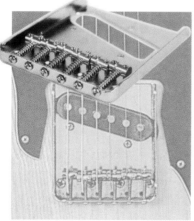

Albert Lee set the frets afire for Head Hands & Feet on, first, a Fender Tele, then a Music Man.

Any guitar's bridge contributes to its sound, but the original Telecaster unit has a character all its own. Brass bar saddles on early models add bite and sustain, while the steel pickup-mounting plate gives zing and twang to the tone. Of course the three-saddle design limits intonation accuracy, too, so many later bridges were upgraded to six saddles for full adjustability. Some purists argue, however, that the original with three brass or steel saddles yields the truest Tele tone.

1   2

solidbodies

WOOD SHED

The wood(s) used to make a guitar's body play a major part in the instrument's sound: 1. swamp ash offers solid lows and sparkling highs, with somewhat scooped, open mids; 2. alder produces a thicker midrange, with firm lows and enough high-end articulation to cut through; 3. mahogany tends toward a dense and warm tonality, combining gutsy lows and powerful mids; 4. basswood produces even, balanced frequency response with a full midrange; 5. the "classic combination" – mahogany body with maple top – offers dense, powerful mids with good definition and balanced high and low response.

Originally devised to save labor and make repairs or replacement simpler, the bolt-on-neck guitar (the neck is in fact screwed on in most cases) has a tonality all its own. It offers a bright, edgy, cutting tone (the classic "twang"), a woody resonance, and decent natural sustain (particularly from through-body designs), as well as a good tuning stability.

Not only did the new era in guitar construction help make the guitar the star in dozens of popular country and swing bands, it saw the electric guitar virtually taking the job of an entire orchestra, ushering in guitar groups (typically two guitars, a bass and drums) that would change the face of popular music forever and pave the way for rock'n'roll. More than merely a point of evolution in the look and feel of the instrument, however, the solidbody electric triggered a giant leap in the sound and power of the guitar-based band. There was little point developing large, high-powered amplifiers when guitars would only squeal with feedback after a certain volume was reached. With the solidbody, suddenly the sky was the limit in amp design – and in the volume wars the guitar was the new victor.

Since those early days countless other brands have followed the form of Fender's production-line original, and it has proved – with a number of variations – to be one of the most successful templates for the solidbody electric guitar.

1. '53 FENDER TELECASTER
Materials: *solid swamp ash body; bolt-on one-piece maple neck/fingerboard; 25½" scale.*
Electrics: *dual single-coil pickups; single volume and tone control; three-way switch (originally selecting neck p'up with bassy sound, neck p'up with tone control; bridge p'up).*
Features: *through-body stringing; brass saddles.*

A rosewood-neck early '60s Tele provides Steve Cropper's signature tone with the MGs.

2. '63 FENDER CUSTOM TELECASTER
Materials: *solid bound ash body; bolt-on maple neck with rosewood fingerboard.*
Electrics: *dual single-coil pickups; single volume and tone control; three-way switch (switch selections as on '53 Tele description, left).*
Features: *through-body stringing; threaded steel saddles; three-ply pickguard.*

3. '77 MUSIC MAN STINGRAY I
Materials: *solid two-piece alder body; bolt-on maple neck and integral 22-fret maple fingerboard.*
Electrics: *dual humbucking pickups; bass, treble and volume controls; four-way rotary switch and active preamp switch.*
Features: *through-strung non-vibrato 'hardtail' bridge.*

4. '94 ERNIE BALL/MUSIC MAN ALBERT LEE
Materials: *solid ash body; bolt-on maple neck with maple fingerboard cut from same timber.*
Electrics: *three single-coil DiMarzio pickups; single volume and tone control; five-way switch.*
Features: *through-body stringing; six-saddle bridge; four/two headstock layout.*

A lifetime Tele man, Roy Buchanan shows what Leo's creation can do.

The designs of many the single-coil pickups in use today – in basic technical terms – are largely unchanged from those seen at the dawn of amplification, but there are many variations on the theme. The classic Tele bridge pickup is biting, snappy and punchy, while its neck-position partner is mellower and more rounded in tone. Vintage Strat units tend toward the thin and edgy, with piercing highs. Now seen on plenty of bolt-neck guitars too, the Gibson-style humbucker is characteristically fat, warm and powerful.

Telecaster bridge pickup

Tele neck pickup (covered)

Strat pickup (uncovered)

Gibson-style humbucker

3

4

Gibson's Les Paul managed to do most everything that Fender's Telecaster could do, if somewhat differently (see following pages). So Fender needed a new trick to bring the spotlight back in their direction. In 1954, with the launch of the Stratocaster, they found it. While the Tele set the prototype for bolt-neck solidbody electrics, the Strat took the format right out of this world, introducing the most-played and most-copied electric guitar design of all time.

Aside from its radical shape, if the Strat had been fitted with Tele pickups and hardware it would have sounded and performed much like a Tele. But two major areas of design development significantly altered the instrument's sound and playability.

The first innovation came in the Strat's electronics. Ostensibly much like the single-coil units on the Telecaster, new pickups were developed by Fender for the Stratocaster. They were brighter, with sharper highs (though often somewhat less powerful than the Tele

bridge unit) in an era when cutting through a muddy bandstand "mix" in order to be heard was a key priority. Also, the three-pickup switching with dual tone controls offered a broad range of voices.

Second, there was an even more radical advance: the Strat's fully-adjustable self-contained "tremolo" tailpiece. This allowed more down-bend than any previously available production unit, in an age when heavier string gauges made left-hand bends more difficult, and offered reasonable tuning stability when set up correctly. Even when not in use it changed the guitar's core tonality, shifting the path of string routing and tapping off some of the acoustic resonance through a bridge block and the unit's associated springs.

The Strat vibrato – now taken for granted – ushered in a whole new range of playing styles, from the new hard-twang country styles, through the sproingy, heavily vibrato'd surf instrumentals of

---

1. '56 FENDER STRATOCASTER
Materials: *solid ash body in two tone sunburst; bolt-on maple neck with integral 21-fret maple fingerboard; 25½" scale.* **Electrics:** *three single-coil pickups; tone controls for neck and middle p'up; master volume; three-way switch.* **Features:** *vibrato tailpiece with internal rear-mounted springs single ply white pickguard.*

No single player displayed the Strat's capabilities better than Jimi Hendrix.

2. '61 BURNS BISON
Materials: *solid alder body; one-piece un-bound bolt-on maple neck and rosewood fingerboard.* **Electrics:** *four single-coil 'Super Sonic' pickups; four-way selector; mode switch; volume control.* **Features:** *Burns vibrato.* **Historical note:** *Britain's answer to the Strat in its rare four-pickup incarnation.*

3. '89 IBANEZ RADIUS 540R
Materials: *solid alder body; one-piece un-bound bolt-on maple neck and rosewood fingerboard.* **Electrics:** *single F1 humbucking pickup in the bridge position plus two C1 single coils; single volume and tone, five-way selector.* **Features:** *Ibanez-made locking vibrato tailpiece.*

4. '97 JACKSON STEALTH TH2
Materials: *solid ash body; glued-in maple neck with unbound 22-fret rosewood fingerboard.* **Electrics:** *two Jackson humbucking pickups plus center-position single coil; master vol and tone; five-way selector.* **Features:** *two-post Jackson vibrato bridge.*

5. '89 G&L COMANCHE
Materials: *solid swamp ash body; bolt-on maple neck with unbound 22-fret rosewood fingerboard.* **Electrics:** *three G&L single-coil-style hum-rejecting 'Z-coil' pickups; five-position selector plus mini toggle switch for neck+bridge or all three p'ups.* **Features:** *G&L 'dual fulcrum' vibrato bridge; GraphTech string tree.*

Blueser Stevie Ray Vaughan squeezed hot, wiry tones from his beloved Stratocasters.

An Ibanez 'superstrat' proves the weapon of choice for Joe Satriani's virtuoso shred-rock.

1   2   3

solidbodies: bolt-on neck

**Vintage style
Strat vibrato**

**Modern two-post
vibrato**

**Floyd Rose-style
locking vibrato**

In developing the ingenious vibrato tailpiece for the 1954 Stratocaster, Leo Fender listened to musicians' requests, and worked to build what they wanted. The result was a self-contained unit with full adjustability and impressive down-bend. Improvements on the theme have included two-post knife-edged fulcrum designs for improved tuning stability, and locking units for serious rock divebombing action.

Just another solidbody? On the contrary, Danelectro's famous minimalistic look appears solid outside, but the body hides a lot of airspace between the hardboard front and back and central solid wood core. Like this reissue U-3, most are characterized by a bright, thin tonality with ringing highs and somewhat limited sustain.

the early '60s, to Hendrix's wild divebombing and air-raid effects. Taken to new levels in subsequent decades by the likes of Eddie Van Halen and Jeff Beck, it has proved one of rock's most expressive tools.

In purely visual terms, the Stratocaster has become a design icon honored and loved even by non-guitar players, and has a surprisingly timeless appeal. More than just a radical stylistic coup, however, the Strat's body contouring made it a more comfortable, even intimate instrument to play. The upper back contour made it easier to tuck in under the ribcage for long sets, while the chamfer at the top of the lower bout braced the player's right forearm without cutting into it as a Les Paul or Tele's square edges did.

As familiar as we are today with the Strat's look, sound and feel, any consideration of the inherent "rightness" of all its ingredients reminds us once again of what a great leap forward Leo Fender's second solidbody represented at the time.

The Strat has been the subject of countless upgrades and modifications, most of which have evolved into production models available off-the-shelf, including single and dual-humbucker models, locking nut and vibrato, deluxe wiring and switching layouts and other "superstrat" configurations. It remains the most emulated basic template for the solidbody electric some 50 years after its arrival – and, in most cases, without straying radically from its original form.

NECK WOODS & FRETS
Not as influential on a guitar's overall tone as its body wood, the neck wood can nevertheless add its own special flavor to the brew. (Below, L-to-R: maple; rosewood; mahogany.)
1. A solid maple neck (with maple fingerboard) lends tightness and definition to both the low and high end, bringing notes into sharp focus.
2. In the maple neck/rosewood fingerboard combination, the rosewood lends some roundness and looseness which can be perceived as a louder bottom end and more "sizzling" highs.
3. A mahogany neck with rosewood fingerboard – the classic Gibson combination – is characteristically full and warm, with a balanced response. An ebony fingerboard, the other most common variable (and usually found on a mahogany neck in solidbodies), adds note definition and clarity – and makes for an extremely hard-wearing option.

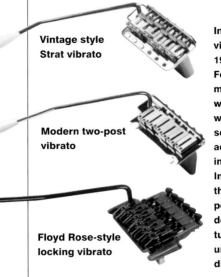

Fret widths also affect the guitar's feel and – some say – tone. High, narrow frets (below left) offer good chording and accurate noting; wider frets (center) are more bend-friendly. Some players believe wide, low frets (right) also allow more neck resonance into the sound, though it's much debated.

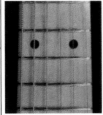

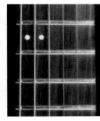

4

5

solidbodies: superstrats

29

Distinguished not only by their glued-in or bolt-on neck/body join, the differing neck angle between traditional Fender-style and Gibson-style guitars gives them very different playing feels. Note how the Les Paul's neck leaves the body at a much steeper pitch than the near-parallel Strat neck.

Strap on a Les Paul today and one thing comes instantly to mind – and fingers: rock. It's incredible to think, then, that when the model arrived in 1952 there was no such music. Gibson's premier solidbody was a response to the growing success of the Telecaster. But, mindful of their reputation and eager to tap a market with more traditional players still put off by Fender's bolt-together radicalism, Gibson wasn't about to offer their own slab-styled canoe paddle.

Instead, Gibson applied its skill with carved archtop "jazz" guitars to a maple cap atop a solid mahogany body, sticking with their time-tested set neck construction, and attaching a pair of the P-90 pickups already in use on hollowbody f-hole models in the late-'40s. In this way, Gibson arrived at the "other electric" – the archetype for the solidbody with glued-in neck. Perceived as more classy, with a big nod toward tradition but with all the

power needed to pump out the new music, the Les Paul has evolved in many directions, but remains the third significant electric-guitar blueprint. Several elements define its character.

Perhaps most important is the Les Paul's body construction. The chunky mahogany slab lends sustain and a generally warm, rounded resonance to the tone, given a degree of brightness and "cut" by the maple top. Tonally, the glued-in neck aids sustain and sonic depth somewhat, and can introduce a certain darkness to the overall sound. As for playability, Gibson's neck pitch, or angle to the body, which is significantly steeper than that of Fender's, brings the neck more within reach of the left

1. GIBSON LES PAUL STANDARD
Materials: *solid mahogany body with two-piece carved maple top; glued-in mahogany neck with bound 22-fret rosewood fingerboard; 24¾" scale length.*
Electrics: *dual humbucking pickups with individual vol and tone controls; 3-way switch.*
Features: *stop tailpiece and Tune-o-matic bridge.*

2. '58 GIBSON LES PAUL JUNIOR
Materials: *double cutaway solid mahogany body; glued-in mahogany neck with unbound rosewood fingerboard; 24¾" scale length.*
Electrics: *one P-90 single-coil pickup; single vol and tone control; 3-way toggle switch.*
Features: *wrapover 'stop' tailpiece/bridge; Kluson tuners; yellow 'TV' finish.*

Who said 'fat tone?' The LP that sealed it for the Les Paul and British blues-rock.

3. '59 GIBSON FLYING V
Materials: *solid korina body; glued-in korina neck with unbound rosewood fingerboard.*
Electrics: *dual 'Patent Applied For' (PAF) humbucking pickups; individual volume and master tone controls; 3-way toggle switch.*
Features: *through-body stringing via 'V' tailpiece; Tune-o-matic bridge; Kluson tuners.*

4. '59 GIBSON LES PAUL SPECIAL
Materials: *double cutaway solid mahogany body; glued-in mahogany neck with unbound rosewood fingerboard; 24¾" scale length.*
Electrics: *dual P-90 single-coil pickups; individual volume and tone controls; 3-way switch.*
Features: *wrapover 'stop' tailpiece/bridge. Plastic-button Kluson tuners.*

5. '97 PRS ARTIST III
Materials: *solid mahogany body with bookmatched quilted maple top; one-piece mahogany neck with rosewood fingerboard; PRS's regular 25" scale length.*
Electrics: *dual humbucking pickups; five-way rotary switch; master tone and volume.*
Features: *PRS wrapover bridge; abalone-bound neck and headstock.*

1

2

BRIDGE WORK
The bridge and tailpiece used on a set-neck solidbody have a lot to say in determining its sound. The simple one-piece Gibson-style wrapover unit – the original hardware for this type of guitar if you exclude the ill-conceived "wrap-under" trapeze tailpiece of the first Les Pauls – has long been admired by tonehounds for its stability and solid, resonant string anchoring, but has clear limitations for intonation adjustment. PRS's update of the type was designed for improved intonation. The classic stop tailpiece/Tune-o-matic combination offers solidity with precise intonation adjustment. If wobbles are desired, a Bigsby fits the bill – though tone can suffer due to lost string tension over the bridge.

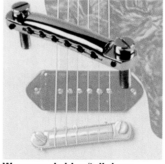

Wrapover bridge/tailpiece.

PRS wrapover bridge.

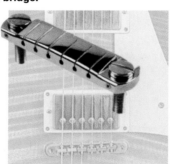

Tune-o-matic bridge.

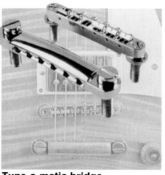

Bigsby with Tune-o-matic.

solidbodies: set-neck

hand, which some players find more comfortable. The slightly shorter 24 3⁄4" scale, meanwhile, also makes it somewhat slinkier and more bend-friendly than Fender's 25 1⁄2" scale length. However, the glued-in neck construction makes repairs and major adjustments difficult and often costly.

As for electronics, a Les Paul fitted with P-90 pickups is biting and edgy, with gritty highs and punchy mids. With humbuckers, it's generally a smooth, warm, powerful and sustaining guitar. Either way, output is hotter than standard Fender-type single-coil pickups, driving tube amps into distortion more quickly.

Other post-Les Paul Gibson-style solidbodies such as the Les Paul Special and Junior, Flying V, Explorer and SG, along with roughly similar designs from other makers, leaned more toward slab body construction, cut from a single type of wood and without the Les Paul's elaborate carved maple top. While the voice of some of these guitars is determined by body and neck woods, the set-neck join which they share with the Les Paul still lends them a round, warm and full-throated tonality, particularly when partnered with humbuckers.

Today, myriad combinations of bolt-on and set-neck designs provide tonal performance and playability that range between the two camps. PRS offers some roughly Gibson-like designs with bolt-on necks; big rock-axe companies like Jackson or Ibanez build superstrat-style models with set-necks, hot humbuckers and double-locking vibratos. With the borders demolished, it's no longer simply a matter of choosing between Fender and Gibson.

Gluing together bookmatched maple tops at the PRS factory.

Before the neck is fretted, the 10" fingerboard radius is applied.

Pre-cut frets are hand-installed and pushed into the radiused fretboard.

Finally, PRS "robots" buff the finished body to a high sheen.

One respected latter-day builder, Paul Reed Smith, manages to come close to doing most of the sonic and stylistic tricks previously ascribed to one side or the other of the set-neck/bolt-neck divide. A single PRS guitar can run the gamut from Les Paul-like warmth and power to Strat-like cut and twang – while excelling at a range of voices in between. A look inside the PRS factory, above, reveals the cohabitation of computer-aided assembly techniques and tried-and-tested hand craftsmanship. In addition, PRS were among the first production builders to extend the use of dramatic natural wood figure – in flamed, quilted and tiger-striped maple tops particularly – combined with striking translucent finishes, as illustrated below.

3   4   5

solidbodies: set-neck

According to the prophecies of makers such as Ibanez, Yamaha, Alembic, Carvin and a number of others in the late '70s and early '80s, the through-neck guitar was the way of the future. They preached about added constructional stability, increased resonance and sustain, and an all-around improved instrument. The through-neck guitar was being touted as the new top of the line, the crème de la crème, the ultimate evolution of the solidbody electric guitar.

So what happened? Not a lot. Just as through-neck designs existed well before the 1970s, they continue to be built today, but they've always been at the fringe of constructional techniques. Three things seem to account for this. First, the manufacturing complexities required of some designs didn't justify any

"improvements" gained over set-neck guitars – improvements that are, arguably, negligible anyway. Second, according to some builders and players, the apparent advantage of a central body core and neck carved from the same piece (or laminated pieces) of wood only proved detrimental to tone. And third? Well, these old bolt-on and set-neck guitars that were lying around all sounded pretty good already. Why go to the trouble of redesigning the wheel?

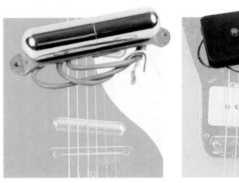

Danelectro's lipsick tube.   **Fender's Jazzmaster pickup.**

Fender Strat and Tele-style single coils and Gibson-style humbuckers may have set the templates for the majority of pickup derivations found today, but a number of quirkier units have made their mark on music history, and found fans in particular genres. Danelectro's bright, wiry lipstick pickup and Fender's punchy, rounded Jazzmaster unit have both been favorites of the new wave, indie and alternative camps.

Slide supremo Johnny Winter gets it on with a 'reverse-body' Gibson Firebird.

1

Thin and toppy? Pah! Pete Townshend let his Ricky go wild with The Who.

2

3

Used as a marketing tool around 1978, a "through-neck" hailed the ultimate in tone and sustain. In reality, many players noticed no quantifiable improvement in resonance, power or general sound over glued-in or even bolt-on necks. Interestingly, many classic makes and models of solid or semi-acoustic electrics that employed through-neck construction in the late '50s and early '60s, notably a number of Rickenbackers and Gibson's first "reverse body" Firebirds, usually did so without calling much attention to the fact.

There's little doubt, though, that the integral neck/body core design lends great structural stability to a well-built guitar, and the mere fact of the effort required to build a quality instrument using this technique generally signals that extra craftsmanship has gone in elsewhere, too. And the strength of such a neck makes it easier to design a guitar with deep cutaways and excellent upper-fret accessibility since it's no longer necessary to leave enough solid body wood free from the upper and lower cutaway to secure a sturdy neck join.

In any case, the major through-neck designs offered from the 1970s onward tended to be high-end models, and generally powerful, weighty, humbucker-loaded guitars aimed at the rock or fusion player. Yamaha's SG-2000, first introduced in 1976 and reissued recently (though always available in Japan), was the first Japanese guitar to gain wide acceptance among Western pros, with an important early endorsement from Carlos Santana.

Even before this, Alembic – best known for deluxe active-electronics basses – were building some of the most expensive production solidbodies then available, all with through-neck designs, exotic woods and elaborate active electronics. These designs further inspired more affordable models from Ibanez, Carvin and others… until the way forward was found by looking backward to "retro" fashions.

---

1. '65 GIBSON FIREBIRD V
Materials: *solid mahogany through-neck/body core with mahogany body 'wings' in original 'reverse body' style; bound rosewood fingerboard.*
Electrics: *dual covered mini humbucking pickups; individual volume and tone controls; three-way toggle switch.*
Features: *vibrato, Tune-o-matic bridge; banjo tuners.*

2. '61 RICKENBACKER 460
Materials: *bound maple body with maple through-neck and rosewood fingerboard.*
Electrics: *dual single-coil 'toaster-top' pickups; individual volume and tone controls; three-way lever switch; Rick-O-Sound (stereo) blender control.*
Features: *shark fin position markers.*

3. '59 RICKENBACKER 360
Materials: *semi-solid maple body with maple/mahogany laminated through-neck and rosewood fingerboard.*
Electrics: *dual single-coil 'toaster-top' pickups; individual volume and tone controls; three-way lever switch.*
Features: *'cooker' control knobs; two-tier gold plastic pickguard.*

4. '78 ALEMBIC SERIES I
Materials: *carved solid body of exotic hardwoods including walnut and others; laminated 'sandwich' through-neck of maple and walnut, with 24-fret unbound rosewood fingerboard.*
Electrics: *low impedance single-coil pickups with rotary selector and low-Z XLR out.*
Features: *brass nut & saddles.*

5. '84 YAMAHA SG-2000S
Materials: *bound solid mahogany body with carved maple top; bound laminated maple/mahogany through-neck with ebony fingerboard.*
Electrics: *dual humbucking pickups; individual vol and tone controls with push/push coil taps; three-way switch.*
Features: *brass sustain block mounted under bridge.*

6. '78 IBANEZ MUSICIAN MC500
Materials: *solid walnut/maple/walnut body with maple/mahogany laminated through-neck and ebony fingerboard.*
Electrics: *dual humbucking pickups; active on-board preamp and coil-split switching.*
Features: *brass bridge and tailpiece; abalone vine inlays.*

Carlos made that note sustain for days on his SG-2000 with early-'80s era Santana.

4

5

6

Are you seeking the power and versatility of a solidbody electric but with some of the vibe of an archtop jazzer – or just desperate for a little weight reduction? Step this way. The dictionary defines the prefix "semi" as meaning half or partially, hence its use in descriptive terms such as semi-detached and semi-precious. When applied to the electric guitar it is generally associated with the words "acoustic" or "solid," and in each case the description refers to the method of construction involved. However, the two terms do actually overlap to some extent and on some instruments the distinction is sufficiently blurred so that either definition can be correct.

The designation "semi-acoustic" relates to an instrument that usually employs the same or similar frontal dimensions as those of a full-size acoustic-electric – although proportions may be more compact – but with significantly slimmer body depth. The amount of air within can vary considerably; some guitars described as "semis" (incorrectly, technically speaking) are completely hollow, while others incorporate differing quantities of internal timber, ranging from small reinforcing blocks to full-length or full-width solid sections.

Those electrics that contain an appreciable amount of wood rather than open space may also be described as "semi-solid," which is where the duplication of terminology arises. On a strictly solid guitar, the body mass has a major effect on tonal properties

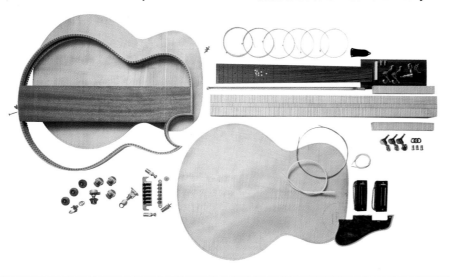

Most players know what is meant by the term "semi," though they may be coming at it from opposite directions. This photo of the constituent parts of a semi-acoustic electric reveals the solid mahogany block between the arched top and back of an otherwise hollow body.

Looking, from the front, every bit a full-bodied jazzer like the Super 400CES or L-5CES, Gibson's Byrdland was among a trio of "thinline" electrics launched in 1955 which reduced the standard body depth of approximately 3½" to nearer 2". Still a hollowbody instrument – as were its new thinline cousins the ES-225T and ES-350T – it showed the early evolution of Gibson's thinking toward semi-acoustic lines with a bid to improve playing comfort and reduce feedback while still retaining some of the feel and look of a traditional archtop.

1

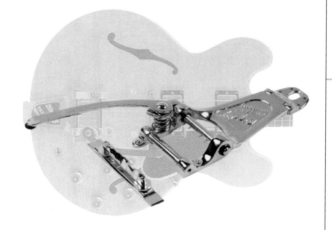

BIGSBY VIBRATO

Though it has made an appearance on most styles of electric guitar over the years, the Bigsby is the vibrato tailpiece of choice for the semi-acoustic. A rather crude device mechanically – causing tuning instabilities unless set up well and allowing pitch bends of only a semitone or so – it nevertheless has a distinctive sound loved by many players.

and sustain, while the inherent natural sound of a full-depth acoustic-electric exerts a great influence on the character of its amplified output.

In keeping with its name, the semi (whether considered acoustic or solid) represents something of a halfway house between the two. The idea is that the resonance created in the hollow chambers of the body audibly contributes to the overall amplified performance. Even playing a semi "unplugged" should reveal a louder acoustic response than that derived from a solid six-string, although it's still appreciably less than the volume produced by a deep-bodied, all-hollow equivalent. But this will of course only be of minimal importance when it comes to practical performance, because an amplifier will naturally negate any such discrepancies in volume.

Warranting much greater consideration are the overtones generated, because these can have a discernible effect on the

1. '57 GIBSON BYRDLAND
Materials: *thinline hollow body with laminated spruce top and maple back and sides; maple neck with ebony fingerboard.*
Electrics: *dual single-coil 'alnico' pickups, with individual volume and tone controls; three-way toggle switch.*
Features: *trapeze tailpiece and floating Tune-o-matic bridge.*

2. '55 GRETSCH CHET ATKINS
Materials: *hollow body with laminated maple top, back and sides; maple neck with bound rosewood fingerboard.*
Electrics: *dual single-coil DeArmond pickups with individual volume controls, master tone, master volume and three-way selector.*
Features: *fixed Bigsby vibrato.*

Chet's fluid style perfectly spotlights the semi's warm yet articulate tone.

3. '59 GIBSON ES-335TN
Materials: *semi-hollow body of laminated maple with mahogany center block; mahogany neck with bound rosewood fingerboard.*
Electrics: *dual 'PAF' humbuckers, with individual volume and tone controls; three-way toggle switch.*
Features: *Bigsby vibrato and Tune-o-matic bridge.*

An ES-335 (among others) proved to have power aplenty for Cream-era Clapton.

4. '61 HOFNER VERITHIN
Materials: *hollow body of laminated spruce and other woods; laminated maple neck with bound rosewood fingerboard.*
Electrics: *dual single-coil pickups with master vol and tone controls and 'Solo' switch.*
Features: *Bigsby vibrato and floating Bigsby bridge.*

Former Suede guitarist Bernard Butler used an ES-335 for his fiery indie riffs.

end results – although it must be said that the differences so derived are more marked with some guitars than others. The aim is that these qualities should enhance rather than impede the sound, but exactly how such benefits are perceived and employed is really down to the individual player. In general, the semi-acoustic's extra resonance imparts a degree of sweetness and often mellowness to the sound, but with the low end staying well defined and treble content relatively unimpaired.

In recent years the semi-solid concept has become considerably more popular, with most company catalogues now offering at least one obviously more airy alternative. But to most players, the word "semi" conjures up images of big but slim electrics, epitomised by the creations bearing the Gibson brandname. This company was the first to offer the convenience of thinner-bodied archtop-electrics, beginning with the Byrdland

in 1955. The absence of much body depth made the instrument much more manageable, while still retaining the friendly familiarity of conventional cosmetics, and this policy was soon extended to include slender equivalents of existing instruments, including the ES-350T ("T" for "thinline"), while the ES-225T was an even slimmer six-string. All employed single-cutaway styling, but in its size the 225 model paved the way for an innovative design approach.

In 1958 the company debuted the ES-335TD, featuring a body with novel twin cutaways and an internal solid centre block. Gibson correctly reasoned that the latter restricted the body's resonant properties, in turn reducing the risk of inducing the feedback cycle often apparent when using acoustic-electric instruments (thick or thin) in close proximity to an amplifier. The end result was certainly less prone to the horrible howl. It was still

---

1. '62 EPIPHONE SHERATON
Materials: *semi-hollow body of laminated maple; mahogany neck with bound rosewood fingerboard.*
Electrics: *dual 'New York' mini-humbucker pickups, with individual volume and tone controls; three-way toggle switch.*
Features: *'Frequensator' tailpiece, Tune-o-matic bridge.*

2. '61 GIBSON ES-330
Materials: *hollow body of laminated maple; mahogany neck with bound rosewood fingerboard (note 16th fret neck/body join).*
Electrics: *dual single-coil P90 pickups; individual volume and tone controls; three-way toggle switch.*
Features: *trapeze tailpiece, Tune-o-matic bridge, plastic-button Kluson tuners.*

3. '64 RICKENBACKER 360/12 12-STRING
Materials: *carved and routed semi-hollow maple body; laminated mahogany and maple through-neck with bound maple fingerboard.*
Electrics: *dual single-coil 'toaster-top' pickups with individual vol and tone, three-way switch and blend control.*
Features: *two-tier pickguard, semi-slotted headstock.*

4. '90 RICKENBACKER 381V69
Materials: *carved and routed maple body, laminated mahogany-maple through-neck with bound rosewood fingerboard.*
Electrics: *dual single-coil 'toaster-top' pickups with individual vol and tone, three-way switch and blend control.*
Features: *'R' tailpiece, 'German carve' body.*

5. '77 FENDER TELECASTER THINLINE
Materials: *routed semi-solid ash body; bolt-on maple neck and fingerboard.*
Electrics: *dual humbucking pickups; master volume and tone controls; three-way lever switch.*
Features: *through-body stringing; fully-adjustable six-saddle bridge; 'bullet' truss rod adjuster.*

6. '98 PRS HOLLOWBODY II
Materials: *carved and routed mahogany body with bookmatched carved flame-maple top; glued-in mahogany neck with bound rosewood fingerboard.*
Electrics: *dual humbucking pickups; master vol and tone controls; three-way toggle.*
Features: *PRS wrapover bridge; locking tuners.*

Eight miles high, 12-strings, and one Roger McGuinn – and classic Ricky jangle is born.

1   2   3

semi-acoustics

not as safe as a full solid body, but it was at least a significant improvement. Almost at once Gibson exploited this advantage, adding the more deluxe ES-355TD and ES-345TD to make up a line of slimline semi-acoustics.

Also introduced at this time was the similarly styled but fully hollow ES-330TD, while sister brand Epiphone boasted respective equivalents in the form of the Riviera, Sheraton and Casino. The popularity enjoyed by Gibson's twin-cutaway quartet soon prompted most competitors to revise their ranges. The slimline treatment had already been adopted by a great many makers worldwide, and the company would now exert even greater influence on styling.

Gretsch, Guild and Harmony were among the many US manufacturers who opted to champion the twin-cutaway cause to a greater or lesser degree, usually adding their own touches to the overall outline. Surprisingly, none initially perceived the benefit of employing a solid centre block as Gibson did, although for a while Gretsch removed f-holes on some semis in an attempt

Modern mechanization means PRS hollowbody archtops are built somewhat differently than those of more traditional makers. After the solid body section has been "scooped out" by a computer-guided router its rough-cut top is glued in place (top right). The rough arch is then carved into the top by one router (near right), then finished by another – and the final result is now beginning to take shape as a PRS guitar.

4   5   6

to curtail feedback. Gibson's twin-cutaway concept was taken up by numerous contemporaries in many countries, with virtually all the European makers offering their own interpretations.

Again the constructional aspects were ignored in favor of retaining an all-hollow interior, but this position would change over the next two decades as the practical performance advantages became clear. The Japanese were quick to copy both cosmetics and construction methods for their more upmarket repros of the Gibson originals. The same principles were adopted when some of the makers in that part of the world decided to employ more original thinking, and the better examples of semis bearing brand names such as Aria, Ibanez and Yamaha certainly put Gibson's groundbreaking work to good use.

More recently there has been a less slavish adherence to the long-established twin-cutaway styling, with PRS in particular breaking with tradition – at least visually – by applying tried and tested semi-acoustic construction principles to the brand's own ideas on design.

Regardless of price, most semi-acoustics employ laminated wood for the body front and back as this lends itself to the manufacturing methods involved. This contradicts the choice made for solids, where the use of plywood indicates penny-pinching production. Internal differences affect the choice of certain hardware components, and in many instances the bridge and tailpiece in particular can provide clues as to how much

wood actually lurks within a semi. A floating bridge points to an all-hollow interior offering no purchase for body-mounted supports, and the same often applies to a trapeze-type tailpiece or vibrato unit secured to the side of the guitar. Instruments that incorporate some sort of center block tend to employ it to provide adequate anchorage where necessary, allowing the use of well-secured hardware such as bridge pillars and tailpiece.

A semi-solid can yield some of the same sonic seasoning as a semi-acoustic, although another prime purpose behind introducing some air into the construction is to reduce the guitar's physical weight. Ever since its inception, the solidbody electric has endured criticism concerning weight, levelled by players and also many makers. With this in mind, numerous competitors to Fender and Gibson's original designs have sought to offset the inevitable increase in ounces.

There's a limit to how light wood will go and still be a practical

Jeff Beck strapped on the requisite Duo Jet for his Cliff Gallup tribute, Crazy Legs.

1 **2**

semi-acoustics

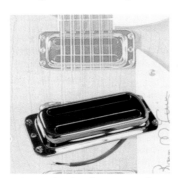

Rickenbacker 'button top' single-coil pickup.

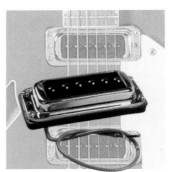

Rickbenbacker 'toaster top' single-coil pickup.

Gibson's legendary single-coil P-90 pickup.

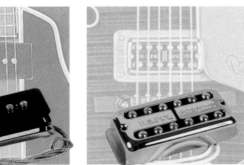

Gretsch Filter'Tron humbucking pickup.

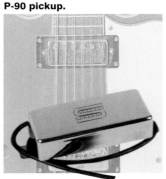

Seymour Duncan mini-humbucker replacement.

DiMarzio's super-hot Super Distortion humbucker.

Like their solidbody cousins, semi-acoustic electrics carry a dizzying number of different pickup types, and these variations in design play a major part in the different voices heard from each model of guitar. Lower-powered single-coil units like the classic Rickenbacker pickups exhibit pronounced high-end response with plenty of sparkle, while Gibson's meatier P-90 single-coil packs more midrange punch. Humbucking designs do anything from solid twang (Filter'Tron) to bright-with-bite (mini-humbucker) to full-on rock (DiMarzio Super Distortion).

proposition for guitar building, so the obvious solution is to incorporate some space inside the body. It's surprising how many makers have adopted this approach over the years, and with the absence of any soundholes to confirm the presence of cavities within, such semis successfully masquerade as straightforward solids, often helped by marketing that does little to alter this impression. Early so-called "solids" from famous US names such as Gretsch, Guild, Harmony, Kay and Rickenbacker employed degrees of hollow construction in an effort to shed pounds and make their creations more appealing, weight-wise, than those from Fender or Gibson, but of course these changes also altered tone and sustain.

Other major names flaunted the routing of a little wood from an otherwise solid body – Fender's Tele Thinline being perhaps the most notable – as a variation on a tested theme, appealing to players seeking only a small step toward an airier semi.

They may look much alike at a glance, but Gibson's ES-330 and ES-335/345/355 are very different. Aside from the pickup differences, the ES-330 (far left) has a truly hollow body, with a 16th-fret neck joint. The ES-345 beside it has a central core of solid wood and neck joint at the 20th fret.

Generally, the semi suits a player who wants to hear a little more of the unplugged tone of the instrument in their amplified sound. Sure, this can sometimes introduce unwanted problems – feedback, occasional muddiness – but many guitarists are willing to overlook or overcome any drawbacks in return for the alternative aural texture of a good semi.

---

1. '58 GRETSCH DUO JET
Materials: *semi-solid routed mahogany body with laminated pressed arched top; glued-in mahogany neck with bound 22-fret rosewood fingerboard.*
Electrics: *dual Filter'Tron humbucking pickups, with individual tone switches and vol controls plus master vol.*
Features: *Melita Synchro-Sonic bridge.*

2. HARMONY STRATOTONE JUPITER H-90
Materials: *semi-solid body with spruce top; bolt-on maple neck and 20-fret rosewood fingerboard.*
Electrics: *dual single-coil pickups; selector switch; individual volume and tone controls plus master volume.*
Features: *floating two-piece rosewood bridge.*

The man whose name defined the beat, with a Jet Firebird in pre-rectangular-body days.

3. '00 GUILD BLUES 90
Materials: *semi-solid chambered mahogany body with carved solid maple top; glued-in mahogany neck with 22-fret rosewood fingerboard.*
Electrics: *dual single-coil P-90 style pickups; 3-way selector switch; individual volume and tone controls.*
Features: *Grover tuners; Tune-o-matic bridge with stop tailpiece.*

4. '79 HAMER SUNBURST
Materials: *semi-solid chambered mahogany body with carved solid maple top; glued-in mahogany neck with 22-fret rosewood fingerboard.*
Electrics: *dual humbucking pickups; 3-way selector switch; individual volume and master tone controls.*
Features: *strings-through-body bridge design; Grover tuners.*

5, '00 BRIAN MOORE M/C1
Materials: *semi-hollow composite body with solid 'tone' block and solid bookmatched quilted maple top; glued-in maple neck with 24-fret ebony fingerboard.*
Electrics: *Seymour Duncan pickups: one humbucker and two single-coil size Hot Rails.*
Features: *Wilkinson vibrato; elaborate abalone neck inlay.*

3   4   5

Nine hundred and ninety-nine players out of a thousand might feel that the electric guitar has evolved about as far as necessary – or possible. But there is always that one dissenter who's looking to get something more from the instrument. It's this kind of musician who inspires designers to search for the un-tapped tone, to forge new combinations of voices, to coin a radical feature or a fresh new feel – with one ear always cocked toward the musical horizon.

Guitars generically dubbed "hybrid" usually combine two or more means of sound reproduction for entirely new blends of tone and playability. This is more than just giving new shapes to the old familiar formulae – as did, say, Steinberger with the headless design or Floyd Rose with the locking vibrato. Typically, the new aural melange appears in the form of traditional magnetic and acoustic-like piezo pickups mounted on the same guitar; as an otherwise trad electric carrying MIDI/synth access; or simply in the form of an instrument with the look and feel of a solidbody

Despite his guitars' versatile pickup systems and slinky playability, Ken Parker has sometimes been taken to task for the modern, even "synthetic" outer appearance of some of his instruments. This advertisement (far right) was an effort to prove once and for all that there really is timber inside a Parker guitar. In 1996 Parker introduced the wood-bodied NiteFly (near right) aimed at more traditional tastes.

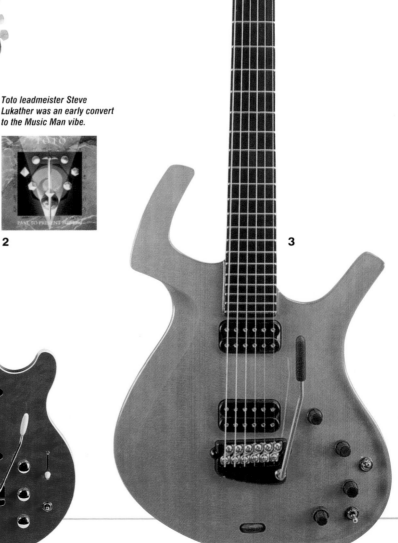

1

Toto leadmeister Steve Lukather was an early convert to the Music Man vibe.

2

3

but delivering feedback-free amplified-acoustic performance. Many also use this futuristic sonic template as a springboard for nouveau looks and radically re-thought features. The result is an ever-expanding array of makes and models which, in fairness, can hardly be categorized.

"I hate the term hybrid," says Ken Parker, co-founder with electronics expert Larry Fishman of Parker Guitars. "I build the best electric guitar I know how to make." Yet despite the objections of the man behind probably the best-known and defining example of the breed, it's a term the general public can latch on to. There's little doubt, however, that other visionaries in the industry share Parker's simple defining goal: "The point of the guitar is to make a guitar sound better."

By allowing the player to combine acoustic and more traditional electric sounds – all treated through the effects and amplification set-up of his or her choice – the piezo/magnetic hybrid offers near-endless nuances of color between the previously isolated primary voices of the guitar. Additionally, it offers an instant leap between the two sounds, an enormous boon for any live performer who previously had to deal with the major hassle of squeezing a dramatic electric lead break into the middle of an otherwise mellow acoustic ballad, for example.

Add synthesizer access to the brew and the sky's the limit sonically, though even with the improved tracking and pitch detection of newer units, the guitar synth remains an under-used musical tool.

Whatever the hardware, the new breed is earning a growing list of name users, from former Red Hot Chili Peppers and Jane's Addiction guitarist Dave Navarro to David Bowie sideman Reeves Gabrels. It's a future just beginning to reveal itself.

---

1. '99 TOM ANDERSON HOLLOW DROP TOP
Materials: *semi-solid 'tone chambered' basswood body with quilted maple top; bolt-on maple neck with 22-fret rosewood fingerboard.*
Electrics: *humbucking and dual single-coil Anderson pickups; individual series/parallel switching; piezo-saddle LR Baggs X-Bridge vibrato with volume control and switch.*

2. '00 MUSIC MAN AXIS SUPER SPORT
Materials: *solid mahogany body with two-piece maple top; bolt-on maple neck with maple fingerboard.*
Electrics: *dual DiMarzio humbucking pickups with five-way switch, volume and tone; Fishman piezo-saddle vibrato bridge with volume, mode switch, and rear-pocket trim-pots for treble, bass and trim.*

3. '97 PARKER FLY ARTIST
Materials: *solid spruce body, top and neck with composite glass/carbon fiber/epoxy strengthening 'exoskeleton' and fingerboard; glued on frets.*
Electrics: *dual magnetic humbucking pickups with three-way selector switch; piezo-loaded 'flat-spring' vibrato bridge with controls for blended or individual use.*

Reeves Gabrels uses his Parker to smash sonic boundaries with Tin Machine.

4. '94 HAMER DUO TONE
Materials: *semi-solid mahogany body with maple top; glued-in mahogany neck with rosewood fingerboard.*
Electrics: *dual humbucking pickups with master vol and tone; piezo-pickup-loaded acoustic-style bridge saddle; controls for blended or separate use.*
Features: *mini soundholes.*

5. '98 GODIN LG-XT
Materials: *solid silver-leaf maple body with carved maple top; bolt-on mahogany neck with ebony fingerboard.*
Electrics: *dual Seymour Duncan magnetic humbucking pickups with five-way switch, volume and tone controls; piezo-loaded LR Baggs vibrato X-Bridge with separate graphic EQ; 13-pin synth output with associated controls.*

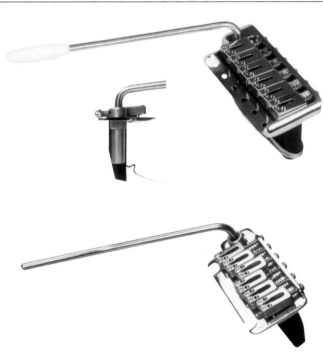

BRIDGE POWER
More than just a factory option these days, the proliferation of retro-fit piezo-saddle bridges means that many guitars with Strat-style vibratos can be converted to "hybrid" operation with relative ease. So far, two models are clear leaders in the field: the Fishman Power Bridge (top) is designed for a six-screw vintage Strat vibrato-type mounting (though other models are available), while the L.R. Baggs X-Bridge vibrato fits more contemporary two-post designs.

4

5

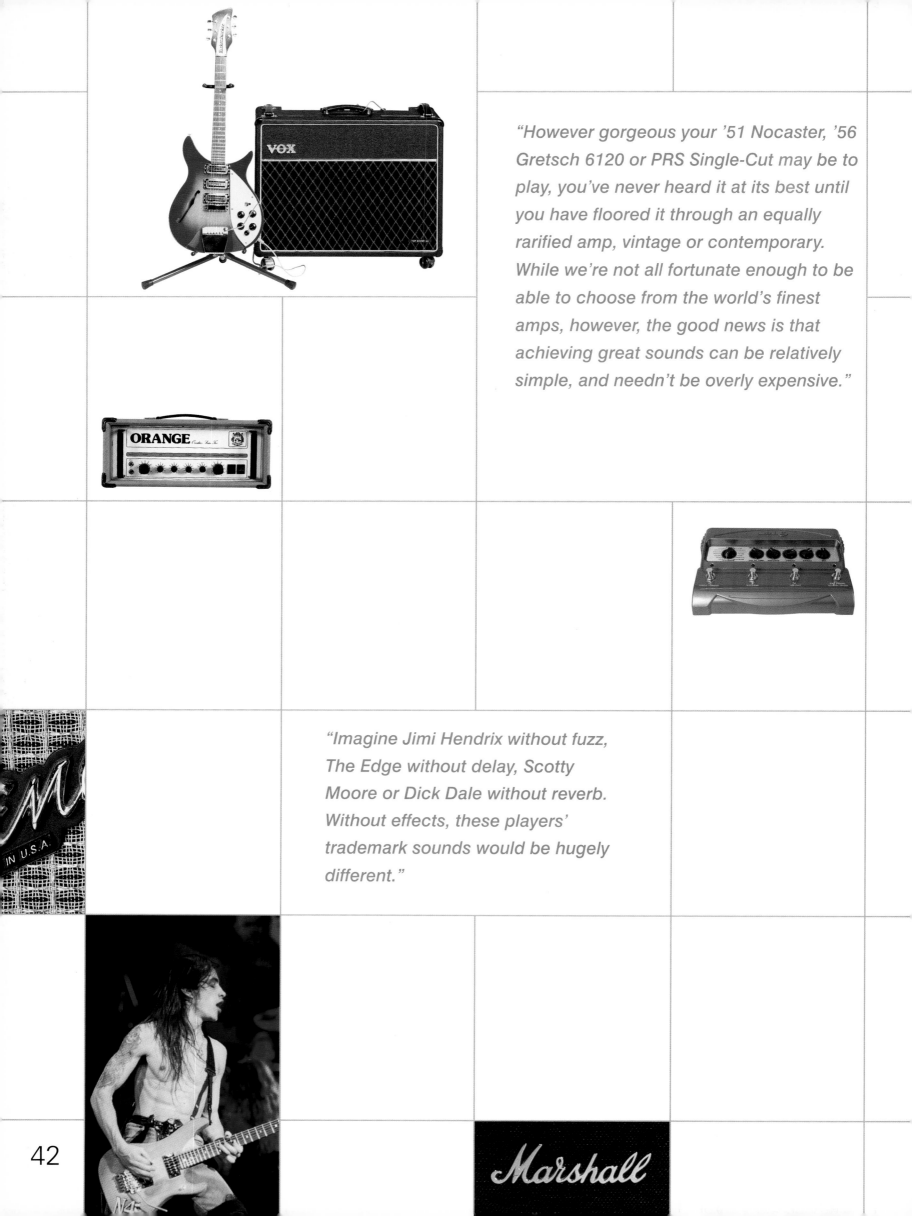

"However gorgeous your '51 Nocaster, '56 Gretsch 6120 or PRS Single-Cut may be to play, you've never heard it at its best until you have floored it through an equally rarified amp, vintage or contemporary. While we're not all fortunate enough to be able to choose from the world's finest amps, however, the good news is that achieving great sounds can be relatively simple, and needn't be overly expensive."

"Imagine Jimi Hendrix without fuzz, The Edge without delay, Scotty Moore or Dick Dale without reverb. Without effects, these players' trademark sounds would be hugely different."

chapter 2

GUITAR
AMPS & EFFECTS

Most players know that their amps and effects play a huge part in the sound chain, but have had little chance to look under the hood of these crucial sonic ingredients to learn what makes them tick. In this chapter, we lift the lid on the ways in which circuit types, tube variations, speaker designs, construction techniques and more can shape your tone.

Players gush and enthuse endlessly about guitars, but relatively little attention is paid to amplification. An amp sits behind you, you switch it on, plug in, play, and the sound comes out. What's to think about? Ah, but there's the key: *the sound comes out!* The amp has the final say in what you and your audience hear of your playing, and adds the final twists that determine "your tone."

TUBE TASTING

In any tube amp, the tubes (valves) themselves are where the real work is done – where your guitar signal is married to high voltage electricity to create amplified sound. It's the way in which tubes distort that, historically, has for many players made them preferable to solid-state, or transistor, systems. Transistors distort too, but without a lot of extra engineering the result tends to be harsh and relatively unmusical. Tubes, on the other hand, make a more gradual transition into distortion, during which the guitar signal gains what our ears perceive as added dimension and a compression-like smoothness. Even "clean" tube amp sounds have an element of distortion, which adds richness and texture to the tone. Different tubes have different characteristics: 6L6 – bright, tight, big-Fender sound; EL34 – the Marshall favorite, with crunchy mids and juicy overdrive; EL84 – the sweet and ringing "baby Brit;" 6V6 – the Jr. Fender-type, creamy and easily distorted. Others include preamp tubes (the 12AX7 is easily the most common) and rectifiers like the GZ34 or 5Y3 that convert AC electricity to DC.

Still unclear about the significance your amp plays in the overall sonic picture? Try this imaginary test: side by side in your mind's ear, plug a Korean-built Squier Stratocaster into a Matchless D/C-30 combo, and plug a Fender Custom Shop Strat into a Squier practise combo. Now play each rig a while. Which sounds better? No competition. That hand-built Matchless can induce spasms of tonal ecstasy, even with a competent but underwhelming budget guitar. Yes, it's an unfair contest – but it's not over yet. Reverse the set-ups and play again. Sure, the D/C-30 is even more heavenly with the Custom Shop Strat injected. But here's the rub: rank all four combinations in order of best to worst. Bet you the hand-built, all-tube amp comes out number one and number two, right?

A foregone conclusion, perhaps, but a good amp – one that's well-built for its price, suited to your style of music, and kept in good working order – plays a major role in taking you closer to aural paradise, however fine, vintage or custom-built your electric guitar. Similarly, however gorgeous your '51 Nocaster, '56 Gretsch 6120, or 2000 PRS Singlecut may be to play, you've never heard it at its best until you have floored it through an equally rarified amp, vintage or contemporary. While we're not all fortunate enough to be able to choose from the world's finest amps, however, the good news is that achieving great sounds can be relatively simple, and needn't be overly expensive.

Your first glance under the hood of many modern tube amps can be a little daunting, but as with cars today a lot of the tangle inside has nothing to do with getting you (or your basic guitar sound) from A to B. Channel-switching circuitry, effects-loop routing and other added features all jumble the picture. But from input to tone-shaping circuit to tubes to output, there needn't be a whole lot of excess science to get in the way.

Consider, for example, the early '50s tweed Fender Deluxe pictured here. Countless rock'n'roll hits were played through such an amp and bluesmen have pushed them into sweet, creamy overdrive, while raw rockers crank them up for excesses

'53 FENDER DELUXE
Specifications: *two channel class A/B all-tube combo; 15W output; cathode biased; single 12" speaker.*
Controls: *individual volume for each channel, shared tone.*
Features: *fully hand-wired circuit (model 5C3); one 12AY7, one 12AX7, two 6V6s and one 5Y3 rectifier; Jensen P12R alnico-magnet speaker (note replacement speaker on this example); open-backed 'wide panel' fingerjointed solid pine cabinet.*

'96 PEAVEY CLASSIC 30
Specifications: *footswitchable two channel class A all-tube combo; 30W output; single 12" speaker.*
Controls: *Ch1: volume; Ch2: gain and master volume, shared: bass, middle, treble, reverb.*
Features: *circuit on printed board (PCB); three 12AX7 preamp tubes, four EL84s, solid state rectification; Peavey Blue Marvel speaker; top-mounted controls; open-backed plywood cab covered in repro tweed.*

After giving birth to rock'n'roll, the tweed Fender Deluxe helped launch the signature "grunge" sound when Neil Young injected his Bigsby-equipped '50s Les Paul for *Rust Never Sleeps*.

tube combos

of distortion and hot, edgy lead tones. Neil Young, for example, is a fan of later-'50s tweed Deluxes, while Ted Nugent recorded with early '60s examples.

A closer look inside shows that there isn't a whole lot to this classic design – and the electronic magic behind most great vintage tube amps is equally simple. In the case of this "tweed" Fender, the only things to come between the guitar's signal at the input and the output transformer and speaker – the team that puts the sound we hear into the air – are a couple of resistors, four signal capacitors, a volume and tone control, and the preamp and output tubes themselves. Everything else contained within the amp's chassis has to do with shaping and filtering the high voltages and getting them to the tubes in the right condition to induce as little unwanted noise as possible.

While this Deluxe only produces 15 watts, bigger tube amps follow the same design principles, adding just a few more components for tone-shaping with larger (and sometimes more) tubes for more power. Still, countless guitar greats have recorded legendary solos on cranked Deluxes and similarly diminutive models (including ultra-tiny 3W '50s Champs), and record-buying fans never suspecting they were hearing anything less than a quartet of 100-watters through a wall of Marshall 4x12" cabs.

Of course, many factors influence great sound, and there's as much variety in amp design and component choice as there is in the world of guitar building. Makers today follow a wide range of topologies to suit players' needs: lower gain preamps coupled with tight, powerful output sections for big clean sounds with plenty of headroom; medium-gain preamps with vintage-style output designs that are easily pushed into crunchy, chunky distortion; multiple high-gain cascading preamp stages coupled with a firm but responsive output stage and master volume, for scorching leads and singing, near-infinite sustain.

At the heart of it all, however, lies a technology not much more complicated than that which produced great-sounding little combos like our tweed Deluxe some 50 years ago.

MARSHALL ARTS

In the early '60s, London music shop owner Jim Marshall saw an opportunity to build his own version of the Fender amps popular with British guitarists, but almost prohibitively expensive to acquire. Using a late '50s tweed Fender Bassman as a template (with initially only a few changes to account for more-easily available British components) he and colleagues Ken Bran and Dudley Craven gave birth to a rock legend. Following a handful of early prototypes the first proper production models arrived in 1963 (pictured above is a "sandwich front" '63 MKII JTM45). Other than the slight variables in components, which originally included the use of great Mullard preamp valves and GEC KT66 output valves, the main sonic distinction from their American-made inspiration was the speaker cabinet – a closed-back unit carrying four low-powered 12" Celestions rather than the four 10" Jensens in the Bassman's open-backed cab. This, as much as the amplifier itself, played a major part in the birth of the "British sound." As Marshall designs evolved they grew further and further from their Fender-inspired roots, though closed-back 4x12" speaker cabs remain a trademark.

'95 MATCHLESS T/C-30
Specifications: *two-channel class A all-tube combo; no negative feedback; cathode biased; 30W output; dual 10" speakers.*
Controls: *Ch1: volume, bass, treble; Ch2: volume, tone; shared: cut, master.*
Features: *all hand-wired circuit; one EF86 and three 12AX7 preamp tubes, four EL84s, one GZ34 rectifier; Celestion G10L-35 ceramic magnet speakers; half-power switch; individual effects loops; speaker phase switch.*

'99 CARVIN BELAIR 212
Specifications: *footswitchable two-channel class A/B all-tube combo; 50W output; dual 12" speakers.*
Controls: *Ch1: volume, bass, middle, treble; Ch2: gain, volume, bass, middle, treble; shared: reverb.*
Features: *printed circuit board (PCB); five 12AX7 preamp tubes, four EL84 power tubes, solid state rectification; two proprietary speakers; open-backed plywood cabinet and speaker baffle covered in reproduction tweed.*

'00 VOX AC30TBX REISSUE
Specifications: *three-channel class A all-tube combo; no negative feedback; cathode biased; 30W output; dual 12" speakers.*
Controls: *volume for each channel (vib-trem, normal, brilliant); shared EQ (treble, bass and cut); speed and vib-trem switch.*
Features: *PCB; top-mounted controls; five 12AX7 preamp tubes, four EL84s, one GZ34 rectifier; Celestion Alnico Blue speakers; open-backed plywood cab.*

'01 FENDER '65 SUPER REVERB REISSUE
Specifications: *two-channel class A/B all-tube combo; fixed bias; 45W output; four 10" speakers.*
Controls: *Normal ch: bright switch, volume, treble, bass; vibrato ch: bright switch, volume, treble, middle, bass, reverb, speed and intensity.*
Features: *PCB; four 12AX7s, two 12AT7s, two 6L6s, one 5AR4 rectifier tube; Jensen P10R alnico magnet speakers; tube reverb and vibrato.*

Belting out its gritty chime with anything from a Rickenbacker to a Gretsch at the input, a Vox AC30 has stood behind The Beatles, Tom Petty, and many,

many more. On the other side of the tracks, Fender's Super Reverb is a classic blueser, favored by the likes of Buddy Guy and Stevie Ray Vaughan.

Like just about any field of technology, the amp world has always had its hot-rodders. Ever since tube amps were first commercially available, players and engineers alike have tinkered with and modified stock units to get more gain, better tone, more distortion, less distortion... whatever it takes to achieve that illusive sonic nirvana that rings in guitarists' heads.

For years most hot-rodding went on as after-market modification. Eager engineers took in standard amp models and adapted circuits and specs to convert them to fire-breathing superbeasts. Inevitably, however, a whole new breed was born –

As with taking your guitar on the road, it's important to give your amp the right protection if and when it is subjected to the rigors of touring. Flightcases are available in many standard sizes or custom-built to fit any combo or stack, and offer the best protection from the truck to the stage and back again.

a genre of small-run, often hand-built and sometimes custom-order "boutique" amps that sought to rise above the perfectly respectable but perhaps rather tame offerings of such mass manufacturers as Marshall and Fender.

In the late '60s and early '70s San Francisco amp tech Randall Smith started converting modest little 12W Fender Princeton amps into high-gain, 60W rock monsters for players on the scene who wanted a little more than most production amps of the day could offer. Smith's "cascading gain" circuit fed multiple tube preamp stages one into the other to create a hotter front end than any amp commercially available. The results were extreme overdrive sounds and ringing sustain of the sort only previously attained by maxing out a large power amp. An early conversion

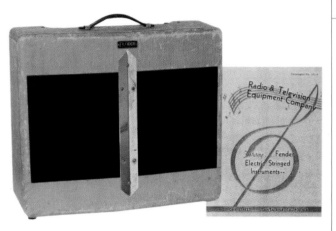

THE FENDER YEARS

Leo Fender's amps were far from the first on the market, but their rugged build, workmanlike simplicity and impressive sound, combined with Fender's knack for discerning and fulfilling the needs of musicians, ensured that they were some of the best available from the very start. Compare Fender amps from as early as 1948 – when their construction quality really began to come into its own – with just about any other production model of the time and the superiority is clear. It's also obvious at a glance both inside and out why modern amps echo these early Fender designs more than they do those of any other 55-year-old combo. When you get it right first try, there's not a lot of room to evolve.

Remember: for Fender, the amp came first. While the K&F company and, later, Fender built a number of electric lap steel guitars in the '40s, the early amps were clearly a cut above their stringed partners. Check out the Fender catalog from 1949, for example, and familiar combo models like the Pro, Super (above), Deluxe, Princeton and Champion are already available, still 12 months before the first production solidbody electric guitar (Fender's first "standard" guitar of any type) was listed for sale.

While makers like Supro, Gibson, National, Premier, Rickenbacker, Gretsch and Ampeg brought us a great amp or two – some before Fender even existed – Leo's successive series of amps have arguably launched more classic models than any other brand.

'00 MESA RECT-O-VERB
Specifications: *footswitchable two-channel class A/B all-tube combo; 100W output; dual 12" speakers.*
Controls: *separate gain, master, bass, mid, treble, reverb and presence controls and voicing switch for each channel; dual shared output controls.*
Features: *PCB; five 12AX7 preamp tubes, four EL34s or 6L6s (with switchable bias), two 5AR4 rectifiers; Celestion Vintage 30 speakers; half-open-backed plywood cabinet.*

'01 VHT PITTBULL FIFTY/CL
Specifications: *footswitchable two-channel all-tube combo with switchable class A/class A/B; 50W output; 2x12".*
Controls: *Ch1: gain, volume, treble, middle, bass; Ch2: volume, treble, middle, bass; boost, shift and bright pushbuttons for each; shared: reverb, graphic EQ.*
Features: *PCB; four 12AX7 and one EF86 preamp tubes, two EL34s or 6L6s (with switchable bias), 5AR4 rectifier; Eminence speakers; plywood cabinet.*

In addition to revealing more controls than the front panels of many standard amps, a rear view of the Mesa R-O-V displays those dual rectifier tubes.

hotrod combos

job tested by Carlos Santana elicited the comment, "Man, that little amp really boogies!" The rest is history.

As used Princetons got harder to find, Smith started building his own amps from scratch, selling by direct order right from the workshop. In just a few years, Mesa/Boogie became one of the most heavily pro-endorsed lines in the rock world. Progressing through the famous Mark I to Mark IV lines of mostly 1x12" 60W and 100W combos and heads to the Dual and Triple Rectifier arena-blasters of today, Mesa/Boogie remains the first and prime culmination of an amp fanatic's quest for more. Now manufactured in the sort of mass volume that lifts it out of the boutique category – using printed circuit boards for consistency and expediency – Mesa/Boogie nevertheless remains at the front of a line of custom-style production builders.

Plenty of other designers have chased the mega-gain dream, and many have become well-known mass-manufactured makers in their own right, even if elevated prices sometimes mean ordinary players rarely get their hands on these amps. Today, fellow Californians like Soldano, VHT, Rivera (run by former Fender designer Paul Rivera) and Budda all offer imposing tube amps with more fire and fury than any rock guitar hero of the early '70s could have imagined. Then there's the creamy, lush drive tones of George Dumble's high-end creations, which were around before Mesa/Boogie but have remained ultra-rare thanks to high costs and low production numbers.

Not all the visionaries are pursuing the ultimate overdrive. Matchless, Bad Cat, Dr Z, Trainwreck, and the many vintage Fender repro guys (THD, Victoria, Kendrick and Clark among them) have crafted their appreciation of simpler vintage designs by Vox, Marshall and Fender into lushly toneful and often stunningly over-engineered homages to the classics. As ever, such quality comes at a price (though many of the tweed Fender-style reproductions are impressively good value), but these builders' work genuinely approaches high art in the amp field.

Not surprisingly, all of the big boys now do their own hotrods. Peavey's Van Halen signature amp is the 5150; Carvin's Steve Vai

MAN VS. MACHINE
Arguments continue to rage about the virtues of hand-wired circuits (as in this vintage Vox AC15, above right) versus more affordable printed circuit board (PCB) construction. Many connoisseurs insist a hand-wired amp will sound better every time, but the difference might be beyond the average guitarist's ability to discern – and, in fairness, could also be down to variations in components and specs. There's no doubt whatsoever that many of the very best guitar amps built today are assembled by hand and individually tuned by artisans at the top of their trade; so it goes with most any craft. Many excellent amplifiers are also built using PCBs, however, which offer greater consistency of performance and better affordability than hand-building could ever hope to achieve.

signature is the Legacy model; Marshall has its Triple Super Lead series; and Fender the flexible, high-gain Prosonic model. All are recent incarnations of these major makers' adaptations of modifications which independent custom builders first applied to some of Fender and Marshall's own basic designs.

Echoing a similar what-goes-around-comes-around philosophy but from a different tack, in the late '80s and early '90s many major manufacturers eventually spotted the popularity so many classic, non-master-volume models had attained – along with the success of the boutique reproduction builders – and released their own "vintage reissue" models. Along came amps such as a more vintage-correct Vox AC30 TBX, Marshall's JTM45 and Bluesbreaker combo, and Fender's tweed '59 Bassman, '65 Twin Reverb, '65 Deluxe Reverb and '65 Super Reverb. They all display that the big corporations are again catching up to players' desires… eventually.

'01 SOLDANO LUCKY 13
Specifications: footswitchable two-channel class A/B all-tube combo; fixed bias; 50W output; dual 12" speakers. Controls: Ch1: bright switch, volume, bass, middle, treble, reverb; Ch2: gain, bass, middle, treble, reverb, volume; shared: presence.
Features: PCB, six 12AX7 preamp tubes, two 6L6s; solid-state rectification; front-mounted Eminence Legend speakers; open-backed plywood cabinet and baffle.

'99 MARSHALL JCM2000 TSL602
Specifications: footswitchable three-channel all-tube class A/B combo; 60W output; dual 12" speakers. Controls: Ch1: volume, treble, middle, bass; Chs2/3: shared treble, middle, bass with independent gain and volume; shared presence, master and reverb; effects loop mix control.
Features: PCB; four 12AX7s and two EL34s; solid-state rectification; Celestion speakers.

'01 RIVERA QUIANA
Specifications: footswitchable two-channel all-tube class A/B combo; fixed bias; 55W output; dual 12" speakers. Controls: dual channels with individual gain, bass, middle, treble, volume and footswitchable boost; shared reverb, presence and focus (resonance).
Features: PCB; five 12AX7 preamp tubes, two 6L6s; solid state rectification; vintage/modern (high/low power) switching; Celestion Vintage 30 speakers; plywood cabinet.

CLASSIC SPEAKERS
A: Celestion Alnico Blue. The British speaker giant's reissue of their 15W alnico-magnet 'Blue Bulldog' which appeared in classic Vox amps.
B: Celestion G12H-30. Reissue of the 'heavy magnet' ceramic driver that powered classic '70s 4x12" cabs.
C: Jensen P12R. Reissue of the alnico-magnet Jensen 12" as featured in countless '50s Fenders and Gibsons.
D: JBL D-120F. Vintage driver known for piercing highs, fat mids, tight lows.

Eric Clapton helped put Soldano on the map when he used an SLO-100 for his appearance on the TV show *Saturday Night Live*.

A

B

C

D

While non-American six-strings barely figure in the early history of the electric guitar, rockers from the other side of the pond were getting one thing right from the very start. British amps rival any in the world for quality, power and sound – and for heavy rock in particular, the Brits set the standards for others to follow.

Removing the otherwise closed back from this contemporary Marshall 4x12" cabinet reveals the four reissue Celestion "Greenbacks" that give it plenty of bottom-end oomph, with juicy, crunchy mids.

The "Brit sound" remains a rock byword, defined by sweetly compressed and saturated drive tones with punchy, often crunchy mids and gut-slugging lows. Although Fender had introduced its radical new piggyback rigs (an amp head atop a separate speaker cabinet) in 1960, before any other large-production manufacturer, we still credit British builders with inventing the "stack" – the high-powered arena-rock head with one or two large speaker cabs, classically 4x12"s. If one setup defines this so-called British sound it's probably a late-'60s 100W Marshall "plexi" Super Lead head and closed-back, slant-front

cab with four 12" Celestion Greenback speakers. But there are many more variations in classic English amplification than any single catchphrase can sum up.

For many players Britain's greatest success – and tone heaven – is contained in one short word: Vox. Organ manufacturer Tom Jennings entered rock'n'roll history in 1956 when he employed designer Dick Denney to mastermind the company's first combo aimed at guitarists, the AC15. Vox lays claim to being the first manufacturer to design an amp circuit from the ground up with electric guitar specifically in mind. Others had been marketed for guitar for years, adapted from such general applications of amplification as broadcasting, PA, and radio, or developed from early lap-steel amps.

As the rock'n'roll craze escalated in Great Britain and bands performed in bigger and bigger venues, Jennings heeded the call for more volume and put Denny on the case again. In 1959 the resulting combo hit stages across the UK – and soon the world – in the form of the AC30 (pictured in reissue form on p45). Undoubtedly one of the finest amps of all time, it used four archetypically British-sounding EL84 output tubes in a class A circuit to pump about 30 Watts through a pair of alnico-magnet Celestion G12 speakers. Today's reissues again follow much the same formula.

If 30W doesn't sound like a lot of power, a quick blast through a good AC30 will show you how much volume these amps can put out. Even so, the quest for more power continued, and when Jim Marshall adapted Fender's Bassman circuit for his JTM45 in the early '60s (see *Marshall Arts*, p45) he addressed the demand

'01 MARSHALL JCM2000 TSL100
Specifications: *footswitchable three-channel all-tube class A/B head; fixed bias; 100W output.*
Controls: *individual gain, volume, bass, middle and treble controls for each channel; individual reverb, presence, FX mix and mid-boost for clean (shared by crunch and lead).*
Features: *PCB; four 12AX7s and four EL34s; solid-state rectification.*

'82 HIWATT LEAD 100 HEAD
Specifications: *footswitchable two-channel all-tube class A/B head; fixed bias; 100W output.*
Controls: *Ch1: volume, treble, bass; Ch2: gain, volume, middle, treble, bass; shared and master volume.*
Features: *hand-wired circuit on tag strips; four 12AX7 preamp tubes and four EL34 power tubes; solid-state rectification.*

From the "crank it and play" non-master-volume simplicity of their '60s JTM45 (main photo, far left) to three-channel rock wonders like the TSL100 (left), Marshall has evolved by keeping with contemporary hotrods.

the stack

for volume and projection head-on. If the popular big-amp speaker formats of two 12s, four 10s or a 15 alone or in pairs still didn't cut it with the day's generally lower-power drivers, why not just keep going? For one, because it makes an unwieldy rig for the average gigging musician without a roadie.

But Marshall's monster 4x12" enclosures with closed backs for improved damping of low powered speakers and tighter lows all round helped usher in a new era in rock firepower. Like to crank your 100-watter to the max? Stick two cabs under it. Got an arena date on the tour? Daisy-chain four full stacks for 400W of music power through 32 12" speakers. From the late '60s the stack was king, a genuine necessity on the big stage until vast improvements in PA systems arrived in the mid '70s. But the "wall of Marshalls" remains the hallmark of a real rock guitar hero.

Not that a "Marshall" has to be a Marshall, in a manner of speaking. The huge-sounding, crunch-of-doom Hiwatt Custom 100s that Pete Townshend made famous, the robust Sound City heads, the funky Orange amps (particularly the 120 Overdrive) of the early '70s, and the big Laneys adopted by Black Sabbath's Tony Iommi and other metal players all belted their own version of the British sound from stages around the world. US makers like Ampeg, Randall, Acoustic, Sunn, Music Man and indeed Fender offered up their own popular mega-watt rigs to the stadium rockers through the '70s and '80s. Meanwhile, most big names and specialists alike offered solid-state alternatives, too.

Like other formats, the stack has evolved considerably, and today many examples couple all the high-gain and channel-switching features of the hotrod combo with ever-more-efficient output sections. Super-deluxe models like Mesa's three-channel,

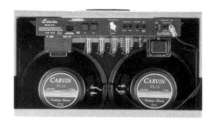

SPEAKER CABINETS

Even the design of a speaker cabinet and the type of drivers it contains will affect the sound your amp produces. Open-backed cabinets accentuate the higher frequencies, with a wider, more "surround-sound" type of dispersion. Closed-backed cabs keep the low end tight and full, with more directional sound projection. Of course, the more speakers a cab carries, the more air it will move and the greater the perceived volume – although the power output from the amp remains the same however many speakers it is driving, with each unit dividing the wattage equally. Speaker size also influences tone. Those 10s have a faster response with super-articulate highs, but still good low-end reproduction when used in multiple numbers, while 12s typically have a wider, more open low-end and full-throated midrange.

150W Triple Rectifier Solo Head are flagships of the field, while major names like Peavey, Marshall and Carvin have similarly put some of their best engineering into high-powered, pro-standard stacks with creative tone-shaping options and instant footswitchability. And even if you don't really need a full stack to get your music across… hey, it still looks great up on stage.

'80s ORANGE OVERDRIVE SERIES TWO HEAD
Specifications: *single-channel all-tube class A/B head; fixed bias; 120W output.*
Controls: *single channel with volume, bass, treble, presence, contour and master volume.*
Features: *hand-wired circuit on tag strips; four 12AX7 preamp tubes and four EL34 power tubes; solid-state rectification; characteristic orange vinyl covering.*

'66 VOX SUPER BEATLE HEAD & 4x12" CAB WITH HORNS
Specifications: *three-channel solid state head with footswitchable effects; 120W output.*
Controls: *Ch1: volume, treble, bass; Ch2: volume, treble, bass; Ch3: volume and tone; shared: fuzz, MRB (wah-like mid frequency shift) and reverb.*
Features: *field effect transistors (FET) on PCB circuit construction; cabinet contains four 12" Vox Bulldog speakers plus two high-frequency horns.*

'01 MESA TRIPLE RECTIFIER SOLO HEAD & 4x12" CAB
Specifications: *footswitchable three-channel class A/B all-tube head; 150W output; four 12" speakers.*
Controls: *separate gain, master, bass, mid, treble, reverb and presence controls and voicing switch for each channel; dual shared output controls.*
Features: *PCB; five 12AX7 preamp tubes, six EL34s or 6L6s (with switchable bias), three 5AR4 rectifiers. Cab has four Celestion Vintage 30s.*

'00 CARVIN STEVE VAI LEGACY HEAD & 4x12" CAB
Specifications: *footswitchable two-channel all-tube class A/B head; fixed bias; 100W output; four 12" speakers.*
Controls: *Ch1: volume, treble, mid, bass, presence; Ch2: gain, volume, treble, mid, bass, presence; shared master and reverb.*
Features: *PCB; five 12AX7s and four EL34s or 6L6s (with switchable bias); solid-state rectification; Celestion speakers in closed-back plywood cab.*

Around back: six output tubes, three rectifiers… *plus* preamp!

Heavy rockers – including Metallica's Kirk Hammett and James Hetfield – have made the big Mesa/Boogies the byword in rock power. The similarly high-gain Carvin Legacy was developed to shredder Steve Vai's specifications.

London-based Orange captured an appropriately groovy vibe to launch its amp range at the end of the '60s, and perpetuated it through some lean times to make a comeback in recent years – still as bright as ever.

A lot of space in this chapter has already been devoted to extolling the virtues of tubes. But good solid-state amps definitely have their fans and their applications, and a player on a tight budget can certainly get a lot more bells and whistles on a new amp by going transistorized. While the components required to build any tube amp are relatively costly by mass-marketing standards, transistors designed to perform similar functions can be had for pennies – and the savings in basic circuitry construction often translate into an abundance of bonus features for the same retail price: clean/overdrive channel switching, reverb and maybe some other onboard effects, headphone outs, recording DIs and more.

Even more importantly, the sound quality of more affordable solid-state amps has improved dramatically over the years, with some models – to many ears – running hard-fought A/B comparison tests against the tube amps they still generally seek to emulate. A breed that was largely received as tonal ly deadweight upon its first widespread introduction to the market in the mid '60s has evolved into a viable playing option, to the credit of R&D teams everywhere.

There were some notable solid-state amps right from the start, and of course some maverick engineers throughout the history of this variety have put time, effort and expense into designing great transistor-based models which are simply excellent guitar amps in their own right, regardless of cost. Models by Standel, Kustom, Polytone, Pignose and – a little later – Roland, Award-Session and Randall have all had their big-name followers.

In recent years even some of the legendary names in tube amps have made great leaps in solid-state development. The models in Marshall's AVT line do carry a lone preamp tube – placing them in a genre generally referred to as "hybrid" – but are for all intents and purposes 90 per cent solid state – and fierce sounding rock amps they are. Fender's Dyna-Touch series

of all-solid-state models is a world away tonally speaking from their efforts of decades past, and even the popular, workmanlike Peavey Bandit has evolved considerably.

It's also important to note that there are certain styles of music to which solid state amps are even considered by some to be better suited, where the low-end tightness and/or cleanness at – often – the massive volume required would be difficult to achieve from all but the most expensive and meticulously over-engineered tube amps.

Odd bedfellows perhaps, but thrash metal axemen and jazz players often choose solid state: the former because of the massive bottom end, fast response, tight punch and lack of spongy "squash" in big tranny amps by makers such as Randall; the latter mainly because of the successful way in which a couple of great models like the Polytone Brute and Roland Jazz Chorus addressed jazzmen's tonal needs right from the start.

The '90s saw a proliferation of hybrid amps carrying a single preamp tube, occasionally a pair, in a bid to bring "real tube tone" – as the advertising team frequently phrases it – to players on a low to medium budget. It's worth being aware that in some amps these tubes are fully functional components, but in others they're mainly there as a marketing tool to lure less-informed buyers who've been told they simply must have a tube amp. In any case, one lonely 12AX7 can't perform all the preamp functions in an amp of this format, so at best such preamps are still 50 to 75 per cent solid-state. At the most cynical end of the genre, "hybrid" amps are functionally solid-state and the tube is just injected with enough voltage to make it glow.

It's also worth noting that many tube freaks argue vehemently that the bulk of any great tone is generated in the output stage, not the preamp. Unsurprisingly, however, adding a single tube to an otherwise solid state preamp and power amp is a lot cheaper than linking a solid-state preamp to an all-tube output stage.

'00 MARSHALL VALVESTATE 2000 AVT50
Specifications: *footswitchable two-channel 'hybrid' combo; 50W output; single 12" speaker.*
Controls: *Ch1: gain, volume, bass, treble; Ch2: gain, volume, bass, middle, treble; shared: reverb depth.*
Features: *transistorized PCB construction with single 12AX7 tube in the preamp, all solid state power amp; CD input; headphone output; closed-back cab with Celestion speaker.*

'01 ROLAND JC-120 JAZZ CHORUS
Specifications: *footswitchable two-channel solid-state combo; 120W stereo output (60W per side); two 12" speakers.*
Controls: *Ch1: volume, treble, middle, bass, bright switch; Ch2: volume, treble, middle, bass, bright switch, distortion, reverb, vibrato speed and depth, chorus/vibrato switch.*
Features: *all-solid-state circuit on PCB; 'riveted' cabinet edge.*

A favorite of jazzers, the Roland JC-120 also helped define the punk-pop sound at the hands of Bob Mould (Hüsker Dü, Sugar, solo artist), who cranked his Strat through two of the big, clean 120-watters paired with two Rivera-era Fender Concerts.

SOLID ROCK

Solid-state amplifiers use transistors rather than tubes to amplify a sound source. Almost every other type of amplifier in the home today – hi-fi, television, clock radio, active PC monitor speakers – uses transistors in roughly the same way. In its raw form, this technology doesn't flatter the electric guitar. In early transistor amps, engineers virtually replaced tubes with discreet solid state components in circuits that, broadly speaking, weren't radically different in their function from the tube-loaded designs. Advertisements touted "better reliability" and "no tubes to replace." The amps worked, certainly, but players with a taste for tonal subtleties quickly gave them the cold shoulder. To be fair, though, some of these early solid-state models built with particular attention to detail are great-sounding amps in their own right, have occasionally been favored by major players, and have provided the voice for a good few classic guitar recordings over the years.

With the tube guitar amp's lasting appeal widely confirmed, many big builders continued to pursue solid state lines not so much because they were more reliable, but because they were considerably cheaper to build.

As with everything in consumer electronics, however, the transistors used in guitar amps have become vastly better, smaller and cheaper over the past 30 years. They can now pack a multiplicity of functions into a single integrated circuit chip to do the work achieved by a Super Beatle-sized head cabinetful of FET electronics in the '60s. The size and affordability, as well as the skill of the engineers, means builders can squeeze in circuitry to shape and filter the signal to more closely mimic the sound of a tube amp.

The fact that solid-state amps don't require costly (and heavy) output transformers and can run off less-extreme high voltages than tube amps also makes them cheaper and simpler to build, and easier to keep within an appealingly budget-minded price range.

Though the tube amp was and is king with the majority of guitar heroes, plenty of major names have played through solid state models down the years – both vintage and modern. This 70W 1966 Vox Conqueror, for example, was believed to have been a temporary choice of The Beatles around the time of the recording sessions for the *Sgt Pepper* LP.

Interestingly, in building some of the first widely available hybrid amps in the mid-'70s, Music Man did just that. Deciding that the output tubes were crucial to the feel, sound and response of a good guitar amp, while a tranny preamp could do the job perfectly well, they reversed the current trend, resulting in a line which drew endorsements from the likes of Eric Clapton and Steve Miller.

When you go shopping for an amp, the best advice is to seek out the model that sounds best to you and carries the features you desire for the amount of cash you have to spend. Ultimately, let your ears decide – and if an all-solid-state amp sounds perfectly good, don't be swayed to spend a little more for a "hybrid" carrying a lonely 12AX7 simply because someone's told you there ain't no mojo without a glowing glass bottle under the hood. And putting the word "tube" or "valve" in the model name without using the real thing anywhere in the circuit does not a tube amp make.

'79 PIGNOSE
Specifications: *solid-state practise and recording amp; 3W output (5W peak); single 5" speaker. Powered by six AA 'pen light' batteries or dedicated AC/DC adaptor.*
Controls: *volume with integral on/off switch; single input.*
Features: *brown vinyl covered cabinet is hinged for battery replacement.*

'01 PEAVEY BANDIT II
Specifications: *footswitchable two-channel solid-state combo; 80W output into 8| (100W into 4|); single 12" speaker.*
Controls: *Ch1: volume, low, mid, high, modern/vintage voicing switch; Ch2: pre-gain, low, mid, high, post-gain, high-gain/modern/vintage voicing switch; shared: reverb, presence, dynamics.*
Features: *all solid-state circuit on PCB; Peavey Sheffield speaker.*

'00 FENDER DELUXE 90
Specifications: *footswitchable two-channel solid-state combo; 90W output; single 12" speaker.*
Controls: *Ch1: volume, treble, mid, bass; Ch2: drive, volume, more drive switch, treble, mid, bass; shared: reverb.*
Features: *Dyna-Touch Series solid-state circuit on PCB; open-backed plywood cabinet and ply baffle; Celestion G12T-100 speaker.*

'02 RANDALL DIMEBAG DARRELL WARHEAD STACK
Specifications: *footswitchable two-channel high-gain solid-state head; 300W stereo output; four 12" and two 15" speakers.*
Controls: *individual three-band active EQ, gain and volume controls; shared 9-band graphic EQ and 14 presets for 16 digital effects.*
Features: *closed-backed speaker cabinets with Celestion Greenbacks (top cab) and 15" Jaguars (bottom cab).*

The ability to get 'good'n dirty' at low volumes has made the wee 3W Pignose a recording favorite since the '70s.

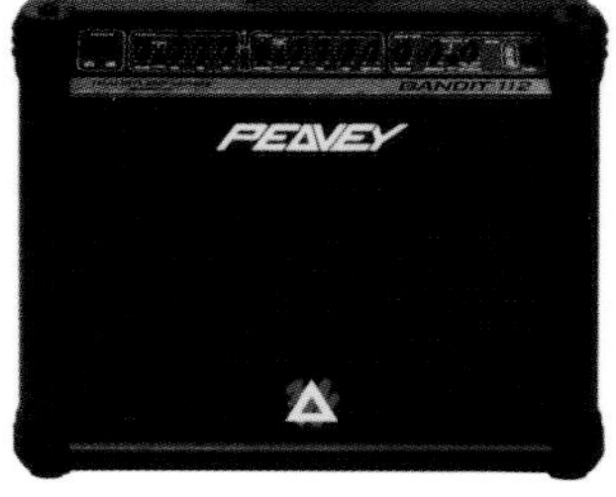

Sometimes solid-state is the only way to go for the huge-and-tight bottom end that thrash-metal players demand – as Pantera's Dimebag Darrell proves in spades with his Randall Warhead stacks, right.

AMPS DU JOUR

The heart of any digital amp is its model "menu," the list of emulations of classic amplifiers which it is able to conjure up. Whoever the manufacturer – Johnson, Crate, Peavey, Fender, or Line 6 (who make the Flextone II shown in close-up below) – the legends ringed around the amp selection control are often thinly veiled codenames denoting great vintage or modern tubesters, and aren't usually too tricky to figure out. For example, "Small Tweed" or "Studio Tweed" usually denotes a '50s Fender Champ or Deluxe, while "Big Tweed" or "Blues Tweed" invariably means a Bassman. Others include:

"Brit Class A" = Vox AC30
"Modern Class A" or "Boutique Class A" = Matchless D/C-30
"Brit blues" = Marshall JTM45 Bluesbreaker
"Recto" or "Rectified" = Mesa Dual Rectifier
"Modern High Gain" = Soldano SLO

STUDIO SMARTS

A good workman selects the right tool for the job. Where guitar amplifiers are concerned, performing live and recording in the studio can be very different jobs indeed. It can be a risky venture to purchase a particular make of amplifier primarily because you like the sound of a certain famous guitarist and have been told it's the amp he uses. Are you blown away by Jimmy Page's sound on *Led Zeppelin II* and looking to acquire just the right mega-stack after seeing him wail away in front of a wall of 4x12s on *The Song Remains The Same*? Think again: legend has it Mr Page recorded most of the first two Zep albums through a diminutive Supro combo (using his '58 Tele, as it happens, not a Les Paul). Busily rigging up high-gain heads in search of an enormous grunge sound? You'll be interested to know that Kurt Cobain recorded most of Nirvana's *Nevermind* album on a 22W Mesa/Boogie Studio 22 and a 30W Vox AC30.

The thing to remember is that most amps sound their best when set to within a very narrow "sweet spot," which usually occurs at or past halfway up on the volume control. Try that with a 100W Marshall Plexi in most studios today and it's just too loud for the room – or the mikes – to handle. Set your Fender Pro Junior to 8, however, with the right mike placed in just the right place in front of its 10" speaker, and the tone on tape might be as huge as you'd hoped for from your half-stack, without deafening the engineer into the bargain.

Big amps played at lower volumes often sound dull, flat and lifeless. Crank them up until they sound good, then trap them inside a too-small room, or record them using poor technique or a mike that can't handle the sound pressure levels, and you might get ragged, harsh results. Your precious 100-watter ends up a blur in the mix, or it swamps the other instruments fighting for a place in the frequency spectrum.

A growing number of artists are finding a use for digital modelers in the studio, too, using DI products such as Line 6's POD. Where to some ears digital amps may still sound a little "cold" in the real world, once placed in the track – which more often than not, after all, is digital anyway – many amp emulations provide another solution to the trick of miking and recording a large, raging amp in a small studio space.

Born out of more hours in the R&D lab than any guitar tool which has come before, the modeling amp is neither tube (though some employ one or two) nor solid-state as we have commonly come to know it. This is a third breed. Rather than being engineered to present a sound of its own, it has been designed to mimic many of the best-loved tube amps of all time. This, then, is the paradox at the heart of the digital amp movement: a truly computer-age product claiming to be the way forward, but only acceptable to its own marketplace so long as it successfully emulates the technologically-archaic designs which have gone before.

Pioneered by the likes of Line 6 and Johnson, later taken up – and given further acceptability – by Fender, Peavey, Crate and others, modeling amps are mainly based on the same sorts of digital signal processing that allows a multi-FX unit to mimic a spring reverb and a tape echo, or a keyboard to hop between a Hammond B-3 organ and a Rhodes piano at the push of a button. By digitally mapping the parameters of a great tube amp's sound and performance, designers of the better modeling amps have gone to great lengths to program in not only the basic tones of the classics, but to emulate things like their playing feel, response to pick attack, and EQ quirks.

Though it generally looks like a modern but traditional guitar combo, a digital amp's very format approaches signal reproduction in an entirely different way, right down to the choice of speaker. Rather than being the final link in the tone-coloration chain as in many tube or tranny amps, the speaker functions in a context more akin to a speaker in the hi-fi world. It is there to accurately project the full sound of the amp itself, which in most cases already includes the appropriate speaker emulation to suit the amp model selected.

There's no doubt that digital amps can sound pretty incredible. Most experienced reviewers continue to agree that even the best few sounds in any make's emulation menu still don't quite capture the nuances of the real thing. But digital amp designers are pushing the envelope all the time and certainly many players would have trouble distinguishing the model from its inspiration in

'02 LINE 6 VETTA

Specifications: *footswitchable multi-channel digital modeling combo; 100W output (optional mono/stereo); dual 12" speakers.*
Controls: *too numerous to mention: includes full array of buttons and controls for programming and preset selection.*
Features: *45 amp models; 28 cab models; 64 factory and 64 user presets; numerous onboard 'stomp' and digital effects; DI facilities.*

'01 CRATE DXJ112

Specifications: *footswitchable multi-channel digital modeling combo; 60W output (mono cab, stereo headphone and line out); single 12" speaker.*
Controls: *master output, amp selector, gain, bass, mid, treble, channel level, effects selector, effect adjust, reverb level and depth, plus keypad.*
Features: *16 amp models; 8 digital effects; DI facilities; headphone out; footswitchable presets; MIDI sync; Eminence speaker.*

Line 6's broad palette of tones has already lured a diverse following, from country picker Pete Anderson to rocker Art Alexakis of Everclear.

a number of cases, a verdict upheld by the ever-growing lists of pro endorsements for digital modeling amplifiers.

Even more impressive for the average buyer than the virtue of any individual emulation is the sheer number of amp tones which most digital makes now offer. While players happy with just a few variations on the one good sound or professionals who can afford a large collection of vintage amps are still likely to turn to the real thing, the modeling amp presents an incredible sonic playground to the average Joe who couldn't hope to ever own a '62 Vox AC30, a '68 Marshall Plexi, a '59 Fender Bassman, an '83 Mesa/Boogie MkIIC, and a Matchless D/C-30… or to get them all into the trunk of his Ford.

And there's that paradox again. By including amps like the above and many others on its emulation menu (the true identities of which are often thinly disguised on the control panel rotary selector – see *Amps Du Jour*) the new breed continues time and again to re-confirm just how much we love the old. But so it goes with much in the guitar world. The basic tonal templates for rock, blues and country were laid some 50 years ago, and we as players don't often want sounds that are new and original, but yearn for sounds that take us somewhere close to the heroes that have gone before. The point is, of course, that most guitarists simply don't want their new Digitone Space-O-Matic to sound like a Digitone Space-O-Matic. They want it to sound like a '65 Twin Reverb, a '68 Plexi, a '57 tweed Deluxe and a Soldano SLO – all within the same song, at the tap of a footswitch.

The resurgence in acoustic gigs has brought us another new breed of amplifier. In the early days of large-venue acoustic performance it took a skilled live sound engineer to mike up a guitar in a way that would keep it sounding natural but powerful, while still minimizing feedback. As soundhole and under-saddle piezo pickups improved, life for the small-club troubadour became easier, and it was often enough just to inject the guitar straight into the PA or – preferably through a dedicated acoustic preamp – into a standard guitar amp. Neither tended to render particularly pleasing sonic results (generally sounding rather dead and muted on one hand, or tinny and lacking any punch on the other) but they were an easier option than miking-up for the novice soundman.

The unplugged music revolution of the early '90s changed the scene dramatically: if so many players wanted to perform acoustically, they might as well sound acoustic. A new amp market had been clearly defined, and the manufacturers eagerly hopped to it.

In crude terms, acoustic guitar combos lean more toward hi-fi design than they do toward the traditional electron-tube-based electric guitar amp. Firstly, on the electronics side, they seek to reproduce as realistically as possible the natural sound of the acoustic guitar plugged into them, rather than coloring, warming and distorting the signal as most guitar amps do. Secondly, on the speaker side, the drivers – rather than adding their own further coloration – aim to transfer the signal with accuracy and high fidelity into the moving air which the human ear perceives as sound (much as with the modeling amps discussed earlier).

This approach has somewhat more in common with bass amp design than it does with building amplifiers for six-string electrics. Unsurprisingly, great bass amp builders like Trace Elliot, SWR, Ashdown and others have introduced some impressive models for acoustic, with deserved success. Creative features like dual active and low-impedance channels, XLR inputs, mid notches and feedback filters have set new standards of tone shaping for acoustics, and secured a lasting place for the genre in the player's arsenal.

Many big manufacturers have made forays into the field, with some worthy offerings from most. The achievements of Marshall's AS50R and AS100D and Fender's Acoustasonic line prove neither was content to merely re-badge a tranny practise amp – as some ultra-budget models from occasional B-list makers have certainly done. On one hand, the acoustic amp now seems yet another piece of kit the cash-strapped player feels pressured to buy; on the other, if an acoustic is your main tool of choice, you'll want and need an amp that does it justice.

'01 FENDER CYBER-TWIN
Specifications: *footswitchable multi-channel digital modeling combo with tube preamp; 130W output (optional mono/stereo); dual 12" speakers.*
Controls: *trim, gain, volume, treble, middle, bass, presence, reverb, master; pushbuttons for programming; rotary model selector.*
Features: *35 amp models; 85 factory and 85 user presets; 28 effects types; DI facilities; stereo headphone outs; motorized main amp controls.*

'98 TRACE ACOUSTIC TA200S
Specifications: *three-channel solid-state acoustic combo; 200W output; eight 5" speakers.*
Controls: *individual gain and EQ for each channel (piezo/low-level, active/high-level, balanced XLR); shared: master volume, shape and notch; controls for 16-bit digital effects and reverb (footswitchable).*
Features: *balanced DI; phantom power for XLR mike input; link/line out; effects send and returns.*

'99 ASHDOWN RADIATOR 2
Specifications: *two-channel hybrid tube/solid-state acoustic combo; 120W output; 8" speaker and dual tweeters.*
Controls: *Ch1: phase switch, input level, seven-band EQ (on rotaries and sliders), mid feedback, reverb; Ch2: phase switch, input level, tube drive, seven-band EQ, low feedback, reverb; shared: reverb type, output level.*
Features: *XLR, piezo and active inputs; XSL DI out; solid cherry hardwood cabinet.*

'99 SWR STRAWBERRY BLONDE
Specifications: *single-channel solid-state acoustic combo; 80W output; single 10" speaker and piezo tweeter.*
Controls: *gain, master volume, aural enhancer, bass, midrange, treble, effects blend, reverb.*
Features: *balanced XLR out; spring reverb; parallel effects loop; strawberry red control panel; blonde Tolex-covered cabinet.*

Ever since the magnetic pickup was first mounted on a guitar, electronics designers have sought ways to enhance, augment and affect the signal from the source. The very first "effects" were often integrated into the amplifier itself, although the Rocco Company, owned by Epiphone, manufactured stand-alone units in the 1930s. Guitar effects pedals as we know them, however, really date from the early '60s.

Two very popular effects – reverb and tremolo – were included within many amps' electronics from the 1950s. Compared to modern IC-chip-loaded units these and other early effects employed relatively bulky circuitry and often mechanical devices and even moving parts to enable them to manipulate the sound of an electric guitar or other amplified instrument. The Leslie rotating speaker cabinet (originally built for use with the Hammond organ) was an early attempt at a chorus effect – and sonically very successful, if extremely cumbersome – while the first echo units employed moving loops of recording tape. They

were complicated, but sounded quite fantastic. Great guitarists throughout the ages have utilised these tools with stunning effect. Imagine Jimi Hendrix without fuzz, The Edge without delay, Scotty Moore or Dick Dale without reverb. Without effects, these players' trademark sounds would be hugely different.

A lot of early experiments with effects can be traced back to Les Paul himself who, innovator that he was, created some of the sounds we take for granted today. He built a delay unit, for example, by linking a pair of tape recorders together and recording the signal from the guitar back and forth between the machines to achieve a repeating echo effect.

Guitar pedals perform a vast array of sonic functions; this chapter will outline many of the most popular, along with some quirky options. The possibilities that can be created by using and combining effects are almost endless. Although pedals can be broadly cast into the categories defined here, the fact that each manufacturer uses different components means that few units sound identical. So an Ibanez and, say, an MXR phaser certainly do sound different, with their own quirks and tonal characteristics.

DISTORTION PEDALS
1. *Maestro FuzzTone,* **2.** *Colorsound Tonebender,* **3.** *Electro-Harmonix Big Muff Pi,* **4.** *Ibanez Overdrive,* **5.** *Ibanez TS808 Tube Screamer,* **6.** *Ibanez TS9 Tube Screamer. Opposite page: Dallas/Arbiter Fuzz Face and Boss OD-1.*

COMPRESSORS
1. *MXR Dynacomp,* **2.** *Ross Compressor,* **3.** *Marshall ED-1 Edward The Compressor.*

CHORUSES
1. *Boss CE-1 Chorus Ensemble,* **2.** *Boss CE-2 Chorus. Following page: Uni-Vibe.*

PHASERS
1. *Early issue Electro-Harmonix Small Stone and* (**2.**) *later issue Electro-Harmonix Small Stone,* **3.** *MXR Phase 45, Phase 90* (**4**) *and Phase 100* (**5**).

FLANGERS
1. *Electro-Harmonix Electric Mistress,* **2.** *Electro-Harmonix Deluxe Electric Mistress,* **3.** *Ibanez FL-305 Flanger,* **4.** *MXR Flanger,* **5.** *Ibanez FL-301 DX Flanger,* **6.** *Ibanez FL-303 Flanger.*

DISTORTION PEDALS

COMPRESSORS

PHASERS

FLANGERS

CHORUSES

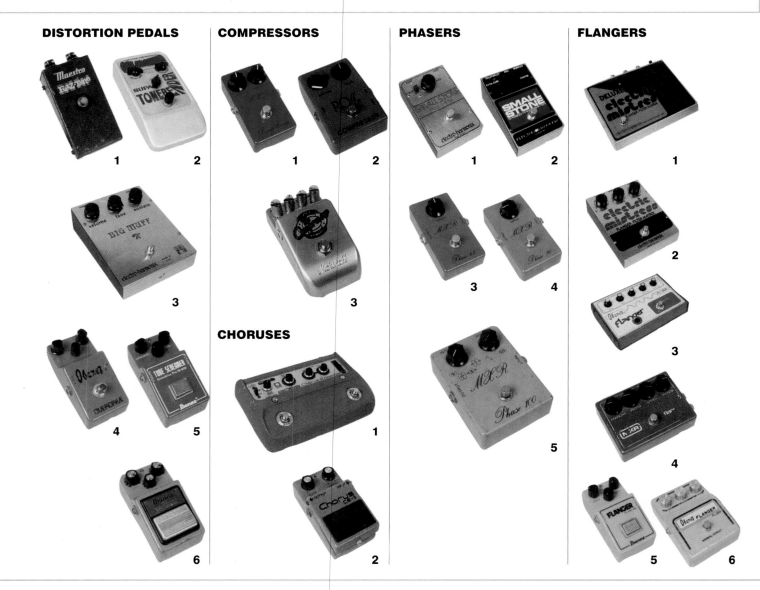

classic pedals

The way the guitar's signal can be "effected" can be divided roughly into five categories.

BOOST AND DISTORTION EFFECTS

These overdrive your amp through use of a boosting circuit, or add fuzz or distortion to the sound, without affecting pitch. In the beginning guitarists turned their amps up full to get tube distortion. When it became apparent this wasn't enough – or required oppressively loud volume levels – creative engineers developed fuzz and distortion pedals, and the guitar world was never the same again. There have probably been more fuzz and distortion pedals produced than all other pedals combined.

The Maestro Fuzztone, manufactured by Gibson, was arguably the first commercially produced fuzz guitar pedal, although the Sola Sound Tonebender Fuzz was also introduced at around this time. The Fuzztone is reportedly the unit Keith Richards used to create the guitar sound for the famous riff on The Stones' 'Satisfaction'. The example pictured opposite is also interesting in having a Gibson "Patent Applied For" sticker on its base. These, of course, are more usually found on Gibson's first humbucking pickups. The Fuzztone has two controls, one for Volume and one for Attack. The Attack control varies the amount of distortion while Volume controls the volume level of the pedal when it is activated. This unit creates a harsh, rambling fuzz.

The Tonebender was the brainchild of Larry and Joe Macari. It was initially produced under their Sola Sound banner until the company was renamed Colorsound. This early, no-holds-barred fuzz was much loved by Jeff Beck. This famous unit, with the orange "fuzz flash," has three controls: a Volume control, a Bass/Treble control to adjust the tone, and a Fuzz control to set the amount of distortion required.

Electro-Harmonix's Big Muff was first made in the late '60s. It went through four cosmetic facelifts. The third version is the most commonly seen and it's the one that has been reissued, too. It features the classic metal E-H case with three controls – Volume, Tone and Sustain – all of which have drastic ranges. Volume, of course, sets the required boost when activated, Tone does pretty much what it says, and the Sustain control determines the amount of distortion (which also, indeed, influences the sustain of the note). A compression control was added to the cocktail for the late '70s mains powered version. All Big Muffs create an enormous wall of dense fuzz; no subtle overdrive here.

Ibanez, the Japanese company better known for its electric guitars, started offering guitar pedals in the early '70s. Their units were actually produced by the Maxon company. The first overdrive unit they made was simply called Ibanez Overdrive, and came in an orange case with script lettering. It has three controls: Distortion, Volume and Tone. Most fuzz pedals have similar variations on these basic controls. This pedal evolved – through about three incarnations – into the legendary TS-808 Tubescreamer Overdrive Pro, much admired by Stevie Ray Vaughan and many others. The TS-808 produces a very natural sounding and smooth overdrive supposedly recreating the tone of tube distortion. The essential component to this circuit is the RC4558 chip, which many believe is crucial to the pedal's sound. The 808 was succeeded by the highly regarded TS-9, which replaced it in the early '80s – and has since been seen on thousands of stages worldwide. It has also now been reissued.

The Dallas/Arbiter Fuzz Face was introduced in the mid '60s and was distinctive thanks to its round "smiley face" design. With two controls for Fuzz and Volume, the circuit is pure simplicity.

ROLAND SPACE ECHO
For years regarded as one of the finest-sounding delay units available, Roland's classic tape-loop-based Space Echo still sounds great by any standards, and has become a highly desirable vintage unit. This version adds chorus and reverb to the brew.

Fuzz Faces most commonly came in red, blue or silver-grey, although there are other colors, including black. Constantly reissued by an ever-changing host of manufacturers, including Jim Dunlop, the originals from the '60s are most sought after on account of their components. Many argue that circuits containing "top hat" style NKT275 germanium transistors sound the best. The Fuzz Face is a true fuzz rather than distortion pedal, creating thick fuzz tones that compress and break up more as the Fuzz control is turned up. Jimi Hendrix is a well documented early user of the Fuzz Face, though at times he played through a Big Muff and a number of custom-built Roger Mayer pedals as well.

The first series of small-case Boss pedals from Japan included

Something old, something new(ish): the Dallas/Arbiter Fuzz Face is a true '60s original, while Boss's OD-1 is more typical of latterday pedals – but both offer some serious drive tones.

the Boss OD-1 overdrive, a great little distortion unit, favored by Pete Townshend. The OD-1 has just two controls. One for volume, in this case labelled Level, and one for the amount of distortion, which Boss labelled Overdrive. Some of the newer Boss distortion and fuzz units, such as the popular DS-1, offer unbeatable value for money. The DS-1 features three controls: Level sets the overall volume, Tone adjusts just that, and Distortion sets the severity of the overdriven sound. The Boss line is now manufactured in Taiwan.

COMPRESSION EFFECTS

These units amplify any signal detected above a given level to add sustain and "squash" to the sound. Relatively basic compressor pedals work by performing a simplified function akin to the more complex and expensive studio units, maintaining a constant level of volume by boosting quiet passages and "limiting" loud ones. A compressor is commonly used to give sustain and definition to jangly arpeggiated chordal parts or to soften and "warm up" lead lines, and is one of the classic ingredients in many Nashville session guitarists' bag of tricks. Compression is also the effect that gave Byrds guitarist Roger

McGuinn's 12-string playing its trademark chime and ring. Without it, McGuinn has said, his Rickenbacker sounded relatively dull and sustainless.

One of the all-time classics, the MXR Dynacomp, has been around for years and has two controls: Output for overall volume, and Sensitivity for the amount of effect. It can also be useful as a straight booster for solos if Output is put on full with Sensitivity kept low.

Many players and pedal collectors regard the Ross Compressor from the early '80s as an improvement on the Dynacomp, though this gray box can be even harder to find. It too has two controls, this time labelled Sustain (for the amount of compression) and Level. Beloved for its rich, warm tone, it is one of the key stompboxes on the pedalboard of Trey Anastasio, guitarist with Vermont-based alt-rockers Phish.

Often misunderstood and generally underappreciated, compressors have been manufactured by most big pedal makers at one time or another. For functional low-budget squash, Marshall recently issued the very acceptable sounding and cleverly named Edward The Compressor. It carries more functions than most of its breed, with four controls to govern Emphasis, Volume, Attack and Compression.

MODULATION EFFECTS

Taking many forms, modulation alters all or part of the pitch of the original sound to create spacial effects such as chorus, flanging, phasing and octave-below effects. In the early days,

chorus was closely related to vibrato (which, correctly speaking, is the sound created when a note is modulated upward and downward, as opposed to tremolo, merely a rhythmic fluctuation in the volume of a signal). Accordingly, many units performed both effects, or something in between. The massive rotating speaker cabinets – such as those built by Leslie – were an early means to create a chorus effect, and Uni-Vox's legendary Uni-Vibe unit of the '60s was largely an effort to produce the sound of a rotating speaker in a smaller, more portable box. It has a Chorus/Vibrato switch to select the desired function, along with controls for Volume and Intensity, and a footpedal to control the rate. A Uni-Vibe is responsible for the hypnotic swoosh on Jimi Hendrix's 'Machine Gun' and 'Star Spangled Banner,' and it can also be heard on much of Robin Trower's work.

Modern choruses are more efficient, high-tech affairs but achieve their results in much the same way, by splitting off a portion of the signal, modulating its pitch slightly in relation to the original, and blending it back to create a multi-voiced sound. Flangers, on the other hand, sweep a modulated portion of the signal up and down against the original at a (usually) variable rate to create a familiar swooshing, spacey effect.

Phase pedals appeared slightly before modern-style choruses and flangers and simulate the sound of tape phase, where two tape machines are run very slightly out of sync. Early versions were made by Ibanez, Jen and Maestro.

Boss started making pedals in the late '70s. Their first units were offered in a large metal case before the more familiar small

---

DELAYS
1. *Boss DM-2*, 2. *Boss DD-5*, 3. *Electro-Harmonix Deluxe Memory Man. Previous page: Roland Space Echo. Following page: Line 6 DL4 Delay Modeler.*

TREMOLOS
1. *Selmer Tremolo*, 2. *Boss PN-2 Tremolo/Pan*, 3. *Nobels TR-X Tremolo.*

WAH-WAH PEDALS
1. *Vox Wah*, 2. *Colorsound Wah-Wah*, 2.. *Jen Cry Baby.*

ENVELOPE FILTERS
1. *Electro-Harmonix Queen Triggered Wah*, 2. *Musitronics Mu-Tron III*, 3. *Ibanez AF201 Auto Filter*, 4. *Electro-Harmonix Dr. Q*, 5. *MXR Envelope Follower.*

OCTAVE DIVIDERS
1. *MXR Blue Box*, 2. *Boss OC-2 Octivider.*

WEIRDOS
Shinei Siren/Hurricane.

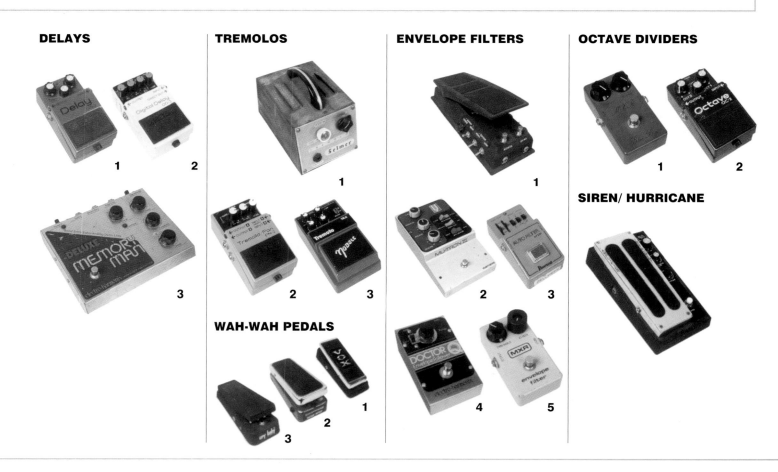

DELAYS
1 2 3

TREMOLOS
1 2 3

WAH-WAH PEDALS
1 2 3

ENVELOPE FILTERS
1 2 3 4 5

OCTAVE DIVIDERS
1 2

SIREN/ HURRICANE

size pedal case was introduced. The Boss line is vast and the pedals are consistently popular, having been around for over 20 years with little change, although some of the early pedals have now been deleted. From the first "large case" line, the CE-1 Chorus/Vibrato is regarded as a classic – liked by artists ranging from Lenny Kravitz to Pantera's Dimebag Darrell – and it can be heard on a large array of '80s recordings. It features mono or stereo outputs with a Level control and an Intensity control for the amount of effect. A footswitch enables the player to change the unit between chorus and vibrato modes. Vibrato uses a Depth and Rate control. The large-case line was deleted in favor of the "small case" models in the early '80s.

As the '80s progressed the range of Boss pedals available grew extensively. The CE-1 chorus was replaced by the CE-2, which is available to this day and is a very decent sounding unit. Simple to use, it carries two controls: Rate and Depth.

The Electro-Harmonix Electric Mistress is described on its case as being a "Filter/Flanger Matrix," and it sounds like no other pedal. It has three knobs: a Rate control determines the speed of the flanging, Range governs the amount of oscillation, and Color sets the amount of effect. First offered in the early '70s in a battery powered unit, it evolved a few years later into an AC-powered version and has now been reissued. In short, it offers flanging and other great modulation effects. Essential! The Boss BF-2 has been another mainstay in the flanging world for many years. This little purple pedal is inexpensive and sounds good.

Ibanez made a host of flangers from the early '70s onward, including the large FL-305 and FL-303, and the FL-301 from the same series as the famous TS-808 overdrive. These were followed by the Ibanez FL-9, which is still an inexpensive bargain on the used market. Four controls determine Speed, Width and Regen ("regeneration," which controls the depth and sweep) and Delay Time which controls how quickly the flanging begins.

MXR's acclaimed mains-powered gray flanger also has four controls, three of which bear the same description as the FL9. The exception is the "delay time," which MXR labelled "Manual." You can hear this unit on much of John McGeoch's playing with Magazine and Siouxsie And The Banshees.

Electro-Harmonix introduced the famous Small Stone in the early '70s. It boasts a unique Color switch, which adds more depth to the effect, as well as a Speed control, which adjusts the speed of the phasing.

When MXR introduced its line of pedals in the early '70s their three phasers – the 45, 90 and 100 – were instant hits. The most popular was probably the Phase 90, which was used extensively by Mick Jones of The Clash, as you can hear prominently on 'Lost In The Supermarket' on the album *London Calling*. The Phase 90 only has one control – to adjust the speed of the phase. Many phasers have a depth control too. Boss, Dod, Danelectro and many other modern makers manufacture excellent phase pedals.

Octave dividers add one or two octaves below the note struck by the guitarist. The MXR Bluebox was one of the first. It featured a Blend control to adjust the amount of dry and effect signal. This pedal was sometimes used by Jimmy Page.

Another very useful Boss pedal is the OC-2 Octivider, which adds two lower octaves if required, with separate blend controls for each. This brown unit has been around for over 20 years. Of the three knobs, the one in the center controls the Blend between normal and effect signal. The other two are labelled Oct 1 and

A classic '60s Uni-Vox Uni-Vibe, the pedal loved by Jimi Hendrix and Robin Trower. (There is also a foot control, not shown here.)

Oct 2 and control the amount of the first or second octave sounded below the source signal.

A true oddball in the pedal world is the Siren/Hurricane pedal manufactured in the '70s by the Shinei Company of Japan. The unit adds white noise (surf), pink noise (hurricane) or, by clicking the switch on the side, a police siren! This pedal was used for the siren effect on The Sweet's '70s UK hit 'Blockbuster.'

TIME-BASED EFFECTS

Units in this category repeat or recreate the original signal without altering its tone or pitch (unless they mix in chorus or flanging), and come in different forms, including delay, tremolo and reverb. Delay is one of the most widely used guitar effects. The pedal or unit repeats the source signal generated by the guitar. The speed of the delay (delay time) and number of repeats (feedback) can usually be controlled by the unit.

The first delay units used moving tape, recording and playing back the signal between different tape heads. The further away the head which recorded the original signal from the one which played it back, the longer the gap between the direct and repeated sound. Delay times are usually measured in thousandths of a second or "milliseconds." Typically, analog pedals produce delay times up to a maximum of about 500 milliseconds, whereas digital and rack mounted units can produce repeats of up to two seconds or more. But beware: digital pedals eat batteries, so a mains adaptor is useful here.

The Watkins Copicat was one of the first tape units available and was widely used in the '60s, in Britain particularly. Good working units, particularly the early tube models, are still great sounding delays. As the tape motor can be turned off, they also make excellent tube preamps. Maestro's Echo-Plex is a similarly desirable American-built tube-driven delay unit that is getting extremely difficult to find.

Roland introduced its famous Space Echo line in the '70s, and at the time these gave what seemed a very modern twist to the echo unit. The final version, the RE-501, added chorus and reverb. There are six delay modes, each accessing a different tape head, as well as Delay-Time and Feedback controls. It also has controls for Bass and Treble along with pushbuttons to access chorus, echo and "Sound on Sound," a control that adds further delays to the actual repeat signal. Any combination can be used at once.

Boss introduced delay pedals with the rest of its line. The early analog pedals, such as the DM-2 and DM-3, were succeeded by digital versions like the DD-3 and DD-5. The DM-2 features three controls: Repeat for the time between the source and delay signal, Intensity for the amount of effect, and Echo for the number of repeats or feedback. The digital DD-3 offers much longer delay times. The four controls each determine Level of effect, Feedback, Delay Time and Hold – which sets the unit's starting point at 50, 200 or 800 milliseconds.

MXR, Ibanez and Electro-Harmonix all made analogue delay units. The E-H Memory Man has been extensively used by The Edge of U2 (you can clearly hear the effect's analog "dirtiness" on the track 'I Will Follow,' among others). This pedal, which has now been reissued, has three controls: Blend for the ratio between the direct and effect signal, Feedback, and Delay to set the delay time.

Tremolo is a long standing guitar favorite. In effect it cuts the guitar signal in and out at a consistent speed, as if you were turning the volume control on the guitar up and down. It is often built into amplifiers. Many Beatles recordings feature the tremolo built into Vox amps. Tremolo pedals have been made by most of the major manufacturers, including Colorsound, Electro-Harmonix and Dallas-Arbiter, who made the Trem Face to match their famous Fuzz Face distortion.

Distinct from tremolo – although the term is sometimes used as a misnomer for tremolo – vibrato achieves a similar bouncing, volume-cut effect, but in its truest sense does also alter a portion of the pitch of the original signal in the process. A more complex effect to achieve electronically, vibrato is less often seen in stand-alone units (though Matchless once made an intricate tube-powered pedal, and others have offered variations) and is rarer than tremolo as an on-board amp effect. It was included on a few early-'60s Fenders, '50s Magnatones and the early Vox AC30s. Gibson offered the now-rare GAV1 vibrato unit in the '50s, designed as an "add-on" between guitar and amp, and Selmer made a tube powered stand-alone unit in the '60s. Simple to operate, each had controls for depth and speed.

The now-deleted Boss PN2 Tremolo/Pan pedal can be used as a straight tremolo unit or as a stereo pan box, panning the signal between the left and right channels in a stereo field. This requires two amps, of course. It has a Rate (speed) control, a Depth control (for the severity of the effect) and a Mode control. Four modes can be accessed, two each for tremolo and panning – each with a differing waveform. It has been succeeded by Boss's TR2 pedal which lacks the panning facility.

Tremolo has come back into vogue in recent years, and newer pedal versions of the effect are beginning to surface, from Voodoo Lab's deluxe and lush-sounding Tremolo, to Nobels' affordable but extremely functional option. The latter features four controls – Depth, Speed, Tone and Level – plus a four-way switch to set the "hardness" and wave shape of the tremolo.

EQ-BASED EFFECTS

This category of effect alters the frequencies of the signal's tonal range, and includes EQs and wah-wahs – the latter among the most widely used of all guitar effects pedals. Many players are happy to go on stage with no pedals at all except a wah-wah.

In widespread use since the mid '60s, wah-wahs contain a potentiometer which governs what is essentially a tone circuit within the pedal that is altered by a foot control. The further forward the foot control is depressed the more treble is produced. A similar effect can be achieved by turning the tone pot on the guitar itself, but obviously a greater versatility is achieved by leaving the guitarist with both hands free, and the active circuit of the wah pedal generally has a broader frequency

range, used in combination with coloration and boost in some models of wah-wah.

The visually appealing Vox Wah was made by the Italian company Jen, and was electronically identical to their own Cry Baby Super. Hendrix, of course, was famous for using one (for a classic example listen to the intro to 'Voodoo Chile'). The tonal sweep isn't as broad as that of, say, a Colorsound Wah of the same period, but the narrower range makes the effect somewhat more controlable for the guitarist.

Colorsound produced their Wah in the early '70s. It had a very

Digital technology has brought us affordable processors which perform a dizzying number of functions and are often designed into a format which combines floorboard switching options, too. Zoom's GFX-4 (1) is styled to capture nostalgia for older pedals but offers six simultaneous effects out of a possible 44, as well as 60 user and 60 factory presets, plus amp and cab simulation. Boss's relatively upscale GT-3 (2) does much of the same and more, with unusual pickup simulation, acoustic-electric preamp, impressive routing facilities, and nearly 350 user and preset patches.

At the forefront of digital technology in today's guitar world, "modeling" units are blurring the lines between effects processors and amp emulators – and most of the frontrunners pack in plenty of both. Johnson's J-Station (3) is a handy desktop unit for home recording, while Line 6's POD Pro (below) expands upon the features of their own similarly styled desktop POD, but improves the routing and connecting facilities for studio use.

large sweep which resulted in a trademark sound. Colorsound also produced a Fuzz/Wah which combined fuzz into the wah pedal by clicking a second rocker switch.

The Dunlop Cry Baby reissue is a great wah pedal; robust and functional. It's not a true reissue in that some of the components differ from the original Jen version, but it captures much of the same sound and is good value for the money.

Envelope filters or followers are basically automatic wah-wahs, but the tonal change and sweep are triggered automatically by how hard the string is hit: the harder you pick, the more it "wahs." They were extremely popular with funk guitarists and bassists in the late '70s and early '80s, and have come and gone from fashion ever since.

The Boss T/Wah was a big hit in the '80s. It is a sensitive unit, with three controls: knobs for Sensitivity and Peak determine the amount of effect and the range of the sweep respectively, while a Drive switch presets the sweep range. It has been succeeded by the Boss Auto-Wah.

Many consider the Musitronics Mu-Tron III to be one of the best sounding envelope filters ever. It boasts three knobs, one each for Mode, Peak and Gain, with three switch controls: one to turn the unit on and off; the other two for Drive and Range. It offers a huge range of possibilities and is often used by bass players – think Bootsy Collins. Ibanez offered its first auto wah in the AF-201. It had three switches: two for Mode and one for Range, combined with two slider controls for Sensitivity and Peak. This pedal was succeeded by the AF-9 unit.

Electro-Harmonix manufactured the Dr. Q envelope follower along with a deluxe version, The Zipper. The Dr. Q has a slider switch which augmented the bass response and a "Q" knob to control the range of the effect. The Zipper has a switch for a high or low range, marked 1 and 2, a Range control for the range of the sweep and a "Q" control for sensitivity – the speed at which the high peak is reached.

MXR originally made their Envelope Follower, now reissued, in the late '70s. The company named the range and sensitivity controls Threshold and Attack respectively.

One of the rarer Electro-Harmonix pedals is the '70s Queen Triggered Wah. This unit can be used as a conventional wah-wah – and a very good sounding one too – or as an envelope follower/auto wah. The unique aspect of this pedal when used as an auto-wah is that the position of the pedal determines the tonal range accessed. So if the pedal is fully upright the tonal range is in the lower registers; fully depressed, the effect is in the higher registers. The sensitivity, or amount, of auto wah or "Q" is determined by a control on the side. It's an impressive box.

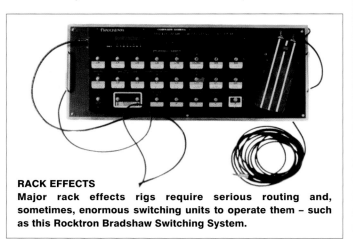

RACK EFFECTS
Major rack effects rigs require serious routing and, sometimes, enormous switching units to operate them – such as this Rocktron Bradshaw Switching System.

Capitalizing on the popularity of vintage delay pedals, Line 6 has employed its amp modeling experience to produce a series of floor units which model a broad range of classic stompboxes. The DL4 Delay Modeler emulates 15 delay units, from the Space Echo to the Memory Man, and adds a 14-second loop sampler.

MULTI-FX UNITS

Pedals doing all of the above jobs – and sometimes combining two or three sounds – have provided the portable answer to altering the guitar's straight sound since the early '60s, with a resurgent popularity again in recent years. But digital technology has signaled a major revolution in what this or that box of tricks can do for you. Studios and large concert stages have long seen the use of powerful, sophisticated rack units, at first usually dedicated to doing one job well (reverb, delay, chorus), and then capable of complex multi-functions.

But the cost of digital components has decreased while their processing capabilities have dramatically increased. It's this particular combination of changes that has put a vast array of previously complex effects in the hands of everyday musicians – whether they are hardworking sidemen, amateur guitarists, or dedicated hobbyists.

The largest portion of this new market in relatively affordable digital effects comes in the form of multi-FX pedals, or "floorboards." These combine the processing power of rack units but do away with the need to string separate patch-triggering footswitches across the stage or practise room floor. They do this by incorporating their own stomp switches and expression pedals. Such units are designed to sit on the floor in the usual front-line pedal position for easy and instant access.

Most of the prominent music electronics manufacturers offer multi-FX units – names like Boss, Zoom, Digitech, Korg and others – often in a range of prices broad enough to suit any budget. Even basic and astoundingly affordable models like Zoom's GFX707 offer capabilities that would have sounded impossible 10 (and certainly 20) years ago: nine effects simultaneously, multiple user and factory patches, even a built-in drum machine. The power of some of the more heavy-duty units truly boggles the mind.

While different makers do have their own sound and character to some extent – one excelling at reverbs, for example, while another does great vintage-style chorus – the nature of digital technology does homogenize the business. Price and the number and combinations available of effects, therefore, often decide what you might buy as much or more so than the inherent sound qualities of different makes and models.

Many guitarists still prefer the sound created by older-style analog units, too, which they argue are warmer and more natural in tone. Plenty of records which contain classic guitar effects were made before digital technology was invented, so there's certainly a valid argument in the claim that the old analog boxes sounded pretty good already. But there is a trade-off. Analog effects are noisy, and linking a number of such units together can produce unacceptable hiss or "white noise" – and of course you would need to string together nearly all of the stompboxes pictured on the preceding pages to get the sonic options of, say, a single Boss GT-3 processor. For quantity, digital technology is unrivaled – but for quality, the jury is still out.

"Learning to change your strings efficiently is the first stage of guitar maintenance, and it can be surprising how many people who've been playing for years still put on a fresh set in a manner that may impede their ability to stay in tune and sound their best."

"Setting intonation is one of the main goals of any set-up. Without getting this crucial step right, your guitar will never quite sound in-tune, nor will the resonance and harmonic content of its natural voice ring true."

chapter 3

GUITAR
MAINTENANCE

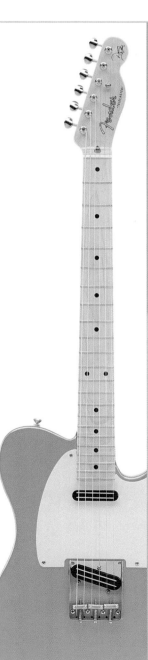

In order to play your best, you need a guitar that is optimized for peak performance. By doing the work yourself, you can both save money and keep your instrument in the best possible shape for your own style and sound. This chapter shows you how to string up correctly, adjust all factors crucial to "action" and feel, change pickups, perform wiring mods, and much more.

STRINGING UP

Chances are you're constantly aware, if only subconsciously, of the effects that the feel and freshness of your strings are having on your playing and sound. Even so, it's all too easy to overlook this vital first link in the chain – the component which most directly connects you to the music you're making. The type of strings you use, their condition, and the stability of their attachment and contact with all points of the guitar will all affect both tuning and tone. When all of the above are at their optimum, there's that much less to get in the way of your playing. Appropriately, then, we'll begin by looking at options for correct string loading and ways of maximizing their condition and effect on tuning stability.

STRING TYPES

You've probably given a lot of thought to the type and style of guitar you want and struggled to find the money to buy it. But have you ever given a thought to the strings you're going to use, or how frequently you should change them? Let's face it, the type of strings you use on your guitar and their general condition will form the starting point of good guitar tone.

The variety of string choices available can be dizzying, though you need to keep in mind that the majority of brands are produced by just a few string manufacturers. In fact, you should try to choose the strings you use based on their consistency and their availability as well as their "feel" and tone.

The most common type of strings for electric guitar are "nickel"

If your strings are poorly attached there's little chance of good tuning stability, and your tone will probably suffer too. Even plenty of experienced players load their strings in ways that fail to optimize their performance, but it's easy to learn a stable and efficient technique for stringing-up – either a basic wind or more advanced locking technique.

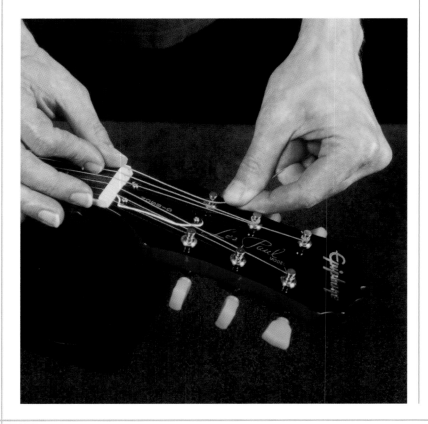

roundwounds. What that means is that the wound strings – typically the three low strings – have nickel-plated steel windings (wraps) around a steel core. The unwound strings – typically the top three – are "plain" high carbon steel. A small metal "ball" is wound onto each string at one end; this is the "ball-end" that secures the string into the anchor point at the bridge. You'll need to cut this off before you can use a string for a Floyd Rose vibrato (see the discussion of vibrato adjustmnent that follows). Some special strings do come already without ball-ends for this purpose.

You will also see "stainless steel" strings. D'Addario introduced this type back in the mid-'70s, and they now use "400-series magnetic stainless steel" instead of nickel-plated steel wraps. D'Addario use this material on their flatwound Chromes (where a flat-section outer winding is used). They also use it for their Half Round strings (where the oversized stainless steel winding is partially ground down to offer some of the smoothness of flatwound strings) which offer reduced finger-noise and less fret wear, but without abandoning all of the brightness of roundwounds.

Stainless steel strings typically sound a little brighter initially, but become duller more quickly than nickel. Nickel-plated strings usually sound slightly more mellow, but tend to die less quickly. Custom string pioneer Ernie Ball has recently re-introduced their original pure nickel wrap strings, which offer an even warmer tone than the nickel-plated variety.

Do bear in mind that these are generalizations, and that you're advised to experiment with different strings. However, when you do experiment, it's more useful to compare the different winding types of the same brand and the same gauge, to keep the variables at a minimum.

STRING LOADING I: BASIC

Learning to change your strings efficiently is the first stage of guitar maintenance, and it can be surprising how many people who've been playing for years still put on a fresh set in a manner that may impede the strings ability to stay in tune and sound their best. There are many ways to attach the strings to the tuners. You need to establish your own working practice, one that secures the strings efficiently and suits your own guitar and the style you play in. Here's a basic method:

1 Lay your guitar on your worktop in front of you with the headstock to your left (supported if it's back-angled) or whichever way is most comfortable. Unless you need to clean your fingerboard, or do any other maintenance or modification, always replace your strings one at a time, which helps to keep neck tension fairly regular and to hold any "floating" bridge or tailpiece parts in place. Use a string winder to quickly slacken the string and remove it from the tuner's string-post – start with the low E-string.

2 Remember that the plain end of the string was probably cut to length with wire cutters and will be extremely sharp, so watch your fingers, eyes and guitar finish. Remove the old string from the bridge and discard it. Set the tuner so that the hole in its string-post (diagram a, following page) is parallel to the nut. Thread the new string through the tailpiece or bridge and carefully pull it down to the tuner's string-post. Place the string against the inside edge of the post and pull it tightly, as pictured on the left.

3 Now wind the string around the string-post counter-clockwise for one full turn (diagram b), keeping the tension on, and thread it through the string-post hole (diagram c). This will add another turn above the first.

4 Pull the string out of the other side of the string-post hole and pull it as tight as you can (pictured right). Bend the loose end of the string at a right angle and slightly downwards immediately at the point it emerges from the string-post hole. Tune up to pitch. Repeat this procedure for the A-string and D-string. If you have a six-a-side headstock, use the same technique for all strings; if you have a three-a-side headstock the procedure is the same except it becomes a mirror image for the second set of three tuners, which are mounted on the opposite side of the headstock.

5 Now wind on your plain strings. Whereas you have ended up with just a couple of turns around the string post on the wound strings, the plain strings need a few more turns. Wrap the string neatly around the string post three or four times before poking the loose end through the post hole. Stretch your strings (a process described in depth later in this section), tune the strings up to pitch, and then check that your intonation is accurate and reset it if necessary.

6 Finally, clip the loose end of the string a few millimetres away from the post for a tidy finish. Some players like to curl the loose string in a circle, which is fine – but never leave the loose ends hanging because they can be dangerous.

a   b   c

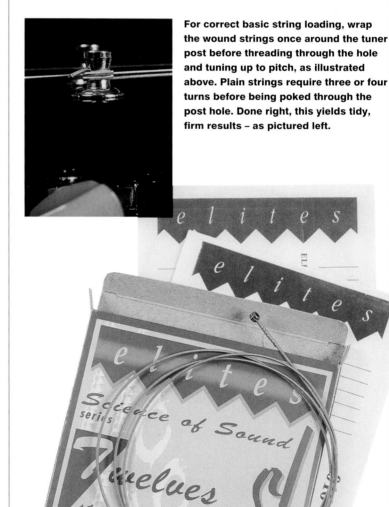

For correct basic string loading, wrap the wound strings once around the tuner post before threading through the hole and tuning up to pitch, as illustrated above. Plain strings require three or four turns before being poked through the post hole. Done right, this yields tidy, firm results – as pictured left.

STRING LOADING: GOLDEN RULES

Don't wind the string around the post from the speaking length side. Some people place the un-cut string in the post hole and then wrap the slack, by hand, around the post. This is not advised as it may well distort the windings on the wound strings.

Never cut a wound string without first making a right-angled bend. This is recommended by most string makers and will prevent the winds (wraps) from distorting or unwinding.

Never have any overlapping winds around the post. Keep things neat and tidy and always wind the string in a downward direction under the string-post hole.

Never leave any slack in the string as it winds around the string-post. This could cause future tuning problems.

Never leave excess string hanging from the end of the tuners. Either cut the strings close to the post or wind the free length into an interlocking circle.

  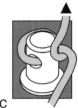

a   b   c

Slightly more involved than basic string loading but potentially very effective – and favored by many players – this locking wrap provides a high degree of tuning stability thanks to minimal string slippage around the tuner post.

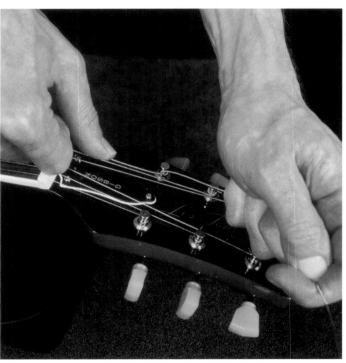

STRING LOADING II: LOCKING

Many players and repairmen prefer to lock the string around the tuner's string post for additional security and tuning stability, and it makes sense to do this if you have a vibrato (without a locking nut or locking tuners). This method requires a little more dexterity and, because of the lock, it may not be quite as quick to remove the strings – something to consider if you break a string on-stage and you haven't got your own guitar tech. However, practise makes perfect.

1 Start off exactly the same as the basic method but this time turn the tuner's string post so that the hole is approximately 60 degrees to the nut. With your left hand, pull the string to the inside edge of the string post but hold it with your right hand to create some slack length (top left). Holding the string firm at the tuner with your left hand, move your right hand down the string to the tuner, and grip the string. (Alternatively you could poke the string through the string post first and then estimate your slack, but you must be very careful not to bend the string in the wrong place.)

2 Poke the loose end through the string-post hole from the centre of the headstock outwards (see diagram a, left). Pull the loose end through the hole but don't lose the grip on your right hand because that's still creating the slack. Bend the loose end clockwise around the post (diagram b) and under the point where the string is entering the post (diagram c). Hold the string momentarily with the first finger of your right hand, then grab the loose end again with your left hand and pull it tightly as you bend it upwards and over the string (lower photo).

3 Hold the string in place with your right-hand thumb and tighten the tuner so that the "speaking length" of the string clamps the loose end tightly (the speaking length is the portion that goes from the tuner, over the nut, and on to the bridge). Then, with your string winder in your left hand, carefully wind on the slack, making neat turns below the first turn. If you've estimated your slack correctly you should get approximately two to three turns around the post. Again, if your guitar has a three-a-side headstock, the procedure on the treble strings is a mirror

ALTERNATE LOCKS

Follow the locking procedure described above to the point that you start winding on the slack. Instead of your first wind going under the locked string try one over and the remaining turns under. For extra security try two over and the remainder under. Whatever locking method you use, be flexible. If your tuner has a short string-post, it will not be practical to use a double locking method, especially with heavy gauge strings (see *String Loading: Golden Rules* on the previous page).

Locking Tuners take the guess-work out of string loading. Sperzel's Trim-Loks, for example, require that you simply thread the string through the post hole, pull it tight, tighten the lock on the back of the tuner housing and tune up. One thing to remeber with any locking tuners is that you must always fully slacken the string before undoing the lock – don't undo the lock with the string tuned to pitch.

image. Having attached, tuned, and stretched all your strings, and if necessary re-set your intonation, make a final downward bend where the loose end of each string emerges from the post, and clip off the string as close as you can to the post.

STRING LOADING III: SLOT-HEAD TUNERS

Vintage Fenders and the numerous modern re-issues often use split-post vintage-style tuners (often called Safeti-Post tuners) as originally supplied by Kluson from the early '50s until the mid-'60s. While you can attach your string in any of the ways already shown – the slot is just like an open-topped post hole – they were originally designed so that the loose end is placed down the hole in the centre of the post. This is a very neat and tidy way of string loading and you never have any protruding and sharp string ends. Remember: replace the strings one at a time. If your guitar has a vibrato and you need to remove all the strings at once, place the vibrato's backplate, or a stack of business cards, under the back edge of the vibrato *before* you remove the strings to keep the balance between springs and string tension approximately correct.

1 Lay the guitar in front of you, remove the old string' set the tuner slot so it's parallel with the nut and load the new string through the bridge. Pull it tight against the inside of the tuner post. You need to allow approximately the distance of two machineheads (2"/50mm) for winding on (see *Headstock Angles*, below) so if you're fitting the low E, make a right-angled bend in the string at a point coinciding with the D-string tuner. Cut the string to length approximately ½"/10mm beyond that right-angled bend, as pictured above.

2 Poke the loose end down as far as it will go, into the central hole in the tuner's string post, and bend it down to the bottom of the slot (near right photo). Hold it in place with your right-hand thumb while – with your string winder in your left hand – you tighten the tuner, making sure that the slack string is neatly wound down the post.

HEADSTOCK ANGLES

The type of headstock you have affects the ways in which you need to load your strings. The reason is that the angle at which the string "breaks" from the nut to the tuners plays a part in the tone of your guitar and its tuning stability. If the string angle is too shallow the string can rattle in the nut slot, causing a loss of tone and at worst a sitar-like buzz. On guitars with a standard back-angled headstock (without a locking nut) you need to aim for around two to four neat string turns around the tuner post. Clearly this depends on the gauge of the string and the height of the string-post hole above the tuner bushing (the washer-like or nut-like fitting around the post which sits against the face of the headstock and into the post hole). For example, a heavy gauge low E string on a short tuner post will require fewer turns than a lighter gauge E on a longer post.

On Fender-style, straight headstocks you need to be a little more clever, especially when you only have one string tree on the top two strings. On the low E string aim for two turns (too many here will create too steep an angle which main impair tuning stability, especially if you have a vibrato). On the A string aim for two to three turns; the D string needs around four turns. The G string is the most problematic and you need as many turns as you can down the post almost to the tuner bushing itself. This will

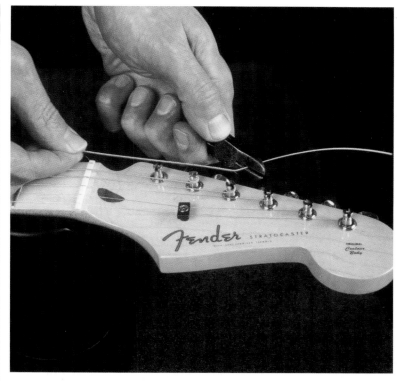

After allowing a distance of about two string posts from the post you're winding onto, make a right-angle bend in the string and cut its remainder, leaving enough length after the bend to poke down into the hole at the center of the slot in the tuner post.

One of the oldest types of tuners found on solidbody electric guitars, primarily because of their use on early Fender models from the '50s to the mid-'60s, Kluson (and similar styled) split-post machine heads are a deceptively clever design. They offer an integral solution to stray, finger-jabbing string ends, while also providing a degree of string-anchoring stability beyond that of a basic wrap.

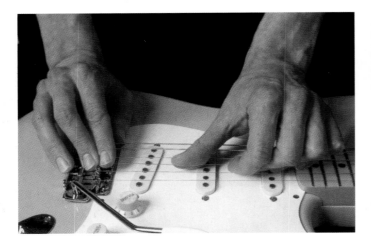  

Correctly stretching new strings is vital to getting them settled and able to hold their tuning. After pulling each string firmly away from the body to seat it, grip and squeeze between thumb and fingers.

Do this for the length of each string to ensure it is evenly stretched in.

And don't forget to stretch behind the nut, where further tuning problems can occur.

create the maximum behind-the-nut string angle. The top two B and E strings, because they pass under the string tree, need only four or so turns. Obviously the more turns you require, the more slack you need to gauge or the longer the length the string must be before you cut it off. It takes some experience to gauge these different numbers of turns, especially with slot-head tuners, but after a few careful re-stringings you'll get the hang of it.

Some locking tuners help the problem, especially on Fender-style headstocks as they have "staggered-height" posts to help you achieve the correct behind-the-nut string angle. Gotoh have recently introduced their HAP locking tuners which allow you to precisely set the height of each individual tuner post.

STRING STRETCHING

Without getting too scientific, a string has three stages in its life-cycle. When you first put on new strings they are extremely elastic and sound very bright and "fresh." Until they settle, however, they won't stay in tune. Once stretched and played in, they're in their optimum state. How long they stay like this depends upon how much and how aggressively you play and how much you sweat. The combination of playing, your sweat and the dirt that will accumulate on the strings will lead to the strings becoming "dead," losing their tonal brightness and physical elasticity, making them much more prone to breakage – especially at friction points at the tuners and saddles. You can prolong the life of the strings by wiping them after every playing session with a cloth or a string cleaner, but you can't alter the physical decay due to playing wear. Any new strings must be stretched. Players have different techniques for this though the aim is the same: to ensure they settle and therefore stay in tune.

1 First, hold the string over the pickups and lightly pull them away from the guitar one at a time. This will relieve any hitching at the tuners, nut and bridge, as pictured above left.

2 Next, lay the guitar in front of you and grip and squeeze each string with your left-hand thumb and fingers, moving along the entire length of the string. Bend each string a few times behind the nut and, if relevant, behind the bridge. We find holding the string over the bridge saddle with your right-hand thumb stops any unnecessary friction wear which could lead – especially on the lighter strings – to premature breakage. Stretch

each string one at a time, constantly re-checking your tuning: when the string no longer de-tunes after some pretty heavy bending, the string is stretched.

String-stretching is a balancing act between getting your new strings to settle in-tune, but not over-stretching them so much that the winds around the core distort and impair your tone.

STRING GAUGES

String gauge (the diameter of the string) is measured in inches. The most commonly used set runs (top E to bottom E) from .009" to .042" – nine thousandths of an inch to forty-two thousandths of an inch – and is usually referred to as a "set of nines." "Tens" typically go from .010" to .046". The thinnest readily available set is "eights" (.008" to .038"), while "elevens" typically run from .011" to .049". Then there are many "hybrid" sets where, for example, the top three of a set of "nines" are combined with the bottom three of the heavier "tens." All this makes for a bewildering choice – as evidenced in the string gauge chart, below – but remember: if everything else remains the same, the thinner the gauge the easier the strings are to fret and bend, but the lighter the tone will be – and vice versa. So while a set of "elevens" may well give you the meatiest tone, they will be a lot harder to fret and bend compared to "nines." Deciding what's right for you will probably mostly come down to feel: whether you opt to work a

Chart of Popular String Gauges

"LIGHT": .009, .011, .016, .024w, .032w, .042w

"REGULAR": .010, .013, .017, 026w, .036w, .046w

"POWER" (med.): .011, .014, .018, .028w, .038w, .048w

"HYBRID" (light top/regular bottoms): .009, .011, .016, 026w, .036w, .046w

Most electric guitar string sets today are made up of gauges selected from a range that runs anywhere from .008" (the high-E on "super light" sets) to around .048". The chart above shows the individual string gauges for four of the more common complete sets. (w = wound)

strings

little harder for the extra power a set of "tens" can give you, or go for the easy bendability of a set of "eights," you're the boss.

TYPES OF TUNERS

On most modern electric guitars, except some of the cheapest, you should find a pretty decent set of tuners (machineheads). Most are pre-lubricated, fully-enclosed units based on the original Grover/Schaller design. These have a high gear ratio, which means you have to turn the button more to get one rotation of the string post, giving finer adjustment. They also have a small tension-adjustment screw at the end of the button.

On some electrics you'll find tuners modeled on the older Kluson design (Kluson-brand tuners have recently made a return to the market, and are proving popular with players looking to replicate an accurate vintage look, though they are now manufactured by a different company than the US-made originals). Japanese reissue Fenders, for example, use this type with a "split" string post and non-adjustable metal buttons. Certain Epiphones use a similar tuner but with a vintage-like green-tinged plastic "tulip" button or a keystone-shaped button, and a standard string post. Despite their vintage look, most have a higher gear ratio than the originals.

A new breed of locking tuners began to appear in the 1980s which "lock" the string onto the string post by clamping it into place in its hole or slot, usually by means of a tension-adjusted internal peg. Specifically designed for guitars with non-locking vibratos, they bring an end to all that fiddly winding of the string-end around the string-post. Installing strings on these is very easy and you can be confident of eliminating any potential movement that can cause string slippage and, therefore, return-to-pitch problems. They are a fine upgrade for any guitar, with or without vibrato, as they make re-stringing very quick and should aid overall tuning stability. The US-made Sperzel heads lead the way, though locking tuners are also available from makers such as Schaller (as used by Fender and Ernie Ball/Music Man), Gotoh, Grover and LSR. There are even some units available which outwardly replicate the look of vintage-style tuners.

TUNER ADJUSTMENT

Little alteration is necessary with most modern tension-adjustable tuners. When you change strings, check that the fixing nut on the face of the headstock is tight. If it's loose you'll need to tighten it with a conventional wrench or socket wrench of the correct size. Never use pliers, or you risk both damaging the edges of the nut and severely scratching the finish on your headstock.

The small screw at the end of the tuner button affects the feel of the machinehead. Technically it doesn't reduce what is called "backlash" or "slippage," the free play of the tuner between clockwise and anti/counter-clockwise rotation. Tightening the screw (pictured right) will create a firmer feel. Don't over-tighten, or tighten it so far that you can't easily move the button. Your aim here is to get an even feel (tight or slack, whatever you like) on all the tuners.

PRS use their own design of Schaller-made locking tuners, without the white nylon washer between the button and the housing, leaving just the bent metal washer in place. PRS tighten their tuners for a positive (some would say stiff) action, based on their belief that the firmer the tuner the more stable the tuning.

Finally, it's worth underlining that tuning problems caused by the nut or by the string tree – or simply by bad string attachment – will not be cured by the tuner, whatever its type.

Schaller: fully enclosed, tension adjustable.

Gotoh Magnum Lock: tension adjustable, locking.

Economy type: non-adjustable.

Kluson-style "vintage" reproduction: non-adjustable.

As shown here (above and left), a wide range of tuner types are available today as stock and retro-fit equipment. While budget guitars may still come with generic types like that pictured above left, most midrange instruments are now fitted with enclosed, adjustable tuners like the Schaller (top left) or similar, while locking units are commonly found on high-end electrics – and are now popular after-market upgrades, too.

Sperzel Trimp-Lok: tension-adjustable, locking.

Most decent tuners today come with a screw set into the end of the button. Not a means of correcting "slippage" as such, it is provided to let the player adjust the feel of the unit for a firm or easy action, according to personal preference.

The same basic principles of loading strings securely and stretching them prior to tuning up as applied to electric guitars will help acoustics hold their pitch longer and more accurately. There are, however, several variations to acoustic guitar bridge and headstock designs – including the classical types – which occasionally require a different approach to string loading.

Most flat-top acoustics have their strings fixed at the bridge by means of push-in bridge pins. Always use the correct tool to remove them.

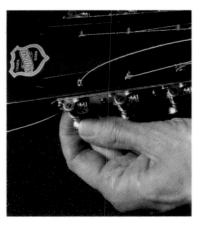

Slot headstocks can be trickier to string up than the standard variety, though the winding procedure is much the same.

TUNING TIPS

An accurate, low-cost electric tuner makes getting your guitar in tune a breeze, and is almost a must for setting intonation (described later in this chapter). As such, it's a worthwhile investment for any guitarist. If you haven't got an electronic tuner to hand, however, you'll need some kind of reference – a keyboard, pitch pipe or tuning fork.

Tune the low E string first, plucking an open string or 12th-fret harmonic, and always tune *up* to pitch from a *flat* note. If the string is already sharp, drop it down below the correct pitch then bring it back up. Carry on from here using the standard "relative tuning" method (fifth fret to open string, fourth fret on G to open B), though be aware that this can introduce inaccuracies to your tuning. Once you feel you're "in tune," play some unison and octave pairs in other positions, then try some low-position open chords to check the "sweetness" of your tuning, and adjust as necessary. These last steps are worthwhile even when you have tuned using an electronic tuner, to ensure your guitar *sounds* good rather than just being "in tune" according to the machine.

ACOUSTIC VARIATIONS

In practise, the majority of acoustic guitars are strung up and tuned just like any electric guitar, but there are several variations worth mentioning. One factor that is different on almost all, however, is the bridge design: most standard steel-string flat-top acoustics use bridge pins to hold the strings in place behind the bridge saddle.

The tapered pins – themselves made of ebony, rosewood, bone, plastic or other synthetic material – fit into holes drilled through the bridge and the face of the guitar, to hold the string's ball ends in place in a slot in the bridge block mounted inside the guitar (for more detail, see the *Acoustic Bridges* section on page 81). Bridge pins should not need to be pushed so firmly into their holes that they are difficult to remove. If they don't come loose after a tug with the fingertips, however, use the slotted handle of your string winder, which is designed specifically for this purpose. Never use pliers or the head of a screwdriver, which may damage the pins – or worse, the bridge or the face of your guitar.

Some other acoustic guitars have different designs for string anchoring at the bridge end – classical guitars especially – which either will be delt with here, or are so obvious as to require little instruction.

STRINGING UP SLOT-HEAD ACOUSTICS

Correctly stringing a guitar makes all the difference to its tuning stability. We have covered conventional electric and acoustic guitars, but there are other styles of instrument which deserve mentioning. Certain vintage style steel strung instruments, such as those based on the early Martin and Washburn designs, as well as most resonator guitars from makers like National and Dobro, have "slot head" side mounted machine heads in a fashion similar to classical guitars. These are much trickier to string up than conventionally mounted machine heads. However, there is a simple method which will make the job easier.

In essence it's the stringing sequence that will prevent you from tying knots in your fingers. Starting with the two E strings, pass the strings through the holes in the metal machine head posts, pulling them through so that only a small amount of string slack is evident over the fingerboard. Now pass the string through the slots between the E and A string posts for the bottom E string, and the E and the B string posts for the top E string. Now loop the string around behind the string where it entered the post originally, so that when you turn the machine heads the string clamps onto itself in a simple locking manoeuvre. Cut off the excess string and tune to pitch.

Now repeat this procedure for the A and B strings, but passing them this time through the slots between the A and D string (for the A string itself) and the B and G string (for the B string itself). Finally repeat the procedure for the D and G strings, passing the strings through the slots between their relative posts and the top of the slots. You can use the same method to re-string a classical guitar. The benefits of this self-locking technique are that the strings reach concert pitch quicker and stay in tune longer – which is normally a problem for classical guitars especially.

CLASSICAL GUITARS

When stringing up a classical guitar you must tie the strings to the bridge first. To do this, pass the string through the hole behind the saddle and pull it through until you have approximately 6cm – 8 cm (2"– 3") of string visible. Now pass the string over the top of the bridge and loop it under the tail end of the string where it passes through the hole. This will create a loop where the string passes over the bridge. Take the remaining few centimetres and pass it two or three times through the loop so that when you pull on the main length of the string it tightens the loops into place.

The strings used for classical guitars are generally made from nylon, or in the case of the lower strings, a multi-fibre nylon core with a metal wrap – usually brass, bronze or a silver alloy. Classical guitar strings are not normally rated by their thickness but by their tension. Beginners often use low tension strings whereas proficient players use medium or high tension strings for a firmer tone. The action height on a classical guitar is also set much higher than a steel strung guitar because the vibration pattern is much greater, and the strings need extra clearance to avoid buzzes against the frets.

STRING TYPES

The range of string gauges for steel strung acoustic guitars is enormous. Before the advent of amplification many acoustic guitars were fitted with heavy gauge strings to aid projection of tone and volume. The tops of these instruments were often more heavily braced than they are today. Typically, a heavy gauge set of strings may range from .013" for the top E to .062" for the bottom E.

Most manufacturers today recommend medium or medium light gauges. Medium gauge strings typically range from .012" – .056", whereas medium light gauge strings normally range from .011" – .052" from the top E to the bottom E. Light gauge or ultra light gauge strings are available nowadays for acoustic instruments with typical gauges of .010" – .047".

Of course the gauges quoted here are typical and not necessarily those represented by any specific manufacturer. Most companies have websites now so you should be able to get the details of a particular set of strings and the range of gauges before you purchase. If you like bending your strings for "bluesy" style playing then we suggest you use light or ultra light gauges. You may sacrifice a small amount of volume and tone but string bending will be easier. For fingerpickers and folk guitarists either light or medium light gauges would be the most suitable. If you want the most projection and volume then you should fit medium gauge strings. Unless the manufacturer of your particular instrument states otherwise, heavy gauges should be avoided due to the possibility of damage occurring because of the tension applied to the modern, lightly braced tops.

Acoustic guitar strings are made from various bronze alloys, with plain metal used for the B and E strings. Some manufacturers even plate the strings with real gold in an effort to increase the life of the string. This works fairly well if you're not string bending, or strumming fiercely, but if you do thrash your guitar metal fatigue will do its damage irrespective of the type or quality of plating.

Other string manufacturers, such as Elixir, coat their steel strings with a Teflon-like substance to keep dirt and moisture from entering the windings, thus improving string life. Some players find these types tend to sound a touch duller and more "played in" from the start, but they have found many fans, too, and all indications are that the technique does increase use able string life considerably.feel (tight or slack, whatever you like) on all the tuners.

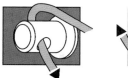

The technique for winding strings onto sideways-mounted tuners in slot-headstock guitars is similar to that used with standard tuners. A simple locking method will suffice, but follow a different sequence, and be aware your perspective is rotated by 90 degrees.

Nylon classical guitar strings need to be "tied" to the bridge for a secure hold before being wound onto the tuners.

The process involves making a loop of the string-end behind the bridge, and winding this under the speaking length to lock it firmly in place.

The same basic self-locking method of stringing up steel-string slot-head acoustics can be used for classical guitars. This simple locking technique is especially useful with nylon strings, which tend to have a longer stretching-in period and therefore can remain "unsettled" for longer periods before holding concert pitch consistently when wound on using less stable techniques.

NECK AND ACTION ADJUSTMENTS

Many perfectly competent guitarists limit their dealings with action and string height to occasionally raising or lowering bridge saddles, scared off from touching a truss rod by legends of warped necks or fractured headstocks. But by following instructions carefully, and using the correct tools, there is a lot you can do yourself to fine-tune the playability of your guitar without ever putting your neck at risk.

TRUSS ROD ADJUSTMENT

When you buy a new guitar you'll usually find included an owners' manual and a truss rod adjustment key, and the manual will provide some basic info on making any necessary adjustments yourself. Conversely, most repairers generally discourage their customers from attempting any truss rod adjustment, which is usually good advice but can leave the beginner understandably confused. So what's the mystery?

Paradoxically, truss rod adjustment can be both simple and

Measuring neck relief is relatively simple, and you can do it with feeler gauges, an accurate steel ruler, or even a plectrum of a known thickness. For all measurements, hold the guitar in playing position (as below) and place a capo at the first fret to free up your left hand. Fret the G string at the 14th fret.

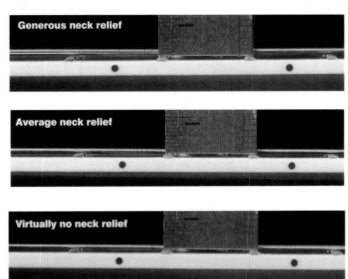

Generous neck relief

Average neck relief

Virtually no neck relief

complex at the same time. On the simple side, a minor adjustment to either straighten a neck with too much concave bow (achieved by tightening the rod) or to relieve a convex bow (by slackening the rod) is possibly all that's needed to make some dramatic improvements and can easily save you a trip to your repairman. On the complex side, adjusting the rod will simultaneously alter other aspects of the set-up such as overall action, the string height at the nut, intonation, and so on. Furthermore, the actual effect any rod adjustment has on the neck will vary between instruments according to the type of rod and the different woods used for the neck's construction. Even on two identical models, the rods can have differing effects. It also sometimes occurs (even with new guitars) that fully slackening the rod won't have the desired effect and other measures are necessary, but with new instruments that's what the warranty is for. Also, don't forget that necks are subject to movement caused by changes of temperature and humidity, so be prepared to tweak the rod when necessary.

CHECKING RELIEF

For any guitar to play with a low, buzz-free action, a slight amount of concave forward bow is necessary due to the elliptical shape of a string's vibration. The small amount of gap (concave bow) in the neck is called "relief," which is usually (but not always) necessary for a buzz-free action. This concave bow, in really, occurs between the first fret and approximately where the heel of the neck starts – typically between the 14th and the 16th fret depending on the guitar. Relief is measured at the mid-point: the 7th-8th fret.

With your guitar in playing position, fret the low E string at the first fret with you left hand and the 14th fret with your right hand. Now look at the seventh/eighth fret. There should be a small gap between the fret and the fretted string. That's the relief.

The amount of relief varies according to string gauge, action height and how hard you actually play. For example, if you use light gauge strings with a low action and a light touch, you'll probably need less relief and a virtually straight neck.

Before you make any adjustments you need to measure the relief and evaluate the neck's condition...

MEASURING NECK RELIEF

Just playing your guitar (normally thorough an amp) can give you a good indication of how much relief you need. If, for example, you're getting fret buzz on most strings when you play on the lower frets it could mean you don't have enough relief. If the lower frets sound fine but as you move up the neck you're getting more buzz it may mean you've got too much relief. Note, however, that this latter scenario could also mean that there's a more serious problem that the truss-rod can't cure. Part of any guitar neck is held firmly in the body. The main, unsupported length is pulled slightly forward by the string tension; the resulting concave bow can be corrected by the truss-rod. However, if there's a fault in the neck itself (maybe the truss-rod is too short, or the timber too weak) the neck can bend at this fulcrum point creating an "up-tilt" which can't be corrected by the truss-rod.

If you don't realise this and continue to tighten the rod, you may create an S-shape bend, where the main playing area has a convex bow (because you over-tightened the truss-rod) and the final part of the neck still tilts up because the neck itself is at fault.

This Washburn D-61 dreadnought's truss rod adjustment is very easily accessed through the soundhole, with strings slackened slightly and the correct allen key applied.

ACOUSTIC NECKS/ADJUSTMENTS

There are many variations in acoustic truss-rod adjustment facilities, though most follow similar procedures to those used on electrics. The through-soundhole approach used for Martins and others (such as the Washburn above) is similar to that used for vintage-style Fender solidbodies, with truss-rod adjustment accessed at the body end of the neck. Others, including Gibsons, are accessed under a plastic cover on the headstock behind the nut.

With these types and others, however, be aware that acoustics may be more sensitive to any adjustment which alters string tension as this has greater structural implications on the glued bridge and the thin wooden top of the guitar, which is much more vulnerable to distortion caused by the strings' pull than a solidbody electric guitar. For this reason, it is all the more important to slacken strings slightly when making any truss-rod adjustment on an acoustic, and to make all adjustments only by small fractions of a turn at a time, letting the guitar rest, then bringing strings back in tune, and carefully gauging the changes before proceeding further.

1 Place a capo at the first fret. Press the G string down at the 14th fret. Look out for a small gap of about. 0.25mm (.010") between the top of the seventh-to-ninth fret and the underside of the string. You can measure this gap with feeler gauges, even a steel ruler (or use a light guage plectrum, approximately 0.5mm thick, as a rough guide).

2 Move the capo to the seventh or eighth fret, and with your right hand fret the last fret. Now measure the gap over the 14th fret (as described above). If this second gap is a lot more than the first relief measurement, it could mean that your neck is at fault. In this case do not attempt to tighten the rod; take your guitar to a pro.

ADJUSTING THE TRUSS ROD

Once you've followed the steps to evaluate the relief you can adjust the truss-rod if necessary. *Always* follow the manufacturer's recommendations and use the supplied truss rod key or allen wrench. Before you touch the truss-rod read, *If In Doubt... Don't* (following page). For guitars with nut-end adjustment the basic procedure is relatively simple. If you need less relief, tighten the truss-rod adjusting nut (turn it clockwise). Obviously you may need to remove the coverplate behind the nut. If you have too little relief, slacken the adjusting nut (turn it counter-clockwise).

Vintage Fender-style guitars have the rod adjustment at the body, end which is a little more involved...

1 Having evaluated the relief, slacken the strings and place a capo at the first fret. Turn the guitar over and undo – but don't fully remove – the neck screws. Slip the neck upwards so you can see the cross-head truss-rod adjusting nut.

2 Make your adjustment as above, re-tighten the neck screws, remove the capo and tune up. Check the relief again and if you need to make further adjustments repeat the above steps.

Note that when tightening the truss rod it is advisable to slightly slacken the string tension. Because the metal strings are in contact with the metal frets you must always expect a certain degree of fret buzz, magnified by how hard you hit the string. With electric guitars, always listen for fret buzz through an amp. Minor un-amplified buzz that occurs when you play "acoustically" on an electric but which can't be heard through the amp doesn't necessarily indicate a real problem.

Headstock-end truss-rod adjustment is simple: just remove the coverplate (if one exists) to access the adjustment nut and proceed according to instructions.

Vintage Fender-style body-end truss-rod adjustment can be somewhat more involved, often requiring loosening the neck to access the adjustment nut.

IF IN DOUBT... DON'T

A neck is a precious thing, so it's not surprising that even many pro players won't attempt truss-rod adjustments. But if you feel inclined to try any small adjustments in accordance with the manufacturers' manual, here are some tips.

Always use the correct tool for the job.

Never force the adjuster if it feels very tight.

Make any adjustment in very small degrees at a time and monitor progress. Usually the correct adjustment is achieved within about a quarter turn in the appropriate direction. Avoid making adjustments greater than this.

Leave some time for the neck to settle between adjustments

If you have any doubts, take the guitar back to the shop or a qualified repairer.

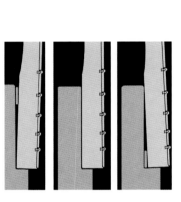

The angle of a guitar's neck relative to its body face is called "neck pitch." Short of major surgery, a set-neck guitar's neck pitch – as with that of the Les Paul pictured near-right, which has quite a steep pitch – is set during the manufacturing process, but there's a lot you can do to fine-tune the neck pitch of a bolt-on guitar. The exaggerated drawings above show three types of bolt-on neck pitch: fingerboard parallel to body face without a shim (center), increased neck pitch with shim placed deep into the neck pocket (right), and an upward tilt created by placing a shim at the front edge of the pocket (left) – the latter a rare scenario.

ADJUSTING A BOLT-ON NECK

In theory, the face of a bolt-on neck will be parallel to the face of the body. In practice the neck often tilts back slightly (this back angle is called the "neck pitch") so that the correct action height can be set. With its carved top, the neck of a Les Paul – or similarly designed guitar – leaves the body at quite an acute angle, which many players find much more comfortable to hold and play.

It's important to understand the relationship between the bridge height and the neck pitch. On a bolt-on Stratocaster, for example, the individually adjustable saddles – especially the pressed steel-type of a vintage tremolo bridge – have a limited range of height adjustment. You may find that even with the saddles as low as they can go the action is still too high. By slightly increasing the neck pitch the action can be made lower. Viewed from the side of the guitar, the tip of the heel (that "lip" of wood at the underside of the body which supports the end of the neck) acts as the fulcrum point. Think of a see-saw: behind that point the neck drops, in front of that point the neck rises.

Imagine the reverse situation: that even with the saddles adjusted to their full height, the action is too low, so you need to reduce the neck pitch – possibly even creating an upward tilt. The saddles-at-lowest/action-too-high scenario is the most common, whereas the saddles-at-highest/action-too-low scenario, where you need to reduce the neck pitch, is actually quite rare.

Fender's American Standard series guitars have a four-screw neck-to-body fixing plus a micro-tilt adjustment which makes neck pitch adjustment easy. For bolt-on necks without this micro-tilt adjustment – the majority – you'll need to add a neck shim: a small piece of thin hard material (ideally wood veneer, hard plastic sheet or hard cardboard – cigarette packets or business cards will work in an emergency). Here's what you do…

1 If the guitar is fitted with a vibrato, place a stack of business cards or the vibrato backplate under the back of the vibrato bridge. This keeps your vibrato close to its correct in-tune setting, and makes it quicker and easier to get back to correct string tension after adjustments have been made.

2 Slacken strings, place a capo at the first fret. Remove the vibrato arm if one is fitted and lay the guitar on a flat surface, face down.

3 Using a correctly sized cross-head screwdriver remove the four neck screws. Turn the body and neck over and place the neck to one side.

4 Cut a shim with scissors to the appropriate size and place it between the end of the neck pocket and the two screws furthest into the body. A couple of small dots of PVA glue (any basic wood glue – alternately use double sided adhesive tape) will hold the shim in place, but don't use so much that's it's difficult to remove the shim for further adjustment at another time.

5 Re-assemble guitar. Put some tension back on the strings and reset saddles. If everything seems OK carefully reset the action (as described in the *String Height* and *Vibrato Adjustment* sections which follow from page 78). If the shim is too low or too high don't worry – remove the neck, take out the shim and try again.

TECH'S TIP: NECK ACHE

It's pretty rare that a misaligned bolt-on neck cannot be corrected, even if you have to take it to a pro. A set-neck guitar, however, is a different matter. But, as top London repairman Charlie Chandler points out, "It's pretty rare these days that set-neck guitars with alignment problems get through quality control – if they can't set them up properly they don't leave the factory." If you're unlucky enough to have problems, unless it is a valuable instrument, re-setting the neck is probably not worth the time and trouble.

"The majority of less-expensive guitars have a thick polyester finish," continues Chandler, "so even if a neck reset is undertaken it will always be evident that it's been repaired. Unlike older cellulose finishes, where we have numerous techniques to disguise the repair, with polyester it's virtually impossible to hide."

Sometimes the bridge and tailpiece can be repositioned, however, especially on a Gibson-style guitar with a Tune-o-matic bridge and stud tailpiece. This may also mean that the pickups have to be slightly moved, yet these methods are a more cost-effective answer than a total neck reset.

So, while the problem is rare, it's worth checking on a new purchase that the neck is aligned correctly. You can visually check (or take a 6" ruler with you) that the outer strings sit approximately equidistant from the fingerboard edges at the 12th fret. Remember, the distances should be the same – or, if anything, a greater distance on the treble side (as previously discussed) is preferable.

A set-neck may also be glued in at the wrong neck pitch. If the angle is too flat you might not be able to get the bridge low enough for your required action, and vice versa. Again, this can be a serious problem and, as Chandler says, "if you're thinking of buying a set-neck guitar ask the store to set it up to your requirements. If they can't or won't... don't buy it.'

On vibrato-fitted guitars, begin by placing the vibrato backplate (spring cover) or a stack of business cards under the back edge of the bridge to maintain your bridge angle for easy re-tuning.

Place a capo at the first fret to keep strings clamped in the correct position at the nut end.

Remove the neck screws – *always* using the correct size screwdriver – and set the neck aside.

DESIGN STRENGTH
While their glued-in nature gives the impression of being universally "stronger" than bolt-on necks, not all set-neck guitars are created equal. For example, a Gibson Les Paul (above left), has much more wood to adhere to on the bass side of the guitar's body than a Gibson SG (above right) with its deep cutaways on either side of the neck. Before the SG design was modified in other ways in the late-'60s, neck breaks were a significant problem for these models.

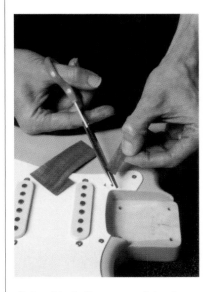

Cut a shim to the appropriate size – wood veneer or other hard material is preferable for this.

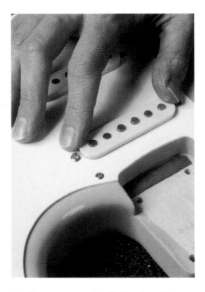

To increase neck pitch, place the shim between the end of the neck pocket and the inside screw holes.

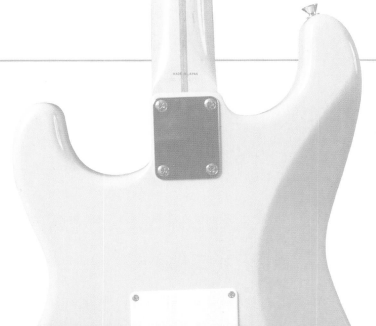

Under normal conditions, many bolt-on necks will exhibit some side-to-side movement, which can usually be corrected. You may be able to simply manhandle your neck into better alignment, then tighten slightly.

To accurately assess alignment, measure the clearance between low and high E and fretboard edge.

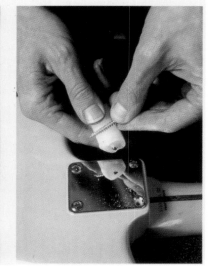

If re-alignment requires heavy tightening of the neck screws, apply some candlewax first to ease the job.

MORE BOLT-ON NECK ADJUSTMENTS

Unless a bolt-on neck is really well fitted, the chances are it may move sideways if it's roughly handled or knocked. This movement is usually pretty subtle, but the first check you want to make is to see if your neck moves.

Hold the guitar in a seated playing position and push down quite roughly on the neck. Did you feel it move, did it creak? Don't worry. If it did move, yank in the opposite direction and it should move back again. What you've established is the likelihood that your guitar neck will move in the future – that's not ideal. But the cure can be simple.

Firstly, measure the distance from the outer strings, at the 12th fret, to the edge of the fingerboard. The distance should be the same. If anything a greater distance on the treble side facilities hammer-on and pull-off techniques and stops you slipping off the board.

Manhandle the neck until you achieve the right position. Lay the guitar face down on your work surface and tighten (don't over-tighten) the neck screws. Sometimes this is all you need to cure any movement. Now see if you can move the neck under reasonable pressure. If you can't, you've solved the problem: most bolt-ons just need a little tightening from time to time.

If the neck still moves, remove it and check the condition of the neck pocket and bottom of the neck. Are there any loose wood shavings? Are the surfaces rough? The flatter the surfaces, the more neck-to-body contact and the more stable the joint will be (also, the better your tone). We're not advising trying to smooth the neck pocket – take it to a pro – but one thing that may help is to apply some dry lubricant (candle wax is ideal) to the neck screws and re-assemble the guitar. This simple tip may allow slightly more pressure to be applied without damaging the screw heads and thus cure any movement.

Removing a bolt-on neck may seem dramatic on your first attempt but so long as you use the correct tools, lubricate the screws and don't over-tighten them you'll be okay. Never force a screw. If it doesn't want to move, *leave it* – and seek pro advice.

CHECKING NUT HEIGHT

Our main concern with the top nut is to ensure that it is cut to the "correct" height and has friction-free string slots. Altering or replacing a nut is definitely a pro's job, and nut replacement is usually necessary when you have your guitar re-fretted.

Most new production guitars have nuts that are cut a little too high. This may make it harder to press the strings down and fret them (and might cause intonation problems), but it is simpler for a repairer to lower your nut height than to increase it. To check your top nut height, first fret each string between the second and third frets (pictured opposite). Ideally there should be a very small gap above the first fret and the bottom of each string. Even if it is almost touching, don't worry – the open, unfretted string may still vibrate cleanly. If the open string buzzes, then it probably means that the nut slot is too low – but check both your neck relief and string action height.

To check if the string groove in the nut is impeding the return-to-pitch of the string, pick an open string and bend it by pushing down on the string behind the nut. Can you hear any clicks? This will indicate a tight string groove in the nut. Does the string come back into tune? Re-tune and try again. So long as your strings are properly stretched, a behind-the-nut up-bend of around a semitone should come back in tune. Again, getting the string grooves perfectly smooth is a tricky job. If you've got problems,

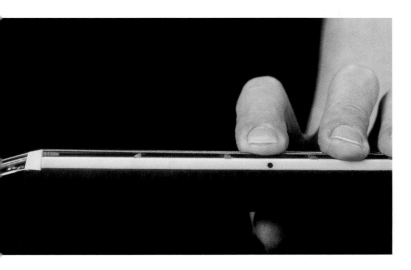

A little pencil lead (graphite) still makes a simple and effective lubricant for curing minor string-hitching problems. To check nut height, fret each string between second and third fret (above). The string should be touching or *just* above the first fret...

... Then, if the nut's string groove is impeding string-movement on bends etc, rub a soft pencil lead in the groove, and return the string.

Once nut grooves have worn too low, replacement is the only option, though Gordon-Smith's adjustable nut (above) offers a longer lifespan.

lift the string out of the groove, rub a soft pencil lead (graphite) into the groove (as pictured above, center), and return the string. Try those bends again. The graphite lubrication may have helped, but won't necessarily cure the problem.

The ever-resourceful British maker Gordon-Smith uses a height-adjustable brass nut (far right). It's a neat idea. If over a long period the nut slots become worn you can loosen the nut with the two screws, place a thin shim under the nut to raise it, and if necessary re-cut the slots. Of course, if you just want to raise your string height – for slide or bottleneck playing – it's very easy: just use a thicker shim.

FINGERBOARD FUNDAMENTALS

The fingerboard holds the frets and provides the playing surface of the instrument. Obvious, really. But, as ever, the role of the fingerboard is more complex and worthy of some examination. Made from a hard-wearing hardwood – typically rosewood or ebony – the fingerboard is usually unfinished. Only if a light-colored wood such as maple is used will a finish be applied, to protect it from getting dirty.

Some makers such as Music Man use a light oil finish on both the maple neck and fingerboard, and this does get dirty. Some players like it; others (including store owners) often don't. Back in the 1970s Fender used a very thick finish on their maple fingerboards, and this may be why people think that maple and rosewood 'boards feel different.

With the modern choice of typically higher-gauge fretwire, the fingerboard material really makes little difference to its playing feel. Tonally, however, the fingerboard will have an effect. Maple is perceived to have a bright and twangy tone, contrasted by the warmer tone of the softer rosewood. Ebony is the hardest and smoothest wood used for the job, and creates a bright sound with a lot of definition. But, as ever, the "sound" of wood is a highly subjective area.

FINGERBOARD RADIUS

Much more important to the player than the wood from which the fingerboard is cut is its slight radius (camber, or curving from side to side). Combined with the size of the frets and the overall set-up, this is what contributes most to different fingerboard

feels. Radius is measured by considering the fingerboard as a wedge from a cylinder of a certain radius.

Fender originally used a small 7¼" (184mm) radius, although US/Mexican-made Fenders now uniformly use a flatter 9½" (241mm) radius. Gibson went for a flatter 12" (305mm) radius, PRS uses an "in between" 10" (254mm), and Parker uses a "conical" radius increasing from nut to top fret, from approximately 10" to 12" (254mm–305mm) so that the board is flatter in its upper reaches. Modern rock guitars typically use a flatter radius of anything from 14" (356mm) upwards.

So why all the options? Fender's vintage radius feels great for comfortable chording, but with a low action, high-fret bends can lead to "choking" (the bent string colliding against a higher fret, thereby killing off your note). The only way to stop this is to raise the action or flatten the fingerboard radius, hence Fender's current 9½" (241mm) radius. But fashions constantly change.

TECH'S TIP: NEW NUTS FOR OLD

Hugh Manson, a UK repairman and custom-builder for the likes of former Led Zeppelin bassist John Paul Jones, says the main reason to replace a top nut is because it's too low, either from the abrasive action of the strings, or when a re-fret sets the new frets higher than the old ones.

Another problem occurs when players increase the gauge of strings they use. "Never try to force a heavier-gauge string into an old nut slot that was cut for a lighter gauge," advises Manson. "At worst, you may crack the nut, or suffer from tuning problems as the new string sticks in the old slot."

A repairman will use special tools to cut and/or widen the slots. When it comes to nut replacement, some guitars are problematic. "The ones I hate are those 1970s Fenders where the thick polyester finish is sprayed over the nut. Getting the old nut out is difficult" says Manson.

The same can apply to many Gibson guitars where the nut sits at the end of the fingerboard but is partially recessed into the neck wood and then sprayed over. Many modern guitars, including those of PRS for example, have the nut fixed after finishing, so nut replacement is relatively easy. "A nut has a finite life," concludes Manson. "It must be solidly fixed, but removable in the future when replacement becomes necessary."

The Parker Fly (left) uses a rare conical-radius fingerboard, with a smaller radius at the nut end for comfortable chording, and larger radius at the higher frets for fast lead work.

Most production electric guitars use a fingerboard radius that is constant throughout the length of the guitar. Vintage Fenders (and reissues) use a very rounded-feeling 7$\frac{1}{4}$" (184mm) radius, above left; Gibsons use a flatter 12" (305mm), center; while Floyd-Rose equipped guitars use an extremely flat 16" (406mm), right.

Currently we're seeing 9$\frac{1}{2}$" to 12" (241mm–305mm) radiuses – which suit virtually any playing style – fitted with high but not too wide frets, and neck shapes that are chunkier in cross-section. This is a distinct contrast to the '80s and early-'90s virtuoso "speed-is-everything" designs which used a much flatter fingerboard fitted with heavy-gauge frets and a thin-depth neck.

At first such thin necks seem very comfortable, but many players find them tiring for extended sessions, since they don't fit into the hand as naturally as more rounded neck shapes. But the "conical" (sometimes known as compound) radius makes a lot of sense, as it provides comfort in the lower positions and very easy high-fret bendability.

But, unless your guitar uses very small-gauge fretwire, its the frets rather than the fingerboard that provide the real playing surface. Made from nickel silver, the fret is pushed and sometimes glued into sawn fret-slots on the fingerboard. Once seated, the frets are levelled and polished to provide a smooth, buzz-free playing surface. Originally both Fender and Gibson used very narrow and quite low frets.

Wider frets became popular for a smoother feel, but as string gauges came down and string-bending became much more popular, makers and players realised that higher frets made strings easier to bend. Wide and low frets were popular for their smooth feel, but if the top of the fret (the "crown") is too flat you can get intonation problems. Likewise, if the fret is very high you have to be very precise about how you fret each note, as it's easy to sharpen notes by applying uneven finger pressure, especially within a tricky chord.

CHECKING FOR FRET BUZZ

Fret buzz can be caused by too-low string height, too much or too little neck relief – as already discussed – or isolated individual height problems (where, for example, one fret has popped out of its fingerboard slot). Always test for fret buzz through your amp. Bear in mind that minor buzzing due to hard playing and the proximity of metal-to-metal (string against fret) is unavoidable. Nonetheless, play every string at every fret and if you hear a deadening clonk at, for example, the 12th fret, it could mean either that this fret is too low or that the next fret (the 13th in this example) is too high. Note the problems, and have a pro check your guitar.

WHAT IS ACTION?

For many players the "action" of a guitar is the height of the strings above the frets, typically measured from the top of the 12th fret to the underside of the outer two strings: the low E (bass) and the high E (treble). But if only it were that simple. In fact "action" is a general term used to describe the combination of the entire playing "feel" of the guitar. You'll hear comments like "this guitar has a really low action", or "the action's really high on this one" and the reasons are not just to do with the physical distance of the strings from the frets. Neck condition is crucial: the neck's straightness and relief, the fingerboard radius in relation to the bridge's saddle radius, and the nut and even fret height all contribute to the player's perception – that's you! – of action.

For example, as we discussed earlier, the relief of the neck, when you think about it, will alter the string height. More relief (concave bow) places the frets further from the strings, and vice versa. Big, high frets often give the impression of a higher action simply because the fret's top, or playing surface, is further from the fingerboard face. Of course, without having your guitar re-fretted you can't do anything about this yourself, but what you can do – having adjusted the neck is – set a string height that's most suitable for you.

Many players simply strive for the lowest possible action "without buzzes". As we've already discussed, that may never be achievable and is not always the "best" set-up. The best set-up is simply the one that suits you and your playing style, your guitar, and the frequency at which you practise and play. If you're too busy to play for more than a short while every other day or so, a medium to high action will probably feel a little hard on your fingers. But if you practise every day you could cope well with a higher action, and you might prefer the tone this affords.

There is of course a fundamental that we've purposely left until last: your strings. We've already discussed the effect of string gauge on the neck itself and the feel of the strings in relation to your guitar's scale length. But those aspects aside, a heavier gauge will simply feel harder to play (initially at least). Likewise the higher the string height of your guitar the tougher the guitar feels to fret and bend. Certainly, the additional mass of the heavier gauge should give you a bigger sound, and a higher action should mean a cleaner, less buzzy tone, but it's going to require more physical effort and practise. A guitar with a low string height and light gauge strings will feel fine for bedroom practice; but on-stage – with all that adrenaline pumping through you and the natural tendency to play harder in front of an audience – a heavier gauge and possibly higher action might be more suitable. So changing your string gauge is a lot more complex than just re-stringing your guitar.

Fretwire is available today in a wide variety of sizes, though most is still identifiable in simple terms by the era from which it originates or a maker by whom it is commonly used. The illustrations below show the cross-sections of three types of wire, inset against photos of the actual frets on different types of guitars. Fender's "vintage" fretwire (below left) is of a relatively small gauge, while Gibson traditionally uses fretwire of a larger cross-section (center). The Jackson fingerboard (right) carries an even larger wire, usually called "jumbo", which has become popular on guitars favored by some rock and metal players.

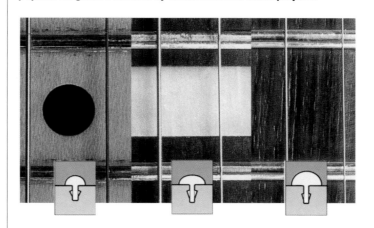

TECH'S TIP: FRETFULNESS

Fret wear, unless extreme, rarely requires a total re-fret; usually the repairer can level the frets and then re-shape them (also called "crowning" or "dressing") to a smooth, dome-like section. Of course, as experienced repairer Tim Shaw (Manager, Product Development of Acoustics – both for Fender and Guild – at Guild's Custom Shop) points out, "The more times frets are re-crowned the flatter they get. In extreme cases they become so flat that your intonation goes down the tubes and your only option is a re-fret.

"But one of the main reasons for a re-fret is when you get a twisted neck that can't be straightened by the truss rod. Similarly, guitars with a small fingerboard radius, which can lead to string choking, are another candidate. On occasions the radius in the upper fret areas can be increased (by careful levelling and re-dressing) but in other cases the old frets must be removed and the 'board re-radiused. Then there are players – especially those who like a high fret – who will prefer a re-fret rather then re-crowning. Of course, you may simply want to change to a different gauge of fretwire.

"The hardest – and therefore the most expensive – are guitars with bound fingerboards. Finished maple fingerboards are problematic too, especially those old '70s Fenders with a really thick finish. You have to re-fret and re-finish the 'board. Rickenbacker often combine binding with a finish; they require a lot of work."

Conversely an unbound, unfinished rosewood board is probably the most straightforward. "Yeah," agrees Shaw, "an old '56 Gibson Les Paul Junior… the necks are really stiff and if you can't re-fret one of those you're in trouble."

CHART OF 12th FRET STRING HEIGHTS

String Heights	12th fret treble	12th fret bass
LOW	³⁄₆₄" (1.2mm)	¹⁄₁₆" (1.6mm)
MEDIUM	¹⁄₁₆" (1.6mm)	⁵⁄₆₄" (2.0mm)
HIGH	⁵⁄₆₄" (2.0mm)	³⁄₃₂" (2.4mm)
SLIDE	³⁄₃₂" (2.4mm)	⁹⁄₆₄" (3.6mm)

The measurements listed above are merely approximate guides and will depend on string gauge, neck condition and nut height.

You can easily check your string heights using a ruler with fine gradations. Measurements are traditionally taken at the 12th fret, from the top of the fret to the underside of the outer strings.

STRING HEIGHT

Assuming that your neck is pretty much correctly adjusted and your nut isn't too high or too low, you can proceed to setting the string height.

Using a steel ruler with fine gradations for tight measurements, measure the string height at the 12th fret – from the top of the fret to the underside of the string – of the outer strings (as pictured, center left). A basic guide would be approximately ¹⁄₁₆" (1.6mm) on the treble side (high E), ⁵⁄₆₄" (2.0mm) on the bass-side (low E). (See chart, left.) What about the other strings? They should gradually curve from the low E to high E heights, creating a radius that will follow that of the fingerboard. That'll give you – with all the previous considerations taken into account – a slightly high, but hopefully clean, buzz-free playing guitar: This is a good starting point from which to fine-tune to your own taste.

To adjust the string height you need to raise or lower the bridge or the individual saddles. If you have a new guitar, the chances are you'll have an owners' manual. *Always read this thoroughly!* The most specialist tool you'll need is the correctly sized Allen key, for the height adjustable saddles and tremolo pivot posts.

TUNE-O-MATIC

The Tune-o-matic type bridge, as fitted by Gibson and Epiphone, for example, has overall height adjustment either via two thumb wheels or a slot-head screw. The radius created by the bridge is not adjustable except by notching the saddles, a job for a pro.

To lower the action, turn the wheels or slot screw clockwise (the pitch of the strings will drop slightly); to raise the action, you must slacken the strings to achieve any upward movement, then turn the bridge's set screw or thumbwheel counter-clockwise. Tune back to pitch and re-measure.

Once you've achieved the correct string height, check the stud tailpiece – the strings should run from the back of the Tune-o-matic saddles to the tailpiece *without* touching the back edge of the bridge. You may need to raise the stud tailpiece, but keep the angle as steep as possible. The adjustment of this tailpiece is the same as for the one-piece wrapover bridge (as described on the opposite page).

The radius of a Gibson-style Tune-o-matic brige is fixed, but usually allows for a fairly wide range of string-height adjustment. Simply turn the set screws or thumbwheels at either end clockwise to lower the action. To raise it, slacken strings slightly to allow movement, then turn screws or thumbwheels counter-clockwise to raise the bridge. Some units are too tight for easy thumbwheel movement, so you'll need to apply the correct-sized screwdriver anyway, as pictured left. After adjustment, set the stud tailpiece for the correct break angle over the bridge saddles (above left).

set-up: string height

ONE-PIECE WRAPOVER

Gibson's one piece wrapover bridge/tailpiece (or any of the variants) has two large slot-head studs which adjust the string height. (Again, like the Tune-o-matic, the radius of the bridge is preset.) It's doubtful you'll have a big enough screwdriver – don't use one with a blade width that's smaller than the stud slot, because you'll damage the stud. Instead…

Slacken off the string tension and you may find you can simply move the studs by hand or with the aid of a stiff (or a couple) of plectrums – some find a small coin ideal – placed in the slot. A tip passed on by the late Sid Poole, a top UK luthier, is to slacken off the string tension and place a piece of paper towel over the slot and insert the curved end of your 6" steel ruler, as pictured right. The edges of these rules can be very sharp – you may also want to wrap a piece of paper towel around the rule. Make a turn on the bass stud then the same on the treble stud, tune up and re-measure you string height. Take your time otherwise you'll damage those stud slots. *Always remember to slacken your strings before adjusting these studs!*

OTHER SIX-SADDLE TYPES

Bridges with six saddles usually have height adjustment for each string. For non-trem, six-saddle Tele or Strat bridges, for example, the adjustment is the same as for the Stratocaster tremolo bridge (below). Three-saddle Tele bridges don't give as much precise height control as a six-saddle bridge. But by setting the height screw next to each string – thereby angling the paired bridge saddles – you can achieve the necessary radius.

If you have a bolt-on guitar and for any reason you don't have enough or have too little saddle adjustment to achieve your desired action, you will probably need to shim your neck slightly, as discussed in previous pages.

VIBRATO BRIDGES

The Floyd Rose-style vibrato is quite a complex piece of hardware, but thankfully setting string height is dead easy. There are two height adjustable pivot posts; because the saddles are preset in terms of height – and therefore radius – these are the main way to adjust the string height (pictured near-right). Usually a Floyd Rose has a flat-ish saddle radius of about 16" (406mm). If your fingerboard radius is smaller you'll have to put up with the outer strings being slightly higher than the inner ones to avoid fret rattle, so here measure your action height firstly from the G and D strings, not the outer E strings. (Tip: You can alter the height of a Floyd Rose's saddle with very thin shim steel – try your local hardware store. Simply cut small pieces to fit under the saddles, therefore rasing the height and creating a small radius.)

A Strat – especially with tremolo – is more complex, as there are six saddles, individually adjustable for height. Having set the outer two strings for height, use the steel rule to measure the inner four, and, gradually increase the height from the treble to the bass strings. As we've said, if you have a vintage spec Fender guitar with its small (7¼") fingerboard radius, you may encounter upper-fret choking. So once the string height is set try some upper-fret bends. If the string chokes on a higher fret, raise the saddle further.

You might find that using a radius gauge (pictured right as available from Stewart-MacDonald, or you can make one yourself) is a more convenient way to match the radius of the saddles to the radius of the fingerboard once the outer two string heights have been set. Current Fender USA/Mexican guitars have

In theory, the Gibson-style wrapover bridge/tailpiece is simple to adjust – but you're unlikely to have a big enough screwdriver handy. After slackening the strings, place a paper towel over the stud slots and then insert your steel ruler to make the adjustment.

The Floyd-Rose style vibrato, as on this Jackson, allows for overall height adjustment only.

A Strat's six individually-adjustable saddles allow for precise string-height and radius setting.

A radius gauge, as pictured above (this one from leading guitar-tools supplier Stewart-MacDonald) provides a quick-fire means of setting your bridge to accurately reflect your fingerboard radius.

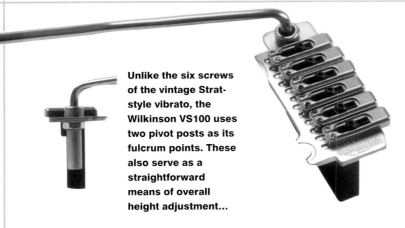

Unlike the six screws of the vintage Strat-style vibrato, the Wilkinson VS100 uses two pivot posts as its fulcrum points. These also serve as a straightforward means of overall height adjustment...

To adjust string height on the Wilkinson VS100, first slacken off the saddle lock-down screw, then set the outer saddles flat against the bridge plate and adjust the overall height accordingly, raising or lowering the pivot posts...

...while fingerboard radius is matched by raising or lowering the six individually-adjustable saddles. When introduced, the Wilkinson VS100 – seen in detail at the top of the page – represented one of the more significant advancements in non-locking vibrato tailpieces.

a 9½" fingerboard radius; Japanese Strat reissues (and some older spec USA models) still have a smaller 7¼" radius.

Using a radius gauge is a fine starting point, but no adjustments are written in stone. Once you've set the saddle radius you might, for example, want to slightly reduce the height of the centre strings, but you must retain a gentle curve.

Alternatively, with any multi-saddle bridge you can set the action totally by "feel". Simply lower each string until you get continuous buzzing on most frets, then raise it until most of the buzzes disappear.

Wilkinson's VS100 bridge has adjustment both for pivot-post height and individual saddle height. The pivot posts are for height adjustment and the individual saddles are to match the fingerboard radius. *Before making any height or intonation adjustments on a Wilkinson tremolo, slacken off the saddle lock-down screw.* The outer saddles should be flat on the tremolo base-plate. Adjust these accordingly, then turn the pivot posts clockwise, lowering the vibrato until the outer strings just touch the last fret on the fingerboard. You can then alter the heights of the other saddles to just touch that last fret, thereby perfectly matching the fingerboard radius of your guitar. Now raise the pivot posts until you achieve the correct action height. This works with an American Standard Strat vibrato too, only the outer saddles should sit approx ³⁄₃₂" (2.4mm) from the face of the baseplate. As with the saddle adjustments, always slacken off string tension before you raise these pivot posts.

VINTAGE-STYLE STRAT VIBRATOS

The vintage-style Strat vibrato pivots on its six front-mounted screws and does not float above the body like a Floyd Rose or Wilkinson vibrato. Therefore the back of this Strat vibrato usually tips up to create up-bend. But you can, for example, have the vibrato set flat on the body so you only have down-bend, with the advantage that if you break one string the others won't be pulled out of tune by the springs. Another option is to make the guitar into a totally non-vibrato instrument by setting the vibrato hard down on the body and leaving the arm in the case.

Achieving different set-ups is relatively easy. Basically, the strings' tension is counteracted by the tension on the two (or more) springs in the vibrato cavity in the rear of the body. Remove the vibrato backplate and you'll see that the springs are hooked at one end onto the vibrato's sustain block and at the other onto the spring "claw". This claw is held to the body with two cross-head screws. The number of springs (and their combined tension) plus the distance of the spring claw from the neck-facing end of the spring cavity will affect the position of the vibrato.

The number and type of springs you fit will affect not only the overall tension but also the feel of the vibrato. Three springs with .010" gauge strings on a Strat is pretty standard. Drop down to two springs and the vibrato feels lighter and its return-to-pitch can be less stable. With lighter .009" gauge strings and two springs it usually feels very smooth, but the firmer feel of three springs is often preferred. Heavier-gauge strings need more springs, and if you want to defeat the action of the vibrato so it sits flat and tight on the body, put all five in. Remember, the "correct" setting of the vibrato is always a balance between strings and springs.

It's worth pointing out that, because of this string-to-spring balance, a Strat vibrato (or indeed any vibrato based on this principle) has limitations. If you bend one string, the rest go flat (try it). You have to bend the string further to achieve the same degree of pitch change as you would on an equivalent fixed-bridge guitar. Country-style bends become tricky too. You might bend one string upwards while fretting and voicing another string… and the un-bent string will go flat. Products like the Fender/Hipshot Trem-setter and WD's Tremolo Stabiliser aim to reduce this problem, but they are not easy to set up and you'll need a pro's help. If this type of bending is important to your style you might want to consider a fixed-bridge guitar, or set the Strat vibrato flat on the body so it doesn't move. Keep in mind that if you don't use a vibrato in your playing, keeping one on your guitar – and dealing with the inherent tuning and set-up difficulties – is almost certainly more trouble than it's worth.

Different springs vary in tension. Combine this with how you like your vibrato to feel and there really are no set rules. So long as the set-up works for you and stays pretty much in tune, then that's the right one.

Typically, however, a vintage Strat vibrato is set so that there is a gap of approximately ⁵⁄₆₄"–⅛" (2mm-3mm) between the back of the bridge and the face of the guitar. This should give an up-bend of approximately one semitone on the top E-string and around a tone on the low E-string, assuming that .009"–.042" gauge strings are fitted.

VINTAGE-STYLE STRAT VIBRATO SET-UP

Assess your existing set-up. Measure the height of the tip-up angle – if there is one – at the back of the bridge. Remove the backplate cover and check the springs. For a lighter feel, use two springs set from the sustain block's outer holes to the spring claw's two inner hooks. For a firmer feel, use one more spring from the block's central hole to the claw's central hook. Move the springs one at a time if necessary; lift off the springs at the block first, then hook them onto the claw and reposition the other end into the block.

The length of the spring cavity differs between Strat models, and of course springs (and strings) vary in tension, so there is no one set position for the spring claw. However, to give you an idea of how it moves, we measured a Fender reissue Strat fitted with a set of .009"–.042" gauge strings. The spring claw with three springs measured approximately ⅝" (16mm) from the neck-facing edge of the back cavity to the neck-facing edge of the claw, and when fitted with two springs measured about ⅜" (9mm-10mm). If you're using .010"s you're better off with three springs – we set the claw ½"–⁹⁄₁₆" (13mm-14mm) from the cavity edge. Make sure the claw is parallel to the neck-facing edge of the cavity.

Yet another of Leo Fender's surprisingly dead-on innovations, the vintage-style Stratocaster tremolo is still a favorite nearly half a decade after its introduction. While cumbersome and difficult to set-up in some ways, it provides a wide range of smooth down-bend, and is highly adjustable for string height and radius.

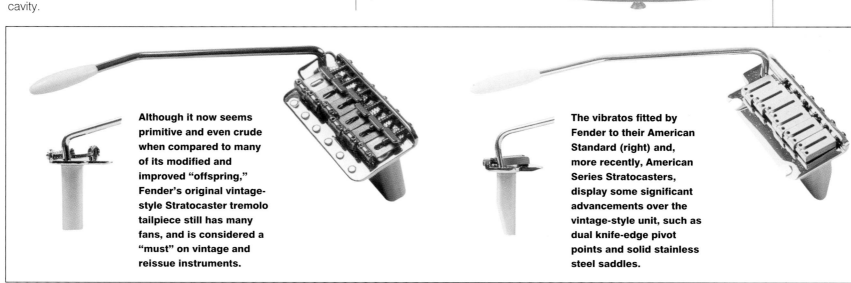

Although it now seems primitive and even crude when compared to many of its modified and improved "offspring," Fender's original vintage-style Stratocaster tremolo tailpiece still has many fans, and is considered a "must" on vintage and reissue instruments.

The vibratos fitted by Fender to their American Standard (right) and, more recently, American Series Stratocasters, display some significant advancements over the vintage-style unit, such as dual knife-edge pivot points and solid stainless steel saddles.

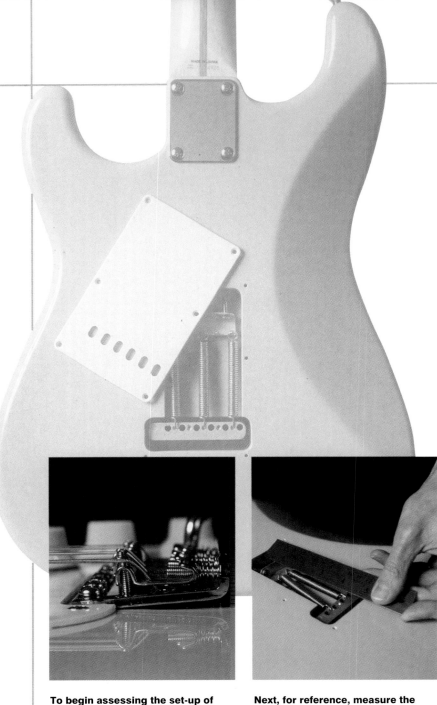

Tune to pitch. Measure the height of the tip-up angle and adjust both the spring-claw screws. If you need more tip-up angle undo (turn anti/counter-clockwise) the two claw screws. Start with two full turns per screw and keep the spring claw parallel with the cavity. Tune the guitar back to pitch and re-measure the up-tilt. If you've gone too far, tighten both screws; on the other hand, if you need more tip-up, loosen the screws. After every small adjustment it's important to re-tune to pitch and then re-measure the up-tilt. When you've got about ³⁄₃₂" (2.5mm) of tip-up angle, check the amount of up-bend. You should find, with the vibrato pulled all the way up, that you have about a one-semitone up-bend on the top E-string, that the low E-string will easily rise by two or maybe even three semitones, and that you can achieve around a tone up-bend on your G-string. You can precisely tune this up-bend by adjusting the spring claw screws.

Now check the position of the six pivot screws at the front of the bridge. Undo the center four screws a couple of full turns so they sit slightly above the vibrato. Hold the vibrato flat down on the body with the vibrato arm, and screw the two outer screws down (not overtight) onto the bridgeplate. Release the vibrato arm and unscrew the outer screws until they just clear the top of the plate after the vibrato has rested in its angled position. If you've already set your action (string height), then all you need to do is just re-check it. You're now ready to set your intonation and maximise tuning stability.

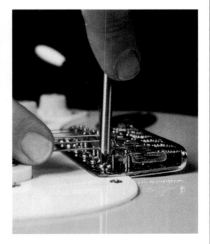

To begin assessing the set-up of your vintage-style Strat vibrato, measure the height of the tip-up angle of the bridge plate.

Next, for reference, measure the distance of the front of the spring claw from the front of the spring cavity.

After adding or removing springs to account for preferences of feel and spring/string tension, re-tune to pitch, re-check height of tip-up angle, and adjust the spring claw as necessary to correct any changes.

TECH'S TIP: BLOCK PARTY

A tip handed on from British luthier Phil Norsworthy (and used by Fender, as reported by Dan Erlewine in the *Guitar Player Repair Guide*) is to use a small, wedge-shaped wooden block, approximately 2" long by 1" (50mm by 25mm) wide with a depth that tapers from around ½" to ⅓" (12mm to 9mm). You place it in the rear trem cavity between the back of the trem's sustain block and the cavity. Because of the block's taper, this allows you to set the precise tip-up angle. Norsworthy recommends a generous ⅛" (3mm), the Fender Custom Shop, ³⁄₃₂" (2.4mm). With the block in place, slacken-off the spring tension so the string tension holds the block. Now you can make your string height, radius and intonation adjustments without the trem moving. Once set, tighten the spring claw. Keep it parallel and, when tight enough, the block just drops out, leaving you with the trem perfectly set and intune. This time-saving block can also be used – because of the taper – on numerous other floating or vintage style trems.

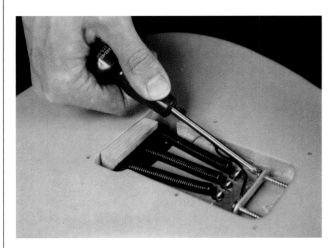

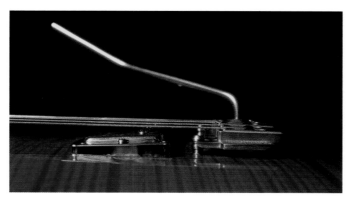

SETTING UP TWO-SCREW FLOATING VIBRATOS

Floating vibratos like the Floyd Rose, Wilkinson and modern American Standard vibratos work on the same principle as the vintage versions – the string tension is balanced by the spring tension. But they all use a more efficient pivot point in the form of two height adjustable posts, and they "float" parallel to the face of the guitar. Note that the American Standard vibrato can float parallel or be set like a vintage, though you will probably need to adjust the neck pitch to alter the set-up.

Setting these vibratos to the correct position is identical to the vintage, and only instead of measuring the tip-up height at just the back of the bridge, you should measure the distance of the underside of the bridge to the face of the body at the front of the bridge, then at the back of the bridge. For optimum performance, these two measurements should be the same.

The distance from the front of the bridge to the body directly affects action height; adjust the spring tension to match the distance of the back of the bridge to that of the front.

ACOUSTIC BRIDGES

Acoustic guitar bridges play a dual role, anchoring the strings and transmitting string vibration through to the top. The size, height and position of the bridge depends upon the instrument's scale length, neck angle and string spacing. On steel strung guitars the bridges are usually made of either rosewood or ebony, or lesser woods that are "ebonised," which means that they are painted black to hide the material's true nature.

Bridge saddles use many materials, some man made, some natural. Popular materials include hard plastics, synthetic bone and natural materials such as animal bone and ivory. The saddle slots are angled to allow for intonation. On some instruments there are two saddles, one for the E-A-D-G strings and another for the B and E strings, placed at different angles for correct intonation of the top B and E strings.

On most steel strung acoustic guitar bridges the strings are held in place with bridge pins which go through the bridge and into the body. The strings are then held securely between the shaft of the pin and the bridge plate (a piece of wood which re-enforces the underside of the bridge). Another method of securing the strings has small holes drilled behind the saddle through to the rear end of the bridge. The strings are passed through the back of the bridge towards and over the saddle. A small brass strip with holes to accommodate the strings is often placed at the back of the bridge for reinforcement. Obviously this style of bridge doesn't require bridge pins and has been a popular feature on budget instruments over the years. The design is good that it makes for easy and quick restringing but it is difficult to shave the bridge height down if the guitar develops a high action (due to the top pulling up) at some in the future.

Classical bridges are simpler in construction and feature a straight saddle with no apparent compensation for intonation. They are generally made of either rosewood or ebony but, like steel string bridges, poorer quality materials are often used which are again "ebonised." The strings are tied to the back of the bridge after being passed through small holes behind the saddle. Expensive models generally feature bone saddles but on cheaper instruments plastic is the material of choice.

Adjusting string height on most acoustics involves precise sanding down of some of the underside of the saddle to reduce its height – a job best left to a professional, as one slip can necessitate replacing the entire saddle.

Though very different in other ways, the non-locking Wilkinson vibrato (top) and locking Floyd-Rose vibrato (above) – and others designed like them – both use two adjustable posts as efficient pivot points. These posts are adjustable for action height, while adjusting spring tension ensures they "float" parallel to the body.

Most acoustic guitar bridges have no means of simple string-height adjustment. Normally, as on the dreadnought above, the strings' ball ends are held secure by bridge pins, with the strings passing over a one-piece bone or synthetic saddle set into a slot in the bridge. Sanding down the underside of the saddle is the only means of adjusting its height. As any slip ups – or simply going too far – will necessitate replacing the entire saddle, however, this is a job best left to an experienced professional.

Resonator guitars, such as the National Resophonic Delphi above, have a bridge design unique to their function – but again, it's a tricky unit to work on, with no easy facility for string-height adjustment. Loading strings into the National's old-fashioned style tailpiece is simpler than with most standard acoustics. But because the bridge saddle is integral with the guitar's resonator cone, its height can't easily be altered by the player. Lowering the action requires deepening the string slots – again, a job for a pro.

acoustic bridges

INTONATION

Setting intonation is one of the main goals of any set-up. Without getting this crucial step right, your guitar will never quite sound in-tune, nor will the resonance and harmonic content of its natural voice ring true. Put simply, correct intonation lets your guitar sound its best. But fear not – this is a job well within the capabilities of most players.

ADJUSTING INTONATION

We discussed the reason for intonation adjustments earlier in the *Neck Relief* section. The making and checking of any such adjustments is crucial. Also, whenever you change string gauge (or indeed brand) you must re-check your intonation.

Fine-tuning the intonation, especially with individually adjustable saddles, is fairly straightforward – but you'll need an electronic tuner. The bridge or vibrato, string height, truss-rod

Intonation adjustment of Gibson-style Tune-o-matic bridges is usually made with a flat-head screwdriver, often from the front side of the bridge. Always slacken string tension before making any adjustment.

Fender's Stratocaster-style tremolo tailpiece – and many others – use a Phillips head screwdriver for intonation adjustment. The job is best done with new strings fitted, and pickup heights not set too close to the strings.

and nut height should be properly set up before you set the intonation, and ideally the frets should be in good condition. Here is the basic procedure for setting the intonation on all guitars, except those fitted with a nut lock, for which see the technique for Floyd Rose-style vibratos overleaf.

1 Tune strings to pitch and sound the 12th fret harmonic of the first string. Now, compare this with the note produced by fretting the same string at the 12th fret.

2 If the fretted note is sharp compared to the harmonic, the string length must be increased by moving the saddle away from the neck.

3 If the fretted note is flat the saddle must be moved forward, towards the neck, shortening the string length. You can remember this by the simple phrase: "Fret, Flat, Forward." This should help you recall that if the fretted note is flat, move the string saddle forward towards the neck. Just remember the three Fs: Fret, Flat, Forward.

Repeat this procedure on all strings, until the harmonic and the fretted notes are the same.

INTONATION AND BRIDGE TYPES

The intonation adjustments just described are usually made with a Phillips (cross-head) screwdriver or with an allen key. But note that Gibson's Tune-o-matic bridge (pictured left) – and the various versions thereof – is a notable exception that is typically adjusted for intonation using its slot-head screws.

Bear in mind, once again, that you must slacken the string tension before you start to move an individual saddle away from the bridge, especially on Fender-style Strat and Tele bridges (*photo below*), although this also applies to the various brands and varieties of one-piece combination bridge/tailpieces.

Always have new strings fitted, and don't have the pickups too close to the strings, especially the neck pickup, as the magnetic pull will interfere with string vibration and distort the pitch.

On bridges such as the one-piece wrapover type (see photo at bottom-right of opposite page) that have overall intonation adjustment, you use the small grub screws that protrude from the back of the bridge to set the overall intonation. Here you need only check the outer strings; the angled position of the bridge itself allows a basic compensation for the rest. You may find that setting the bass-side intonation using the D-string, rather than the low E-string, sounds more accurate.

Similarly, on a three-saddle Telecaster bridge you can only set the intonation per pair of strings. If you start by intonating the first paired saddle to the top E-string, the theoretical result is that the fretted B-string will sound sharp at the 12th fret compared to its harmonic there. If you find the B-string too sharp when you come to play chords in high-fret positions, then move the saddle backwards a little. This will bring the B-string more in tune, but make the top E-string slightly flat.

On the middle G-string/D-string saddle, if you use the D-string to set the intonation, the G-string will probably end up sharp. Again, you can always move the saddle backwards a little to improve this string, but this will in turn make the D-string slightly flat.

These compromise settings are inevitable and will be magnified by all the factors that affect intonation such as string gauge and action height. (Also see *Tele Tuning Hell* opposite.)

TELE TUNING HELL

The Hellecasters' Jerry Donahue is very particular when it comes to setting-up his guitars. Over the years he's evolved a very neat method that not only solves the problems of a three-saddle Telecaster bridge but also, Donahue believes, makes any guitar with a six-saddle bridge play more in tune. So, here's how Jerry sets his three-saddle Teles.

Tune all open strings as normal. But set the center saddle so that the G-string, fretted at the 12th fret, is marginally sharp of its harmonic (which is in tune). The D-string, fretted at the 12th, is therefore marinally flat of the harmonic.

Now, via the machinehead, adjust the G-string so you get that fretted note in tune, effectively flattening the G-string. Use your ears as a guide. A root position E major chord should sound in tune to your ear with the G# (first fret G string) being slightly flat, but not so much that a root positon E minor chord sounds out.

Donahue finds that the top strings are usually fairly in tune, but sets the B-string, fretted at the 12th, very slightly sharp of the harmonic; the top E-string fretted at the 12th and its harmonic should be spot on.

On the low E and A-string saddle Jerry sets the A in tune – fretted at the 12th and the harmonic. Again, he finds the difference here is usually minimal – and he regularly flattens the low E very slightly anyway.

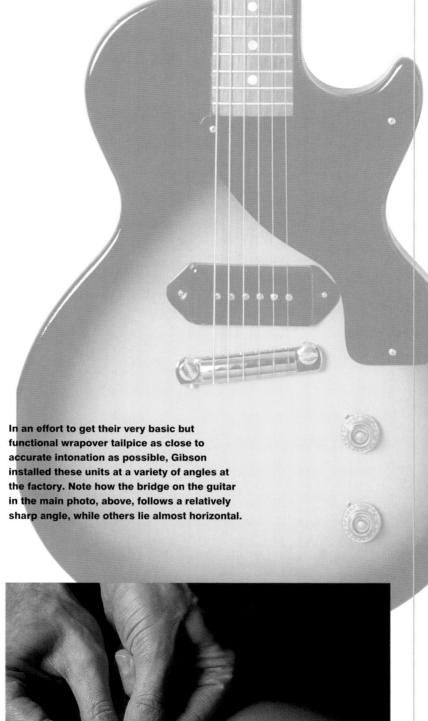

In an effort to get their very basic but functional wrapover tailpice as close to accurate intonation as possible, Gibson installed these units at a variety of angles at the factory. Note how the bridge on the guitar in the main photo, above, follows a relatively sharp angle, while others lie almost horizontal.

Close enough for rock'n'roll? Setting intonation on some earlier electric guitar designs like the Les Paul Junior and Fender Telecaster (right and below) is often a matter of maximizing inherent flaws.

Setting the intonation on the rather primitive three-saddle Telecaster bridge inevitably involves making a few compromises. As you're forced to alter the string lengths in pairs, adjustment here usually means choosing between which of each set of strings to leave a little sharp or flat in relation to its partner.

One of the crudest of all bridge designs for setting intonation, the Gibson-style wrapover unit only allows for adjustment via grub screws at either end of the bar. The angle at which the bridge is installed, however, (and the raised ridge on some types) often helps you get surprisingly close intonation.

Any adjustment of a Floyd Rose-style vibrato starts with loosening the bolts on the locking nut, to free the strings at the headstock end.

Undoing the saddle locks leaves you free to make adjustments. Always use the correct tool here to avoid stripping small screw heads.

Set the intonation in small steps – again using the correct size Allen key – by moving the saddle either forward or backward only about

³⁄₆₄" (1.0mm) at a time. Then lock down the saddle, re-tune, and check intonation again. If still off, adjust further as necessary.

A Saddle Singers insert can help prevent saddle wear and cure many string seating problems, improving tone at the same time.

Often misunderstood, the Floyd Rose string retaining bar is there to ensure that strings sit flat over the surface of the nut lock.

INTONATION OF FLOYD ROSE-STYLE VIBRATOS

Setting intonation on a guitar with a double-locking Floyd Rose-style vibrato is complex and it's best to get the job done professionally. If you want to try it yourself, here's what to do.

1 Unlock the three locking bolts at the locking nut. Compare the 12th fret harmonic with the note at the 12th fret.

2 Remember: if the fretted note is flat, compared to the harmonic, the string length is too long, so the saddle needs to be moved closer to the neck; conversely, if the fretted note is sharp, the string length is too short, so the saddle needs to be moved further away from the neck.

3 Slacken off the individual string tension and visualise the position of the saddle. Undo the saddle lock with the correct Allen key while holding the saddle-locking bolt with your spare hand. Only undo the saddle-locking screw enough to move the saddle either slightly forward or slightly backward as required, and no more than about ³⁄₆₄" (1mm) in the appropriate direction.

4 Having made your adjustment, lock down the saddle-locking bolt and re-tune the string. Re-check the intonation, if it is not correct, make further adjustments as described earlier.

5 When you've completed this for each string, re-check your tuning (see *Vibrato Tuning,* opposite), and don't forget to re-clamp the nut lock.

FLOYD ROSE TIPS

The Floyd Rose and other double-locking varieties may be less fashionable than they once were, but for wide-travel, in-tune bending and serious divebombing, they take some beating. As we've discussed, setting intonation is complex and can be time-consuming, as can re-stringing, but the overall set-up is pretty straightforward.

STRING LOADING

When you're fitting strings on a Floyd Rose vibrato bridge, don't over-tighten the saddle locks. You'll get a feel for the "correct" tightness after a while, and if serious problems occur you should be able to track down replacement saddles from the instrument's manufacturer.

Make sure you always carry in your case or gigbag a good quality pair of wire cutters (and spare strings!) so that prior to loading in the saddle you can cut off the ball-end on the wound strings, at least ¾" (19mm) from the ball-end. Alternatively (and some players do this anyway) load the string (ball-end still attached) through the tuner and then load the plain end into the saddle. This method is used by some players who suffer string breakages at the saddle. You can unwind some of the spare string that has wrapped around the tuner post, and in this way you'll give yourself enough extra length to re-fit the old string into the saddle.

Speaking of string breakage, a UK company markets neat Saddle Singers inserts for Floyd Rose-type vibratos, and they're recommended. These prevent saddle wear – which can lead to premature string breakage – and cure string seating problems, benefiting tone. They're easy to fit when you're changing strings – the photo (far left) shows one in position at a saddle and with the string ready to load.

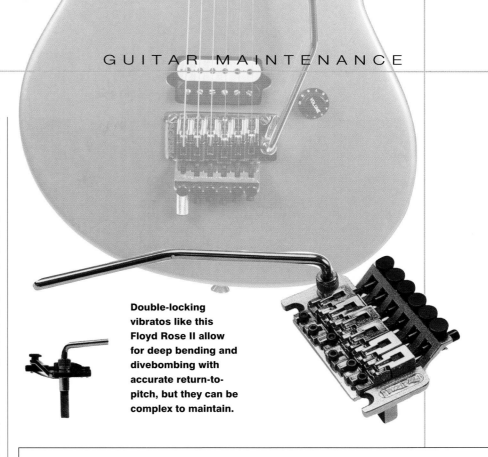

Whenever you're replacing one or all of your strings, remember to "center" the fine-tuners to their mid-way position so that there is plenty of fine-tuning adjustment left in either direction after you've tightened the nut lock.

STRING RETAINING BAR

An often misunderstood feature of the Floyd Rose system is the string-retainer bar situated behind the nut lock. Because the surface of the nut lock is slightly curved, it's important that the string lays flat over the curve, otherwise you will find that when the nut lock is tightened the strings go noticeably sharp.

Visually check that, once threaded under the retainer bar, the strings sit flat over the nut lock. If they don't, then screw down the string-retainer's screws. Now, if any of these screws should feel tight as you screw down, don't force them. Instead, you should first try removing them and applying a little candle wax to the threads for lubrication.

VIBRATO TUNING

Tuning any vibrato can be problematic for the simple reason that as you sharpen one string (increasing the tension) the rest will go slightly flat. A good procedure for any floating (or even vintage) vibrato, especially a Floyd Rose, is to tune from the low E-string first. When that's in tune, go to the A-string. With that one tuned go back to the low E-string, then the A-string again. Only then go to the D-string. With that tuned, return and re-check the previous strings, and carry on using this repetitive back-and-forth procedure.

As with any vibrato it's advisable – even if you're replacing all your strings – to change them one at a time. If you do want to remove all the strings, place a vibrato backplate and/or some stiff card between the back of the vibrato and the face of the guitar to stop the springs pulling the vibrato back. Otherwise the vibrato can come off its pivot points. This is not only inconvenient but can lead to unnecessary wear at these important places.

Finally, having made all your adjustments on the Floyd Rose, you should always remember to tighten the nut locks.

TUNERS AND STRING-STRETCHING

Having set up your vibrato as described you should note once again how careful you must be not to overwind the string around the tuner's string post. Untidy wraps here will be a major problem. Likewise, no vibrato, not even a Floyd Rose, will return to correct pitch unless you've extensively stretched your strings (see *Strings* earlier in the chapter).

On a Strat, for example, not only should you stretch the full length of the string between the saddle and the nut, but you should also make sure you bend the strings behind the nut. This should show up any other problems caused by the string trees and the nut itself.

If you have tension-adjustable tuners fitted, tighten the screws at the end of the button so the action of the tuner feels tight but not too stiff.

STRING TREES

On a Strat, for example, you'll have one or two string trees of varying design. Not only can the tree itself cause the string to hitch up, but if the tree(s) sit(s) too low on the headstock then the behind-the-nut angle will be too steep and, even with the best cut nut slot, the string may hitch in the nut. Graph Tech make excellent friction-reducing string trees which are inexpensive.

Double-locking vibratos like this Floyd Rose II allow for deep bending and divebombing with accurate return-to-pitch, but they can be complex to maintain.

KEEPING YOUR VIBRATO IN TUNE

Don't consider any vibrato bridge in isolation. The problem of the vibrato returning all the strings to pitch after use is invariably down to a combination of factors. It's not always the vibrato bridge or tailpiece that is the main culprit; more often it's the points beyond the bridge. The nut, string trees and tuners – and the way you attach your strings – create the major problem, which is friction. The Floyd Rose vibrato system, by locking the strings at the nut and saddle, not only eliminated any friction points but also the effect of the "dead" string length (that is the portion of the string behind the nut and behind the saddle – within, for example, the sustain block of a Strat vibrato).

A simple device, the string tree plays a crucial role in many guitars' tonal integrity and tuning stability – and some vintage designs can be a headache when they misbehave.

Friction-reducing string trees – like those built by Graph Tech, shown above – can go a long way toward reducing hang ups and improving your ability to stay in tune.

To prevent string breakage at the saddle, the late Stevie Ray Vaughan's guitar tech slipped wire insulation over the wrapped portion of his strings to protect this often-delicate contact point.

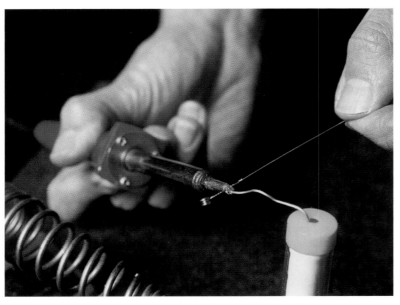

If your strings have a tendency to come unwrapped with extreme vibrato use – inducing tuning troubles with slippage at the ball-end – "tinning" them with solder may help keep them intact longer.

Frustrated by a loose-swinging or ill-positioned Strat vibrato arm? Fitting a small spring in the screw-in vibrato arm hole helps to increase the tension on the screw threads and hold it more firmly in place.

They are moulded to include a spacer, giving plenty of height (and therefore a shallow behind-the-nut string angle).

Should the string angle be *too* shallow – you'll hear a slight buzzing and consequent loss of tone on the open strings if this is the case – you can simply rub the string tree over a piece of medium abrasive paper laid on a flat surface in order to reduce its height. You may be able to remove the G-string/D-string tree altogether, but adding a couple more winds on the string post when you attach the G-string to the tuner will increase the back-angle and, if this job is done neatly, it shouldn't create any slippage problems.

The best solution for problems with tuners and string trees is to replace your tuners with locking types such as those made by Sperzel, Gotoh and Schaller. The Sperzel Trim-Lok tuner, for example, comes with three different post heights so that the behind-the-nut string angle is nicely graduated – and you shouldn't need string trees at all. Tuner replacement is best left to a pro. While it's also a pro job to sort out a nut, you can apply some useful lubricant (soft pencil lead) in the nut slots and under the strings where they pass over the nut.

VINTAGE STRAT VIBRATO TIPS

The vintage-style Strat vibrato has caused many problems and provoked much debate over the years. The pivot points of most modern vibratos of this type have been improved. For example, the underside of the bridgeplate holes are usually countersunk for a better, more knife-edge-like pivot against the six screws.

Lubrication of these points has little lasting effect and should be unnecessary. However, check for noticeable wear on the screws and bridgeplate; if necessary, replace any worn parts.

The vintage-type Strat vibrato has additional friction points both at the saddle and at the point where the string passes over the baseplate on its way to the saddle. Wear on the pressed-steel saddles can cause friction points – especially on the low wound strings – but with a small needle-file and abrasive paper you can smooth these if necessary. Alternatively, if you retrofit friction-reducing saddles these can help with tuning problems and avoid premature string breakages.

STEVIE RAY'S INSULATION WIRE

A tip passed on from Stevie Ray Vaughan's former guitar tech is to slip over plastic wire insulation (as pictured top-left) at the point where the string bends over the block, to prevent breakage. You can easily try this yourself.

SOLDER WRAP

Tinning (soldering) the wrap at the ball-end of your plain strings is easy to do and will prevent the wrap coming undone with extreme vibrato use.

SPRING THING

Nothing to do with tuning stability but worth considering here is the fact that some players find the screw-in vibrato arms used by Fender (and many others) really annoying: the arms either swing loosely, or tighten up in totally the wrong position.

On the Fender American Standard Stratocaster, Fender's simple cure is to fit a small spring in the vibrato arm's hole which keeps the arm in the right position. Available as Fender spares for a few pennies each, these springs (pictured left) will fit virtually any screw-in vibrato arm hole so long as the hole doesn't go right through the block. Also, keep the arm in the vibrato

permanently – just swing it to its lowest position before putting the guitar in its case.

BIGSBY TIPS

One of the many designs that re-appeared in the retro-influenced 1990s and remains popular today is the Bigsby vibrato. Originally fitted from the 1950s on Gibsons, Gretsches and even Fender Teles, for example, the Bigsby is a rather archaic pitch-bending device that adds as much to the visual appeal of your guitar as it does to your bag of sonic techniques.

The design is simple, yet the large tailpiece to which the strings anchor overshadows the fact that the travel is minimal – around a semitone up or down. Guitars equipped with Bigsbys are notorious for poor pitch stability, although usually it's not so much the actual tailpiece that's at fault as the nut and bridge.

Many modern guitars fitted with Bigsbys – such as Epiphone's Les Pauls and Washburn's "P" series solidbodies – come with Tune-o-matic-style bridges, as well as large back-angled headstocks where the strings splay out considerably, creating a steep angle over the nut and therefore more chance of strings hitching in their slots. Tune-o-matic bridges can be retrofitted with Graph Tech friction-reducing saddles, or you can fit a new roller bridge as made by ABM, for example.

The nut must be carefully cut: again, a friction-reducing material is ideal. But both jobs are for a pro. However, you might cure minor problems by careful string-loading at the tuners, extensive string-stretching, and lubrication of the nut and saddles. Ultimately, don't forget that the Bigsby is intended for light use. Treat it with respect!

The Bigsby vibrato is a favorite for vintage-style wobbles, but is a notorious source of tuning troubles.

BILL'S BIGSBYS

Changing strings on a Bigsby vibrato can be a fiddly, frustrating job. Bill Puplett, one of the UK's leading repairmen, has these tips.

"You'll find that pre-bending the ends of the new strings to match the diameter of the string-retaining roller-bar helps, especially with the Bigsby models B5, B7 and B12 that feature a secondary hold-down roller-bar. Use any cylindrical object which has a similar diameter to the retaining bar, for example a pen or piece of dowel. Hold the ball-end flat against the object and firmly wrap the end of the string about one full turn (as pictured near-right), then release it. This will produce a hook-shaped curve at the end of the string.

"Pass this end under the hold-down bar from the bridge side before attaching the ball-end to the retainer pin (pictured far right). Make sure the string is properly attached to the tuner's string-post and tune up so the string has just a bit of tension – don't tune to pitch at this stage. Repeat the bending and installation for the other strings, and then check the string alignment from the retainer bar through to the bridge. Aim to get the strings evenly spaced and running in as straight a line as possible, and make any repositioning adjustments before tuning to pitch. It helps to apply some thorough sharpened and flatened vibrato with the arm, to help the new strings settle.

"When the strings are tuned to pitch, the vibrato arm should come to rest approximately one inch (25mm) clear of the pickguard or face of the guitar. You can adjust this by adding or removing the fiber disc spacers at the base of the spring housing."

Pre-bending the ball-ends of new strings before fitting them to your Bigsby vibrato can make this job a lot easier, and improve tuning and string stability too. Any similar-diameter pen or dowell will work.

Slip the hook-like end of the bent string under the roller-bar string retainer and hook the ball-end on the small retainer pin. This technique also helps to keep the ball-end from popping off the pin as you tune up.

set-up: retro-fit saddles

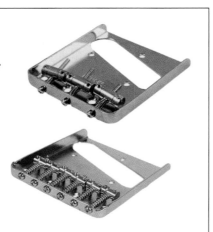

The vintage three-saddle Telecaster bridge (top, right) has a lot of fans, despite its limitations. For those who get annoyed with the oldie's quirks, retro-fit six-saddle alternatives offer more accurate intonation adjustment.

Some players find their guitars benefit from the tuning stability and improved resistance to string breakage that Graph Tech saddles may bring, and it's a job you can usually do yourself...

DEALING WITH SADDLE WEAR

As we've already pointed out, your bridge saddles are very important for tone, sustain, intonation and string longevity. The quality of bridge saddles is often overlooked by manufacturers working in the lower price areas because they need to keep down costs, and consequently the materials used often don't maximize a budget guitar's performance. Combine that with general wear-and-tear and you have a situation that's far from ideal.

Graph Tech's line of replacement String Saver saddles can provide an easy retrofit answer. They are made of a friction-reducing plastic and should cure any string-hitching problems. They can also maximize string life, and should improve your tone a bit too as compared to budget saddles.

Graph Tech also make a synthetic ivory material called Tusq used for some electric guitar saddles, though mostly for acoustics. These will give a slightly different tone, increasing acoustic resonance and "zing".

Graph Tech's saddles come in a variety of sizes for a variety of guitars, so consult your local store to find the right ones (and remember to take along your guitar). You can easily fit them yourself, and the right time to do this is when you're changing your strings. We fitted them to a Strat, as follows.

1 On Strats and Teles (and other similar guitars) fit one saddle at a time. Remove the first string and unscrew the intonation screw and spring, as pictured left.

2 Fit the new saddle and match its position and height approximately in relation to the other saddles. Fit your new string and adjust the height and intonation. Do this individually for all the saddles. Then check the string height. Last, check and if necessary adjust the intonation.

Tune-o-matic saddle replacements are also produced by Graph Tech but not all types are available, and the bridge's saddle screws don't always match the thread of the new saddles (unlike the Strat and Tele types which come with their own new screws). It's really important to get the right ones for your bridge, so replacement here is a little more tricky. Also, the tops of the saddles may need to be notched to achieve the correct string spacing. Consult your store and/or repairman.

Simply remove old saddles and replace one at a time with new units, matching approximate settings and string heights as you go. When finished, fine-tune your intonation (above).

ELECTRICS

These are the mysterious "ghost in the machine" to many players, but there's no reason you should shy away from doing basic electrics repairs and modifications yourself – and even undertaking some more elaborate jobs with practise and experience. Just as learning to set up and intonate your own guitar will optimize its acoustic performance, doing your own electrics adjustments, repairs, wiring mods and pickup replacements is a great way to fine-tune your tone.

ELECTRIC MAINTENANCE

There is a big distinction between the acoustic and electric "sides" of your guitar. The acoustic side of the instrument includes all the factors covered so far: the neck, the truss-rod and the hardware, and how each part is adjusted. Now that we've taken care of the acoustic side, we can move to the maintenance and adjustment of the electric side – as well as looking later at retrofit pickups and wiring modifications.

PICKUP HEIGHT

There are a couple of adjustments to pickups that can improve and balance the guitar's output. Both single-coils and humbuckers have overall height adjustment. The closer the pickup is to the strings, the more output you'll get, and vice-versa.

If the pickup is too close to the strings, however, problems can occur with the magnetic pull of the pickup or, in the worst case, the strings can actually collide with the pickup, stopping them dead. Here's what you do.

1 Fret the outer strings (one at a time) at the top fret (21st, 22nd or 24th). Measure the distance from the top of the pickup to the underside of the string. There is no precise distance at which this should be set. It depends on the pickup itself and, just as importantly, how you want to hear the sound balance between the two or three pickups. A rough guide for full-size humbuckers is to go for a gap of around 3/32" (2.5mm) on the treble and bass sides of the neck and bridge pickups.

2 Plug in your guitar and check the output balance of the pickups. If the neck humbucker dominates then screw it down further into the guitar body, away from the strings. Some pickup makers such as Seymour Duncan offer "calibrated" sets of pickups. Because there is more string movement the further you move from the bridge, the strings' output will be greater over the neck pickup than over the bridge pickup. This can be compensated for by altering the pickup's output. So as a guide, Duncan recommends setting a calibrated set of Duncan humbuckers at 1/16" (1.6mm) on the treble side and 1/8" (3.2mm) on the bass-side (top of pickup to underside of string).

3 For single-coils you can go for a similar distance of 3/32" (2.5mm) on the treble side and slightly more, around 1/8" to 9/64" (3 to 3.5mm), on the bass side. With a Strat (again, unless you're using a calibrated pickup set) you may want to screw further down into the guitar the neck pickup and, to a lesser extent, the middle pickup. Be prepared to sacrifice output by lowering the pickup – especially on the bass side of the neck pickup – to avoid the magnetic string-pull that can distort the strings' vibrational pattern and create a double-note effect which can impair tone and hinder accurate tuning.

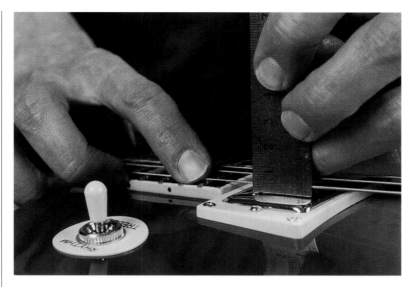

Setting a pickup's height is an important means of adjusting and balancing its output, but your range here will be limited by string clearance and the possible damping effects of magnet on string.

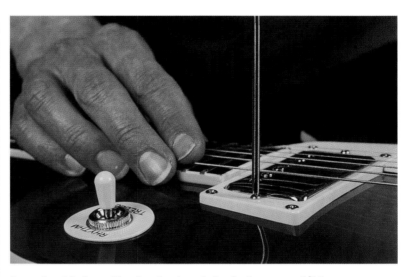

A rough guide for setting humbuckers is to aim for a gap of 3/32" (2.5mm) at the treble and bass polepieces, but there's no hard and fast rule – and some calibrated sets require different settings.

The magnetic polepieces in Strat neck-position single-coils can cause string-pull, resulting in dead notes and ghost tones. You might need to sacrifice some output and set these a little low.

Not so much intended as a means of overall height adjustment, individually-adjustable polepieces can be set to follow a guitar's bridge and string radius, and balance individual string output.

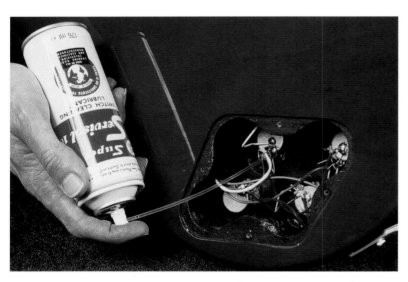

Servisol – or another suitable electrical cleaner/lubricant – can be a great quick-fix for scratchy pots and switches. If this stuff doesn't cure the problem, replacement is usually the only option.

To clean and lubricate a gritty, crackling pot, aim the spray through the intended hole in the pot casing.

To correct scratchy switches, spray the contact/friction points of the lever mechanism.

POLEPIECE HEIGHT

Most humbuckers (and some single-coils) have one or two rows of adjustable polepieces. Once you've set the pickup's overall height you can adjust these to compensate for both the radius of the fingerboard and the strings, as well as their differing volumes caused by varying diameters and whether they're wound or plain types. Start off with the polepieces virtually flush with the top of the pickup.

Play your guitar amplified, preferably with a relatively clean amp tone, and compare the string outputs up and down the neck – and, obviously, one pickup at a time. You may find that the wound D-string is a little quiet compared to the A, so with the appropriate tool – usually either a flat-blade screwdriver or hexagonal Allen key – you can raise the polepiece slightly. Note that you should avoid raising the top E polepiece too far as you could easily catch the string on it, with nasty results. Instead, use that string as your reference and reduce the height, if necessary, on the polepieces for the B and G-strings.

CLEANING POTS AND SWITCHES

Even brand new guitars can suffer from scratchy-sounding pots and selector switches (especially the Fender-style lever switch). Plug your guitar into your amp and continually rotate or activate the scratchy pot or switch. Does the scratching become reduced? If it does, all you need is an aerosol can of pot-and-switch cleaner such as Servisol.

Expose the controls of your guitar and spray the cleaner into the small hole at the front of the pot or into the lever switch. Again, plug in your guitar and quickly rotate the pot or move the switch. You may need a couple of goes at this before the scratchiness is gone. If the pot still sounds scratchy or clicks, replacement is advised. On some guitars you may need to remove the control knobs and the pot itself to clean it, so next we'll show you how to do this.

STAGGERED POLEPIECES
Vintage Fender Strat (and some Tele) pickups have staggered polepieces to compensate for differing string-output levels – though these were originally designed with a wound G-string in mind.

ADJUSTABLE POLEPIECES
Gibson's groundbreaking PAF humbucker allowed for a greater degree of player-adjustability from the start, with one row of threaded polepieces which can be set with a flat-blade screwdriver.

electrics: polepiece adjustment

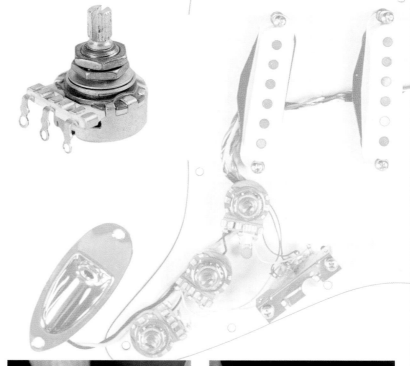

REMOVING KNOBS AND ACCESSING POTS

Disassembling your guitar's electronics is often straightforward, but a few tips can help make the job easier – and avoid costly breakages or mistakes.

To remove a knob, first inspect it to see if there is a grub-screw holding it to the pot. If there is, undo it with an Allen key or screwdriver. Most guitars have push-on knobs, so try lifting the knob by hand.

If the knob is too tight to move by hand, proceed as follows and with care. On Les Paul-style guitars, a tip passed on by UK maker Phil Norsworthy is to wrap a cloth tightly around the knob and gently pull it upwards while gripping the knob with your finger. If it still won't budge, seek pro advice. Do not try to lever it with a screwdriver as it's easy to crack the knob or, worse, to damage the front of your guitar.

On Strat-style guitars the less brittle plastic knobs do not crack so easily – but usually they sit lower on the guitar so you can't get a cloth around them. Here you can protect the pickguard with an old plastic credit card and, using a small flat-blade screwdriver, carefully and gently lever upwards. (Don't turn the screwdriver: this will mark the bottom edge of the knob.) The key here is to slowly rotate the knob as you lever upwards. Once you've moved the knob up a little, wrap the cloth around it; you should now be able to pull it off.

With the knob removed, undo the pot's fixing washer with the correct-size wrench (box spanner). The pot can then be moved, without unsoldering, to allow enough space to clean it. Be careful not to disturb the wiring.

Sometimes pots work loose and rotate, but re-securing the control is easy. Remove the control knob as described and tighten the fixing nut with a box wrench, holding the pot itself firmly in place to stop it rotating. Box and socket wrenches are also very handy for tightening the fixing nuts of the output socket (jack) and the tuners – a job for which you should never consider using pliers.

Lever switches are easily removed and/or secured using the two fixing screws at either end of the switch.

A Gibson-style toggle switch has a ribbed circular nut to secure it onto the guitar. This is tricky to tighten and/or loosen as there is no "correct" commonly-available tool for the job. (Stewart-MacDonald's Guitar Shop Supply offers an appropriate Toggle Switch Wrench, but it's a specialist repairer's tool and perhaps not worth purchasing to use only once every few years.) The late British luthier Sid Poole explained his approach to seemingly basic but rather tricky little job.

"Before I got the Toggle Switch Wrench I dreaded this job. It's all too easy to damage either the nut itself, the plastic rhythm/lead ring, or the guitar's finish. So I suggest that you protect the rhythm/lead ring with masking tape, and then use a pair of pliers held very carefully upright to slowly move the nut. You'll probably need to stop the switch rotating by holding it with a pair of needle-nosed (snipe-nosed) pliers from the rear of the guitar, obviously with the coverplate removed. It's a tricky job." For further protection you can wrap some masking tape around the tips of the pliers. Never attempt to over-tighten this nut. Above all, this apparently simple operation could damage your guitar, and so it really is a job for a pro if you find it isn't successfully accomplished using the above tips.

Unless any component needs replacing, your existing electrics should now be in top condition. It's only at this point that you should consider whether you need a new pickup or maybe want to alter your guitar's wiring.

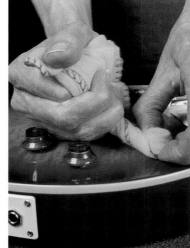

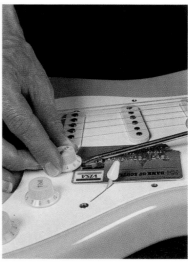

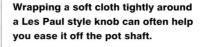

Wrapping a soft cloth tightly around a Les Paul style knob can often help you ease it off the pot shaft.

For tight Strat knobs, slip a flat-blade screwdriver underneath and gently ease it upwards.

The correct sized box wrench is the safest and easiest means of removing a pot retaining nut.

Specialist tools are available for other tricky jobs, but might not be worth buying for occasional use.

ELECTRICS HEALTH CHECK

Check pickup heights are approximately correct.

Check that each pickup and the selector switch is working.

Check each volume and tone control – plus any coil-splits – are working and whether any sounds "scratchy."

Check that the switches, pots and output socket are firmly mounted.

Precisely set pickup/polepiece heights.

Clean pots and switches if needed.

If necessary, remove control knobs and tighten pot fixing nuts and output jack socket nut.

REPLACEMENT ALTERNATIVES

The replacement pickup you choose depends on how you want to alter your sound, and there are hundreds of alternatives to select from today. The list below provides a starting point by suggesting a range of popular retrofit options to achieve different sounds in the bridge position (the most common mod), and presumes your current guitar has stock pickups.

	SOUND	REPLACEMENT PICKUP
TELECASTER		
	vintage	SD Antiquity Tele, JM
	hot vintage	SD Vintage Lead Stack, DiM,
		RioGr Muy Grande
	noise-free	DiM Virtual Vintage
	ultra-hot	SD Hot Rails, Quarter Pounder
STRATOCASTER		
	vintage	SD Antiquity Strat, JM
	hot vintage	DiM FS-1,
		RioGr Halfbreed or Stelly
	noise-free	DiM Virtual Vintage
	ultra-hot	SD Hot Rails or Hot Stack
LES PAUL/SG STANDARD		
	vintage	SD Antiquity
	hot vintage	SD Pearly Gates,
		RioGr BBQ Bucker
	ultra-hot	DiM Super Distortion,
		EMG 81 or EMG 60
LES PAUL/SG SPECIAL/JUNIOR		
	vintage	SD Antiquity
	hot vintage	SD, DiM, etc
		RioGr Bluesbar
	noise-free	DiM Virtual Vintage

SD = Seymour Duncan

DiM = DiMarzio

EMG = EMG

JM = J.M. Rolph

RioGr = Rio Grande

RETROFITTING

If you're happy with the feel, style and overall playability of your guitar but would like a slightly different amplified tone – hotter, brighter or more vintage-like – pickup replacement is often the answer, and it's a job you can probably do yourself.

REASONS TO RETROFIT

There are four primary reasons for considering pickup replacement. First, your pickup may simply have stopped working. Uncovered pickups such as open-coiled humbuckers and Telecaster bridge pickups are susceptible to moisture penetration (beer, sweat, tears, etc) which can lead to corrosion of the delicate pickup coil windings and shorting of the pickup. One answer is to have the pickup rewound, a service that should be considerably cheaper than investing in a new unit.

Second, and a more common occurrence on new and old guitars alike, is that your pickup(s) may squeal, or be "microphonic." These problems have a variety of causes depending on the type of guitar. Covered humbuckers – currently making quite a comeback – can squeal at high volumes. Often this is because the pickup has not been fully wax-saturated (potted); be aware, however, that original-style PAF humbuckers are like this by design. Another reason is that the cover or pickup mounting may vibrate and cause microphonic feedback. Invariably the problem is magnified when you're using a high-gain, high-volume set-up. The options are to get your pickup properly potted and maybe take specialist advice on the pickup mounting, or to fit a new pickup.

The third reason for considering pickup replacement is to do with the original design. Fender Strat and Tele pickups and Gibson's P90 are single-coil types, so they are susceptible to both low-cycle mains hum, and higher-pitched hum and interference from fluorescent and stage lights and computer monitors. If the hum bothers you (or your band), the cure is to replace the offending pickup(s) with humbucking replacements, now available to retrofit most single-coil-size routings.

Finally, and perhaps most commonly of all, you might feel that your pickup is a weak link in your sound chain and you simply fancy a tonal change. Kent Armstrong reckons this is the main reason. Similarly, a technical adviser for EMG says: "It's probably the least expensive and most direct way to change your tone. Most people get pretty comfortable with their guitar, so it's the quickest way to upgrade it." Seymour Duncan concurs that players often look for a tone from their guitar that is not always provided by its stock pickups. "That's obvious," Duncan admits, "but many players are searching for a dream. They want to play and sound like their idol or someone they aspire to. Changing pickups helps further that dream."

PICKUP CONSIDERATIONS

Before we look at what a pickup can do, you need equally to be aware of what it can't do. As we've already discussed, an electric guitar can still be considered as an "acoustic." The combination of the guitar's design, materials, hardware, strings and set-up all contribute to that "acoustic" tone. The pickup then takes that inherent sound and sends it off to your amplifier. While no one is denying that the pickup forms a major part of your sound chain – and of course most pickup makers figure it's *the* major part – it should not affect the acoustic performance of the guitar. Ideally the pickup should take the "information" – the strings' vibration –

and ferry it as effectively as possible to your amplifier. So before you start pointing a finger at your pickups, make sure you've followed the instructions so far to adjust your guitar to its best potential. That includes fitting new strings – and always using a good-quality guitar cord (lead).

CHOOSING A PICKUP

For most of us, choosing a new pickup is always a risk. The only way to know if the new pickup is exactly what you need is to buy it, fit it and sound-test it through your own set-up. So to minimize the possibility of a mistaken purchase, do some homework.

First you need to establish what it is that you don't like about your existing tone – assuming of course that you're happy with your amp, FX and guitar. "That's the key," says Seymour Duncan. "Figure out why the existing pickup isn't happening for you. Does the bridge pickup in your Strat sound too thin? You have to identify the problem. Then you have to work out what you need: better harmonics, chunkier power chords? Think about your guitar and amp. What is the body and neck wood? Do you use a clean tone or melt-down metal? Then you can ask a dealer or repairman a specific question. 'I want a better sound from my Strat,' is too vague, but, 'I want to beef up the bridge pickup on my alder-body maple-neck Strat which I use through a Fender Princeton amp to play blues,' is what we need."

"Ideally you should test before you buy," says Kent Armstrong. "But that's the problem: you can't try everything. Talk to other players who have played them, and get some advice."

Both Seymour Duncan and DiMarzio provide tone charts in their product catalogues, comparing output (high or low) and bass, midrange and treble tone. A high-output pickup will drive a tube amp into overdrive more easily than a lower-powered pickup. The down-side is that you can often lose dynamics: there will be less distinction between light and heavily picked notes and the sound will be more compressed. You should be familiar with bass, midrange and treble from your hi-fi, but the electric guitar is really all about midrange. A classic Les Paul tone, for example, has a strong lower midrange helping to create its notorious thickness, but with enough upper midrange bite to cut through. But a classic Strat pickup will have less pronounced midrange, resulting in a "flatter," more acoustic tone. It'll also have plenty of upper-mids and highs for its classic sparkle.

Artist endorsements can help your choice too. All the big three companies – Seymour Duncan, DiMarzio and EMG – list in their catalogues many players and the set-ups they use, and this will at least give you some idea of the stylistic application of a certain pickup. "There are too many brands out there," says EMG, "and you can't hear them all. We'd suggest looking at your favourite players, finding out what they play and then taking a listen." For example, if you're after a vintage tone from your Les Paul you shouldn't buy a DiMarzio Evolution humbucker designed for Steve Vai, but go for their more classic-sounding PAF model. "As far as we're concerned," says EMG, "if an artist uses our pickups, it's their choice and they found them."

But in the end you're going to have to buy a pickup and live with it. If it's not 100 per cent right for you, at least by following the company's various comparative tone/output information it will be easier to fine-tune your future choice. These charts would tell you, for example, that if you'd purchased a DiMarzio Super Distortion humbucker but found it too aggressive sounding, then a DiMarzio PAF with its close approximation of the original Gibson PAF might be a better choice.

STACKED "SINGLE-COIL" HUMBUCKERS

Looking for hum-free performance in a single-coil-sized package with fairly authentic sound? Some manufacturers achieve this by stacking two coils rather than placing them side-by-side, as with the Seymour Duncan pictured right.

VINTAGE SINGLE-COILS

Not all pickup swaps are in a quest to achieve more power: a large number of players are looking to replicate the tones of the '50s and '60s, and pickups with vintage-correct alnico magnets and precise-spec windings fit the bill.

HOT "SINGLE-COIL" HUMBUCKERS

Fitting a hot single-coil-sized humbucker in the bridge position is one of the most common mods for rock-playing Strat owners, and the Seymour Duncan Hot Rails is a popular choice. With over-wound side-by-side coils and dual blade polepieces, it greatly increases power and sustain compared to standard single-coils, and requires no major alteration of your guitar.

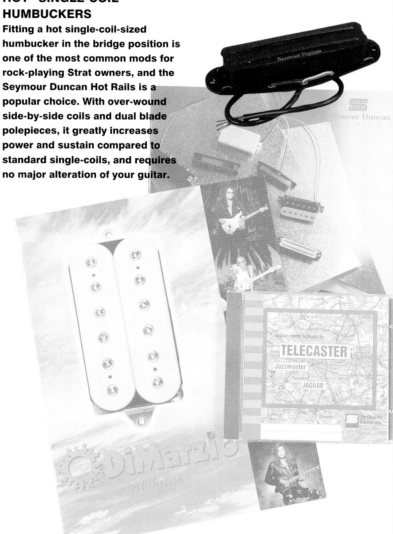

electrics: pickup replacement

On any Strat or similarly constructed guitar, start by removing the pickguard to get at the electrics.

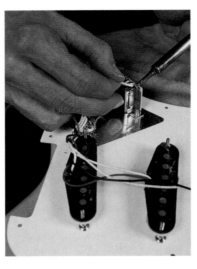

Trace the wires of the pickup you're replacing and unsolder them from the five-way switch.

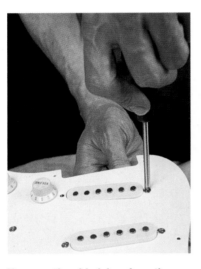

Unscrew the old pickup from the pickguard, setting any mounting hardware carefully aside...

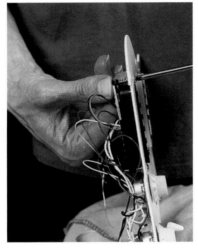

And load in the new unit, using the screws supplied (its mounting holes may differ from your old pickup).

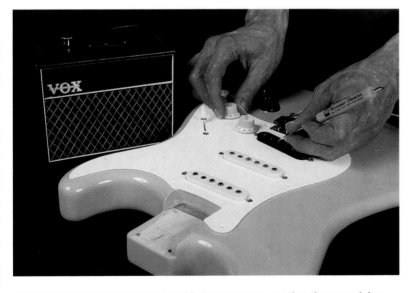

Before re-assembling your guitar, it's important to test that the new pickup and the rest of your electronics are functioning correctly. If all is well, bolt it back together – and give your mod a good playing-in.

REPLACING A SINGLE-COIL PICKUP

Many current Fender Strats are perfect guitars for electrics modification. Under the pickguard there's a large oblong pickup cavity rather than the three separate pickup routs (plus channel) found on a vintage-spec Strat. The oblong rout means that fitting humbuckers is easy, and new pickguards are readily available as spares so you don't have to cut up your original one. The fact that you can remove the neck with the strings still on also makes life easier: the pickguard is accessible, and you can quickly re-assemble the guitar to try it out.

1 Remove the neck (as described in detail in previous sections) and put it aside; unscrew the pickguard and set the screws safely aside – a jar or old film can is useful to keep these safe while you work. Carefully turn over the pickguard and rest it securely on the covered guitar body. Trace the wires from the pickup that you're replacing: one should be already soldered to the five-way switch, the other to the back of a volume pot. Sketch the circuit so you can find your connections again once you have removed the original components, then unsolder the relevant wires by heating the joints and pulling the wires free.

2 Unscrew the old pickup, taking care to keep the springs and the rubber tubing that goes over the fixing-screw between the pickup and the pickguard.

3 Load in the new pickup using the supplied screws and the old springs or rubber tubing. Strip and tin the ends of the pickup wires, but at this stage don't cut them to length. When you've sound-tested your new pickup and are sure that's the one you want, then you can go back into the guitar and tidy up your wiring.

Solder the new pickup wires in place but don't, at this stage, worry about a mechanical fixing – such as hooking the wire through the pot tag – as there's a 50/50 chance that your new single-coil will be out-of-phase with your existing pickup (see *Phased And Confused* on page 97). Before you re-assemble your guitar, plug it into your amp (keep the volume low) and lightly rub (don't tap) the tip of a screwdriver on the pickup polepieces. You'll hear a sound through your amp if the new pickup is working. Then check that the selector switch and the volume and tone controls are all working correctly. Re-assemble your guitar.

4 Test out your new pickup (or any wiring mods) thoroughly before you finally decide it's right. When you've given it the thumbs-up, open up your guitar and tidily cut, re-strip and re-solder the connections, using mechanical joints if possible.

REPLACING A HUMBUCKER

Working on a set-neck Les Paul-style guitar is less easy than a bolt-on. Also, we're showing the bridge pickup; if you're replacing the neck humbucker on a solid-topped Les Paul-type guitar you'll have to remove the bridge pickup too so you can thread the neck pickup's hook-up wire through the bridge pickup's cavity into the rear control cavity.

1 Before you start, make sure the existing pickup heights are about right. Measure and note down the distance from the top of the mounting ring to the top of the humbucker(s) you're replacing.

Remove your strings (or alternatively put a capo at the first fret, slacken off the strings, and remove the tailpiece and bridge). Remove the rear control cavity's backplate. Unsolder the live pickup wire from the correct control, and unsolder the ground (earth) wire from the back of the pot. (It may not be clear which pickup wire goes where. Don't worry, just partially remove the pickup as described in the next step and gently pull on its hook-up wire, and trace which pot it's soldered to by observing which wire moves at the other end. Put two of the mounting-ring screws back, then unsolder the relevant wires.)

2 Turn the guitar over and remove the pickup by unscrewing the four cross-head screws that hold the pickup mounting ring. Carefully pull the pickup, still held in its mounting ring, away from the guitar.

Unscrew the two pickup height-adjustment screws carefully. Make sure you don't lose the two long springs as new ones are not always supplied. Before you mount the new pickup, check to see if the old height-adjustment screws fit the threaded lugs on the new pickup. Don't force them – just use your fingers to see if they'll turn in the thread. If they do, then go ahead and use them. If not, use the screws supplied.

3 Mount the new pickup in the old mounting ring. This is actually quite a tricky job. Insert one screw at a time through the ring, place the spring over the screw, and grip the pickup and mounting ring so that the end of the screw is held over the thread on the pickup's mounting lug. With a small cross-head or slot-head screwdriver (depending on the screw type) carefully turn the screw so that it bites into the pickup's thread. Don't force it – you might damage the thread.

The new height adjustment screws will probably be too long and you'll need a pair of heavy duty cutters to trim them to length. But first screw the pickup down into the ring to match the distance you measured originally. Replace the pickup in the guitar. Does it sit flush on the body, or are those screws stopping it? If necessary, cut them to length with heavy-duty cutters about ⅟₁₆" or so (a few millimeters) past the back face of the mounting lugs.

4 Carefully thread the hook-up wire through the hole that connects the pickup cavity to the rear control cavity (below right), wrapping masking tape around any loose wires so they don't bunch up and catch in the hole. Replace the pickup into the guitar, securing it with just two of the mounting-ring screws at diagonally opposite corners.

At this stage don't cut the pickup wire to length. Strip, tin and re-solder the live wire to the relevant volume control and the earth wire to the back of the pot. If the pickups have four-conductor wiring, make sure you follow the supplied wiring diagram and join the remaining two conductors (for series linkage) as described later in this section.

5 Rub the tip of a screwdriver on the pickup polepieces to check that the new pickup is working and check that all the controls function (as described opposite in *Replacing A Single-coil Pickup*). Fit a set of new strings and tune your guitar to pitch. Set the height of the new pickup. Refit the remaining mounting-ring screws and refit the control cavity backplate. Only after fully sound-testing your guitar should you cut the pickup wires to correct length and re-solder the hot connection using a mechanical joint.

HUMBUCKER VARIATIONS
There are almost as many replacement options for humbuckers as there are for single-coils, and models available perform jobs nearly as diverse as there are styles of music. Seekers of vintage tones generally opt for PAF-style pickups like the Seymour Duncan TB-'59, top, while Joe Barden's dual blade models suit players who appreciate high-end tone without concern for vintage cosmetics. Even more contemporary in design (though they've been with us for years), EMG's active pickups do everything from sweet blues to power metal.

Unsolder the pickup's live and ground wires from the correct control or switch point.

Remove the four screws that hold the mounting ring in place, and lift out pickup and ring.

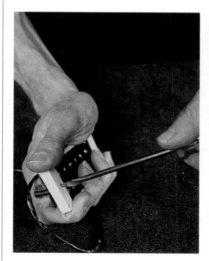

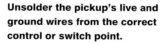

Mounting a new pickup in an old mounting ring can be a surprisingly tricky job – so proceed with care.

Next, carefully thread the wire through the hole connecting the pickup cavity and control cavity.

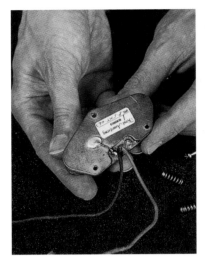

The grounding plate underneath a Tele bridge pickup is a unique part of its design – and must be connected.

The standard-style Tele's controls are easy to get at – merely unscrew the control panel and flip it.

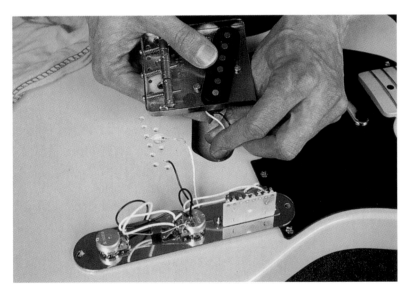

After unsoldering the pickup wires, remove the entire bridge unit before proceeding to swap pickups. This

bridge design is a major part of a Telecaster's distinctive tone – but makes pickup replacement tricky.

Mount the new pickup in the bridge's baseplate before making any solder connections.

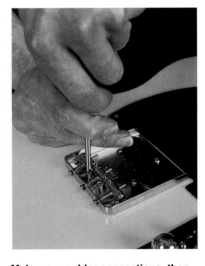

Make your solder connections, then re-mount the bridge unit, string up, and give 'er a play.

REPLACING A TELE BRIDGE PICKUP

Unlike any other electric, the Telecaster and its derivatives has a bridge pickup that is mounted within the bridge's baseplate. It's held with three screws, and under the pickup is a grounding plate. The combination of these design features contributes to the Tele's unique tone – but can also add to microphonic squeal, especially if the pickup's windings are not properly wax-potted and if there's any movement of the pickup and/or the bridgeplate.

In order to replace a Tele bridge pickup, first remove the strings. You have little choice with this, because to access the bridge pickup you'll have to remove the bridge itself. Measure the height of the pickup from the face of the bridgeplate, on both treble and bass sides. Make a note of these dimensions.

1 Unscrew the control plate and sketch the wiring layout. Unsolder the pickup's hook-up wires. As with the humbucker replacement, if you're unsure which wires are which, then remove the bridge's baseplate by undoing the four mounting screws and gently pull on the two hook-up wires to trace one to the three-way lever switch and one to the back of a pot.

2 With the hook-up wires unsoldered, remove the bridge's baseplate and the pickup, undoing the four baseplate screws first if you haven't already. Replace the control plate and place the guitar to one side.

3 Remove the pickup from the bridge's baseplate and mount the new pickup. Some players and makers insist on replacing the pickup's mounting springs with small pieces of plastic or rubber tubing to reduce microphonics. Others stick with the springs. Either way, the key is to make sure that springs or tubing are very tight and firm, and that once the pickup is mounted there's virtually no movement within the baseplate. Set the pickup to the original position. Strip and carefully tin the hook-up wires.

4 Undo the control plate and thread the hook-up wires into the control cavity. Solder them to the correct positions: the live wire goes to the three-way lever switch, the ground (earth) wire to the back of a pot. Place both the control plate and the bridgeplate in position and scratch-test the pickup to check that it's working. Replace all the screws and re-string the guitar. Tune up, and then set the pickup height – then play-test thoroughly.

WIRING MODIFICATIONS

Now that we've covered all the basic aspects relating to your electronics, you can use this *Wiring Modifications* section should you need to replace any components or you want to upgrade and modify your guitar.

REPLACING COMPONENTS

For any component replacement there are some basic rules…

Sketch out your guitar's existing circuitry *before* you start!
Unsolder the component.
Remove old component and re-install new part.
Re-solder new component and scratch-test before re-assembling guitar.

Note that semi-solid guitars like Gibson's ES-335 are popular again but are among the trickiest guitars to work on as far as

electrics: pickup replacement

electronics are concerned. The problem is that these guitars have no backplate. To service the parts or replace the pickups you must remove the pots and switches through the f-holes. For this reason we suggest you take your semi to a professional.

VOLUME AND TONE POTS

To replace these, in most cases a standard split-shaft (splined-shaft) pot of the required value and taper will be fine (as discussed earlier in this section). Before you install the new pot, however, check that the control knob actually fits onto the new pot's shaft. The slotted split shaft can be widened *slightly* by carefully opening it up at the tip with a flat-blade screwdriver, or narrowed by slightly compressing the split with a pair of pliers. *Be warned*: the tips of these shafts are surprisingly fragile.

The tools and techniques for un-mounting a pot are the same as those previously shown for cleaning; here, of course, we completely unsolder the old component and load in the new one in its place.

OUTPUT JACK (SOCKET)

The majority of electric guitars use a mono output jack (socket). The exceptions generally are those with on-board active electronics, where the second "stereo" hot connection serves to make the 9V battery connection when plugged in. A mono output

PHASED AND CONFUSED

When two pickups – humbuckers or single-coils – are combined (positions 2 and 4 on a Strat, the middle positions on a Les Paul or Telecaster) they'll be either in-phase or out-of-phase. If they're out-of-phase (caused primarily by reversed magnet polarity) the resulting mixed sound will be thin (bass light) and "strangled" or overly nasal sounding. Now, you may like this sound especially for high-gain grungy tones or reggae/funk/country clean tones but you may not. (Note that the standard 2 and 4 positions on a Strat, sometimes referred to as "out-of-phase" positions, aren't actually wired out of phase: the thinner, funkier tone of these "notched" bridge-plus-middle or neck-plus-middle settings simply results from the natural frequency cancellations of two closely-positioned pickups selected together in parallel.)

For genuine out-of-phase problems, standard single-coils are easy to cure – simply swap the live and earth connections of one pickup where they connect to the pickup switch. Humbuckers with just one live wire and earth are more difficult because the earth wire – unlike a standard single-coil – is connected to the metal baseplate and the cover (if fitted). Swapping these two around will result in hum. Telecasters can be especially problematic because the earth wire of the bridge pickup is connected to its own grounding plate and the neck pickup's earth wire connects to its metal cover. The most simple solution is swap the connections for the neck pickup but you must rewire the neck pickup's cover to the 'new' earth output, a job for a pro or specialist pickup repairer.

If you're mixing brands of pickups always make sure the humbucker has 3- or preferably 4-conductor and separate earth wires (see *Replacing a Humbucker*) – this way any phase problems for standard pickup linkages can be easily identified and solved.

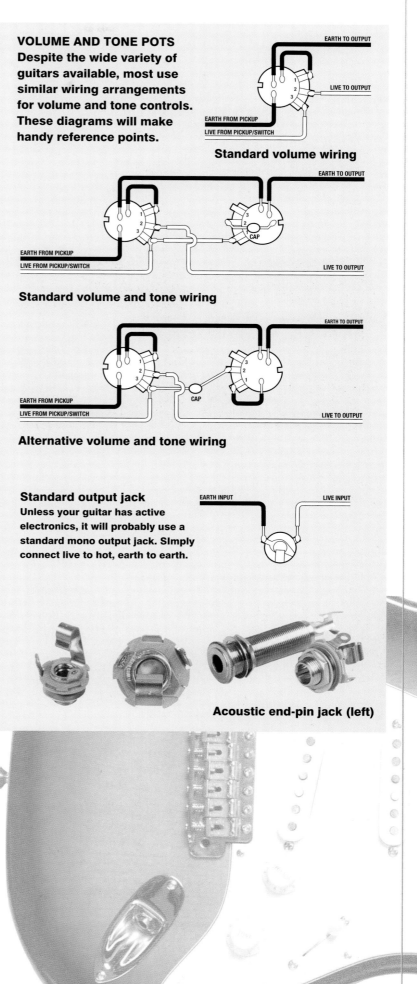

VOLUME AND TONE POTS
Despite the wide variety of guitars available, most use similar wiring arrangements for volume and tone controls. These diagrams will make handy reference points.

Standard volume wiring

Standard volume and tone wiring

Alternative volume and tone wiring

Standard output jack
Unless your guitar has active electronics, it will probably use a standard mono output jack. SImply connect live to hot, earth to earth.

Acoustic end-pin jack (left)

electrics: component replacement

FIVE-POSITION LEVER SWITCH

The top diagram here shows the standard wiring for a US five-position lever switch. The lower diagram demonstrates how Fender wire their lever switches – and this is typically the reverse of the first method. Either way will work.

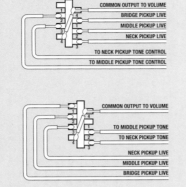

COMMON OUTPUT TO VOLUME
BRIDGE PICKUP LIVE
MIDDLE PICKUP LIVE
NECK PICKUP LIVE
TO NECK PICKUP TONE CONTROL
TO MIDDLE PICKUP TONE CONTROL

COMMON OUTPUT TO VOLUME
TO MIDDLE PICKUP TONE
TO NECK PICKUP TONE
NECK PICKUP LIVE
MIDDLE PICKUP LIVE
BRIDGE PICKUP LIVE

By viewing the contacts in a toggle switch as you move the lever, you can determine correct connections.

Each side of a three or five-position lever switch carries three input/output tags and one common tag.

PICKUP SELECTORS

The five-position Strat-type switch (top right) and three-position variety (center right) are virtually identical in construction, although the former is notched for dual-contact positions between the input/output tags. The type of switch typically used in Gibsons and other similarly-built guitars (below right) looks radically different to the Fender unit, but performs the same job as any three-position Tele switch: selecting bridge pickup, neck pickup, or both together.

THREE-POSITION TOGGLE SWITCH

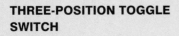

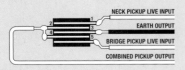

NECK PICKUP LIVE INPUT
EARTH OUTPUT
BRIDGE PICKUP LIVE INPUT
COMBINED PICKUP OUTPUT

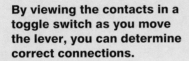

jack simply has one connection for the hot output and another for the ground output. Take care to replace the jack (socket) with one of a similar size, especially on Stratocaster-style guitars where it sits under the separate "dished" mounting plate, or a standard Telecaster where it's mounted in a body rout without much room to spare. Generally, a standard "chassis" type jack is recommended in these situations.

PICKUP SELECTOR SWITCHES

Most Fender-style guitars and many, many others use either a three-position lever switch (for two-pickup guitars) or a five-position lever switch (for three-pickup guitars) to select the pickups. The other industry standard switch is the three-position toggle or leaf switch used on Gibson-style guitars, primarily with two pickups.

THREE AND FIVE-POSITION LEVER SWITCHES

You'll encounter a number of different types within two basic categories: "open" and "closed." A standard US-made open type is preferred, and is featured here. Measure the distance between the centers of the two mounting holes, which can differ, to check that your new switch will fit.

For three or five-position switches, the mechanics are the same. It's a "two-pole" switch – it has two circuits that are switched simultaneously. We refer to these poles or circuits as "sides," simply because of the physical construction of the switch. On each side there are four connection tags: three input/output tags and one common tag.

If your replacement switch doesn't come with a wiring diagram, you can visually check the switch.

1 Hold the switch upside down in front of you with the non-spring side facing you and the selection lever all the way to the right. When the switch is wired in, this position (position one) will select the Stratocaster's bridge pickup.

2 Below the row of connection tags you'll see that the large square lug is in contact with one of those four connection tags. Sketch out the switch and mark this tag as number one. Move the lever to the furthest position to the left (position five) and make a note of which connection tag the square lug is now in contact with, and mark this as number three; this is where you connect the neck pickup.

Mark the tag between these two as number two; this will be your middle pickup connection. (Remember, originally a Strat had a three-way switch – you couldn't combine the pickups. The five-way switch simply joins connection tags one and two and connection tags two and three to create the famous mixed-pickup Strat sounds.)

3 The fourth connection is the common connection. Mark this as number four.

4 Return the lever all the way to the right. Now turn the switch so the spring side is facing you and mark on your sketch which connection the square lug is now in contact with. Mark this as number one. Do the same for all the switch positions as above and mark them, finally marking the common connection. Now, when the switch is in position on the pickguard you can follow your sketch to determine precisely which wires go to which connection tags.

THREE-POSITION TOGGLE SWITCH

Like the three and five-position lever switches, the three-position toggle or leaf-style switch comes in a number of styles and sizes. (Again, not least because you can see which connection tag does what, go for an "open" type as opposed to the square "closed" type.) Typically, a longer switch is used in a Les Paul and a shorter type in a thinner-bodied guitar like an SG. The switch has two input connections (for each pickup) and two output connections, which must be joined on the switch to provide the common output. A fifth connection – usually in the center of the switch – connects to ground (earth). Again, you can visually check which contact does what, as follows.

1 Hold the switch upright so that the toggle moves from left to right with the outer (or both sets) of connection tags facing you.

2 Place the toggle to the left (the up position, which on a Les Paul selects the neck pickup) and you will see that the right pair of contacts are opened, so you wire the neck pickup to the outer connection tag of the left pair, and the bridge pickup to the outer tag of the right pair. With the toggle in the center position you'll see that both pairs of contacts are joined – that's how you get both pickups on together.

BASIC WIRING MODIFICATIONS

If your pickups and controls are working properly, you can use the following simple wiring mods – referring to the diagrams shown on the right and the following page – to alter the way in which the controls affect your pickup's output.

TREBLE BLEED NETWORK

This is a simple modification that can be applied to any volume control. By placing a small capacitor (typically .001μF) between the input (connection tag one) and output (tag two) of the pot, as you turn down the volume control you'll retain the high end of your tone. When wiring in the capacitor you're advised to use a heat-sink (crocodile clip) as you solder each leg.

Some companies prefer the effect of an additional resistor wired (in parallel with the capacitor) between the same two tags. The reason is that you may find the capacitor alone makes the sound too thin with the volume control reduced. "The additional resistor tends to restore the lower (bass) end when the control is turned down," reckons DiMarzio's Steve Blucher. The normal value for this resistor is 150k|, but Blucher thinks this allows too much bass resistance. "The bigger the resistor's value, the less you're limiting bass. I don't use anything below 300k|."

TONE-CONTROL CAPACITORS

Another subtle change you can make involves experimenting with a range of capacitor values in your tone control(s). In this circuit the capacitor shunts off the treble frequencies to ground (earth), in other words the opposite of the treble bleed network. Standard values are .047μF, .02μF and .01μF (all values measured in microfarads, sometimes written as "mf"). Remember, the value of the capacitor determines the frequency point above which the treble roll-off takes place. The smaller the capacitor's value, the higher the frequency point and the less effect the capacitor will have in terms of cutting the treble as the control is wound down.

So, if you find your tone control sounds too dark – and it uses a .047μF capacitor – try a .02μF or a .01μF. Conversely, if it doesn't sound dark enough and you're using a .02μF or .01μF, try a

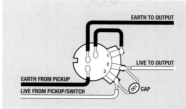

Treble-bleed network

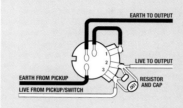

Treble-bleed with resistor

WIRING MODIFICATIONS
Without risking major damage to your guitar or altering it in any irreversible way (especially important for instruments with any collectable value), there are a number of small changes you can make which may open up new tonal horizons that you prefer to the stock wiring. Use these diagrams for reference, and proceed with care and caution. If you haven't yet developed soldering skills through experience, first read the *Soldering Techniques* section which follows these wiring mods on pages 102/103.

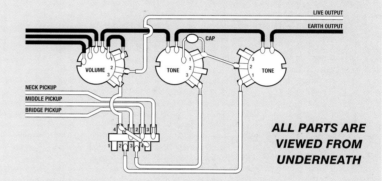

ALL PARTS ARE VIEWED FROM UNDERNEATH

Standard Strat-style wiring

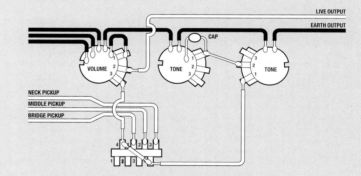

Strat-style wiring with 2nd tone as master tone

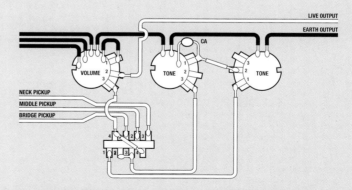

Strat-style wiring with 1st tone for neck and middle pickup, 2nd tone for bridge

electrics: wiring mods

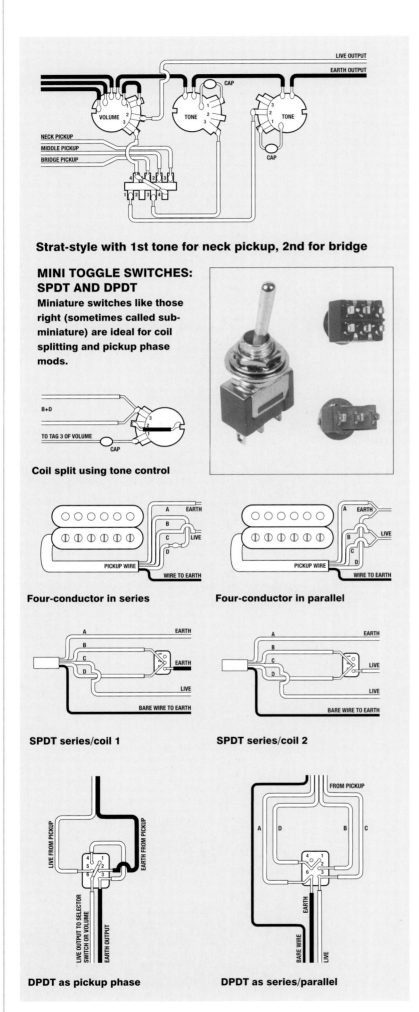

Strat-style with 1st tone for neck pickup, 2nd for bridge

MINI TOGGLE SWITCHES: SPDT AND DPDT
Miniature switches like those right (sometimes called sub-miniature) are ideal for coil splitting and pickup phase mods.

Coil split using tone control

Four-conductor in series

Four-conductor in parallel

SPDT series/coil 1

SPDT series/coil 2

DPDT as pickup phase

DPDT as series/parallel

.047μF. On a guitar with two tone controls, like a Les Paul or Strat, you can use different values to fine-tune the tone controls to individual pickups.

STRAT TONE CONTROLS
Typically a Strat is wired so that the first tone control (the center of the three controls) affects the neck pickup, and the second tone control (furthest from the bridge pickup) works on the middle pickup; there is no tone control for the bridge pickup. Some players like to change this, and it's easy to do. The late Rory Gallagher, for example, wired his Strat so that only the second control functioned, but as a master tone control for all three pickups (refer to diagrams, previous page).

Alternatively, you could use the first tone control for both the neck and middle pickups and the second tone control for the bridge pickup. Another popular option is to use the first tone control for the neck pickup and the second tone control for the bridge pickup, leaving the middle pickup without a tone control. This gives tone control for the often-used soloing pickups (neck and bridge) while the "rhythm" settings (the Strat's combined pickup tones) benefit from the full treble of the middle pickup. Try this with different tone capacitor values.

PICKUP SWITCHES
Fitting a new full-sized humbucking pickup to your guitar, so long as the pickup has four hot conductors and a separate ground, opens up a host of switching options. We've shown the standard wiring for a four-conductor humbucker in series operation (left) and parallel operation (right). Please note that the four conductors are labelled a, b, c, and d, which relate to the *Mister Conductor* chart, opposite. There are, however, numerous ways to switch between these standard wirings – and also to add more sounds – simply by installing an additional switch (or two).

MINI TOGGLE SWITCH MODS
Adding a two-position (on/on) single pole, double throw (SPDT) or double pole, double throw (DPDT), or three-position (on/on/on) DPDT mini switch to your guitar can open up a range of possibilities, some of which are illustrated in the diagrams, left.

An SPDT can be used to coil-split a humbucker from its standard series humbucking mode to either one of the humbucker's single coils. You can achieve a similar effect using the spare lug on a tone control.

An on/on DPDT switch is like two SPDT switches ganged together. To coil-split two humbuckers simultaneously, use either of the SPDT diagrams but assign one to one side for the neck pickup and the other to the other side for the bridge pickup. But this switch also has many other uses. For example, it can be used to switch the phase relationship between two pickups (see diagram bottom-left), or to switch between the way the humbucker is wired, either in series (standard) or in parallel, that will produce a brighter tonal characteristic with a lower output that is noise-cancelling.

An on/on/on DPDT can be used to offer series, single-coil and parallel wiring of one humbucker (as in the diagram near-left), offering three sound variations from a single pickup, all achieved with one switch.

If you want to avoid altering your guitar in any way (for example the drilling through a pickguard required to mount a mini switch) a "pull/push" pot with a DPDT switch mounted on its housing can do any of the jobs assigned here to a standard on/on DPDT.

electrics: tone & switching mods

MISTER CONDUCTOR

Virtually all of the major-brand retrofit pickups come with four-conductor (plus ground) hook-up wire. If you're swapping brands and/or plan to add some wiring options this format is recommended. The four conductors come from each end – the start and finish of the two wound coils, I & II. We've included a color code comparison chart of the three major brands to help you. However, all pickups should come with clear instructions – follow those first and use our chart as reference.

		DiMarzio	Duncan	WD/Sky
COIL I	start (a)	green	green	green
	finish (b)	white	red	white
COIL II	start (c)	red	black	red
	finish (d)	black	white	black

(Note: The uncovered wire is always wired to ground.)

Series humbucker: conductor a) goes to ground; b) and d) are joined; c) is hot. Note that if pickup is out-of-phase, reverse the position of conductors a) and c).

Parallel humbucking: a) and d) joined to ground; b) and c) joined to hot.

Coil I (screw polepieces) single-coil: a) ground; b) hot. Note that if the pickup is out-of-phase, reverse the position of conductors a) and b).

Coil II (slug polepieces) single-coil: c) hot d) ground. Note that if the pickup is out-of-phase, reverse the position of conductors c) and d).

HOT-ROD MODS

Here's a couple of our favorite hot-rod wiring mods, both of which are simple and effective.

THE MAGNIFICENT SEVEN

By changing the volume or one of the tone controls on a Strat (or similar) to a pull/push switched pot (or by adding a separate on/on DPDT mini-toggle) you can, with the pull/push switch pulled up and the neck pickup selected on the five-way switch, add the bridge pickup to the neck pickup for a Tele-like mix (in parallel). Also, if you select the neck-and-middle mix on the five-way switch, by pulling the pull/push up you add the bridge pickup for all three pickups on. This expands the Strat's five pickup selections to a magnificent seven.

STEVE'S WIZARDRY

Designed for Steve Vai in 1986 by DiMarzio's Steve Blucher, this wiring is found on numerous Ibanez guitars that have a humbucker at neck and bridge plus a single-coil in the middle position. Because the set-up uses a master volume and master tone on one side of a standard five-way lever switch, the other side can be used to automatically coil-split the neck and bridge humbuckers.

Blucher's wiring gives us: position one, neck humbucker; position two, bridge-facing single-coil of the neck humbucker plus middle single-coil; position three, middle single-coil; position four, neck-facing single-coil of the bridge humbucker plus middle single-coil; position five, bridge humbucker.

With a reverse-wound middle pickup of opposite polarity to the outer-facing single coils of each humbucker, all positions except number three – middle pickup alone – are hum-cancelling. Note that because this circuit was designed for DiMarzio pickups, to achieve the correct noise-cancelling and phase relationship with other models you may need to reverse one humbucker in its mounting ring.

MOD SQUAD

These hot-rod mods take matters a few steps further than the basics of the previous page. Achieve seven sounds from a standard Strat by adding a pull/push pot, or try Steve Vai's wiring mod.

ALL PARTS ARE
VIEWED FROM
UNDERNEATH

The Magnificent Seven

Steve's Wizardry

103

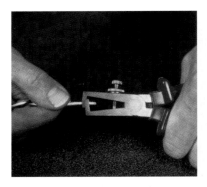

Before soldering any insulated wires, you'll need to strip them with the correct wire-stripper.

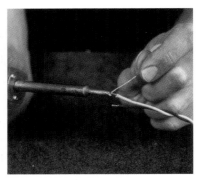

To make a bare wire easier to solder, first "tin" it by flowing a coating of solder over the strands.

SOLDERING TECHNIQUES

Soldering is a process used to join electrical components and wires securely. If you want to fit your own pickup and maybe try some wiring mods, you'll have to learn how to solder. Fear not: it's much easier than learning to read music.

You'll need a small-tipped soldering iron, and it's worth buying a stand for it too. Small irons (25 watts) are fine for small connections but a more powerful iron (40 watts) is necessary for heavier jobs such as when you want to solder ground (earth) wires to the backs of control pots.

First you need to have your iron in good working order. If it's a new iron you'll need to tin the copper tip. If it hasn't been used for a while, clean the tip with fine to medium abrasive paper. Heat up the iron and place your solder (use a 60/40 rosin-core type) on the tip. Let the solder flow over the tip, then wipe off any excess with a damp – not wet – rag or sponge. Keeping your tip conditioned in this way is essential for good soldering. Periodically wipe the tip with a damp cloth. Some soldering-iron stands have a small sponge that can be dampened and used to wipe the iron tip. When your tip becomes blackened with use, re-clean it occasionally and re-tin it as previously described. Good preparation is the key to good soldering.

Having disassembled your guitar so you can access the relevant parts to be soldered, always cover the surface of your guitar with a cloth to stop splatters of solder marking the finish. Make sure you're clear on exactly what you are wiring where. Draw out the existing circuit before your start work, and then draw your modifications. That way you can always return the guitar to "stock." Clearly label these sketches and keep them for future reference.

Most wires you'll be soldering have plastic or cloth insulation. Strip off about ⅛" to ³⁄₁₆" (3mm to 5mm) with proper wire-strippers. If the core wire is multi-strand, twist it so it becomes solid. To "tin" the wire, apply heat from the iron to the bare end of the wire then touch the bare end with your solder, which should flow over the

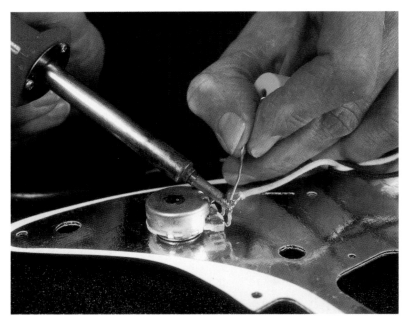

For good electrical connections, heat the joint first then place the solder to it and let it flow. Like anything, good technique takes practice, but you'll develop a feel for it over time.

The small hook made in the stripped wire end, seen in this close-up photograph, represents a "mechanical" connnection in the joint, to help hold it more strongly than solder alone. Make such connections only after you are sure the modification or repair is correct.

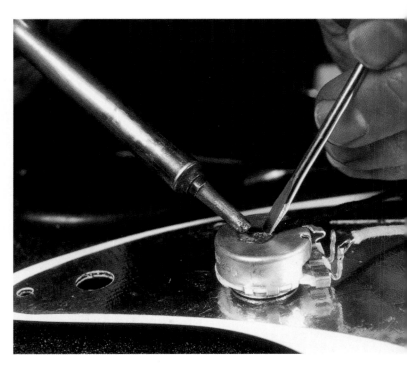

When soldering to the back of a pot, use a small flat-blade screwdriver to hold the wire firmly in place while you wait for the dome of solder to cool sufficiently to form its own solid joint.

soldering technique

exposed metal. You don't want too much solder. If a large blob transfers itself to the tip of the wire, re-heat and wipe off excess with a damp cloth. A helpful addition to your soldering kit is a desoldering pump, or "solder sucker." Its spring-loaded piston is held over a fluid solder joint; when released it sucks away any excess solder. It's handy for working on mini-toggle switches.

Wherever you can, make a "mechanical" joint before you solder the wire to the component. For example, pass the tinned wired halfway through a lug on a pot and bend it back on itself with a small pair of needlenose pliers. This will help secure the wire prior to soldering.

Place the iron on the joint. Leave for a few seconds to heat. You'll get a feel for this, depending on exactly what you're soldering and how powerful the iron is you're using. Then place the solder on the joint and let it flow. Remove the solder, then the iron, and let the joint cool. Don't blow on it. When it's cool, just tug on the wire to make sure the joint is secure. It should look shiny and chrome-like. A grey and dull appearance is a sure sign of a "dry" joint, where the solder hasn't flowed – and neither will the electrical signal. You'll need to resolder the connection.

Securing wires to the back of the pots is always difficult. First, prepare the pot. Rough the soldering surface with medium abrasive paper or score with the edge of a blade-tip screwdriver, wipe off any debris (with a cloth, not your greasy finger) and tin the back of the pot, creating a small dome of solder. Lay your tinned wire in place, hold it, and heat it with the tip of your iron. Apply solder. When the solder has flowed, place the tip of a small screwdriver or probe on the wire, to keep it in place while the solder cools, and remove the iron.

Wire insulation can melt if subjected to excessive heat, while small components like capacitors can be damaged. So when soldering a capacitor, for example, use a crocodile clip as an absorbing "heat sink" by placing it on the relevant "leg" between the component and the joint. Don't forget the most important rule: soldering practice makes perfect.

SOLDER-FREE SOLUTIONS

If the idea of soldering frightens you, don't worry. Many stores will wire up your new pickup for you free of charge (or for a minimal fee). Also, some companies – a good example would be EMG – offer pre-wired pickguards that have new pickups and controls already mounted and wired, requiring just a couple of connections to get them up and running in your own guitar.

Before purchasing any new replacement pickup, check carefully what the manufacturer's and/or guitar store's returns policy is. Some will let you swap a pickup you have tried out but found unsatisfactory for your needs, as long as you haven't trimmed the unit's wires in the process of making your connections.

Plastic wire insulation and smaller capacitors can melt when exposed to the high temperatures of a directly-applied soldering iron. You can use a crocodile clip as a makeshift heatsink that will disperse any excess heat.

MARVELOUS MULTI-METER

Not an essential tool for a basic home guitar workshop, a good multi-meter can nevertheless be extremely handy at times. With settings for reading AC/DC voltages, capacitance and resistance – and many other features – they're good for checking the validity of suspect solder joints, for reading the DC resistance of pickups and for determining whether a pickup short or other malfunction has occured.

LEAVE IT TO THE PROS!

With a little care, and attention paid to the advice given in the rest of this chapter, there are plenty of things you can do yourself to maximize the playability of your guitar. Even so, many jobs remain that should be consigned to a professional – unless of course you are extremely experienced in such work, or are testing your hand on a guitar of little or no value. In addition to the jobs covered here and on the following four pages, other pro jobs might include:

- Repairing body cracks in acoustics, or headstock breaks in acoustics and electrics.
- Finding and fixing loose top braces.
- Routing jobs to install Floyd Rose vibratos, humbuckers, etc.
- Re-wiring semi-acoustic guitars.
- Fret removal and replacement.
- Tuner replacement where headstock drilling is required.
- Unsticking tight or frozen truss rods.
- Refinishing work on valuable instruments.

A veteran guitar tech who has tackled countless repair, maintenance and modification jobs for notable pros and local amateurs alike, Charlie Chandler (below) runs the workshop at the much-respected Chandler Guitars store in Kew, London, with a staff of five skilled repairmen.

PROFESSIONAL MAINTENANCE

There are some maintenance jobs you might consider but that are best not approached by the player. Many require the skill and experience of a trained pro, and taking them on yourself – and messing them up – can result in repairs along with the replacement of major components that end up being far more costly than the original job would have been. A quick look at some of these procedures, however, will show you how a pro might approach the job, and help you understand what is required if you ever need to take your guitar into the shop for similar work. Respected London-based guitar tech Charlie Chandler takes us through four of the most called-for jobs in his workshop.

FITTING AN ACOUSTIC PICKUP

Fitting a pickup to an acoustic guitar may seem a simple enough job, but it requires a pro's touch. It's been an extremely popular modification in recent years, with the "unplugged revolution" sending countless guitarists back into the coffee houses and acoustic club. The necessary precision of connecting pickup and preamp wiring, and the delicate nature of working on acoustics in general means mistakes can be costly to put right. Fitting an end-pin jack may require drilling to widen the hole accordingly – a bad job for an amateur to get wrong – and internal electronics can be difficult to access and connect. Also, if an under-saddle piezo pickup is to be installed as part of the job, as with the Fishman blender-style unit featured here, this usually means

precise measuring and sanding-down of the bridge saddle, along with the other mounting requirements. The good news is that all of this is straightforward work for a trained repairman, and shouldn't cost an arm and a leg to get done.

"Getting the end-pin jack hole right in the first place is one of the hardest things," says Charlie Chandler. "Usually you have to enlarge it. We tend to use a reamer, then countersink it. Once the hole is correctly positioned, most end-pin jacks are easier to fit than they used to be, because you can adjust them and tighten them outside the guitar."

Before setting the jack in place, however, Chandler says it's important to make all soldering connections, and to get the cable lengths correct. "You don't want yards of spare cable rattling around inside the guitar; fortunately, these days most systems come with cable restraints to help you get this right." Once all the connections have been made, Chandler inserts a screwdriver in the end-pin hole to help guide the jack into position, then holds it firmly while tightening it into place.

Mounting the soundhole pickup can seem a simple enough job, but even this has its tricks and fine points.

"With most of them, the positioning is ordained by the soundhole itself," says Charlie. "With the Fishman pickup, which is currently our most popular one – and also with the Sunrise pickup – there's a jaw that will butt up to the narrowest points on the inside dimension of the soundhole. This usually works fine, but the problems you can have are that sometimes a pickguard comes up to the edge of the soundhole on one side, or there's a reinforcing ring underneath the rim of the soundhole. In either case it can prevent the jaws closing evenly. Ideally, you want the mounting jaws to close as evenly and as flush to the guitar's top and underside as possible." In such cases, rather than cut into the pickguard or reinforcing ring, the only solution is to tighten the mounting jaws enough to hold the pickup firmly in place in whichever position minimizes the unevenness of the closure.

Most factory-ready electro-acoustic guitars purchased new today come with rim-mounted preamps already installed. According to Chandler, however, customers who these days are having pickup systems mounted in formerly acoustic-only instruments rarely request the major work of adding a rim-mounted preamp where no hole already exists for one.

"That would be a whole different thing, because you get involved with cutting out a portion of the side of the guitar and then reinforcing it. There are very few people now who have a guitar they will entertain putting something like that on. If they want that style of guitar, they'll go out and buy one. They are so readily available that the cost of converting a guitar not originally built in that way is almost prohibitive."

The popular alternative for after-market fitting is the straight-out system such as the Fishman unit pictured – for use with an external preamp – or a system with a small preamp housed in the end-pin jack.

The key, then, to getting satisfactory work of this type done begins even before the tech sets hands on your guitar. Seek the advice of repairmen and dealers, of friends who have had the work done already, and of pros whose sound you admire, to determine which pickup system is right for you and how invasive the "surgery" required to install it will be. Most techs will hesitate to drill or cut into an especially valuable or vintage acoustic unless the owner convinces them he or she is aware of the consequences and still wants the job done, so be sure you know what permanent changes may result before the work is underway.

Soldering above or in proximity to the face of the guitar can be a real danger to the instrument's finish. A piece of heat-resistant cloth is used for protection while making this wiring connection to the end-pin jack.

A screwdriver placed through the slightly-widened end-pin hole helps to locate the jack held inside the guitar with the other hand and to slide it into place for mounting – which can be a fiddly job otherwise.

The end-pin jack is held firmly in place while the fixing nut is tightened with the correct wrench.

Finally, the magnetic pickup is mounted and adjusted to sit tight and flush in the soundhole.

Chandler uses a calliper to measure the height of the saddle above the face of the bridge.

Measuring the overall height of the saddle determines how much material has to be removed.

Finishing the sanding-down with wet and dry paper laid in a flat bed made from a length of aluminum.

Feeding the piezo pickup cable into the pre-drilled hole in the bridge's saddle slot.

ACOUSTIC SADDLE ADJUSTMENT

Want lower action on your acoustic? Usually the only satisfactory solution is to reduce the saddle height by the required amount. Similarly, if the installation of a new pickup system includes fitting an under-saddle piezo strip, the saddle height might need to be reduced to account for the thickness of the piezo pickup and restore the guitar to its original playing action.

In our sample procedure pictured to the left, Charlie Chandler performs both jobs for a customer: a piezo strip is being fitted as part of the "blender" pickup system installed on the previous page, and a reduction in string height has also been requested.

"The first thing to do," says Chandler, "with the guitar still strung up, is to measure the height from the saddle top to the face of the bridge. Do that at three different points and use it to cross-check how much you are taking off the bottom of the saddle." Next, Chandler removes the strings, takes the saddle out of the bridge's saddle slot, measures its height outside the guitar, and marks it to remove the required amount of material.

"You can take most of it off with a belt sander," he explains. "Then you need to get a very flat bed – we use a piece of aluminum here in the workshop – and put wet and dry paper on it and sand the saddle until it's perfectly flat to the correct depth."

Even with a perfectly flat sanding bed to finish the saddle, however, the job can throw up a few obstacles. "For example, quite often acoustics belly-up slightly around the bridge, and if you've got a bridge that's slightly arched but a saddle that has been sanded perfectly flat, it won't sit flush in its slot. There are a number of things you can do here. For one, companies like Fishman recommend using man-made saddles because they're uniform, whereas anything organic – like bone – may have different hardnesses in different parts of the saddle. Another one is that companies have made saddles, like Fishman's Clear Tone, with slots cut on the underside between the string positions so that it's almost 'sprung' and can curve to the shape of the guitar top's arch."

Other points to look out for? "You need to satisfy yourself that the saddle slot is clean and flat, so the saddle will sit flush inside it. Most guitars now come with a hole pre-drilled at the end of the saddle slot for the piezo pickup lead, or if they don't pre-drill it then indent it, so that part of the job is usually done for you."

From there you insert the strip, make the wiring connection to the system, replace the saddle, string up and tune and, finally, check that the new action is satisfactory. After a saddle has been lowered, slight truss-rod adjustment may be required too.

To level the frets on this '53 Fender Esquire, our tech first reduces their height with a diamond file.

A special slotted guard protects the fingerboard from scratches and gouges while individual frets are polished up.

FRET LEVELING AND DRESSING

Most any fret work is a job for a pro. The owner of this vintage '53 Fender Esquire (brlow, opposite) has asked Chandler to level and reshape its upper frets, where uneven crowns were starting to mean the guitar wouldn't note accurately up above the 12th fret. Taking on a job like this without knowing exactly what you're doing risks major damage to frets and fingerboard, perhaps necessitating an entire re-fret – or more, if you slip up badly.

The work itself is fairly straightforward for an experienced repairman, and shouldn't be an especially costly procedure to have done, certainly much less than re-fretting the whole neck.

"The first thing I do in any job like this is tape off the guitar body and pickguard surrounding the neck join to protect them from any slips with the files. Then I start by taking the frets down to even heights with a diamond file," Chandler explains. "Next, I use a fret file to reshape them to get the roundness back into the crowns, and use another fret file to round off the ends. Finally, I cover the fingerboard with a little slotted guard to protect it – letting only one fret show through at a time – and polish each individual fret to get out any marks left by the files."

Often, "professional" guitar maintenance is as much about having the correct, specialized tools handy as it is about experience and skill. With this fret work, using the wrong type of file can damage frets badly, while one slip without protection can put an ugly gouge into a precious fingerboard.

CUTTING NUT SLOTS

Before a repairman even begins to cut a new nut or adjust an old one, he will ensure that the truss rod is correctly adjusted and the desired action has been set at the bridge. "If you've got a new nut on there to start with," explains Chandler, "you put a capo on at the first fret to take the nut right out of the equation."

To begin, Chandler needs to decide how deep the nut slots need to be cut – which is determined by fretting each string at the third fret and looking at the gap of the string over the first fret.

"The amount of clearance you leave here depends upon the playing style of the guitar owner. If he plays hard, you're going to have to leave more clearance than if he plays soft or you'll get some buzz against the frets. If he plays real fast legato style then you get it as low as you can. If he really digs in, or plays a bit of slide too, leave it a little higher. But again, if he's picky about his intonation you need to get it as low as you can."

Experienced techs will generally know the gap they need by sight, but as a rough rule Chandler says he doesn't want a gap of less than ten thousandths of an inch (0.010") – the width of an average high-E string. "Take it below that and you can expect problems. Allow that gap and, as long as you don't play real hard, you'll probably be all right."

Although all good repairmen will have a set of fret files made to correct sizes for each popular string gauge, there's more to the cutting than simply picking up the right tool and hacking away. "You've got to cut the slot so that the witness point of the string – where the nut surface first meets each string – is at the start of the scale length. Otherwise it'll never play in tune."

Also crucial is to provide enough support on either side of the slot so the string won't pop out when bending and vibrato are applied, but not such a tight fit that it sticks and impedes tuning. "If you look at a PRS, they tend to cut slightly V'd grooves that come down to the right size at the bottom, so it doesn't move side to side." To finish the job, Chandler usually applies dry graphite powder to the slot to keep it well lubricated.

With this Firebird correctly set up and action adjusted at the bridge, the nut slot height is checked by fretting each string at the third fret, then measuring its clearance over the first fret.

Files specially sized to each popular string gauge are essential tools of the trade.

Chandler uses a finger to guide the file and protect the fingerboard while smoothing a newly cut slot.

A well-cut nut slot should support the string on both sides, but without pinching it too tightly. Even so, a touch of lubricant – such as liquid Teflon or graphite powder, as used here – helps make for trouble-free tuning.

CLEANING PROCEDURES

Keeping your guitar clean not only helps it look better, but can improve the life of its finish, strings, hardware and even the electronics. Grime, sweat, grease, dust, moisture, beer, blood, tears – they all contribute to eroding and corroding the various parts of your instrument, and it's fair to say a proper regular cleaning can even help your guitar sound better, by keeping all components in top working order. As with every aspect of guitar maintenance, however, there are a series of dos and don'ts, and by following a few pointers you can maximize your cleaning efforts. Your guitar will thank you for it – and you'll feel better too.

If your finish gets shabby enough to require more serious attention than a regular rub-down and an occasional rub-polish, buffing cream could do the trick. Remove the strings, apply a little cream to a soft cloth, and work in small circles – using plenty of elbow grease.

Most rosewood or ebony fingerboards can be kept clean with a basic, regular rub-down. Using a soft cloth, with strings pushed aside – and always with the back of the neck well supported – wipe gently but firmly, paying particular attention to the grime that can collect at the edges of frets.

CLEANING "PLASTIC" FINISHES

The majority of modern electric guitars are finished with a high-gloss "plastic" finish like polyester or polyurethane. Some major brands still use nitro-cellulose based finishes (Gibson, for example) though due to a combination of factors, not least air-pollution regulations and drying time, cellulose finishes are rarely used, apart from occasional high-end "custom shop" guitars.

These finishes are applied from a spray gun and are then flattened and polished up to a mirror-like gloss on a high speed buffing wheel. It's a time-consuming process requiring numerous coats of finish, and for many production instruments actually forms a major part of the manufacturing time. Apart from looking good, the finish protects the guitar from dirt and grease which, once it gets into the wood-grain, is hard to remove. It also seals the wood from moisture penetration which can cause numerous problems related to the timber's stability.

Most manufacturers simply suggest you polish up your guitar body and other finished wood parts like the back of the neck with a "guitar polish", usually wax-based, and with or without silicone. The problem with products containing silicone is that it makes any future re-finishing and/or repairs even more difficult. So if you do use a guitar polish, make sure it's silicone-free.

The best way to clean your guitar is with a dry, lint-free cloth or duster *immediately* after playing. This will remove all the sweat and grease before it has time to solidify and form a harder-to-remove residue. Stubborn build-ups can be removed with a *barely* damp cloth. Never, never use a wet cloth. Always rub the guitar immediately after with a totally dry and clean cloth to keep any residual moisture from penetrating.

If your guitar is looking a little shabby and dirty then your best bet is to apply to the instrument a *mild* proprietary finish restorer, a fine burnishing cream. Don't use car products. They're too coarse. Mirror Glaze Plastic Polish or Manson's Finish Restorer are ideal. Here's how you go about it.

1 Remove the strings and apply a little buffing cream to a dry, soft cloth and work on the guitar's surface in small, circular areas. The buffing cream will do its job, removing dirt, grease and small scratches.

2 Keep rubbing on the same small area until it achieves a high sheen, then move to an adjacent area, apply some more cream and, of course, liberal amounts of elbow grease.

3 Finally, polish the guitar all over the finish with a new, and dry, soft cloth without any buffing cream.

CLEANING OIL FINISHES

These have had a light oil applied directly to the wood, and enjoy a varying reputation among guitar builders, repairers and store owners. Although there is credibility to the belief that the thinner the body finish the better the tone, a thin oil finish is very susceptible to dirt and moisture penetration. Apart from any tone considerations, many players simply like the look and feel, especially on a neck, of the natural wood.

An oil finish requires very regular maintenance – and even then an oil-finished maple neck and fingerboard will inevitably look dirty very quickly. First, you must always wipe an oil finish after playing. You may notice, especially if you sweat a lot, that the back of the neck begins to feel "furry" where the sweat has caused the grain to rise. You can flatten it with wire wool or

cleaning and polishing

preferably a very fine abrasive paper, and then apply a little furniture wax on a soft cloth. Occasionally you may need to re-oil the wood, for which some makers recommend lemon oil while others promote a tung-based oil like Behlen Master Tung Oil Finish. Certainly you can achieve a very good-feeling neck with this regular maintenance program, but even if you're extremely careful an oil finish will rarely give you the protection of a proper finish that seals the guitar's wood parts. Consequently, some manufacturers now use a very light matt finish to simulate the look of an oil finish, and this requires less maintenance and offers better moisture protection.

CLEANING YOUR FINGERBOARD

The majority of fingerboards are unfinished rosewood or ebony. Most maple fingerboards have a finish much like the body and can be cleaned in the same fashion. Be careful, however, with old, fragile and cracked finishes where bare wood is showing; you won't get these clean, and if the discoloration really bothers you then you should consult a professional, who may suggest some preventive repairs.

For bare rosewood and ebony fingerboards you need an *occasional* application of a lemon oil-based fingerboard cleaner. Several companies offer such a fingerboard cleaner which has a lemon-oil base.

Make sure you always use a preparation intended for fingerboard cleaning. Remove the strings and apply a small amount of lemon oil to a soft cloth or paper towel and rub it into the fingerboard. (It's worth noting that some makers discourage the use of lemon oil or indeed any oil-based preparation for fear that it could have a softening effect on the fingerboard. Used sparingly and occasionally, however, it's unlikely to do any damage.) Leave the oil to penetrate for a few minutes then rub it off with a clean cloth or paper towel which should remove most of the grime and leave the board looking brand new.

Grime can build up right next to the fret, so work some lemon oil into these areas by dabbing a drop on a cloth wrapped around your fingernail (a plectrum will work if your nails are too short or too valuable).

Stephen Delft's Boogie Juice is a fingerboard cleaner with a felt tip that makes it ideal to remove hard-to-access fingerboard grime. Always use lemon oil sparingly and occasionally; again, your best line of defence against fingerboard grime is to rub down the strings and fingerboard after every playing session with a dry, soft cloth.

CLEANING STRINGS

There are various string cleaning and lubrication products available. Washburn Guitar Juice String Cleaner or Manson's String Cleaner or similar work well to remove gunk from strings. Apply a little directly to the strings then wrap a piece of soft cloth or paper towel around and under each string and move it quickly up and down the entire length. (Any residue that goes onto the fingerboard itself can be cleaned off in the same fashion and actually helps to remove fingerboard grime.) Fast Fret is another string preparation that many swear by. It won't make you play faster (only practice does that) but a little application on the plain strings helps to keep the strings in good condition. Avoid any "lubricating" string preparations with an oil base, especially on the wound strings. These can actually attract dirt in between the wrap wires and so you'll find those strings go dead more quickly.

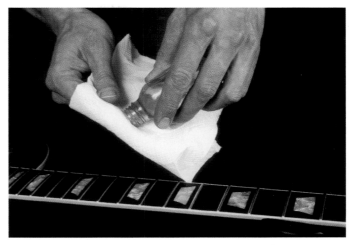

Far less regularly, an application of lemon-oil-based fingerboard cleaner will help get your rosewood or ebony fingerboard into top condition, and keep the wood from drying out. Remove the strings, apply a small amount of oil to a soft cloth, and rub it in...

... Leave the oil to penetrate for a few minutes, then rub off thoroughly with a clean, soft cloth. To get at the grime along fret edges, dab a drop of oil on a piece of cloth wrapped around your fingernail, or around a plectrum if your nails are too short, and work at the fret edges.

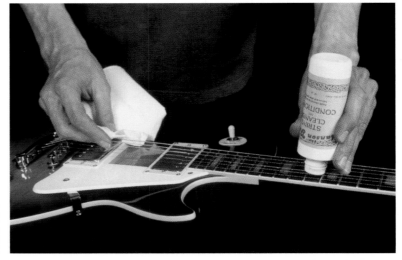

There are a number of specialist products available to ease the work of cleaning, some with clever twists to the usual formula. Stephen Delft's Boogie Juice (above) has a felt-tipped applicator to help you get at the muck that can clog your fingerboard's grain and fret edges.

HARDWARE AND PARTS

The metal parts on your guitar typically have a nickel, chrome, or gold plating. Sweat (or any moisture) is the major enemy, and again that post-playing soft-cloth rubdown is your best defence. Saddles often become caked with grime and can corrode – or in some cases rust – after years of playing and non-maintenance.

Remove the strings, then the saddles, but be very careful with the small screws for intonation and height adjustment. If these are tight they may have corroded, so remove the whole bridge assembly and, away from your guitar, spray on some penerating oil like WD-40 (never spray oil anywhere near your guitar).

Give the penetrating oil some time to do its job and then carefully try (without excessive force) to turn the problem screw again. If it's still tight, leave the part to soak over-night. Still stuck fast? Well then you may have to consider replacement, or professional help. For mildly corroded saddles, a good rub with WD-40 will not only clean off any debris but stop, for the short-term, any further corrosion.

If your guitar requires an occasional deeper cleaning than the casual after-play wipe-down, remove the pickguard or other hardware that might be in the way...

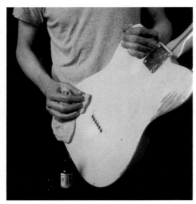

... Then you can apply appropriate buffing cream – and plenty of elbow grease – to help dig out years of accumulated grime from the wood grain and the hardware edges.

As described on the previous page, an *occasional* application of lemon oil to a rosewood or ebony fingerboard (perhaps not more than every couple of years or so) will help restore its rich luster and keep it from drying out. Equally as important as the correct application procedure is that you ensure all excess oil is wiped from the fingerboard with a dry cloth, and that none gets into other components of the guitar.

If your guitar's plating has become dulled, or if the metal part is unplated brass or aluminum, a brand-name metal polish will restore most of the sheen. Even the mild buffing cream works very well too. Black hardware was popular a few years back. In some cases this amounted to little more than thin black paint which wears off very quickly. Proper black-coloured plating or black chroming should have the same lifespan as standard plating methods and should be cleaned accordingly.

Plated pickup covers should just be cleaned with a dry cloth; you really don't want any "wet" polishing compound getting into the pickup. But for a little extra cleaning power, take a cloth you've used to apply metal polish elsewhere and use that on your pickup covers, without applying any more polish to either the cover or the cloth.

Plastic pickguards, knobs and pickup covers can be simply wiped down with a dry cloth or cleaned and polished, if necessary, with the fine buffing cream. You don't want to get any cream in the pickup or control components, however, so remove the plastic pickup covers from the pickups and remove any other components from the pickguard before you clean it. Uncovered pickups should be cleaned with just a dry cloth (or one that's slightly dampened – but never dripping – if the grime is stubborn. Make sure you rub any slight moisture away immediately with another dry cloth.

YOUR WORKING ENVIRONMENT

It's well worth considering your working environment before you attempt even the most basic adjustment techniques described in this book. A comfortable, efficient workspace makes it less likely you'll rush the job and screw something up, and you'll also enjoy your work more. To get started, all you need is a firm table or work-surface in an uncluttered, well-lit area.

Always protect the table with a blanket, a thick towel or newspapers, or a non-slip rubber mat. A neck support is very useful; in fact, any solid block protected with cloth will suffice.

Keep tools away from your main working area and somewhere accessible where you can pick them up one at a time as you need them. Wherever possible, protect the finish of your guitar with a cloth or duster, especially when soldering. Get in the habit of keeping old cotton t-shirts for this purpose and to use as cleaning rags, rather than throwing them out. Always put screws and other tiny parts in a small container so that they don't get lost or damage your guitar.

A quiet, calm environment really is essential so that you can concentrate. Distractions like young children and family pets should be removed.

Wear safety glasses when soldering and snipping wires or strings, and never leave tools or string-ends just hanging around. Remember that they are potentially dangerous.

Always double-check that you've switched off and unplugged your soldering iron, and leave plenty of time for it to cool down before your pack it away.

TOOLS AND MATERIALS

Most of the tools you'll need will be available from a good hardware and/or electrical store.

Your basic equipment certainly must include an accurate steel ruler (and ideally a set of feeler gauges) for all kinds of measurements. Screwdrivers are essential too, especially Phillips head (cross-head) drivers, and you'll need a small, medium and large size to fit, for example, pickguard and intonation screws (small), and neck and spring-claw screws (medium/large). A small and medium-sized flat-blade screwdriver will serve most other applications. Remember: always use the right tool for the job; don't be tempted to undo or tighten a cross-head screw with a flat-blade screwdriver. There are exceptions. A medium-sized flat-blade screwdriver can be used to adjust the cross-head truss rod adjustment nut on vintage-style Fenders, for example.

A small collection of Allen keys (also known as hex keys) is also essential. Most new guitars come with the correct size Allen keys for truss-rod and bridge. You should always keep these in a safe and accessible place.

American-made hardware invariably uses Imperial-size Allen keys; European and Far Eastern-made parts (from Japan and Korea, for example) invariably use metric sizes. To adjust the saddle heights on a Japanese-made reissue Strat, for example, you'll need a 1.5mm Allen key; to adjust the same on a US-made American Series Strat you'll need a slightly smaller .050" or marginally smaller ³⁄₆₄" key.

Imperial-size keys of .050", ¹⁄₁₆", ⁵⁄₆₄", ³⁄₃₂", ⁵⁄₃₂" and metric-size keys of 1.5mm, 2.5mm, 3mm and 3.5mm will get regular use on most types of bridges and vibratos. Truss-rod adjustments are made with either a larger Allen key, around the ³⁄₁₆" to 7mm sizes, or a supplied socket-head nut wrench typically either ¼" or ⁵⁄₁₆".

Other basics like needlenose pliers, wire snippers and wire strippers are also likely to come in handy, along with the soldering iron and related accessories mentioned earlier in the *Soldering Techniques* section.

> For many home guitar toolboxes, it's enough to have a steel ruler, a selection of Allen keys, a couple each of flat and Phillips-head screwdrivers, needlenose pliers, wire snips and a string winder. If you plan to do more involved work or a great variety of repairs and modifications, then keeping a few extra tools to hand will make these jobs easier and generally more successful.

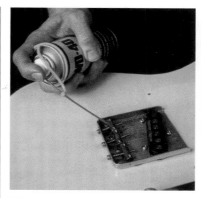

Where would we be without it? Stuck, probably. A quick squirt of WD-40, the mechanic and guitar tech's friend, will usually help loosen corroded adjustable components...

... While a little of the same on a soft cloth is great to clean grime from metal parts – though ensure you protect pickups and other electronics from any stray spray.

Heavy rust usually requires more drastic measures, but for deep-down grime on metal hardware, wrap a cloth soaked in WD-40 around a fingertip (as shown above) and dig in. This generally removes most of the surface crud and helps prevent further corrosion from setting in for a while. If a plated part has become dulled, on the other hand – or you want to clean unplated brass or aluminum – a name brand metal polish will usually help restore much of its sheen. Rub on, allow to dry as per instructions, then buff vigorously as below.

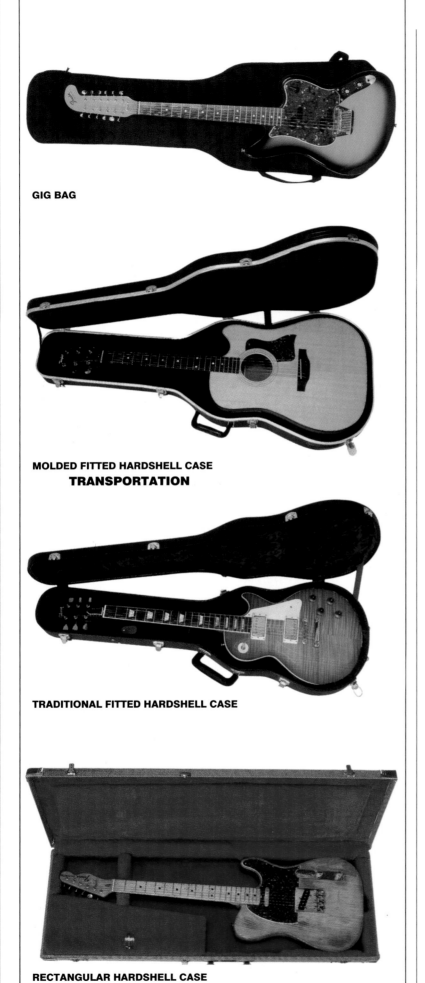

GIG BAG

MOLDED FITTED HARDSHELL CASE
TRANSPORTATION

TRADITIONAL FITTED HARDSHELL CASE

RECTANGULAR HARDSHELL CASE

FULL FLIGHT CASE
If you want to offer your guitar total ATA-approved protection, the padded armor of a full flight case is the only way to go.

It's a false economy to rely on a cheap or flimsy case to protect your beloved guitar. This is especially true for acoustic instruments, where their fragility makes them particularly vulnerable when traveling. Gig bags come in all shapes, sizes and prices. If you're not intending to travel far and the weather conditions are not too hot (or too cold), a padded gig bag will suffice – so long as you don't throw it in the back of a truck.

The next best form of protection for your guitar is a hardshell case. These come in either rectangular form, or are shaped to fit your particular instrument. They are made from either plastic or plywood. The ply versions are covered in tough Tolex-style material. These cases are best suited for medium/light duty and offer reasonable protection from the elements and the knocks and scrapes encountered when travelling. Ironically some high-end versions can be as expensive as a heavy duty flightcase. You might like to ponder the fact that most new high-quality instruments come supplied complete with a hardshell case.

For medium to heavy use a light flightcase is a good choice. These are generally like a tougher version of a hardshell case and are molded from a heavy duty plastic such as ABS. The inside is also moulded to fit the particular guitar it's made for and lined with a soft fabric for protection. These are suitable to fly in the hold of an aircraft with certain electrics, such as Strats or Teles, but not more delicate electric or acoustic instruments.

For ultimate protection you should opt for a proper "full" flightcase. These are of seriously heavy-duty construction and made from high grade ply faced with tough metal or plastic sheet, with aluminum extrusions on all edges. They are normally rectangular in shape and have large metal corners and heavy duty latches. On the inside of the case is a thick foam panel which is cut out to receive the guitar. If you manage to get that gig with an international touring band a case like this is essential. Makers such as Anvil, probably the biggest name for this type of case, offer lines which meet ATA specs (Air Transportation Association). Such ATA-approved cases are the only types that some airlines will accept as adequate protection for a guitar stowed in the luggage hold of an aircraft.

The only drawback with flightcases – other than their price, generally considerably higher than standard hardshell cases – is their weight, although new, lighter materials are being tried in an attempt to improve the weight/strength ratio. If you're carrying your own guitar to and from the gig, propped carefully in the trunk or back seat of your car, a full flightcase probably isn't necessary – or worth the backache.

SHIPPING GUITARS

If for any reason you need to send your guitar by carrier for repair or some other reason, then you must make sure that it is adequately packed prior to shipping. Most people think that the case alone is sufficient ... but it's not! We have seen many damaged cases over the years which have suffered in the hands of shipping companies.

The ideal method of packaging is to place the guitar securely in its case, with the strings de-tuned, and then place the case in a large cardboard box. To prevent the guitar rattling around in the box, roll up sheets of newspaper to act as padding to fill the space around the case. Then tape the lid of the box securely with proper parcel tape and not ordinary cellophane tape.

Label the box clearly on both sides with the destination address and also your address as the sender. Make sure your address is smaller than the destination address and use the words "to" and "from" to ensure that you don't get your guitar returned straight back to you.

LONG-TERM STORAGE FOR YOUR INSTRUMENT

Should you wish to store your guitar for any length of time it's wise to take the following suggestions into consideration. First, de-tune all strings by one tone so as to prevent any possibility of the neck pulling forward should there be some fluctuation in temperature. Second, make sure the instrument is cleaned and polished. Then place it in its case with a small bag of silica-gel to absorb any moisture generated by fluctuations in humidity. Finally, place the case in the largest plastic bag you can find (a large trash bag will suffice) and store it in a cool, dry place out of direct sunlight and away from sources of heat or moisture.

The following places are not suitable for storing a guitar long term: your garage, attic, kitchen, bathroom, cellar, garden shed or anywhere there may be changes in temperature or humidity. Suitable storage locations are closets under the stairs (as long as they are not damp), a dry closet in your living room or bedroom, or under your bed.

EFFECTS OF ATMOSPHERIC CONDITIONS

Two of the main enemies when you try to maintain a healthy acoustic guitar are extremes of temperature and humidity. A sudden change in temperature can cause lacquer checking (fine cracks on the finish surface) and, in extreme cases, cracks in the guitar itself. To avoid this, as far as is possible always transport an acoustic guitar in a hard case, or at the very least in a padded electric-guitar type gig-bag.

If the guitar has been transported in extremely cold conditions (below freezing point), allow the instrument to rest in its case for an hour or so before opening. If this is not possible for any reason, open the case lid for a few seconds then close it for a minute or so. Repeat this operation several times until the instrument has acclimatized.

Keeping a guitar at a constant humidity can be even more difficult. If an instrument gets too dry the timber will crack or split and the action height may increase. Conversely, if it gets too

damp the tone may not be so clear or resonant and action may also be adversely affected.

Specialist acoustic dealers often stock devices for the guitar's case to help maintain the correct humidity for your instrument. Even electric guitars can be affected by humidity – too much and the hardware may tarnish and the neck may warp. Too little and the fingerboard may dry out and split. To avoid such damage it helps to keep your guitar in its case whenever possible.

IMPORTING AND EXPORTING INSTRUMENTS

If you wish to take your guitar abroad, or you want to import or export a new instrument, there are certain things that you should be aware of to avoid problems with the authorities at home or in the country of destination. First, if you wish to take an instrument owned by you to a foreign country, then you would be wise to obtain a "carnet." This is a document which is generally obtained from the port of embarkation, or alternatively from your local Customs office in advance. A carnet allows you to temporarily export your guitar without having to pay duty and local taxes at the destination country, although a small refundable bond may be payable upon entry. Professional touring bands obtain carnets for their entire road rig.

If you are a UK resident traveling within the EC, then it's wise to carry proof of ownership. Something as simple as a purchase receipt will suffice. If this is not possible for some reason then it may still be a good idea to obtain a carnet. Carrying proof of ownership is also sensible for American musicians traveling regularly around the US, even if not actually crossing foreign borders.

If you buy a guitar in a foreign country and it exceeds the current allowance for free importation into your country of residence of goods bought abroad, you must declare it at Customs upon entry with proof of purchase. You will be liable for import duty and local sales tax (or VAT in the UK) at current rates. Don't be tempted to lie about the purchase price, or obtain a false purchase receipt, as Customs departments can easily determine the purchase price of most new and secondhand instruments. They have access to current dealer-price lists and have experts on hand to provide a realistic value for collectable secondhand guitars. The penalties for this type of fraud can include confiscation and a heavy fine.

It is important to remember that levels of taxation as well as local rules and regulations change often, so it's wise to consult the Customs authorities in both relevant countries before you travel.

If you buy a guitar on the internet from overseas you will have to arrange for it to be shipped by a company that specialises in exportation and who will arrange all the necessary paperwork and will then bill you for the relevant amounts due for duty and import tax. This is often all taken care of by the seller, especially if they are a dealer who often sells online to overseas customers.

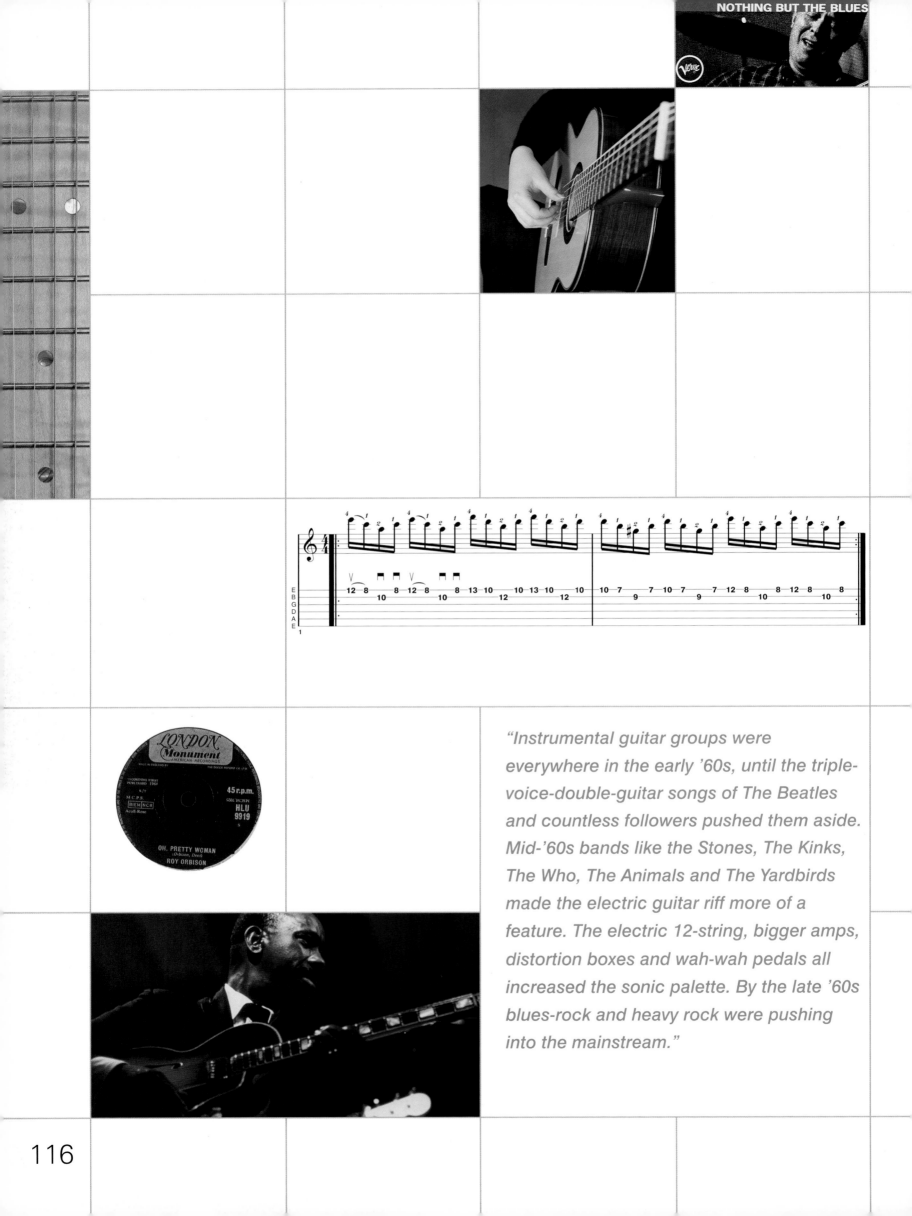

"Instrumental guitar groups were everywhere in the early '60s, until the triple-voice-double-guitar songs of The Beatles and countless followers pushed them aside. Mid-'60s bands like the Stones, The Kinks, The Who, The Animals and The Yardbirds made the electric guitar riff more of a feature. The electric 12-string, bigger amps, distortion boxes and wah-wah pedals all increased the sonic palette. By the late '60s blues-rock and heavy rock were pushing into the mainstream."

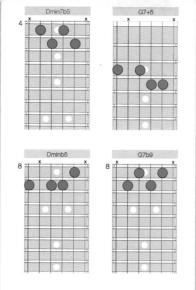

chapter 4

GUITAR
PLAYING STYLES

Music today has pushed beyond conventional boundaries of easy categorization. Whatever your main playing style, broadening your chops in other directions will help you to be a better all-around guitarist, and could open up entirely new avenues for further exploration. This chapter offers detailed primers in ten of the most important guitar styles.

More than ever before, the modern guitarist needs to be able to adapt to a number of playing styles in order to be considered a comprehensive musician. Most players will still specialise to some extent in one type of music or another, but the degree of cross-fertilisation between genres today is considerable – and as a guitarist you stand to benefit enormously from the inspiration offered by previously unfamiliar forms. Jazz can influence blues, classical can influence metal, Latin can influence pop, country can influence jazz... and on it goes, in a near-infinite variety of combinations.

This section will give you a grounding in ten of the most popular forms of guitar playing today, with the dual aim of improving your skills in your favourite style and also broadening your awareness of an eclectic mix of fascinating and useful genres. None of them is pitched at the absolute beginner (although *Acoustic* does start with more basic lessons than the others), but each offers a range of exercises suited to everyone from novice to advanced player – even the most skilled pro should be able to take away a few new licks from a chapter or two. Nor does any of them attempt to be the final word on a particular style (though a few, such as *Pop-Rock*, *Blues* and *Metal* are comprehensive primers), but each provides enough new chops to give your playing a serious freshening-up. Should you get hooked on any of the new techniques – which is a distinct possibility – you'll at least be well prepared for more intensive pursuit of the style elsewhere.

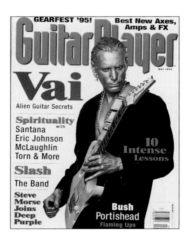

THE *PLAYING* AUTHORS

Acoustic, Blues and ***Rock-Pop*** by Rikky Rooksby
Rikky is a UK-based teacher, songwriter, and author of nearly 30 books on playing, including *How To Write Songs On Guitar*, *Inside Classic Rock Tracks*, and *Riffs*.

Country by Lee Hodgson
Lee is a UK-based country session guitarist and performer, a contributor to numerous guitar publications, a tutor at the London Guitar Institute, and author of the book *Hot Country*.

Rock'n'Roll by Max Milligan
Max is a performing and recording guitarist, songwriter, and journalist of more than 20 years experience, as well as a tutor at the London Guitar Institute, specialising in R&B and Soul.

Metal by Martin Goulding
Martin is a London-based session guitarist and live performer, and a tutor at the London Guitar Institute, specialising in Rock and Metal styles of the post-Van Halen era.

Latin by Nestor Garcia
Nestor, based in Spain, has published several articles on playing Latin guitar, taught at Goldsmith's College, London, and performed with Björk, Tumbaito, and the Afro Cuban Allstars.

African by Kari Bannerman
Kari is a renowned Ghanaian guitarist who has played with Hugh Masekela, Peter Green, Osibisa and his own band Boombaya, and led workshops at Goldsmith's College, London.

Classical by David Braid
David is a London-based classical guitar tutor, performer, writer and composer, magazine contributor, and author of *How To Play Classical Guitar*.

Jazz by Carl Filipiak
Carl is a Baltimore-based jazz guitar tutor, a recording artist with six albums released on Geometric Records, and presenter of the tutorial video *Use What You Got*.

CHORD BOXES

A chord box is simply a diagram representing a portion of the guitar neck, with strings running vertically, so that the line on the far left side represents the low E- string. The thick horizontal bar at the top of the box represents the nut in diagrams depicted in the first position, while the thinner horizontal bars represent frets, with position markers (dots) given to help you find your way. For chords higher up the neck, a number alongside the box provides a fret number for positioning.

The Xs and Os across the top of the box indicate which strings should be played open (0), and which muted (X).

GUIDE TO NOTATION SYMBOLS

If you're not familiar with the symbols used in standard music notation and tablature (TAB), this page and the following two will provide an introduction to most of what you will encounter. As the range of musical symbols is vast, this primer won't necessarily be exhaustive, but it will provide enough to get you through the *Playing* chapters. You'll find further guidance to any new symbols or instructions encountered – particularly in more advanced notation – within the explanatory text accompanying the exercises themselves. All exercises, other than those of pure rhythm notation, will be represented in both standard notation and TAB; be aware that while some symbols are common to both, others are used only on one or the other. While many exercises will include suggested chords for accompaniment below the bottom TAB line, chord boxes will not always be given, unless the chords themselves are the point of study, or the author feels some guidance to unfamiliar chords will be particularly helpful. Note also, as in the Sample Exercise below, that indications of rhythm will be given only in the stave (the standard notation), through the use of traditional note values. For example, the first bar's notation line offers quarter, eighth and 16th-notes, while the TAB indicates finger positions only.

READING TABLATURE

A complete course in reading music in standard notation would take more space than is available here (though the *Classical* section does offer an excellent lesson in this which will at least get you started). But tablature – or TAB for short – is easily explained.

TAB is essentially a method of showing finger placements that correspond to the notes shown on the stave of music directly above it. If you're new to TAB, the key points to note are that it uses no traditional "notes" as such but carries numbers in their place, is made up of six horizontal lines instead of five, and carries no clef or key signature. Each of the six horizontal lines represents a string on the guitar – beginning with the lowest line representing the low E-string. To help you remember which way is up, these string-note values are written alongside the TAB lines (see right top). For exercises in "alternate" tunings, the altered string-note values will be given instead, as in the exercise in DADGAD tuning (right below). Numbers on the lines indicate the fret at which to play that string, while a zero (0) indicates an open string is to be played.

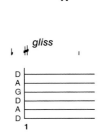

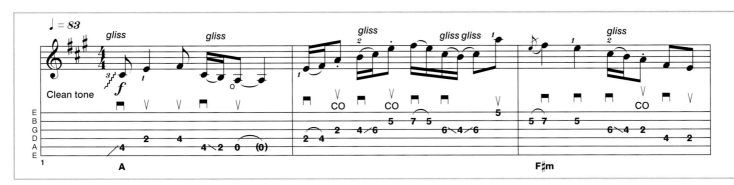

The majority of notation symbols are used to instruct you in the nuances of finger movement required to play a piece with the correct "feel." The dots on the stave – or string/fret number combinations on the TAB – tell you which notes to sound, but without the symbols it would be nearly impossible to determine the subtleties of playing technique that make a particular style of riff recognisable.

Bends

String bends are indicated by a starting note to be played before the bend occurs, and a small "arch" symbol linking it to a second note (sometimes in parentheses), which is the note achieved at the peak of the bend (or, in TAB, to the fret number which equates to that note, even though the bending finger stays at the same fret).

"BU" instructs you to "bend up." Bend releases are signified in the reverse, "BD" telling you to "bend down" (below-left).

When the pre-bend note is not to be sounded but merely provides a starting fret position to bend from, it will be in parentheses, with "PB" for "pre-bend" (below-right). "LD" means "let down."

You will also see an upside-down arch below notes where the symbol would otherwise clash with an un-bent note on a higher string (below-left). Where an up-bend is intended as more of an inflection, without a concluding note a full tone higher, you will see the initials "BSS" for "bend semitone sharp" (below-right).

Fingering

Some exercises offer fingering guidance in the form of arabic numerals alongside the notes in the stave, which tell you which finger to use for fretting that note, where 1 = index. (If a riff is repeated, these fingerings will generally be given for the first example to avoid cluttering the stave.)

In the *Classical* chapter, where the traditional fingerstyle technique is used, the right-hand fingerings will also be indicated with a special code, but a thorough guide to this is offered in the chapter itself.

Gliss

Gliss is short for "glissando," the term used in classical music to indicate a steady slide between notes. In more contemporary forms the technique is often referred to as a "slide" or "finger slide," but still indicated as a gliss in the notation. A gliss can go either up and down (below right).

With a gliss from one note to another, an arch symbol – similar to that used to indicate a bend – appears in the stave, with an arch or adjoining line in the TAB. The technique involves simply playing the first note, then sliding across the required number of frets to reach the second note.

A gliss symbol placed before or after a single note (below) tells you to slide to or from an unspecified pitch, but to land on the note given.

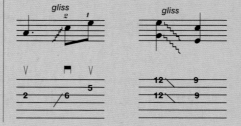

Hammer-ons and Pull-offs

Notes generated by hammering-on or pulling-off a string at a particular fret are indicated with a linking arch and the absence of a picking symbol. Other runs are generated with a picked note to start, with those following hammered or pulled.

Interpreting which is required is based on the direction of the musical line. Ascending notes are hammered, and descending notes are pulled off. This applies whether a phrase is totally hammer/pull generated (below-left) or is launched with a pick stroke (below-right).

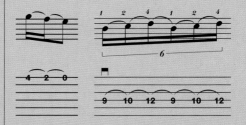

Two-handed Tapping

Found particularly in the *Metal* chapter, two-handed tapping combines right-hand taps with hammer-ons and pull-offs from the left hand. The right-hand taps are indicated in the stave with a downward arrow pointing to the tapped note, and in the TAB with a circle around the fret position at which the string is to be tapped.

Notes which come after the right-hand tap follow the rules for hammer-ons and pull-offs, with ascending notes hammered and descending notes pulled.

When a key note is to be generated by a left-hand tap, however, this will occasionally be indicated, with a symbol like an inverted upward arch – as with every third note in the example below.

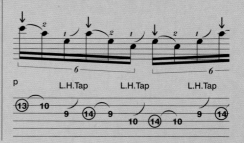

reading notation

reading notation

Harmonics

Natural harmonics – those achieved by damping a string directly over the 12th, fifth or seventh fret for example – are indicated by a diamond-shaped note in the stave accompanied by a "Nat harms" direction and a broken line extending the length of the harmonics' duration. The same is indicated in the TAB by the letters "Nh" followed by a broken line (below).

Artificial harmonics – those performed by fretting a note and damping the same string 12 frets higher – are indicated in the stave with the fretted note in parentheses and the damped (harmonic) note in the shape of a diamond, an octave higher and accompanied by the letter "T" followed by the fret number (example below). In the TAB, this is indicated with a number given for the fretted note followed by the damped note an octave higher given in parentheses, along with the "Ah" symbol.

Picking Symbols

Pick strokes are indicated with two types of symbols:
 = downstroke
 = upstroke

They are not universally given in all exercises, but are generally included where picking direction is critical to the feel of the piece.

Rake

A rake – where the pick is dragged smoothly across the strings, hitting each string individually but in swift succession – is indicated by a wavy vertical line concluded with an arrow pointing in the direction in which the pick should flow (usually from low note/string to high in these chapters). This is generally accompanied by the word "rake" between the stave and TAB line.

Rhythm Patterns

Lines representing pure rhythm patterns without tonal note values occur in a couple of different forms, and generally appear in the *Latin* and *African* chapters, where non-melodic rhythm patterns played by drums and/or percussion are crucial to the genre. These may be represented as one-line "staves" with beat values given per instrument…

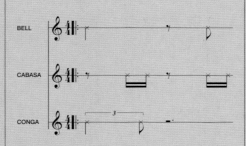

…or as normal five-line staves with atonal beat values given, or ordinary notes falling all on the same space, indicating a lack of tonal value.

The correct interpretation of each will be explained within the relevant individual chapters themselves.

Triplets

Whatever the rhythmic value of the individual notes (which, of course, is always the same for each note of a three-note grouping), triplets are indicated by the number "3" and linking brackets above or below the appropriate notes in the stave.

Similarly, sextuplets (which occur in astonishing numbers in the *Metal* chapter) are indicated by the number "6" and linking brackets above or below the appropriate notes in the stave.

As for septuplets and "fivetuplets"

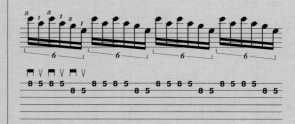

(quintuplets) – yes, they exist – the same applies.

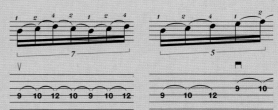

Vibrato

Generally encountered as "finger vibrato" in these chapters, vibrato is represented by a wavy horizontal line above the stave, accompanied by the abbreviation "vib".

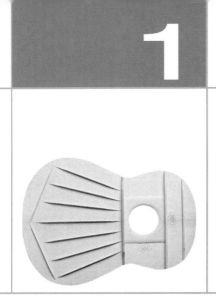

Guitars

NOVEMBER 1959
EDITION IV

BELL MUSIC LTD.
158 EWELL ROAD . SURBITON . SURREY

PLAYING
ACOUSTIC

COLUMBIA

The acoustic guitar is one of the most common instruments right across the whole spectrum of popular music. Whether it's country, traditional folk, blues, soul, pop, indie, rock'n'roll, rockabilly, protest, or rock, the acoustic guitar is there, somehow, even if it's not up front in the mix. The acoustic ethos even led to the launching of the MTV *Unplugged* shows, where performers put aside their electric instruments and renewed their music (and sometimes their careers) by dipping their feet in the "pure" spring of acoustic performance. In turn, that series helped to spawn an acoustic rebirth, and the "unplugged" ethos continues to be popular. ● **RIKKY ROOKSBY**

Whether it's a classical model or steel-strung "folk," for many players the acoustic guitar is where they begin. Generations of would-be rockers have heard their parents say they should start on an acoustic before thinking about an electric. Is there any sense in this beyond a parent's understandable desire to protect their ears and their wallet from too much guitar-induced stress?

Much of what is learned on an acoustic guitar can be transferred to an electric and vice versa. Despite their different appearances, both types of guitar are tuned the same and have the same configurations of notes laid out on the fingerboard. If you know how to play an Am or D7 or F#m9 chord or an E major or D pentatonic minor scale on an acoustic, you can play it on an electric, and vice versa.

Working first with an acoustic can build more strength into the hands. An inexpensive acoustic guitar is more likely to be harder to play – by virtue of its heavier gauge strings and higher action (the height of the strings from the fretboard) – than an equivalent lightly-strung electric, and therefore isn't necessarily a preferable instrument for a beginner. This is why it is important to get an acoustic properly set-up, to have its action checked, so the initial phase of learning isn't needlessly made more difficult.

You'll also find that lead guitar solos with plenty of string-bending cannot be played effectively on an acoustic. So if you're sure that's the direction you want to go then start on electric. Young women in particular with smaller hands, who tend to get saddled (no guitar pun intended!) with nylon-strung "Spanish" guitars with no regard to the type of music they want to play, should certainly consider an electric. This is because they often are put off playing guitar by the physical struggle involved in forming unfamiliar chords around a wide, flat neck. An electric can reduce this struggle with its generally slimmer, more comfortable neck. Just because you play an electric doesn't mean you have to make a racket with it: strummed unplugged, there's still plenty of volume to hear yourself for practise, and more and more good headphone amplifiers are available on today's market, often with built-in effects.

Acoustic guitar has always been popular because it is a relatively portable instrument,

and doesn't need electricity or an amp in order to function. It is ideal for accompanying yourself singing songs, and many people only desire to learn enough to take them to this point. To do this the technical requirements are straightforward: first, learn chord shapes; second, practise changing chord shapes until you can do so fast enough to keep up with a song; third, learn to strum evenly.

The chief hurdle in learning chords is getting to grips with the "barre" chord – the chord in which several notes are held down with one finger. The barre is often first encountered with the F or B chords. Moving these a little further up the neck can assist, where string tension is not as great as it is right by the nut.

A further refinement of accompanying yourself on guitar is to be able to finger-pick the chords instead of strumming them. This is especially useful in slower, quieter material. Initially such finger patterns will be in a simple rhythm. Later, they can be syncopated and incorporate an "alternating thumb" in the bass part. This is where the thumb moves between the bass strings while the fingers strike the higher ones, creating a tapestry of sound. Further refinements come with the ability to add little melodic phrases and riffs into the accompaniment without wholly abandoning the supporting harmony.

Beyond this lies the realm of guitar instrumental music in all its diversity, whether in the classical repertoire or the "folk baroque" of players like Davy Graham, Bert Jansch, John Renbourn, Gordon Giltrap, Pierre Bensusan, Leo Kottke, John Fahey, Stefan Grossman, Michael Hedges and many others. It is in this arena that players have looked for new sounds from the instrument. Most obviously this has come from altered tunings, where the standard EADGBE is changed by one or more strings being tuned to a different note.

In this section we will look at basic rhythm and finger-picking techniques, chords, how to use a capo, and finish with a quick look at the types of altered tunings that are so rewarding on the acoustic guitar – covering, in the process, a range of exercises appropriate to beginners, intermediates, and even some more advance players less experienced with these styles.

MAJOR AND MINOR CHORDS

It makes sense to start with some chords, so here are the shapes for the most-used major and minor chords. Notice that in comparison to the majors, the minors sound sad. The emotional contrast of "bright" major with "sad" minor is crucial to the vast bulk of Western music.

As you tackle the shapes check that each string that should be sounding *is* sounding. When the fingers are in the right place play each string individually. If notes do not sound the usual causes are: a finger on the metal fret, a finger too far away from the metal fret, not pressing hard enough, or a fretting finger touching and therefore muting an adjacent string.

A special word must be said about the shapes for B, Bm, F and F#m. These involve playing a barre, but you can use the version without the full barre for now, until your fingers get used to the required positions. With B and Bm the bass note on the 5th string is therefore optional.

SEVENTHS

The next most common group of chords is the sevenths. Here are two types formed by adding a single note to the major chord. Don't worry if you can't play the B7 and F7 barre chords initially. The B7 barre version will give you a different A7 if you take off the barre and move the fingers two frets toward the nut. The little finger with F7 is optional.

The major seventh chord has a richer sound than the first type. Again, leave the Bmaj7 and Emaj7 if you find them difficult. The F#maj7 has the advantage of being a movable chord that doesn't have a barre. Make sure that all the strings that should be sounding are, otherwise you may miss the seventh!

USING A CAPO

In order to make playing in difficult keys easier, guitarists use a device known as a "capo." This may look like a medieval instrument of torture but, as a guitarist, it's one of your best

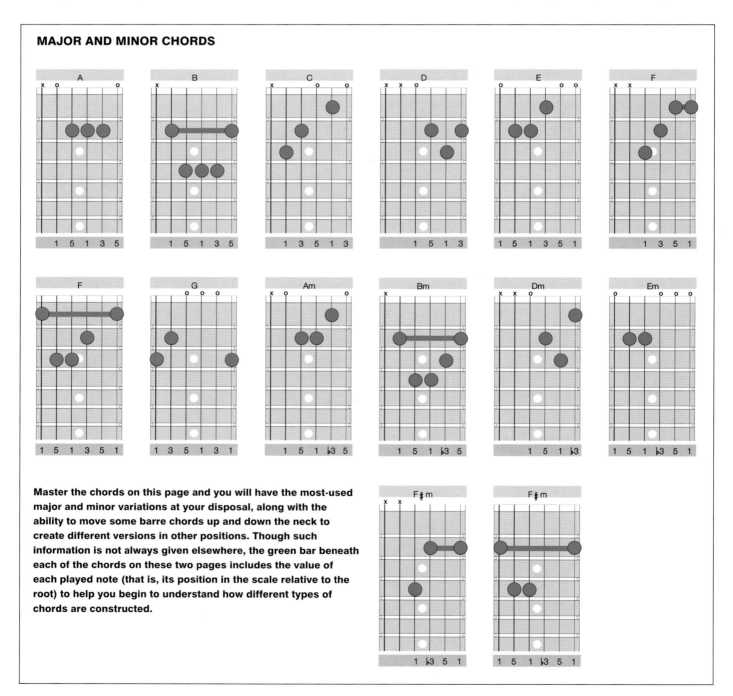

MAJOR AND MINOR CHORDS

Master the chords on this page and you will have the most-used major and minor variations at your disposal, along with the ability to move some barre chords up and down the neck to create different versions in other positions. Though such information is not always given elsewhere, the green bar beneath each of the chords on these two pages includes the value of each played note (that is, its position in the scale relative to the root) to help you begin to understand how different types of chords are constructed.

friends! It acts as a first finger substitute holding a barre, or can be alternatively thought of as a movable nut. If a key would normally mean lots of barre chords (and an aching hand) the capo will allow you to turn most of the barre chords into open string shapes.

Here's an example: you need to play a song that was recorded in Ab major and uses Ab, Bbm, Cm, Db, Eb and Fm – all barre chords. If you put the capo at the first fret each chord can be played with the shape of the chord a semitone below it.

Actual pitch:	**Ab**	**Bbm**	**Cm**	**Db**	**Eb**	**Fm**
Capo I shapes:	**G**	**Am**	**Bm**	**C**	**D**	**Em**

Much easier, and it sounds better too! And that's not the only way we could do it…

Actual pitch:	**Ab**	**Bbm**	**Cm**	**Db**	**Eb**	**Fm**
Capo IV shapes:	**E**	**F#m**	**G#m**	**A**	**B**	**C#m**

Or, for an extreme contrast…

Actual pitch:	**Ab**	**Bbm**	**Cm**	**Db**	**Eb**	**Fm**
Capo VIII shapes:	**C**	**Dm**	**Em**	**F**	**G**	**Am**

You will notice that as the capo goes up the neck the timbre of the guitar will change. This is something that songwriters use deliberately. They also use a capo to shift a chord sequence up or down a key to better suit their voice, which saves learning a new set of chords. Lastly, if you play guitar with a friend, using a capo high on one of the guitars can create a resonant sound with the two guitars playing the same chords high and low:

Actual pitch:	**G**	**Am**	**Bm**	**C**	**D**	**Em**	**F**
Guitar 1 open chords	**G**	**Am**	**Bm**	**C**	**D**	**Em**	**F**
Guitar 2 capo VII shapes	**C**	**Dm**	**Em**	**F**	**G**	**Am**	**Bb**

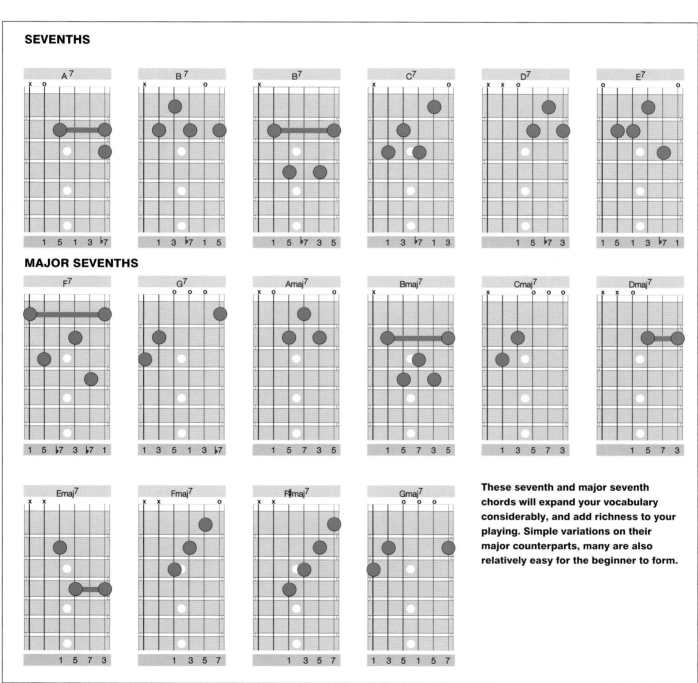

SEVENTHS

MAJOR SEVENTHS

These seventh and major seventh chords will expand your vocabulary considerably, and add richness to your playing. Simple variations on their major counterparts, many are also relatively easy for the beginner to form.

125

British acoustic ace John Renbourn melds ragtime, blues, folk and medieval music into his own brew. From his formative work at the center of the mid-'60s London folk scene to his contemporary recordings, Renbourn's playing always impresses.

MINOR 7, SUSPENDED 4, SUSPENDED 2 CHORDS

By merely moving beyond the basic major chords – where appropriate – to other shapes that aren't much more difficult to play, simple songs can take on added tension and atmosphere. Here are three other types of chord that are often found in songs, and can be useful mood builders. The minor sevenths are the minor version of the A7, B7 and so on previously shown. The Bm7 will yield an alternative Am7 if you take off the barre and move the fingers two frets down toward the nut. The little finger with F#m7 is optional.

The suspended fourth chords are often used to inject drama into song accompaniment because of their tension. In the case of Asus4, Dsus4 and Esus4 all that is required is to add a note to a simple major chord shape. The Asus2 and Dsus2 are popular because the reverse happens: you just lift a finger off a string that would usually be fretted for A or D. The sus2 is not as tense and has an open, "hollow" sound.

A MISCELLANY OF EFFECTIVE ACOUSTIC CHORDS

Here are 16 chords that sound great on an acoustic guitar. Some are created by either lifting a finger off a note with a common barre shape (Bmadd4, F#m7add11, Fmaj7add11) or moving a chord shape up (D6/9, Amaj7), or are unique "voicings" – like the C which has a 12-string resonance because within it there are two Gs and two Es at the same pitch.

Also included are two first inversion chords – G/B and D/F# – which often feature in acoustic songs. First inversion simply means that the root note is not the lowest in the chord, the "third" above it is played instead – the note that is two tones higher than the root in a major chord. Try these out and learn the ones you like for your own playing.

EFFECTIVE ACOUSTIC CHORDS

American fingersylist Leo Kottke, above, is a seminal instrumentalist and one of the true "godfathers" of the acoustic scene over the past thirty years. Running from folk, to jazz, to bluegrass, to blues, his work is consistently inspiring.

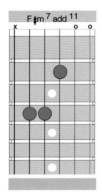
F#m7 add 11

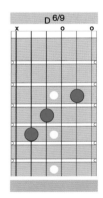
D 6/9

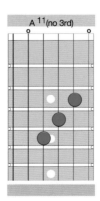
A 11(no 3rd)

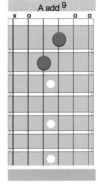
A add 9

MINOR 7 AND SUSPENDED CHORDS

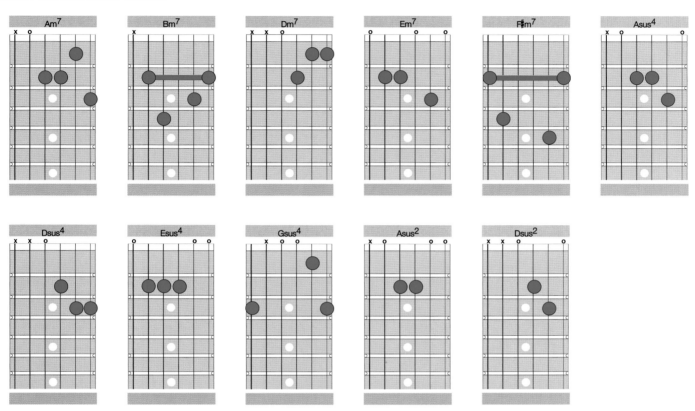

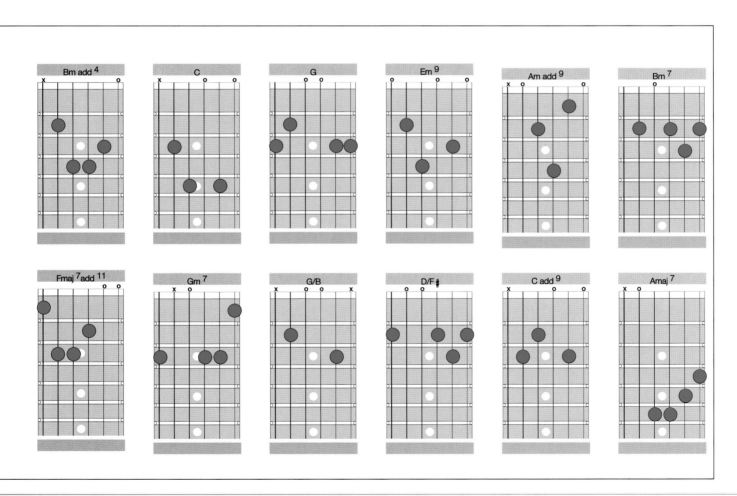

STRUMMING PATTERNS

Now you have plenty of chords to play with! So let's turn our attention to the hand that hits the strings. Although it is possible to strum with your thumb or the upperside of your fingers, the best tone for straight-on rhythm playing is produced by using a pick, or plectrum. These small pieces of plastic are held between thumb and forefinger (don't use your second finger because you might want to pluck a string with it at the same time as holding the pick). The thumb crosses the finger at approximately a right angle. Most of the pick should be gripped – there doesn't need to be much showing to hit the strings. Picks come in various shapes and thicknesses. For acoustic strumming a thin one is easiest to begin with and might give the best tone for jangly but not-too aggressive rhythm playing. Thick picks put up more resistance against the strings and take a little more effort, while also inducing a little more volume. The strumming action is mostly from the forearm as it hangs off the top of the guitar but the hand sometimes contributes a little for emphasis.

The essence of good strumming can be summarized as follows: evenness of tone, avoiding bass strings that are not meant to be hit, the ability to strum up and down with equal facility, controlling the volume, and keeping steady time. It also means knowing when and how to leave out strums.

Exercise 1 gets us started. Hold down an E major chord. Tap your foot, count to yourself, or set a metronome going at a medium tempo (around 80 to 90bpm). This exercise is in 4/4, which means four beats to each bar. Strum downwards every

other beat, then on each beat, then twice on each beat (8ths or quavers), then four times on each beat (16ths or semi-quavers). Depending on how fast or slow you're going you may find that strumming twice and four times to a beat is too difficult just going downwards. The answer is to strum down and up, alternating.

Exercise 2 gives nine strumming patterns. The first is a strum in straight 8ths. Notice how with each example some strums are taken away; the chord is allowed to ring. The rule is: the faster the tempo the longer a gap you can leave. With IV there is the introduction of a "tie." This is the line joining the 5th quaver to the 4th. A tie means you strike the first of the joined pair but not the second. Instead, the first lasts for the length of time of both notes. In any song you could use any one or a mixture of strumming patterns. Your choice will depend on mood, tempo and "groove."

One way to make your strumming more interesting is to pick some of the bass notes of the chords individually and then hit the chord, as in **exercise 3**. This style is known as pick'n'strum. The bass note is usually the root note of the chord. Here is a well-known chord sequence that lends itself to this approach.

In **exercise 4** the bass notes are not all root notes, though the technique is the same. Introductions to songs and links between choruses and verses sometimes feature a phrase played in single notes, with chords in between, as in **exercise 5**. A song like *Wish You Were Here* by Pink Floyd or the intro to Led Zeppelin's *Over The Hills And Far Away* are examples of this popular approach to pick'n'strum.

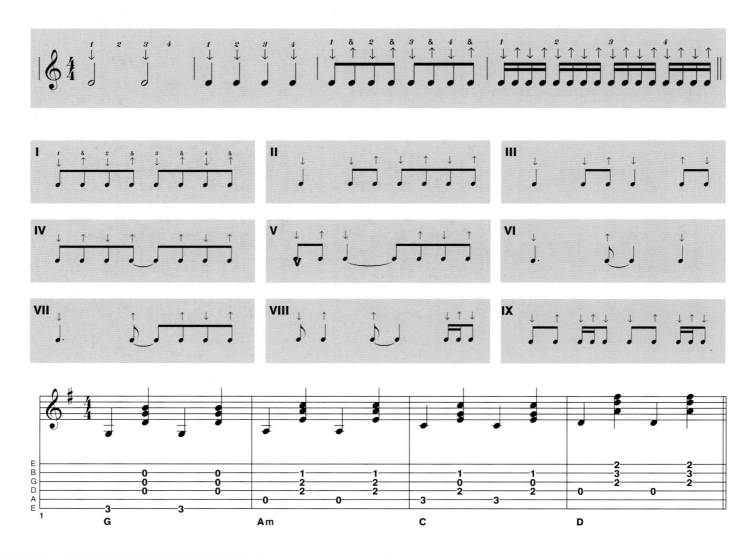

Look no further for acoustic inspiration: 12-string specialist Leo Kottke, DADGAD wizard Pierre Bensusan, and eclectic stylist Michael Hedges offer different techniques with equal virtuosity (albums, left, from left to right respectively).

Far from being limited to the extremes of the campfire sing along, the folky, or the blindingly nimble fingerstyle soloist, the acoustic guitar is found somewhere in the mix in a lot of straight-on rock'n'roll too – as Rolling Stone Keith Richards demonstrates, right.

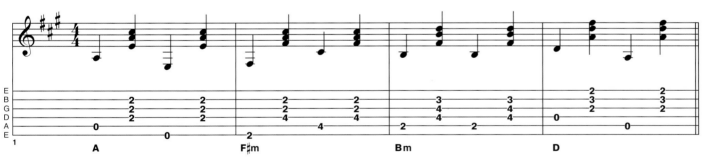

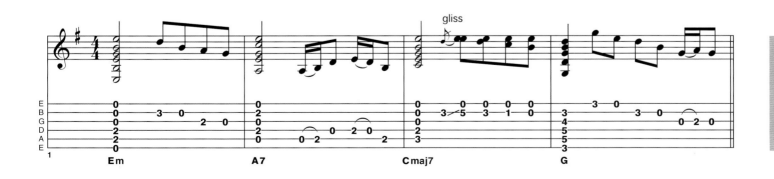

strumming patterns

Exercise 4

Exercise 5

More than just an easy-strummin' singer/songwriter, Bob Dylan is a gifted – if underrated – musician in his own right. Check out his early work in particular, such as 1963's *The Freewheelin' Bob Dylan* (above left), for a quick education in compelling fingerstyle accompaniment with simple, effective fills. At the other end of the spectrum, Led Zeppelin's Jimmy Page (below) is best known for his bombastic electric work, but he knew a thing or two about how to use an acoustic guitar in a rock context, and even pushed beyond the genre with Eastern scales and complex open tunings. Examples of both are plentiful on Zep's *Houses Of The Holy* (above right).

BASIC FINGERPICKING PATTERNS

Exercise 6 shows 14 different finger-picking patterns. Notice how the thumb looks after the bass notes. In each case the notes of the chord are sounding but in a different manner to the simultaneous effect of strumming. Fingerstyle playing generates its own rhythm, too. You can easily adapt the patterns for 6/8 to 3/4. Most of the examples use a C chord, a five-string chord with its root on the 5th string. You can find variations of these patterns for chords with their root notes on the fourth or sixth strings. Obviously the more strings in a chord the more patterns you could devise to play them.

Let's continue by trying some slightly more complex fingerpicking exercises. Examples XI-XIV take a bit more work before you can do them unconsciously because of their syncopated rhythm. Remember to work out the thumb pattern first and then fit the other notes to it. Example XIV is a two-bar blues pattern in swung rhythm – each beat divides into the feel of three rather than two.

basic fingerpicking

basic fingerpicking

XI

XII

XIII

The fleet-fingered Adrian Legg, above, rivals the best acoustic artists as a pure technician, but his creative use of effects, amplification, and adventurous string-bending take him well beyond the usual sonic realm of the instrument.

XIV

Exercise 7 is a simple ascending fingerpick applied to a popular chord progression with a descending bass-line. The 6/8 time signature means two beats in a bar, each dividing into three: 123, 456. Take it slowly at first, then build speed and play ad-infinitum until you get the hang of it. It will feel repetitive, certainly, but this is the sort of exercise that really builds your fingerpicking skills.

Exercise 8 also starts on Am but in the later bars move up the neck. Notice the way the open B string is used. Initially the notes are in ascending order, but from bar 3 that pattern is broken up and the pitch order is less predictable.

In **exercise 9** a simple ascending finger-pick is applied to a chord sequence in which a number of inversions are used to join up root position chords. This is common in folk playing. D/F# and C/E are first inversions; the note after the forward slash sign (/) is the lowest in pitch. The Bm7/F# and Am/E are second inversion chords in which the "fifth" of the chord (the note 3 half-tones from the root) is at the bottom.

Exercise 10 also uses some common inversions but the direction of picking is reversed. Notice also that two notes are sounded together for each group of quavers in bars 1-3. Like 3/4, 6/8 time lends itself to up-and-down patterns like this one. **Exercise 11** is another common progression with a descending bass line. **Exercise 12** is a syncopated piece with an alternating thumb playing the bass notes (marked "T"). The progression is similar to Ex.7. Let the notes ring for as long as possible.

Exercise 7

Exercise 8

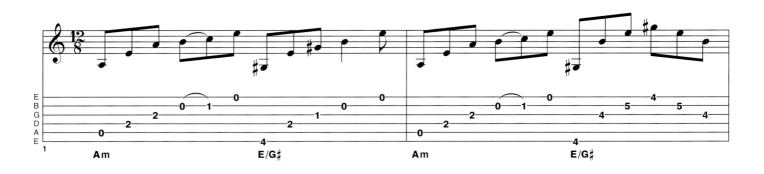

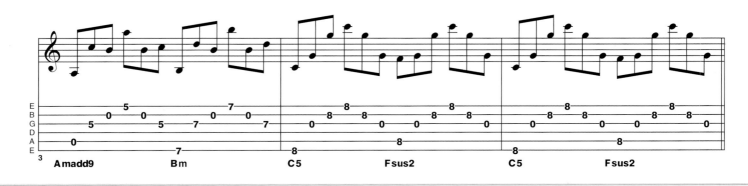

Open tunings have helped a number of great artists find their instrumental voices, from Richie Havens's rootsy, eclectic, world-music-inflected arrangements to the unique jazz-cum-folk of Joni Mitchell (seen in concert, opposite page). Haven's album *The End Of The Beginning* and Mitchell's *Clouds* (both pictured above) are fine examples of what each does best.

ALTERED TUNINGS

Standard tuning – EADGBE – is a wonderful compromise that allows a guitarist to work in many keys, despite its bias toward E minor. Many acoustic guitarists, however, have searched for new tones by altering this tuning. Some players stumble on altered tunings by default – no-one showed them how to tune the guitar properly so they simply used their ear and tuned the strings to an open chord (Richie Havens and Joni Mitchell spring to mind). Others chased new tunings consciously to emulate the droning effects of non-Western instruments such as the sitar, or to make it easier to keep a bass going and improvise a melody.

An altered tuning can create beautiful new chords and stimulate your creativity. These new musical territories come at a

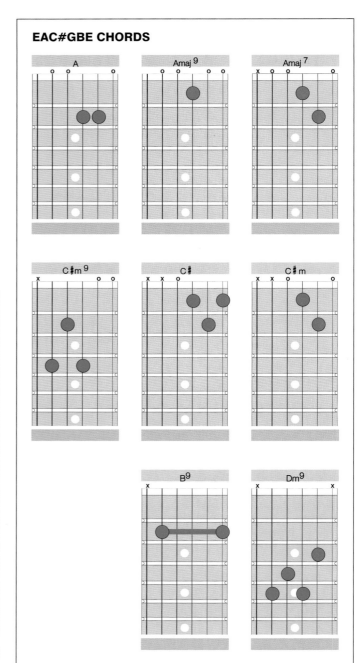

EAC#GBE CHORDS

These chords provide a quick guide to some easy shapes in the tuning of EAC#GBE, which itself makes a simple introduction to altered tunings, having only one string – the D – changed from standard tuning.

A self-styled guitarist of vast creative capacity, Richie Havens stumbled on his own open tunings as a natural means of producing the tones he sought to express, and thus forged an uncategorizable style of his own that remains distinctive today.

altered tunings

price, however. First, there is the tuning in and out of them, with the attendant risk of broken strings and iffy intonation. Second, if you find some beautiful chords you had better write them down. Remembering chord shapes in ten different tunings is okay if you play the pieces regularly, but once they slip from the mind it can be a frustrating job trying to recall what they were!

SINGLE STRING ALTERATION

The simplest way to begin playing around with new tunings is simply to change one string. For this book I've invented a tuning in which the D string is detuned by a semitone to C#, giving us E A C# G B E. To do this, fret C# on the 5th string at the 4th fret and lower the open D until the two are in tune (to get back to standard reverse the process). This implies an A dominant ninth chord. I've supplied eight chord shapes and two short exercises you can play in this tuning.

Exercise 13 is a riff with a bluesy swing rhythm but some unusual chords. Try to keep the bass note steady and fit the higher parts around it. **Exercise 14** is simple upward picking. The idea is to play it slowly and let the strings ring so you can hear the unorthodox chord tones caused by the altered tuning. If these give you some new ideas, you can make up your own.

altered tunings

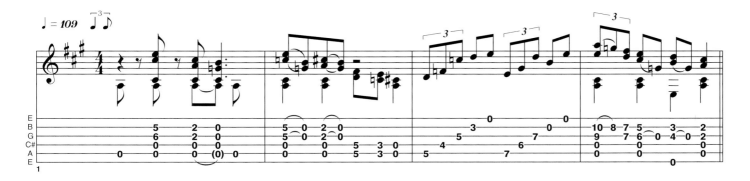

Exercise 13

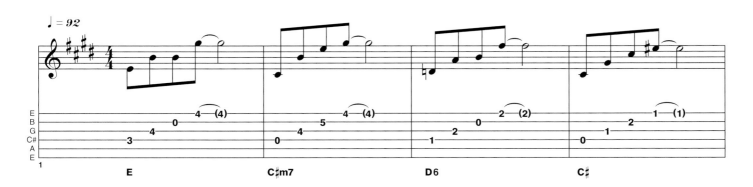

Exercise 14

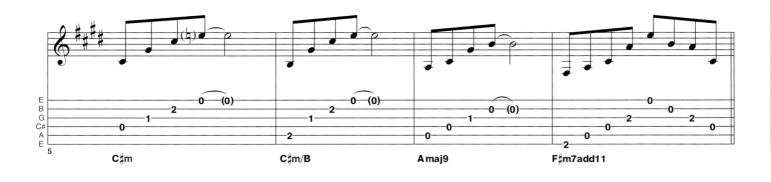

One of the original smashers of musical barriers on acoustic guitar, Davy Graham (near right) melds baroque, blues, jazz and folk into a style entirely his own. John Fahey (center) is another virtuoso forefather of solo acoustic performance, while Gordon Giltrap remains at the center of an underappreciated scene.

DROPPED D

The most famous single-string alteration is known, somewhat confusingly, as "dropped D." More accurately, the bottom E is "dropped" – that is, tuned down a tone to D. This tuning is popular with rock players because the bottom three strings make a power-chord and the low D is good for launching heavy riffs. Folk players like it because it provides an octave open string D with the fourth string for an alternating thumb technique. The fretting hand is thus free to move wherever it wants on the neck. This tuning produces much deeper sounding six-string D and Dm chords.

In **exercise 15** the fourth and sixth open strings are played by the thumb. Above these, a series of thirds and fourths move up and down. This is one way of creating an accompaniment for a voice.

The thumb only alternates on the beat in the 12/8 piece in **exercise 16**. Above, the fingers fret a single-note melody with some decorative hammer-ons and pull-offs. Again, get your thumb working right first, then fit the melody to the steady pulse of the bass notes, not the other way around.

dropped D tuning

Exercise 15

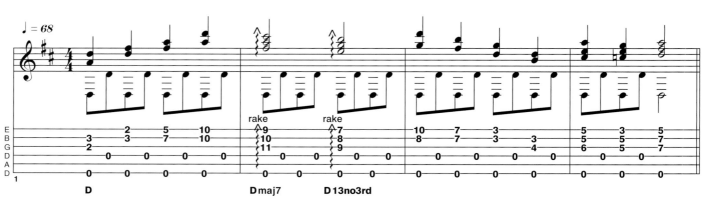

Exercise 16

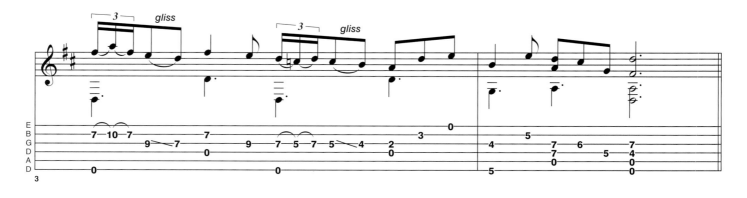

OPEN G MAJOR

After the single-string alteration we have the open tuning proper, where the strings are tuned to make a simple major or minor chord. This means that each of the six strings will be tuned to one of three chord tones. The most popular open tuning is open G (which is also one of the most popular tunings for five-string banjo). The notes of a G chord are G B D. Standard tuning already has those three notes on strings 4, 3 and 2, so the tuning is created by lowering strings 6, 5 and 1 down until they come to the nearest of those three notes. The distance is measured in semitones.

E	A	D	G	B	E
-2	-2	–	–	–	-2
D	G	D	G	B	D

The immediate practical effect of this tuning is that a barre placed across the top five strings at any fret will create a root position major chord. The three chords needed for a 12-bar progression and many other songs will be found on the open strings, at the fifth and seventh frets, with the twelfth fret giving an octave higher. Strong harmonics are also available at frets 5, 7, and 12 by laying a finger across the strings right over the metal fret but not pushing them against the fretboard. Strike the strings and gently pull the finger away and you will hear the ghostly, bell-like tones of harmonics.

Open G makes a very full sound if strummed. If a barre is held down various notes can be added by the other fingers. The first three chord boxes below indicate how this is done. The tuning is also used to provide drone notes as octaves or sixths or thirds are moved up the neck. Try holding down the 2nd fret on the 1st and 4th strings (an octave) and move this up and down as you strum all the strings.

Open tunings also lend themselves to slide playing. Keith Richards has made extensive use of open G with many Rolling Stones classics like *Brown Sugar* and *Start Me Up*. You can also use a capo with an open tuning if you wish to change its key. Open G with a capo at the third fret becomes open Bb major.

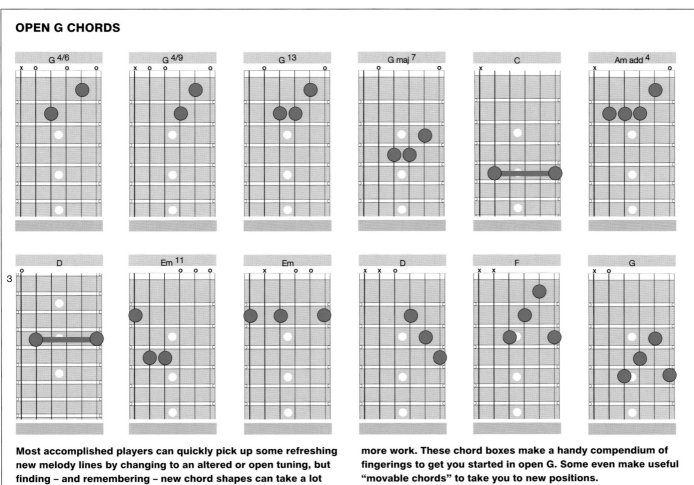

OPEN G CHORDS

Most accomplished players can quickly pick up some refreshing new melody lines by changing to an altered or open tuning, but finding – and remembering – new chord shapes can take a lot more work. These chord boxes make a handy compendium of fingerings to get you started in open G. Some even make useful "movable chords" to take you to new positions.

DADGAD

Altered tunings need not make a simple major or minor open chord. "DADGAD" is one of the most popular examples of a more complex tuning. It has misleadingly been called a "modal" tuning. In fact, it's a Dsus4 chord. DADGAD was introduced into the world of folk guitar in the early 1960s by Davey Graham, a key figure in the English folk scene. It has been used by many players since, including Pierre Bensusan, for whom it is now "standard tuning," and in a rock context by

Jimmy Page who used it for the mighty Led Zep epic *Kashmir*.

Here are some DADGAD chord boxes for you to strum or finger-pick.

To conclude, **exercise 17** is a composition entitled *Postcard To Denys*, a fun piece with lots of bends and decorative hammer-on/pull-off figures typical of the style known as "folk baroque." It should be played with a slightly sloppy touch. In keeping with its humorous spirit the intro alludes to *Purple Haze*.

DADGAD CHORDS

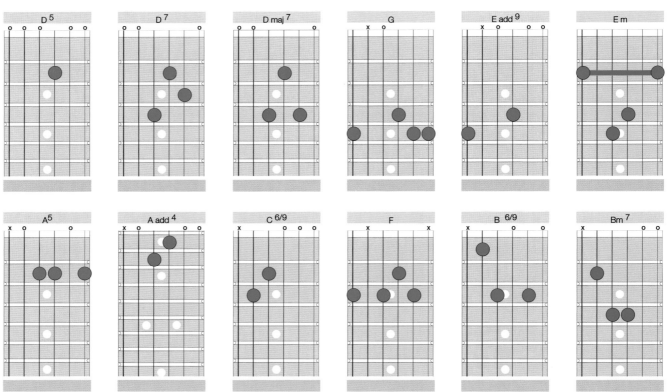

DADGAD tuning

Exercise 17

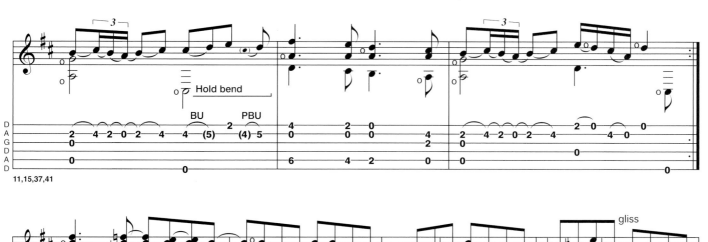

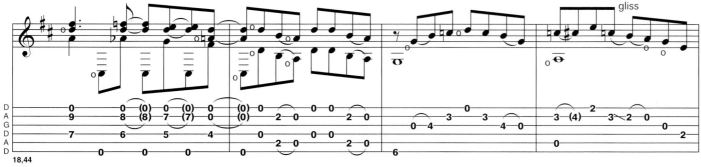

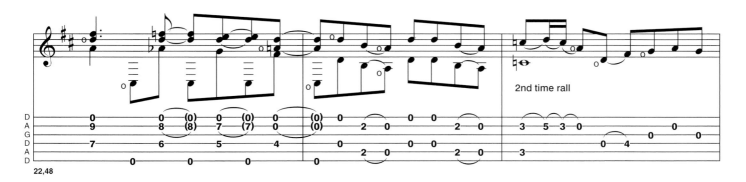

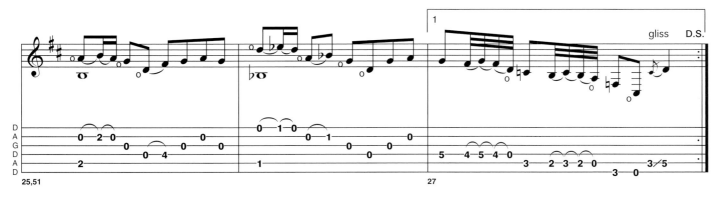

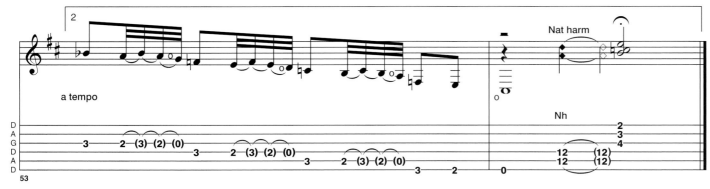

139

PLAYING
ROCK–POP

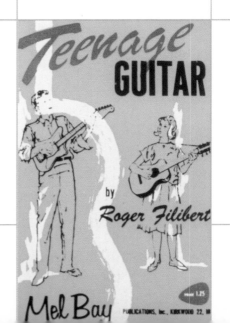

There is no rigid boundary between pop and rock music – and this chapter will deal with playing a range of musical forms broadly classifiable as falling within or between the two, from the late 1950s to the present; in short, the bulk of the most popular music played and enjoyed today. ● **RIKKY ROOKSBY**

By "pop" we generally mean a lighter, less aggressive type of song, more suited to being chart material, possibly with more conservative lyrics, and with less reliance on the blues element that was carried to rock by '50s rock'n'roll. There are also production differences, of course. Rock guitar tends to make more use of distortion. Hard rock styles like heavy metal and the advanced lead techniques that go with it (all covered later in the book) are beyond the scope of this overview. Despite the development of many sub-genres within rock and pop the guitar basics remain quite stable. Eddie Cochran and Kurt Cobain might have had 30 years of rock between them, but from a guitar playing perspective they are still recognisably connected.

It was in the mainstream rock'n'roll of the '50s rockers like Elvis Presley, Chuck Berry, Buddy Holly, and Eddie Cochran that a new instrument, the electric guitar, came to fame. Befitting of this cultural revolution, a new music ensemble was created around the new instrument: two electric guitars, electric bass and drums. This quartet was easy to form among your friends, and the combination of amps and hard-hit drums gave it a strong and dynamic presence. The two guitars could punch out a thick, resonant harmony, underpinned by the bass (up to 16 strings sounding together). In this format, one guitar could play a solo or melody and be supported by the other's chords – thus the roles of rhythm and lead guitar were born.

Players like Duane Eddy, The Ventures, Hank Marvin and Vic Flick (who played the James Bond theme) recorded many guitar-led, echo-haunted instrumentals. Instrumental guitar groups were everywhere in the early '60s, until the triple-voice-double-guitar songs of the Beatles and countless followers pushed them aside.

Mid-'60s bands like the Stones, The Kinks, The Who, The Animals and The Yardbirds made the electric guitar riff more of a feature. The electric 12-string, bigger amps, distortion boxes and wah-wah pedals all increased the sonic palette. By the late '60s blues-rock and heavy rock were pushing into the mainstream,

their groups invariably built around the first generation of guitar heroes who paraded their virtuosity in long, often improvised solos: Hendrix, Clapton, Page, Beck, Kossoff, Iommi, Blackmore, West, Garcia, Santana, and many others. Since then glam rock, late-'70s punk, early-'80s new wave, '80s rock, indie, grunge, alternative rock, Brit-pop and nu-metal have all recycled riffs and ideas and sometimes taken advantage of the stunning expansion of guitar-related technology. The digital revolution has meant the availability of an increasing range of amp tones, many simulated from earlier decades, and the electric guitar has linked up with the wonderful world of MIDI. The electro-acoustic has also been improved to enable an acoustic guitar sound in an amplified quartet.

The relatively limited harmony used in many rock and pop songs means that you can play most styles with quite a small number of chord shapes. When learning chords, first learn the open string shapes. These are easiest to finger and create a resonant, satisfying tone. The most common chords used in songs are A, C, D, E, F, G; Am, Bm, Dm, Em, F#m; A7, B7, C7, D7, E7, G7; Amaj7, Cmaj7, Dmaj7, Fmaj7, Gmaj7; Am7, Dm7, Em7; Asus4, Dsus4, Esus4, Gsus4; Asus2, Dsus2; Cadd9 – all of which, and more, can be found in the *Acoustic* section.

One essential task will be to master the barre chord. A barre chord involves holding more than one string down with a single finger, usually the first. Your aim should be to have two shapes for each type of chord, one with the root note on the 6th string, and the other with the root on the 5th. This will give two options for any required barre chord in any key, including all the sharps and flats. The four most important are derived from open string A, E, Am and Em shapes. At the first fret, turned into barre chords, these become Bb, F, Bbm and Fm. In the exercises that

follow we'll look at many of the key techniques and ideas used in rock and pop since the early '60s. The pages that follow include sub-sections on Rhythm Playing, Riffs, Triads, Intervals, Fifths, Scales and Lead.

the evolution of rock & pop

THE EXERCISES

A tempo indication in "beats per minute" (BPM) is given for each exercise. With a metronome or drum machine you can hear how fast it should be played. Chord indications are given below the stave. These do not necessarily apply to the notes of the exercise. They may be implied chords or chords for a backing. To hear the full tone-colour of these exercises get a friend to play the chords for you, or record them on tape and then play along.

RHYTHM

Let's begin with an easy-to-play rock figure that has been around

since the '50s and almost defines the word "boogie." It's important to master this playing feel for all sorts of music you might want to tackle. For **exercise 1**, play to a steady rhythm, at first with downstrokes of the pick. Later try alternate down/up picking for a somewhat different rhythmic feel. (The "shuffle" variation of this figure can be found in the *Blues* section). This popular rhythm has powered great rock playing from Chuck Berry to Oasis (whose lead guitarist and songwriter, Noel Gallagher, is pictured right).

Exercise 2 is a variation where the note on the fretted string goes a further semi-tone up. Notice also the change from E to A

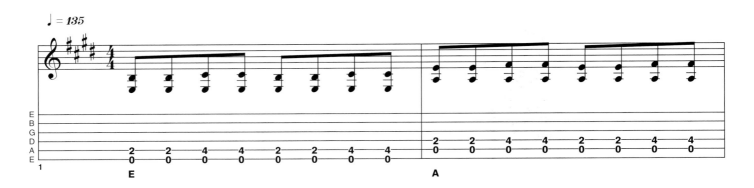

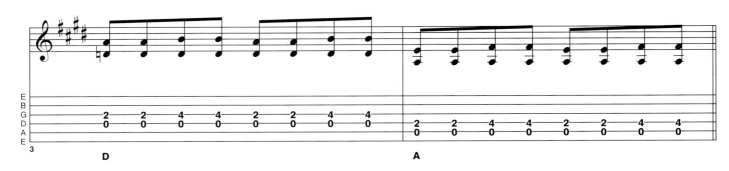

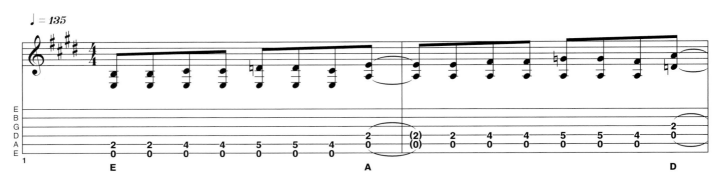

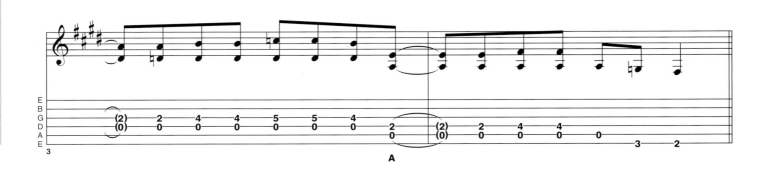

rhythm

comes on the last off-beat of bar 1. This syncopation – with its distinctive "pull" across the bar-line, is typical of rock. Remember to try to get each pair of notes the same volume.

Exercise 3 shows a subtle yet distinctive third variation on this theme, where two notes are introduced that temporarily eclipse the root note in each bar. Syncopation is once again present on the last off-beat.

It is also possible to use this rhythm figure in a new way by turning it into a set of single notes instead of striking two notes at a time, as in **exercise 4**. Watch out for the transition in bar 4 from hitting the 6th string to hitting the 4th string.

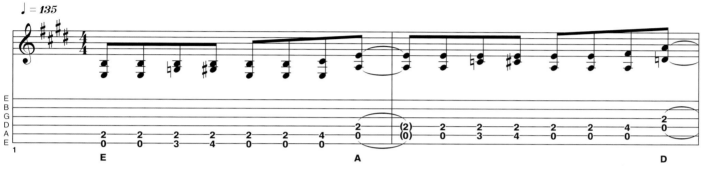

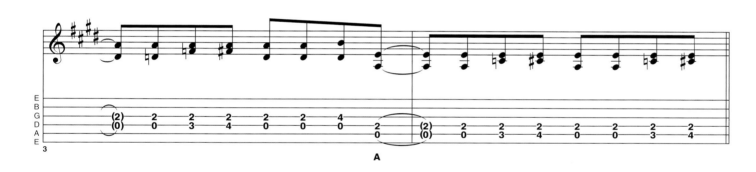

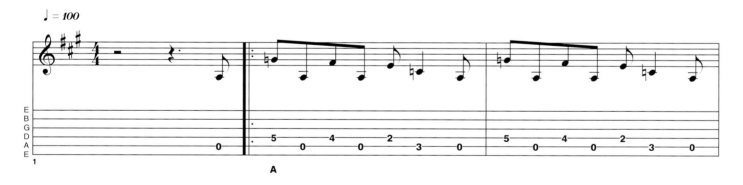

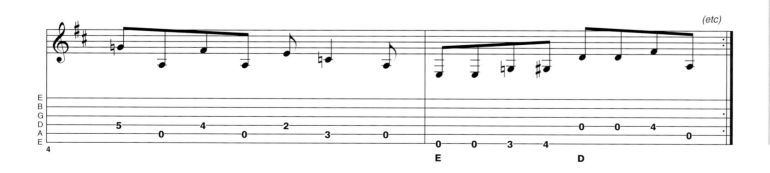

Exercises 1-4 work well in the key of A major. But what if we want to play this rhythm figure in other keys? The answer is to convert it into a fretted figure with no open strings. Don't worry if you find this a bit of a stretch at first. Drop your thumb well behind the neck. That will help your fretting hand open out. **Exercise 5** shows the boogie figure following a common chord progression (chords I, IV and V in B major).

Exercise 6 displays the same idea in E major starting on the 5th string. Starting on either the 5th or the 6th strings enables you to play it in any major key, and to pitch it higher or lower. Songs like Status Quo's *Paper Plane*, Queen's *Now I'm Here* and Super

Furry Animals' *Rings Around The World* feature this.

To help you memorize the pattern that governs the I-IV-V changes, **exercise 7** isolates the root notes. Bars 1-2 give the pattern for starting on the 6th string; bars 3-4 for starting on the 5th. **Exercise 8** shows how original effects can be had with this rhythm figure by moving between less related root notes. Chord VI in E major should be C#m, not C#, and there is no A# in the key of E, which is what the boogie figure demands. You can hear this change in T.Rex's *Mambo Sun* from the album *Electric Warrior* (1971). A further innovation is to flatten the expected note, as in bar 4.

Exercise 7

Exercise 8

rhythm

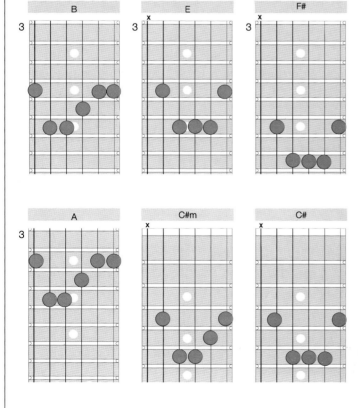

T.Rex's Marc Bolan was a major proponent of the basic boogie rhythm, and applied it to many pop-rock classics. Learning your barre chords – such as those in the diagrams shown left – will help you transpose these useful rhythmic figures to any key.

A related version of the rhythm figure we have been playing occurs on the higher strings and is based on a major triad held by the first finger. Play **exercise 9** to try it in C major.

Exercise 10 is a variation related to Ex.2 where the finger goes up one additional fret. The note you added to each chord in Ex.9 is known as the sixth of the chord. If we add the fourth as well as the sixth we get the rock rhythm figure displayed in **exercise 11**. Bars 1-2 lack a root note. This is suggested in bars 3-4. It is possible but awkward: the little finger must hold down the root and damp the 5th string. In **exercise 12** a related figure adds the fourth and the ninth to the basic triad. Notice the A chord in bar 2 has a powerful sound because the root note is

Exercise 9

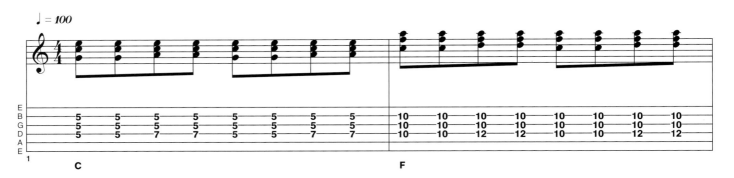

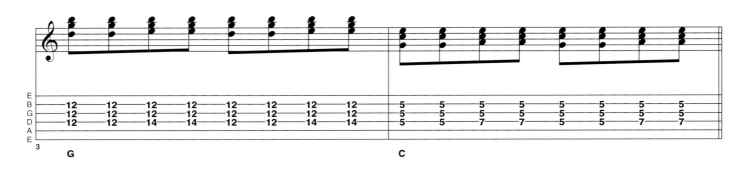

Exercise 10

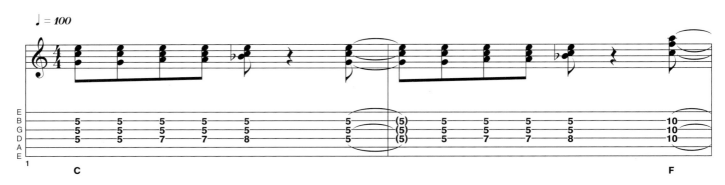

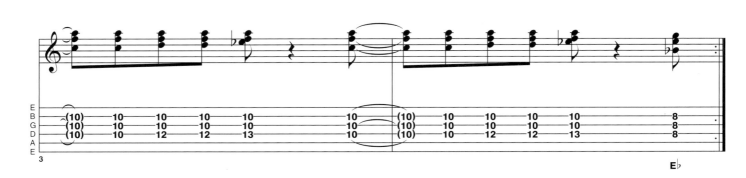

rhythm

merely the open 5th string. This figure on A is very popular for this reason. Exercises 9-12 will remind you of the Rolling Stones, the Faces, and the Black Crowes – good-time rock'n'roll. They are standard tuning versions of figures that occur in open tunings (the *Acoustic* section deals further with open G).

Apart from the A chord in the last example, the other open-string chord that yields excellent results with these 4/6, 4/9 shapes is G. In **exercise 13** bar 1 adds just the sixth, bar 2 the sixth and fourth, bar 3 the ninth and fourth, and bar 4 shows a common pull-off fill making good use of the open strings. Listen to *John, I'm Only Dancing* by David Bowie, or *If It Makes You Happy* by Sheryl Crow (playing live, left; album opposite page).

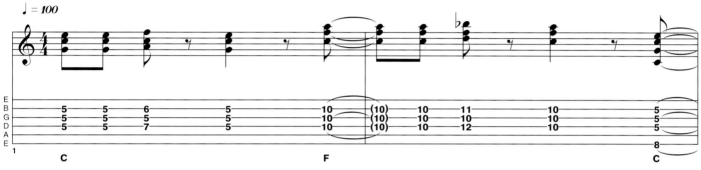

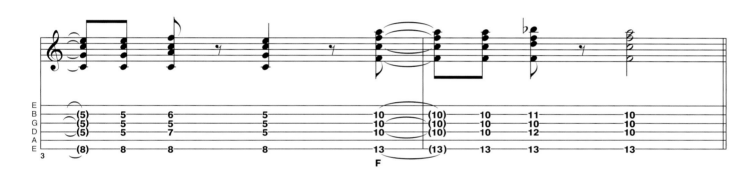

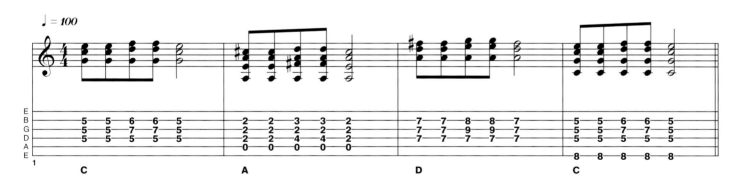

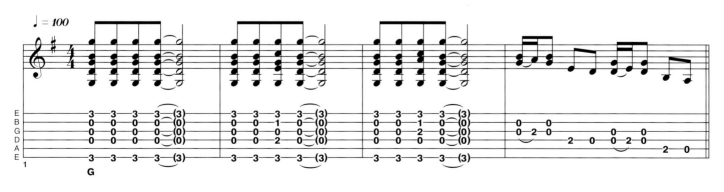

147

power chords

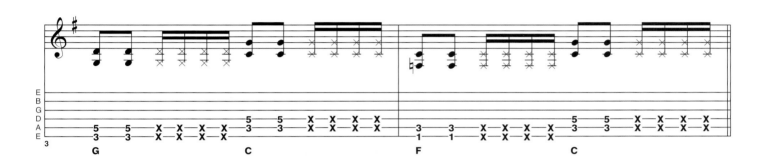

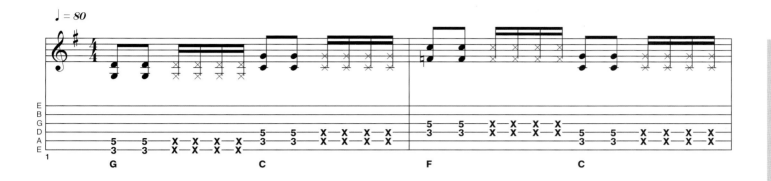

Exercise 14 shows how new effects can be had by giving these shapes a less predictable twist. Bar 2 has an E where we would expect an Eb, and bar 3 has an F where we would expect F#. This is now less Keith Richards and more Jimmy Page.

RHYTHM FIFTHS

In many of the above exercises the interval of a perfect fifth (3½ tones) from E-B, A-E, D-A, dominates. The perfect fifth is crucial to rock guitar. It has a bare, tough, assertive sound and tolerates any amount of distortion. You may already know it under the name commonly used by rock guitarists, the "power chord," and it is essential to master for comprehensive rock playing. The concept will be covered in more detail and with further exercises in the *Metal* section, but the style applies equally to both rock and heavy metal, and it's worth addressing here too.

Strum this sequence in **exercise 15** with open-string chords. Then play it as fifths, as written out. Notice the difference. Even with a clean tone the fifths toughen up the progression if a second guitar plays full chords. Played at various speeds, with or without damping (to give more "thud"), rhythm fifths are a surprisingly diverse tool which occur in rock, metal, punk, new wave and grunge – heard in the music of everyone from Soundgarden to Devo. If you play any form of rock, you'll find a use for them sooner or later.

In **example 16** damp all the strings on beats 2 and 4. If you use your little finger to fret the higher of the two notes in each pair it will lie flat enough to stop most of the strings sounding when needed. To damp the lower note just let the string come off the fingerboard but keep your first finger on it. Notice the F5 occurs in bar 4 an octave lower than in bar 2.

Devo couldn't have made their quirky, jerky bizarro-punk without the help of the muted power chord (and the occasional open G, as demonstrated left in a rare moment *sans* flowerpot hat). For full-blast rock examples of the breed, look no further than Soundgarden's Seattle grunge-metal.

Fifths can be found in the same shape on all string pairs except 3 and 2. **Exercise 17** shows how U2's guitarist The Edge (pictured with vocalist Bono, right) might use a high 5th with an open G string, which is characteristic of his guitar playing and a significant factor of his band's sound in general.

Exercise 18 gives us a fifth with an open G string inside it. As you move the fifth the open G forms different relationships with the other notes, with a moody effect.

Fifths on 4 and 3 can be moved up and down in the key of E or E minor to combine with the top two open strings. Notice the

Green Day guitarist Billie Joe Armstrong offers plenty of great examples of how to use chunky, tight fifths and fourths to power compelling punk-pop tunes.

resonance in bar 1 of **exercise 19** where there are two Bs at the same pitch. As you move the fifths try to let the open strings ring for as long as possible.

Fifths also combine well with sixths. A sixth is produced when you move either the first finger down a fret or the little finger up a fret, as in **exercise 20**. This is an idea frequently explored by Paul Kossoff, the late guitarist of Free.

If you invert a fifth you get a fourth: A-E (a fifth) becomes E-A (a fourth). Fourths combine well with fifths. In **exercise 21** fourths appear in bar 4, but watch out for the way open bass strings add extra interest; this could be Eddie Cochran, Mick Ronson or Green Day – you choose!

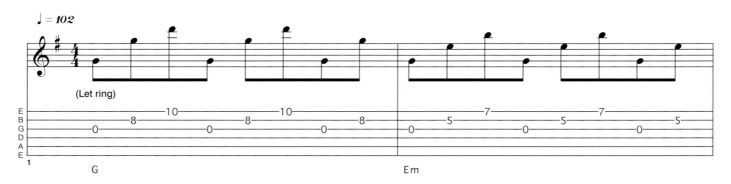

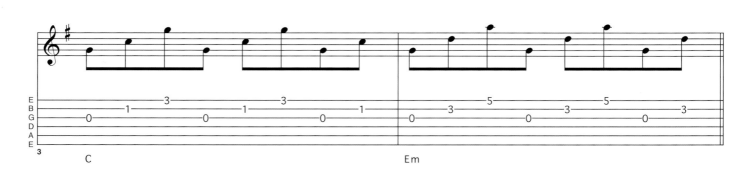

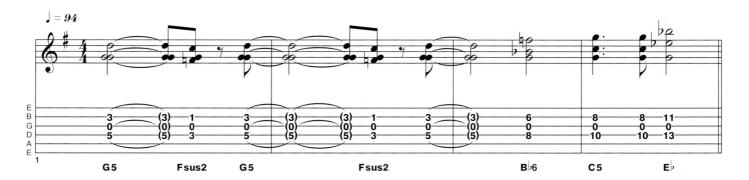

power chords

Exercise 17

Exercise 18

power chords

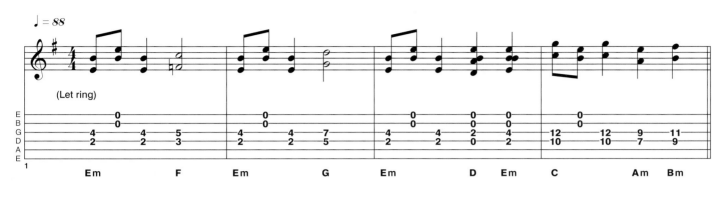

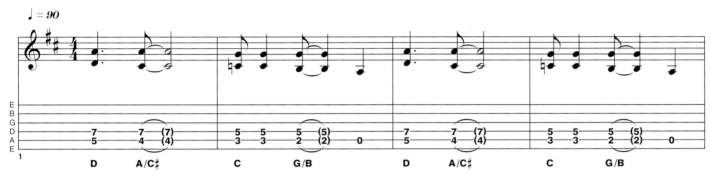

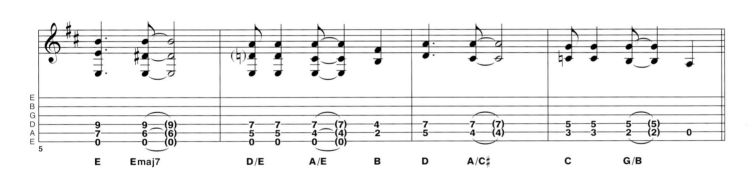

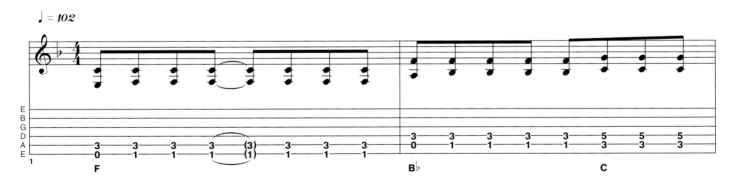

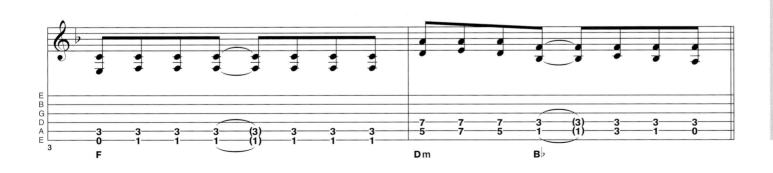

151

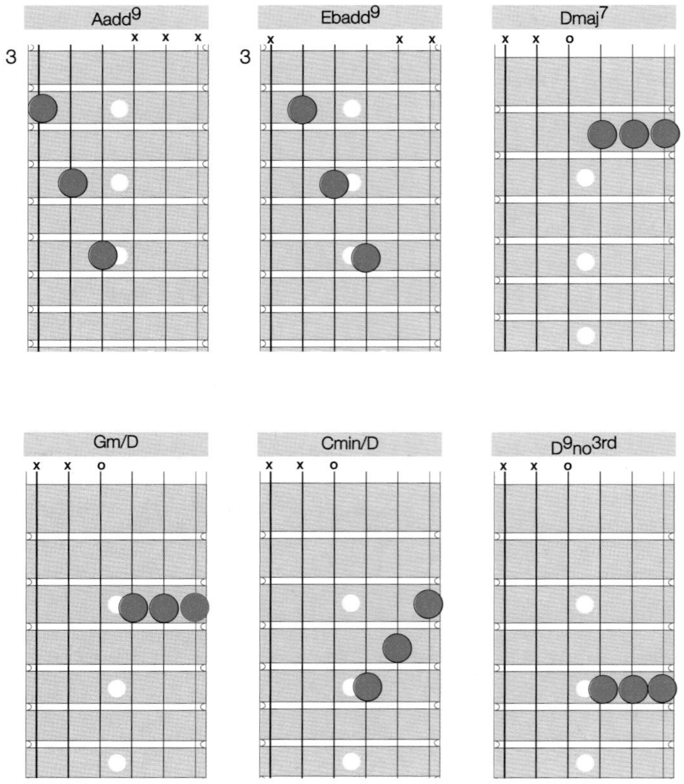

Chord diagrams (top):

Aadd9 · Ebadd9 · Dmaj7

Gm/D · Cmin/D · D9no3rd

The chord block diagrams above offer an added visual approach to some of the concepts explained on this page. Though the chords in these exercises are written out in the notation of each individual example, it might help some readers to try them in this familiar form before exploring the exercises fully.

If you take a fifth and "copy" its shape onto the next string an add9 figure is the result. The chords in **exercise 22** are excellent stretching practice and spice up a sequence of fifths. They are associated with Andy Summers, who used them on Police hits like *Message In A Bottle*. Another fine example of such usage is the song *Palace Of Dreams* by Dubh Chapter.

TRIADS

Though much guitar-playing uses full chords with 4, 5, or 6 strings played at a time, guitarists should not forget the humble triad. It only takes three notes to make a major or minor chord. This builds directly on the fifths we have just been working on, adding just one extra note to the chord – but it's a crucial addition, changing the mood of the chord dramatically between major and minor. Triads are easy to play and lend themselves to rhythm parts, fills, riffs and (as we will see later) even lead solos. (In the *Jazz* section, you will further see how the use of triads can allow any intermediate guitarist to play convincing jazz-style rhythm parts without immediately needing to learn complicated chord forms.)

The fretted notes of an ordinary D chord make a D triad. In **exercise 23** that shape is moved up the neck in a chordal riff. The open D string remains throughout, an example of a "pedal" note (a note which remains unchanged while chords or melody lines change around it). The major triads form different relationships with that D. Watch out for the open top string at the end of bars 1 and 2. This is a simple but effective approach used by Pete Townshend in many Who songs.

There are three major triad shapes on the top three strings. **Exercise 24** shows them over a D pedal. Compare this progression with strumming D, C and G in full chords. You can hear similar effects in Focus's *Sylvia* (intro) and Wishbone Ash's *Blowin' Free*.

There are also three minor triad shapes on the top three strings. In **exercise 25**, notice how the D string modifies their sound quite considerably at certain points, turning the F#m triad of bar 1 into a Dmaj7 chord in bar 2.

Exercise 22

Gadd9 · C#add9 · Aadd9 · Ebadd9

triads

Exercise 26 uses major and minor triad shapes as they occur on strings 2, 3, and 4. This time the pedal note is A. This could be played clean or with a little distortion. Mark Knopfler of Dire Straits is a guitarist whose idiosyncratic picking technique led him to use triads for songs like *Sultans Of Swing* and *Lady Writer*, as in **exercise 27**. It was easy for him to choose triads because he was plucking the strings with his thumb, index and middle finger only. This time there is no pedal note.

FOUR-NOTE CHORDS

Sometimes it's not necessary to include the lower strings. With a strong bass line it can be sufficient for the guitar to play chords on the top four strings only. The Spin Doctors' *Two Princes* is a fine example. A well-known pop and soul recording trick is to put a "stab" guitar chord on beats 2 and 4, as in **exercise 28**. A bright, clean tone is used and the chord is immediately followed by a rest. This chord will often sit with the snare drum. Listen to many '60s soul records, especially from Motown, where the high stab guitar was often played by Joe Messina on a Telecaster.

One of the tricks of professional song-arranging is to know when you don't need to change chord but can let the bass guitar do the work. The G-Gsus4 change stays the same throughout bars 1-3 in **exercise 29**, yet the chords written above change. To hear the effect either get someone to play the root notes of G,

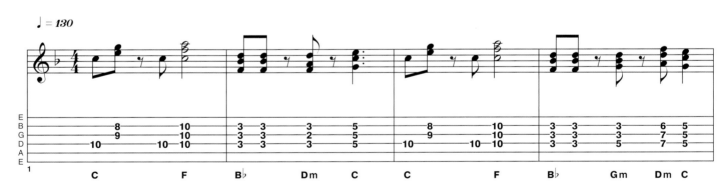

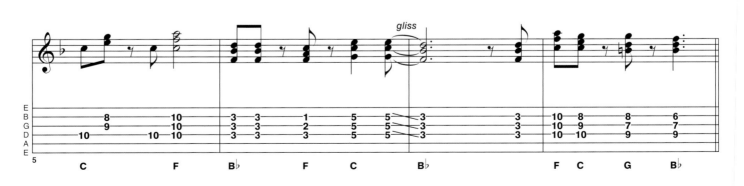

Exercise 26

Exercise 27

stab chords

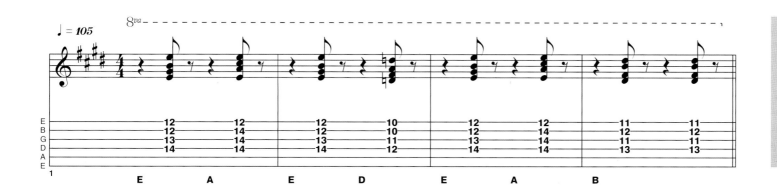

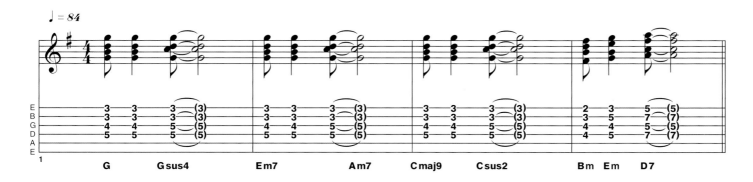

Em, Am and C, or play those chords on guitar or keyboard while you play the written part. The changing root notes change the harmonic value of the written G-Gsus4 change even though it stays the same – so it sounds different in each bar.

RIFFS

A riff is a memorable phrase of between one and four bars. In rock it often focuses much of the energy of the song, and is generally repeated as a central "hook" of the guitar part. Riffs occur in almost all guitar music from '50s rock'n'roll to contemporary nu-metal, and in other genres like reggae, soul, blues and folk; they're the building blocks of countless pop and rock guitar parts. Riffs are quick to write and learn, and great fun to play – and chances are you know a few good ones already. Prepare for some head banging!

Many riffs are derived from the same scales used for rock and blues lead. Bars 1 and 2 of **exercise 30** ascend E pentatonic minor. "Pentatonic" means five notes – in this case, E G A B D. Bars 3 and 4 provide the riff itself, using the lower notes of this scale.

Exercise 31

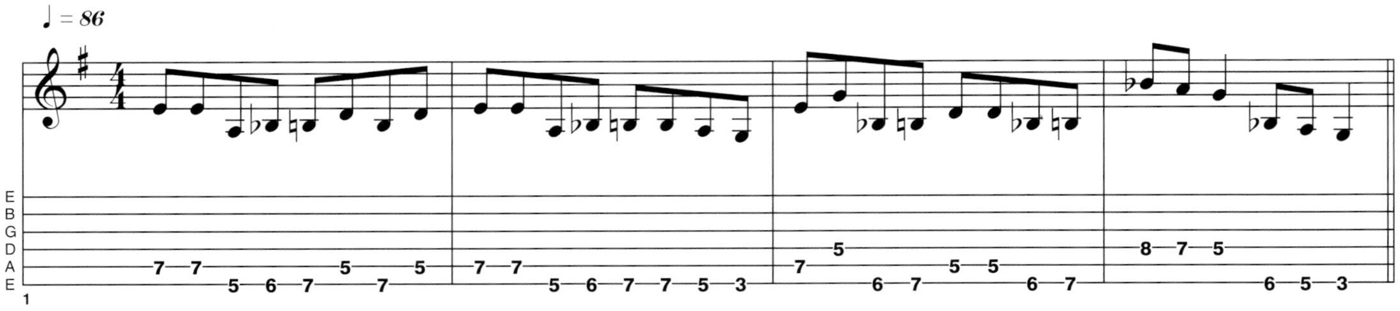

Exercise 32

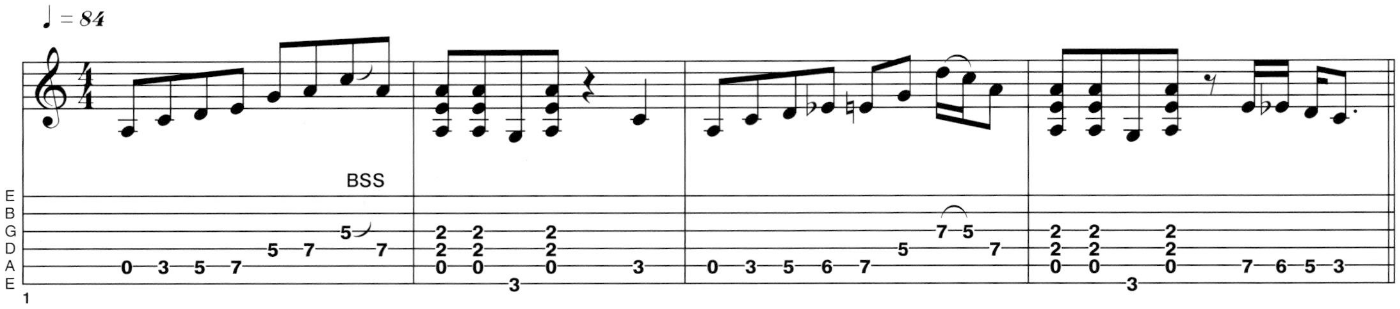

Exercise 33

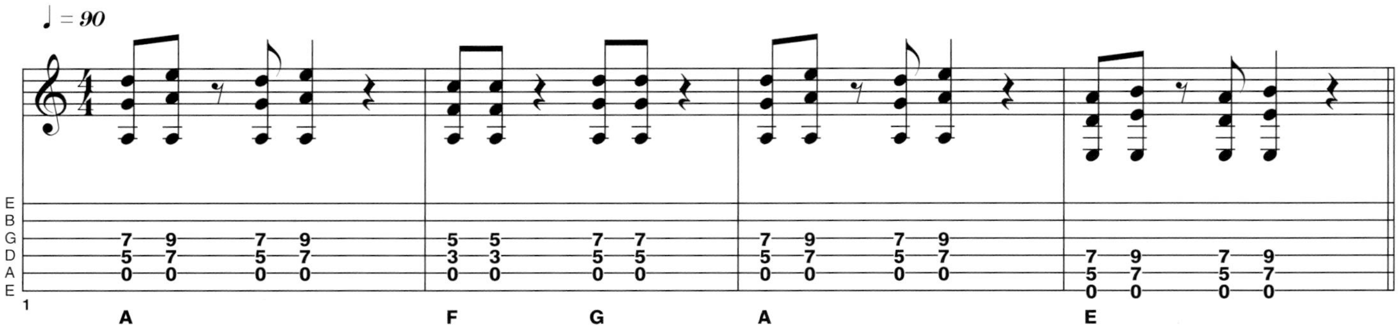

Exercise 34

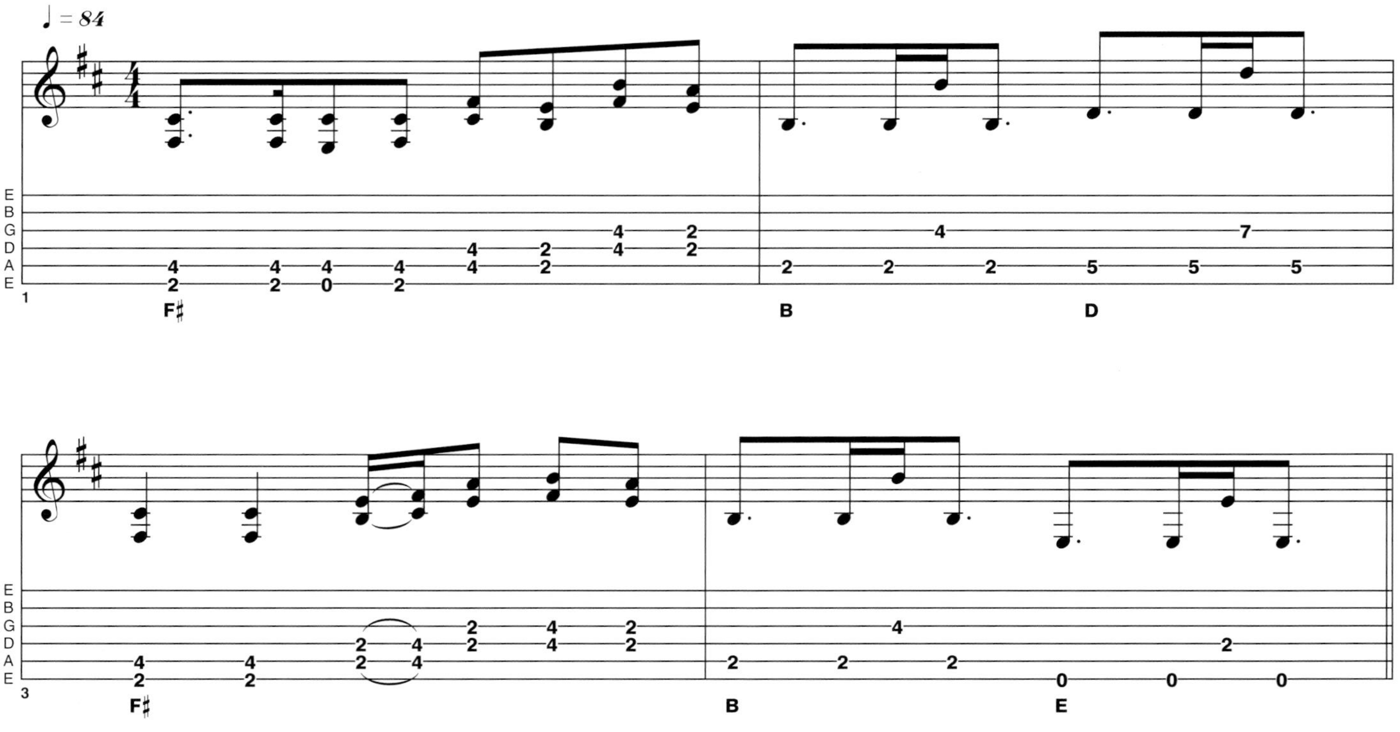

By adding one note to the previous pentatonic scale – Bb – we get the E blues scale, as utilized in **exercise 31**. This extra note is called a flattened 5th and is important for its dissonance: it sounds mean! This note allows a riff with creeping semi-tone movement.

E/E minor are popular keys for the guitar because the strings are naturally biased toward E. However, a pentatonic scale can be played from any note. Since the second lowest open string is A, A pentatonic minor (A C D E G) is also popular. **Exercise 32** is a riff on that scale. Watch out for the powerful A5 chord in bars 2 and 4, and the b5 (Eb) that appears in bars 3 and 4.

Fifths are popular for riffs. In **exercise 33** the fifths are strengthened by the open A and E strings. You can hear this in rock bands like Thin Lizzy and Iron Maiden.

Exercise 34 is a riff that uses fifths, fourths (the pairs of notes here with the same fret number) and octaves (bars 2 and 4). The riff sequence in **exercise 35** uses fourths. Fourths have their own flavor; they're less stable than fifths because the root note is no longer the lower of the two. Ritchie Blackmore used fourths for riffs on many Deep Purple and Rainbow tracks.

Transferred to the top two strings, as in **exercise 36**, fourths become less heavy rock and more new wave. Their slightly "oriental" colour was exploited by Television on their masterpiece *Marquee Moon*, and on the intro to Wings' *Band On The Run*.

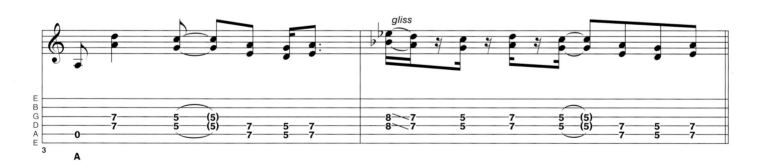

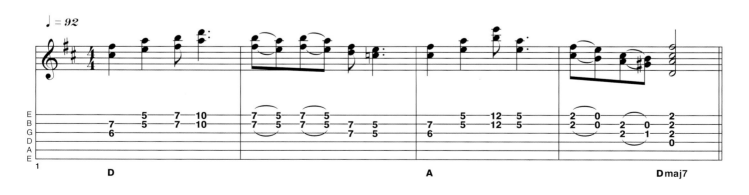

riffs

Bands like Led Zeppelin have forged memorable rock songs from riffs built on octaves, not unlike those in **exercise 37**. These types of riff are especially effective when the guitar and bass are together on the riff. Octave riffs can also make a good accompaniment during a verse structure, as in **exercise 38**. Bars 1-4 feature a basic figure of an octave that falls to the b7 and then the 5th. In bars 5-8 a variation introduces the b5 note previously featured. Here, it's the C# in bars 5 and 6.

Riffs can use single notes over a pedal note, as in **exercise 39**. The pedal note is supplied by an open string. Here over D is a scale known as the "mixolydian mode." You can read more about this mode in the Scales section. It differs from the D major scale (D E F# G A B C#) merely in having the 7th note flattened to C. This effect is featured on The Cult's *She Sells Sanctuary*

and R.E.M.'s *Green Grow The Rushes*.

Exercise 40 is a similar pedal riff, this time using A and having two notes at a time above it. Rock music favors the sus4 chord because of its tension (great for building drama) and its neutrality. Like fifths and fourths, the suspended fourth chord, explored in **exercise 41**, is neither major nor minor. This riff takes a triadic form and moves it down through small changes. Sus4 chords feature strongly in the Who's *Pinball Wizard*, T.Rex's *Cadillac*, Argent's *Hold Your Head Up*, and John Lennon's *Happy Xmas (War Is Over)*.

The bends in **exercise 42** – two strings bent together – were established in rock guitar by Chuck Berry and have been used by many other players ever since. They are very effective at faster tempos, as in Motorhead's *Ace Of Spades*.

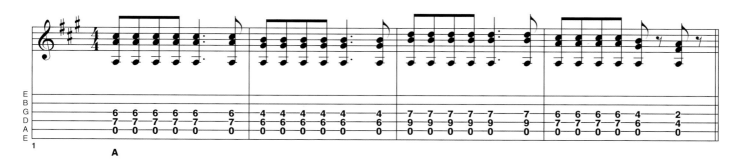

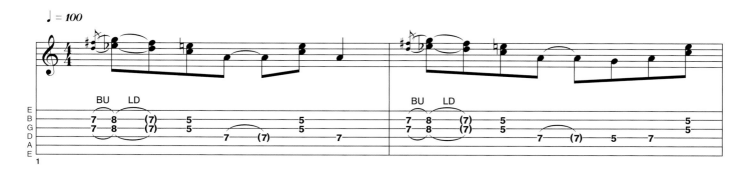

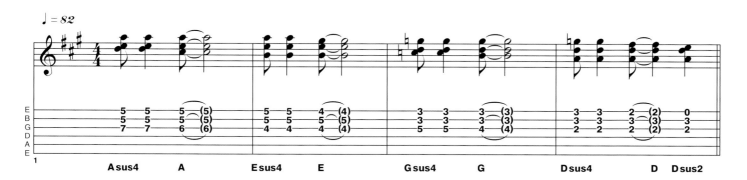

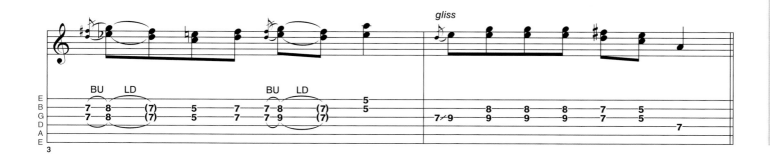

No look at riffs would be complete without the 1-3-5-6 figure, so called after the notes of the scale and explored here in **exercise 43**, which is closely related to the rock'n'roll rhythm parts you played in exercises 1-4.

Exercise 44 is a slightly decorated version. You can hear something similar on Roy Orbison's *Pretty Woman*, though in that song the riff stays on E.

The term "chromatic" refers to the use of extra notes that do not belong to the key, as employed in **exercise 45**. Chromatic riffs have an element of surprise about them. They can sound "jazzy" – as in Pink Floyd's *Money* or toward the end of Hendrix's *Hey Joe* – or sinister, as in Led Zep's *Dazed And Confused*. Look for a fingering that will make use of all your fretting fingers.

USING INTERVALS

Already we've played exercises that use significant intervals. In a major scale the intervals are major second (C-D), major third (C-E), perfect fourth (C-F), perfect fifth (C-G), major sixth (C-A), major seventh (C-B) and perfect octave (C-C). We have seen how fourths and fifths are used in rhythms and riffs. Seconds and sevenths can be discounted because they are not harmonious enough for consecutive playing, so let's move on to octaves.

One use of octaves is to thicken a melody or melodic phrase, as Hendrix did in *Third Stone From The Sun*. For **exercise 46** use a pick and your middle finger, or damp any strings in between and just use a pick. Octaves lend themselves to sliding up or down.

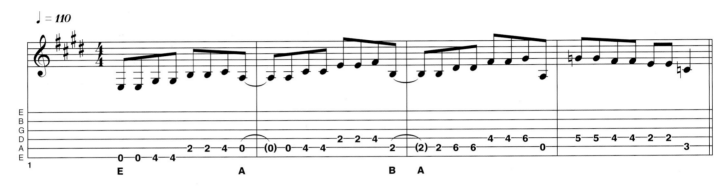

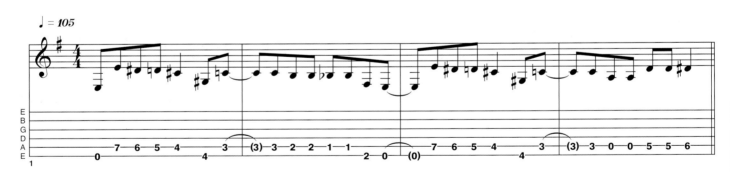

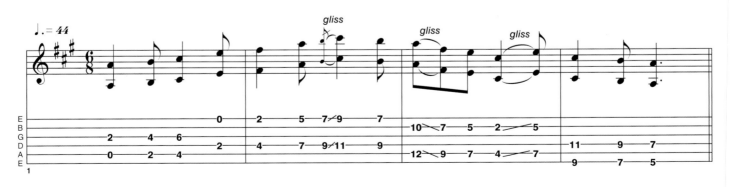

Jimi Hendrix remains a comprehensive single source of inspiration in a wide range of playing styles and techniques. From his jazzy use of chromatic notes to his deft approach to octave riffs, he is still a guitarist very much worth tapping into.

Exercise 47 gives you a chance to practise a 16th-note strum of "damped" octaves. Mute all four of the other strings with your fretting hand, then strum up and down in groups of four with the first of each group accented. When you get comfortable with this you can try cutting out some of the fretted 16ths. By muting more of them in the bar you can generate funk rhythms. There is a hint of this in the last bar.

Here's more muting practice for octave riffs in **exercise 48** – but listen for the altered intervals in the last bar.

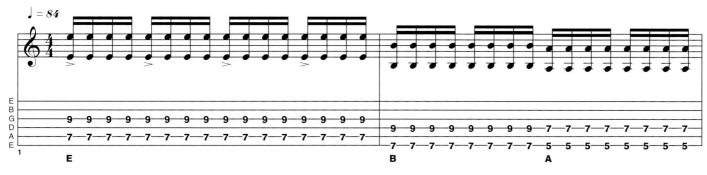

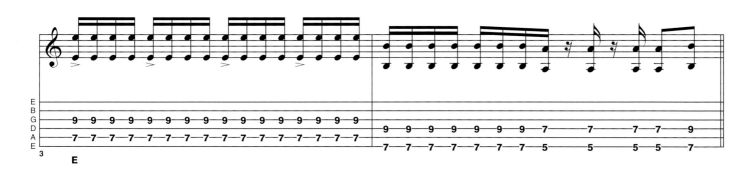

Octaves are crucial to the sound of a 12-string guitar. But what if you don't own a 12-string? Well, **exercise 49** shows a way of generating a 12-string effect on a six-string. It requires some nimble finger-work in both hands but it's a valuable technique, and a great skill builder in itself. Use a pick and a finger and let strings ring as long as you can.

THIRDS AND SIXTHS

The only useful intervals we haven't touched on yet are thirds and sixths. Both have major and minor forms. A major third is 2 tones (C-E); a minor third is 1½ (C-Eb). A major sixth is 4½ (C-A); a minor sixth is 4 (C-Ab).

Exercise 50 shows a sequence of thirds in D major on the top two strings. All the notes on the top string should be fingered with the 1st finger; those underneath are either the 2nd or the 3rd. The 1st finger acts as a guide when you shift position. The key note for the sequence is on the 2nd string at the starting position. If you want to transpose this to another major key simply locate the new key note on the 2nd string and play the same sequence from there.

Exercise 51 is the equivalent sequence in A major on the 2nd and 3rd strings. The guide finger is the 2nd which plays all the notes on the lower string; the 2nd string notes are either 1st or 2nd finger. If this were played from the 7th fret you would have

the same notes as Ex.50.

Thirds have a sweetening effect, and can be used for guitar fills and lead solos. Van Morrison's *Brown-Eyed Girl* and The Smiths' *This Charming Man* use them. They can be played either simultaneously or one after the other, as **exercise 52** shows.

Remember: the harmonic value of notes depends on the underlying harmony. Change the harmony and you effectively change the notes even if they stay still. **Exercise 53** has a two-bar phrase in 3rds. Each time the chord changes it will sound different. Try continuing this riff through another four bars – two bars each against the underlying chords F and G – to hear this effect even further.

Exercise 54 is a sequence of sixths in G major on the 1st and 3rd strings. All the notes on the 3rd string should be fingered with the 2nd finger; those above are either the 1st or the 3rd. The key note for the sequence is on the 1st string at the starting position. To transpose this to another major key simply find the new key note on the 1st string and play the same sequence from there.

Exercise 55 is the equivalent sequence in D major on the 2nd and 4th strings. The guide finger is the 2nd which plays all the notes on the lower string; the 2nd string notes are either 1st or 3rd finger. If this were played from the 8th fret you would have the same notes as Ex.54.

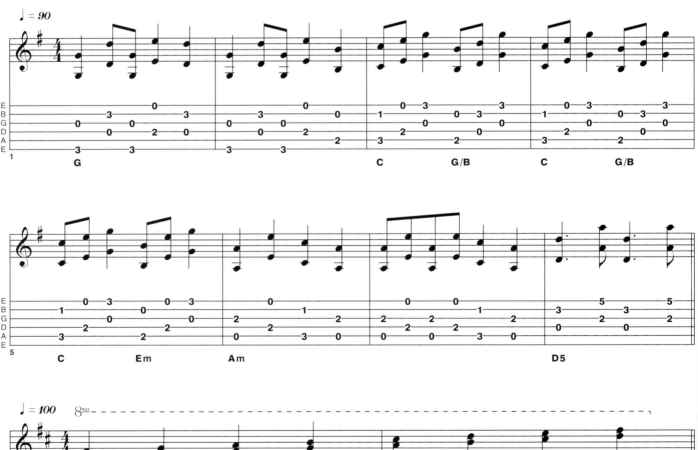

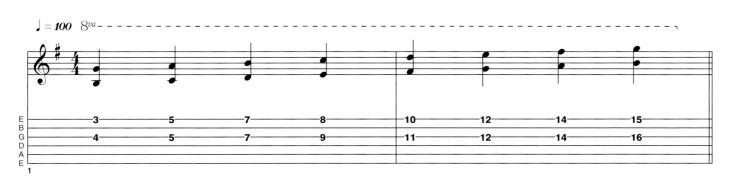

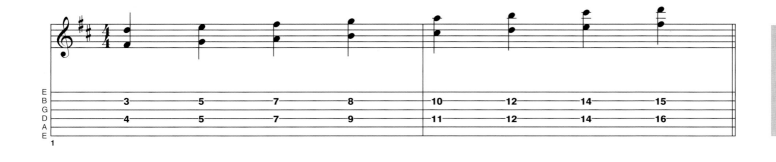

Exercise 51

Exercise 52

Exercise 53

Exercise 54

Exercise 55

Sixths are also used for fills and lead solos, though they don't sound as sweet as thirds. Soul guitarist Steve Cropper is renowned for his use of sixths on many '60s recordings like *Soul Man* and *Dock Of The Bay*. In **exercise 56** the addition of a couple of chromatic sixths emulate Cropper's slinky feel. This is yet another technique that can be simple to master, but has an extremely effective, melodic feel with a little extra bluesy groove to it too – and is usually yields positive results when employed tastefully.

Sometimes in a riff sixths make a refreshing change from fifths or fourths. In **exercise 57** the D G F D change could have been done with either – but here it is in sixths, combined with a D pentatonic minor single-note phrase.

Exercise 58 gives us a look at some thirds combined with an open G string.

Clever choice of key makes it possible to put the open B string in the middle of a run of sixths in **exercise 59**. Taking B as the key note, it is only necessary to find a run of sixths in B major. Andy Summers used a similar technique in E minor in The Police's *Bring On The Night*, where sixths in E minor straddle the open G string (the middle note of an E minor chord).

Learn each of these approaches to sixths, then see if you can make up a few in these keys and others. Use them to spice up your riffs and tunes where appropriate.

THE "JANGLE" STYLE

The last two exercises are reminiscent of a popular style which has become known as "jangle." It is associated with the 12-string sound of The Byrds' Roger McGuinn, Peter Buck's playing with R.E.M. in the '80s, Johnny Marr's work with The Smiths, and many "indie" bands of the '90s. The La's *There She Goes* is a superb example.

Jangle defines a clean, shimmery, ringing guitar texture, sometimes aided by sustaining effects like compression, chorus, echo and reverb. It also involves a certain approach to chord shapes and picking.

Jangle guitar requires open strings to ring out between changes, while chords are turned into arpeggios, the strings picked one at a time, as typified by **exercise 60**. The shapes can be simple but the end result pleasing to the ear and extremely effective in the right context.

In the early playing of Peter Buck there is often a quick picking of the chord to give drive and motion to otherwise fairly simple progressions, and that's the way to approach **exercise 61**. Make good use of up and down pick strokes as you weave among the strings. Notice in bar 3 the "harp" effect of having three notes each a tone apart all sounding at once. Hear Buck's jangle in songs such as *Radio Free Europe* from the album *Murmur* and *Good Advices* from *Fables Of The Reconstruction*.

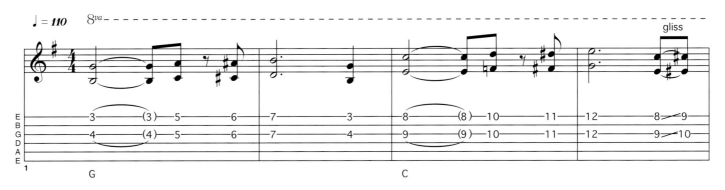

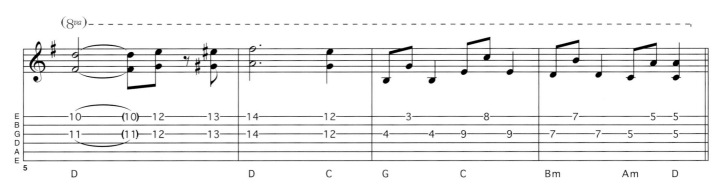

sixths

Exercise 56

Exercise 57

164

jangle

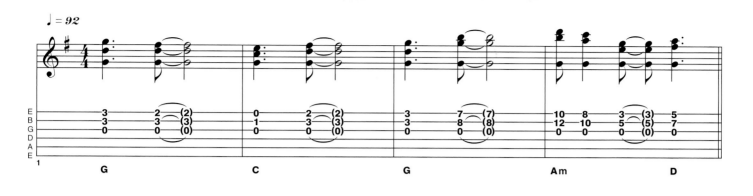

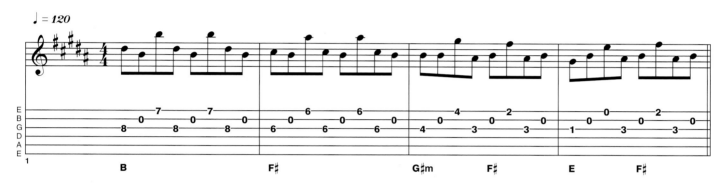

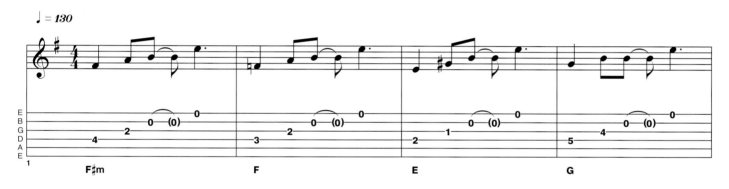

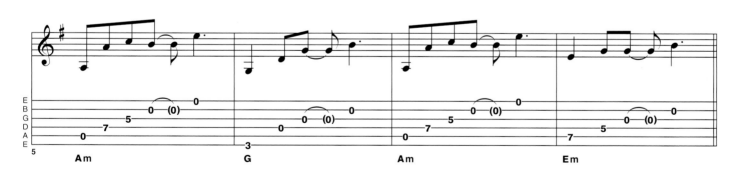

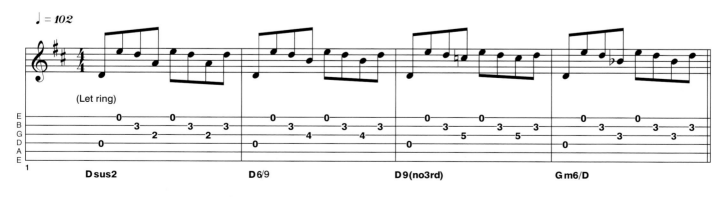

Exercise 62 demonstrates another of those "weaving" picking patterns, with a harp effect in bar 4. Notice the introduction of the open E into the D chord in bars 1 and 2, and the hollow ring of the Asus2 in bar 7. Take care that all the notes in bar 6 ring as long as they can for the full effect.

In **exercise 63** chord shapes are devised away from first position so that open strings can combine with higher fretted notes. Play this with distortion and hear why such arpeggio effects need a clean tone!

ARPEGGIOS

The jangle style plays the notes of a chord one after the other to generate an "arpeggio." Arpeggios are found elsewhere in rock and pop guitar. They are crucial in songs such as Cream's *Badge*, The Beatles' *Here Comes The Sun* and *I Want You*, Bebop Deluxe's *Maid In Heaven* and The Jam's *When You're Young*.

The figures in **exercise 64** exploit the slightly murky tone of low thirds on the guitar. Bryan Adams's *Run To You* and Nirvana's *Come As You Are* do likewise. In **exercise 65** most of the arpeggios are based on a triad, but watch for the C#m7 in bar 7. In **exercise 66** a common sequence moving from C down to G is transformed by the use of arpeggios. This might make a suitable conclusion to a chorus or a whole song.

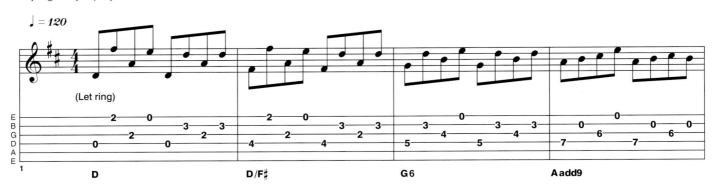

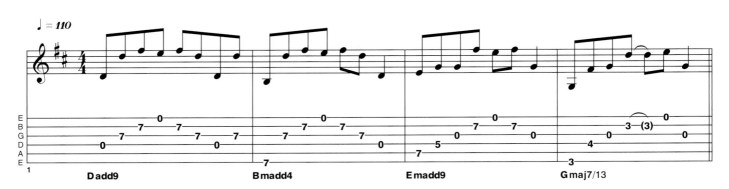

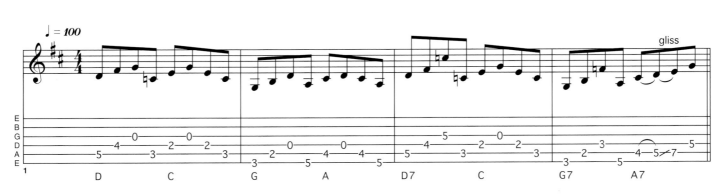

jangle

Exercise 62

Exercise 63

Exercise 64

arpeggios

Arpeggios figure into the guitar parts of songs by everyone from Bryan Adams (left) to The Beatles, Bebop Deluxe to The Jam. More than just a basic 'folky' technique for strumming slower tunes, they run the gamut from sweet and poppy to dark and moody.
Investigate *Here Comes The Sun* for the former, and *Run To You* or *Come As You Are* for the latter.

Exercise 63 features some accompanying chords which might outwardly appear rather complex, but are really fairly simple to play thanks to the use of open strings to double up tones within them for a ringing, jangly feel. The diagrams shown right give a quick visual reference to three of these which you might find useful elsewhere in your playing.

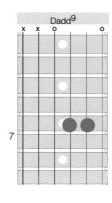

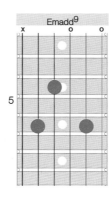

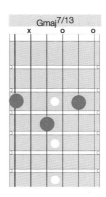

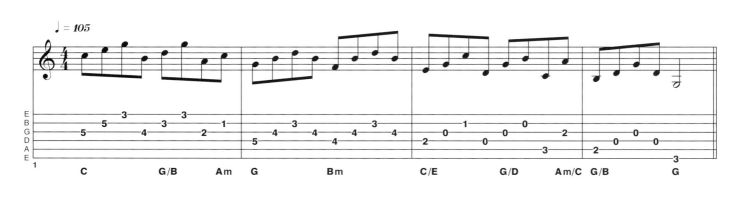

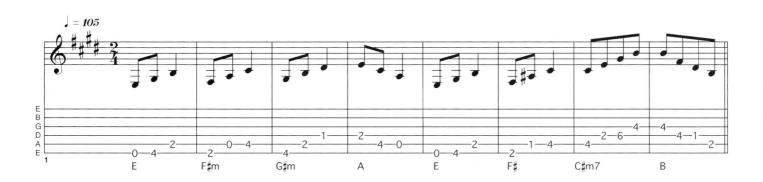

Arpeggios can also be included in a guitar solo. Many of the lead solos in Dire Straits' *Brothers In Arms* begin with a rising arpeggio. The triad in bar 4 of **exercise 67** is played with a "rake": the notes are not struck altogether but fractionally one after the other, either by pushing the pick through the strings, or "rolling" the notes with the pick and two fingers.

LEAD GUITAR

Playing lead guitar competently is a matter of learning a small number of scales and scale patterns, mastering the art of bending and fretting-hand techniques like vibrato, hammering-on, pulling-off, and slides; and gradually finding out which notes work over any given chord sequence.

BENDS

Each bar in **exercise 68** features one of the four commonest bends as measured by ascent in pitch. (Players do occasionally bend further than 1½ tones – but string breakage is always a risk!) In each bar you first play the target note by fretting it; then you bend the previous note up. This "primes" your ear each time so you can listen for when you're in tune. The exception is the final quarter-tone bend which is actually a fraction lower than the C# you play on the 1st beat. In Ex.68 the bends are all done with

the 3rd finger, with the 1st and 2nd on the same string behind it. This means you can push with all three. Try also having your thumb on the top edge of the neck to get more grip.

Welcome to the unison bend. There are some marvellous unison bends toward the end of *Stairway To Heaven*. The higher note (1st finger) stays still. The lower note (3rd finger, 2nd supporting) is bent up until its pitch is the same as the higher. In **exercise 69** the fingers are closer together when you move down a string in bars 2 and 4. **Exercise 70** is a group of ascending unison bends in action. Play them right and the higher they go the more they take on a wailing, vocal quality.

Exercise 71 displays the "pre-bend." This is so-called because you bend the string up before you strike it, then lower it. The listener gets used to hearing notes in a solo bent up, but does not expect to hear a note drop in this manner. The catch is that you have to guess how far to bend to get the starting note.

Exercise 72 contains two essential bend ideas that will give you full-on rock or a country twang depending how you use them. Bend with the 3rd finger as you hit the two notes together. The higher note is held down by the little finger. Notice the note F (6th fret, 2nd string) in bar 2. That note, two frets back from the bend, tells you which chord this phrase fits over. The equivalent is the 5th fret C in bar 3 for the lower bend.

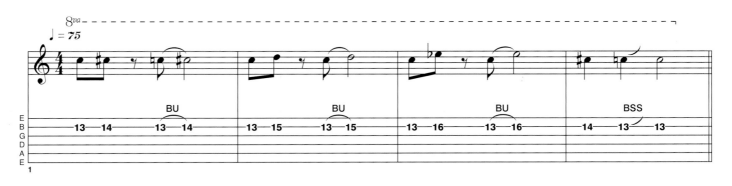

Exercise 73 combines the two individual figures of Ex.72 into one to give a single bend with two notes above it that will generate either a major or a minor chord depending on how far you push the bend. Hold the top two notes down with a little finger barre, and bend with the 3rd finger with 1st and 2nd supporting behind it. You can also play this progression hitting all the notes at once for a slightly different feel. The note on the top string is your root note. Select the root note for the chord you want on the top string, then bend 1/2 or 1 tone to produce the minor or major chord on that note.

It is possible to push a bend up a semitone at a time in order to get a sequence of notes, as in **exercise 74**. The B in bar 2 is pushed up first to C, then C#, then D, after which the E is supplied by the 12th fret on the top string. In bar 3 the idea is used in reverse. The bent E is dropped first a semitone from F# to F and then down to E. You'll see that a similar technique occurs again in bar 5.

Exercise 75 is an A pentatonic minor scale pattern that starts on the 6th string and moves through three octaves to reach A at the 17th fret on the top E.

Part of the same scale can be re-fingered as a two-octave pattern starting on the 5th string, as **exercise 76** demonstrates. This exercise uses triplets – a group of three quavers played on the beat.

Mark Knopfler, above, uses two fingers and thumb to execute his fluid, dexterous lead style – with cascades aplenty.

THE "CASCADE"

In order to make a scale pattern last longer when playing quickly, guitarists sometimes use a technique which we can dub the "cascade." The idea is to play down a few notes and then go back up one or two less. **Exercise 77** is a triplet cascade down the A pentatonic minor scale. You'll notice right away how the cascade helps to give the impression that you're not just running down a scale, but playing a more considered lead line. **Exercise 78** is an 8th note cascade down the same scale. In bar 2 the b5 (Eb) is added to make the A blues scale. Bar 3 is the same cascade idea starting one string lower than bar 1. In bar 4 the same b5 occurs but this time it is bent rather than fretted. Notice the difference in tone.

Exercise 73

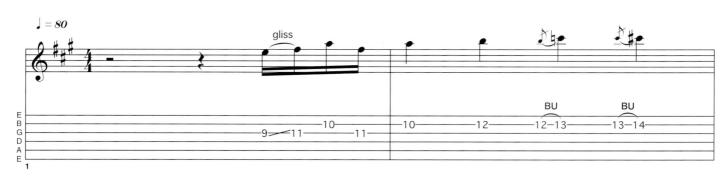

Exercise 74

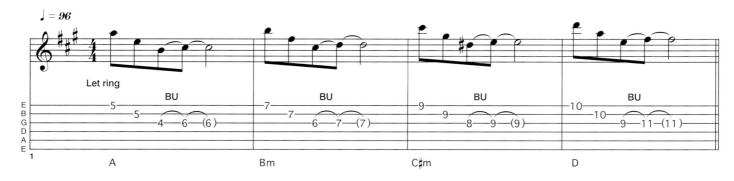

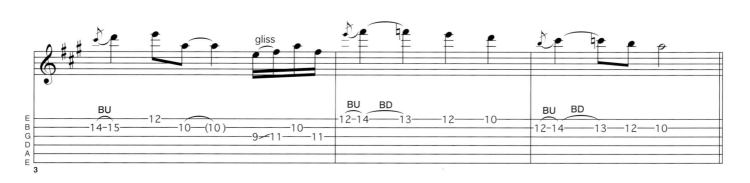

bends

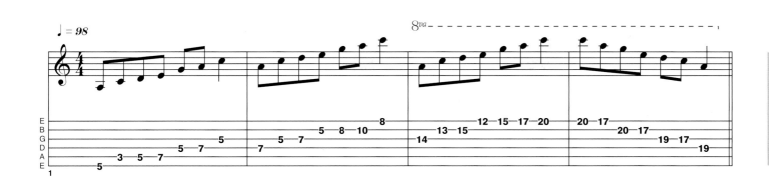

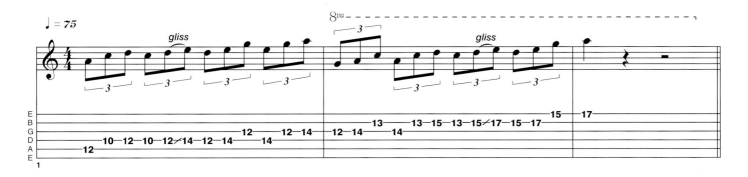

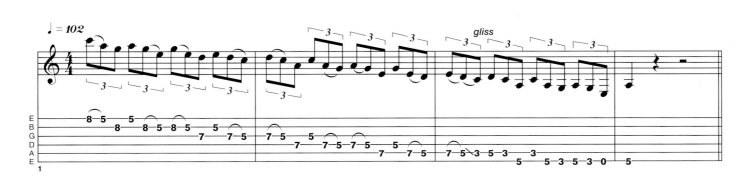

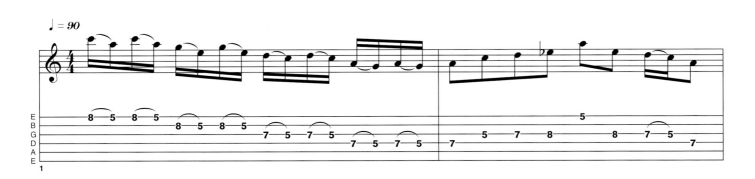

Exercise 79

Exercise 80

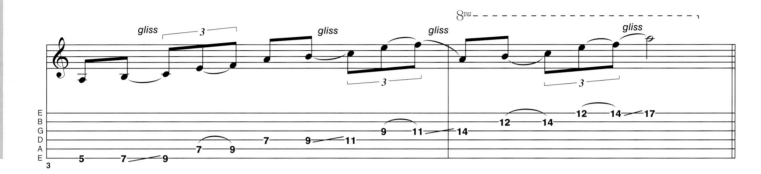

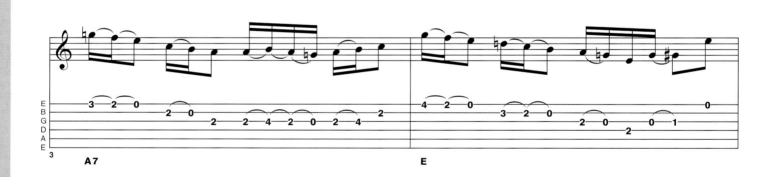

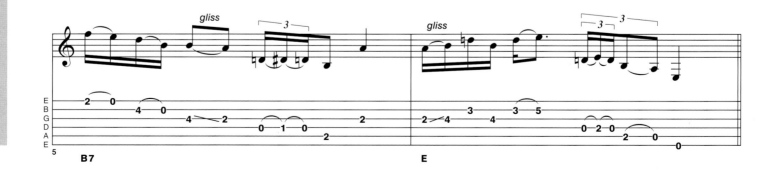

repeat licks

Exercise 79 is a three-octave E blues scale based on the E pentatonic major (E F# G# B C#) but with the addition of a b3, in this case G. This scale has an upbeat feel and is found in lead guitar solos that derive from '50s rock'n'roll.

Apart from string-bending, another decoration used by lead players is the hammer-on/pull-off, seen here in **exercise 80**, where notes are created by the fretting hand. This is based on a six-bar blues pattern. The scale is E Mixolydian (E F# G# A B C D) but with the b3 G also appearing.

REPEAT LICKS

Like the cascade, the repeat lick is a way of getting more from a small group of notes. The idea is to make a short phrase and repeat it for several bars. The one in **exercise 81** uses several that are based on a triad. Mark Knopfler used this idea very effectively at the close of *Sultans Of Swing*. In the right place, as in his energetic solo, these can sound more dynamic and driving than merely repetitive.

The E pentatonic lick in **exercise 82** is possibly the most famous of them all. Keep your 1st finger fretting the top two strings at the 12th fret throughout. Bend the 3rd string with your 2nd finger; do the 15-12 pull-off with your 3rd. Notice that the phrase will sound different with a C chord behind it contrasted with the E.

Mark Knopfler's lead work, especially in the early days of Dire Straits, makes an excellent example of how simple ideas and the careful use of repetition can sound effective and compelling when played with drive, energy and attitude.

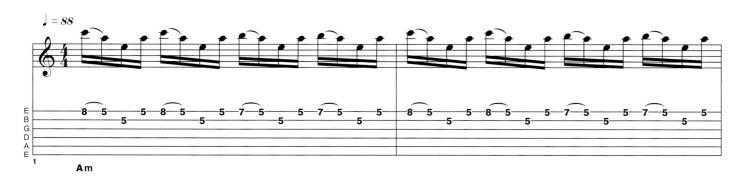

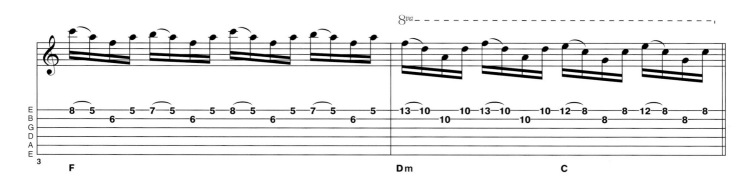

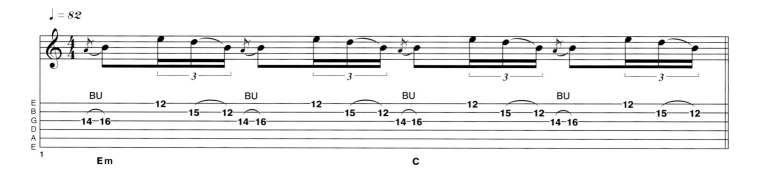

Exercise 83 is a five-note repeat lick that is based on A dorian (A B C D E F# G). Notice the shift up a minor 3rd – a favorite trick of Jimmy Page.

Once you've mastered Ex.83, try squeezing one more note onto the beat to get six – *voila*, **exercise 84**!

THE MODES

The pentatonic patterns are the most used by rock guitarists. A brief look at the group of scales known as the modes, however, will suggest some extra "color." Whether you can use these in a solo will partly depend on the chords over which you're playing.

The Aeolian mode, **exercise 85**, is also known as the natural minor scale. In A it would be A B C D E F G. Listen for the expressive sadness of the 2nd and 6th of this scale (B and F).

Contrast Ex.85 with the non-modal harmonic minor scale in **exercise 86**, where the 7th note is raised a semitone. Rock guitarists sometimes exploit the last four notes of this scale – E F G# A – to get an "Eastern" sound. The Dorian mode, **exercise 87**, can be thought of as the natural minor with a sharpened 6th: A B C D E F# G. It is favored by Santana in much of his lead playing. **Exercise 88** shows the Phrygian mode, which can be thought of as a natural minor with a b2: A Bb C D E F G. Many players consider it to have a Spanish sound.

The Aeolian, Dorian and Phrygian are all minor modes. There are three major modes. The Ionian is our major scale (in G: G A B C D E F# G). The Mixolydian is a major scale with a b7: G A B C D E F G. This is very common in pop and rock. **Exercise 89** shows it in various positions to fit the chord progression.

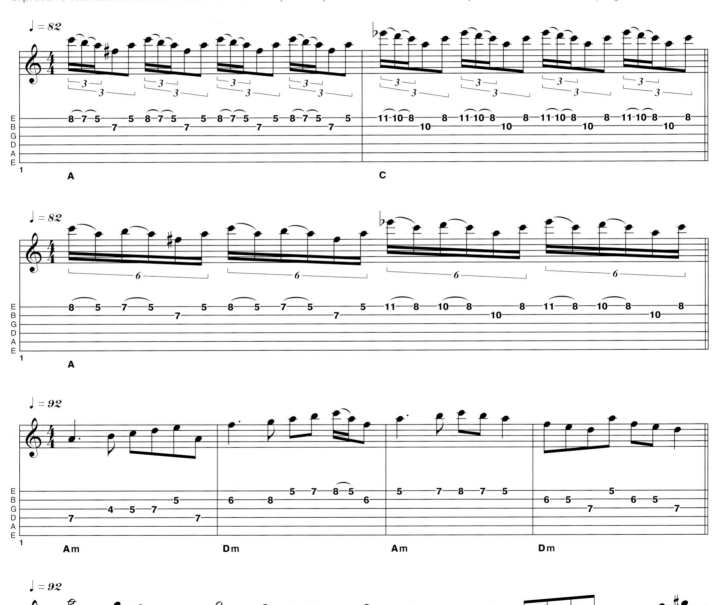

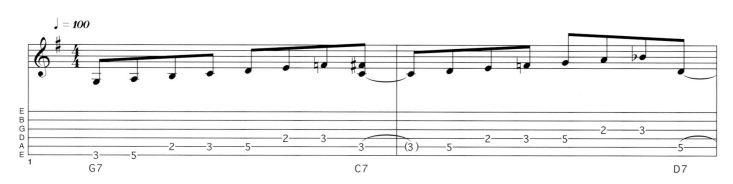

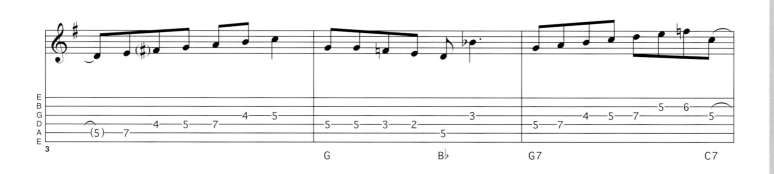

More than just a rock legend, **Jimmy Page is also a great blender of styles, particularly in his classic work with Led Zeppelin. A great British blues-rocker, his playing also incorporates Eastern scales, traditional folk influences, and hard rock dynamics with seamless, fluid results. In addition to his guitar skills, Page's vast experience as a session musician before joining Zep meant he was also a deft arranger and producer right from the early years of the band.**

The Lydian mode, **exercise 90**, is the major scale with a raised 4th: G A B C# D E F# G. The raised 4th gives this mode an edgy, unsettling quality.

To finish, try these two exercises chock-full of well-used bends. First, **exercise 91** is based around the 10th fret and lends itself to playing in D and A. Listen for the bluesy sound of the half bends; then **exercise 92** gives you some classic bends on 12th and 15th fret pentatonic shapes.

When you are working out a solo always check the chords over which you're playing. If the progression is in a single key with no odd chords a single scale will usually work all the way through. Any unusual chords may need an additional scale or perhaps just the adjustment of one note.

Exercise 90

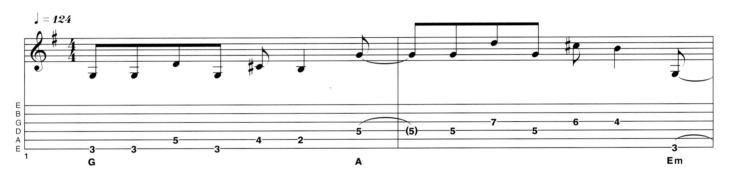

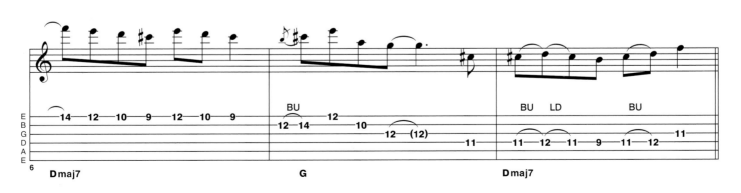

modes

You could do a lot worse than immerse yourself in Led Zeppelin for fine examples of great rock guitar playing, songwriting, arrangement and so on. *Led Zeppelin III*, released in 1970, contains such gems as *Immigrant Song*, *Gallows Pole* and *Braun-Y-Aur Stomp*, while the 1975 double album *Physical Graffiti* offers *Houses Of The Holy*, *Kashmir*, *Black Country Woman* and others.

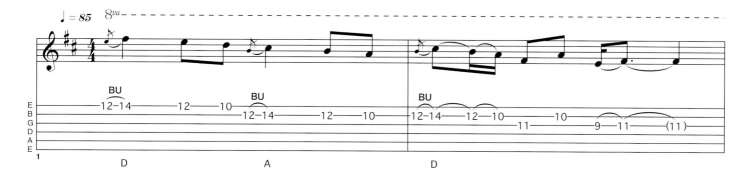
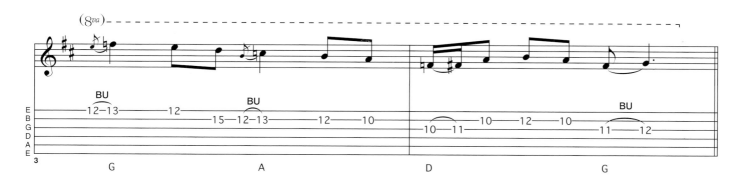

Exercise 91

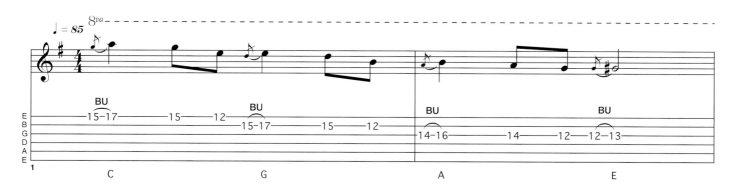

Exercise 92

3

PLAYING THE BLUES

origins of the blues

Blues music in its various forms has influenced many strands of popular music and guitar playing since the 1950s. The blues originated as an acoustic folk music through which African Americans expressed the misfortunes of a disenfranchised people, as well as perennial human themes of frustration, love, sex and loss. Perhaps the ultimate voice for this style was Robert Johnson in the 1930s, though other early blues giants include Elmore James, T-Bone Walker, Son House, and Charley Patton. ● **RIKKY ROOKSBY**

The migration of many African-Americans from the rural south to cities further to the north eventually led to the development of an electric, urban-based blues, most famously in Chicago. During the '50s and early '60s performers such as Muddy Waters, Willie Dixon, Albert King, Buddy Guy, B.B. King, Albert Collins, Otis Rush, Hubert Sumlin, and John Lee Hooker, made their mark with blues played on an electric guitar.

Their sound and songs were emulated in the early to mid-'60s by a younger generation of singers and guitarists attracted to the earthy directness of blues, finding in it a raw energy and authenticity of experience which much pop and rock music lacked. This was especially true in the U.K., where a blues boom occurred. Artists such as the Rolling Stones, Eric Clapton, John Mayall, the Animals, the Yardbirds, Peter Green's Fleetwood Mac, Cream, and Free all either covered blues songs or wrote music in the same vein. In the U.S. a similar phenomenon brought forward talents such as Mike Bloomfield and Johnny Winter. It was highly significant that the most high-profile rock guitarist of the '60s, Jimi Hendrix, played some blues and wrote several classic blues-rock tracks, such as *Red House, Voodoo Chile* and *Hear My Train A-Comin'*.

Despite charges of plagiarism and their music being only a pale imitation of the real thing, it is now evident that the white musicians' interest in blues boosted the record sales and concert-drawing power of the older generation of bluesmen, enabling the latter to enjoy career success and longevity beyond their former expectations. For example, whatever critics think about the way Led Zeppelin played the blues on their 1969 debut album, there can be no doubt that that album (and others like it) acted as a door into the blues for a vast number of listeners. The effects of this new interest panned out through the '70s and '80s, with the result that the blues has taken its place in the broader range of commercial music styles, its legacy carried on by newer talents such as Stevie Ray Vaughan, Walter Trout, Jeff Healey, Robert Cray, Robben Ford and Bonnie Raitt.

Even if it is not your intention to play blues exclusively you will find that many of the ideas in this section can be used in rock and other genres. If you are just beginning to learn lead guitar the 12-bar blues format is a good place to start. This is because the blues style is comparatively "forgiving" once you know a few basic scales and how to use them. Simplicity and feeling are the hallmarks of much blues music, and you don't have to be a virtuoso to express yourself well as a blues guitarist.

At the heart of blues music is a form and a harmony that are easily grasped. Most blues is based on the 12-bar structure. Within those 12 bars there are three chords – chords I, IV and V of whatever key you are in. If the key is E major (the most common blues key on guitar) the chords are E, A and B. To get the distinctive blues sound these chords are often found in the extended form known in theory as "dominant sevenths": E7, A7 and B7. In standard harmony, the dominant seventh is a chord that can only occur naturally on the fifth (the dominant) note of the scale. So in E major that would be B7. Strictly speaking the chords E7 and A7 are not properly part of E major at all. This breaking of the rules, however, by allowing these three chords to be played in the same key, is part of what makes blues sound the way it does.

Most blues lead guitar is based on the pentatonic scale in major and minor forms. The clash between the pentatonic minor scale and the harmony based on the key's major scale creates the blues sound. Blues lead guitar is exceptionally repetitious. In the course of an average-length solo many players will play the same ideas many times over. This is another reason why this is a relatively easy lead style to grasp.

In this section we will begin by looking at rhythm playing and chords aspects of blues guitar, and then progress to the scales and licks that feature in a lot of blues playing to help you begin to improvise. Remember that whatever key the examples occur in, where there are no open strings you will be able to transpose phrases and licks into different keys simply by moving them up or down the fretboard.

RHYTHM

We'll begin with a single-note blues idea. **Exercise 1** has the distinctive "swinging" rhythm so often heard in blues. In 4/4 time each beat can be divided into two 8th notes, or four 16th notes, and so on. The 4/4 bar of 8th notes – counted as "one-and two-and three-and four-and" – is common in rock. In blues it is more usual to divide the beat into three 8th notes. Two 8th notes are thus played as if the first was a 1/4 note and the second an 8th note, giving the rhythm "one-and-uh two-and-uh three-and-uh four-and-uh;" the middle note of each three-note set is silent – it's there for rhythmic feel. There is a time signature – 12/8 – which

expresses this. But for ease of notation reading we will use 4/4 for most of these examples and add the direction to treat the rhythm as a "shuffle", displayed as ♫ = ♩ ♪.

This example is in A major, whose scale is A B C# D E F# G#. In bar 1 you will see a C. This b3 note is a "blue" note. It clashes with the underlying harmony based on the major scale. In bar 5 there is an F which is the b3 of the D major chord and in bar 9 there is G, which is the b3 of an E major chord. Listen for the "tough" quality of these notes. This type of single-note progression will sound good if it is doubled by bass guitar. Just add a drumbeat and away you go: instant blues power trio!

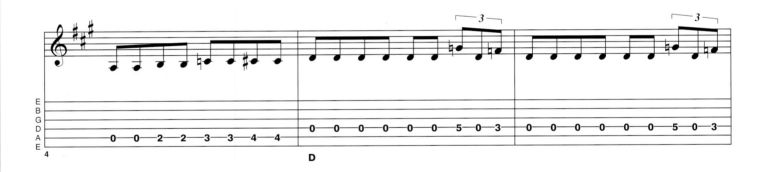

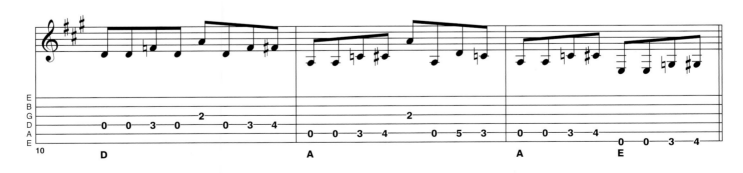

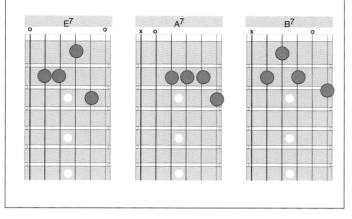

Exercise 2 is another single-note 12-bar, this time in E. Watch out for the syncopation across bars 1-2 and 3-4, 5-6, 7-8, and 10-11. Like Ex.1 this sounds good when doubled with a bass guitar. If you want to solo over either let the bass continue playing the notated progression.

Chord symbols are given in the exercise merely as guides to what you would be playing over. To get an early taste of chordal blues rhythm you can try playing through the exercise not with the straight chord forms below, but using the dominant sevenths as discussed in the introduction – basic examples of which are given left.

Ex 2 - Blues

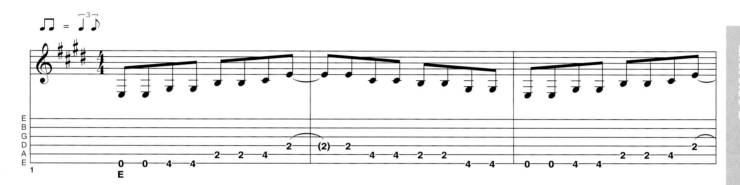

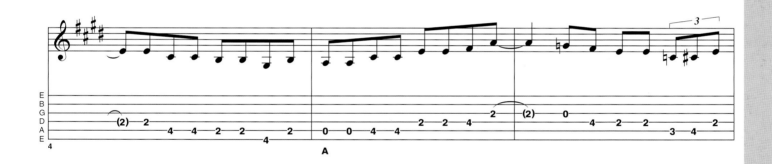

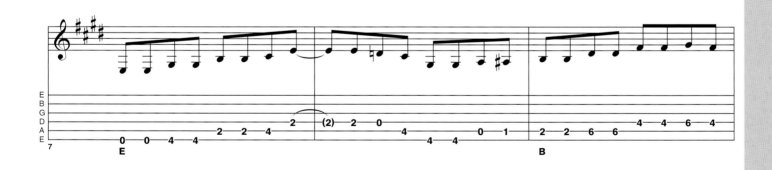

THE SHUFFLE

Here's the easy-to-play rhythm figure that you will find at the start of the Rock section too. The difference here in **exercise 3** is the shuffle rhythm. Watch out for the variation in bar 5, another in bar 6, and a third in bar 12. Also notice that in bar 10 the music does not return to D as it did in Ex.1. Staying on E for two bars is a perfectly valid alternative at this point in a 12-bar.

We need to be able to play this shuffle figure in any key, so **exercise 4** converts this 6-bar blues into a fretted figure with no open strings. If you find this a bit of a stretch drop your thumb well behind the neck. This will help your fretting hand open out. Ex.4 shows the "boogie" figure starting with the root note on the 5th string.

Exercise 5 shows the same idea in G major, over eight bars, starting on the 6th string. Starting on either the 5th or the 6th string enables you to play it in any major key, and to pitch it higher or lower. Notice the G figure in the final bars is an octave above the G figure at the start. Once you've got these down you'll be equipped to transpose this essential blues rhythm into any key required.

Exercise 3

blues shuffle

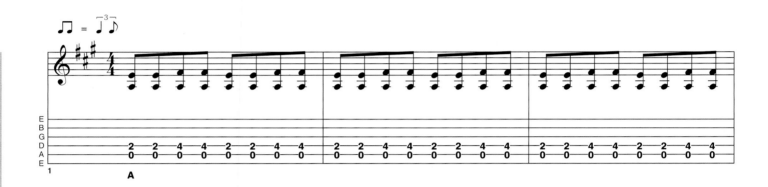

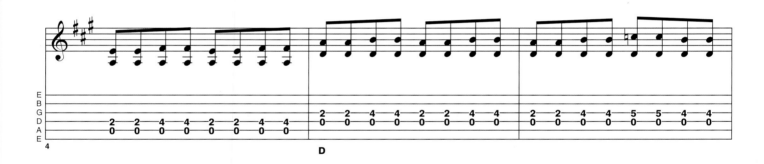

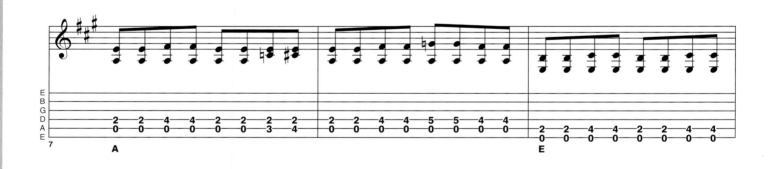

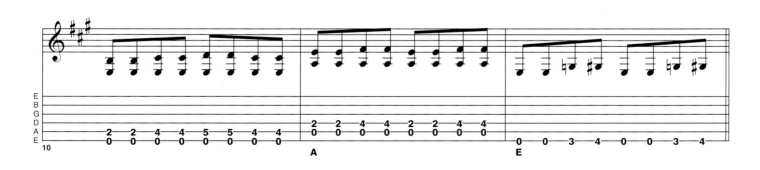

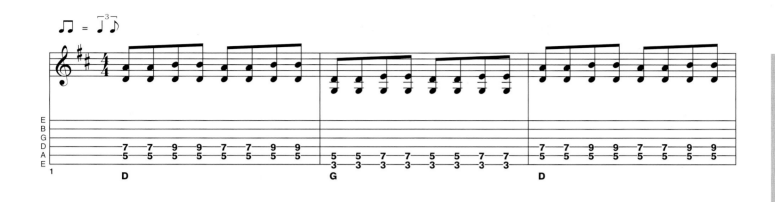

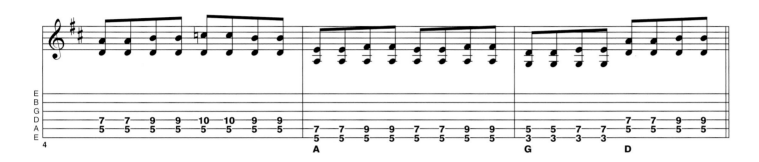

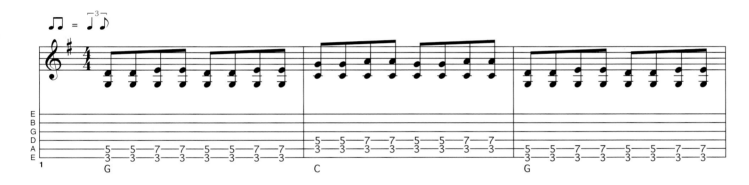

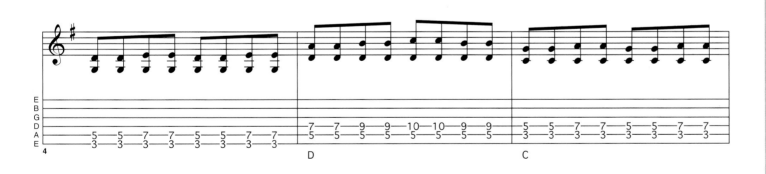

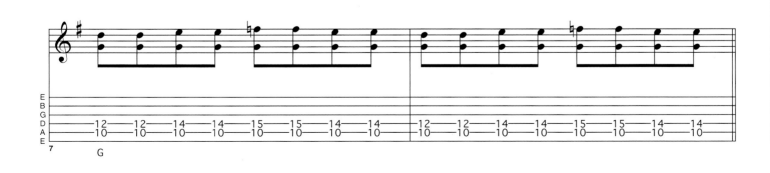

Muddy Waters, left, exhibits better than anyone the great vibe of southern blues played with an electrified Chicago-style energy.

THE IV-bIII-I CHANGE

In blues, movement between the first note of the scale and the b3 is very common. It occurs in vocal lines, in single-note riffs, in lead solos, and in chords. Muddy Waters, for example, features it heavily in songs like *Mannish Boy*, and Hendrix songs like *Voodoo Chile* and *Hear My Train A-Comin'* likewise.

Exercise 6 takes us through a set of variations on the E-A-G change, where G is the b3 blues note or chord. In bar 1 it occurs as single notes, in bar 2 as thirds, in bar 3 thirds with a different termination (in bar 4), in bar 4 as fifths, in bar 5 as triads, and in bar 6 as four-note chords. Each one has a different effect. You can combine these in any way you like during a blues number using the I-IV-bIII change.

We have already discussed a couple of times how the dominant seventh chord is central to blues. Before moving on, let's reinforce that further with another short exercise on its variations. In **exercise 7** D7 is D F# A C. In bar 1 F# and C are played together. By moving them down one fret we get part of G7 and by moving them up one fret part of A7!

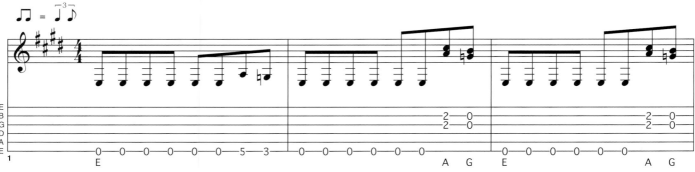

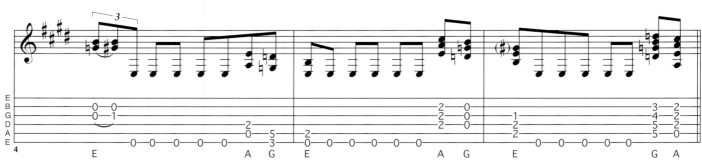

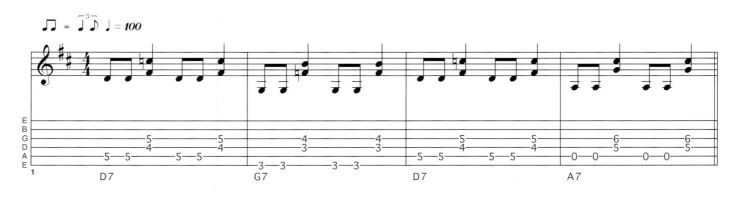

blues IV-bIII-I change

Exercise 6

Exercise 7

TURNAROUNDS

In many blues tunes a musical phrase signals that the 12-bar is reaching its end and is about to start again. It's a short phrase, often going down by steps, sometimes going up. This is the "turnaround." Turnarounds are mainly used in rhythm parts but if you are quick-witted enough you can put them into a lead solo at the end of each 12-bar. Here are eight typical turnarounds, seven in E and one in A.

Imagine that you have already played 10 bars of a 12-bar sequence. Each of these examples represent bars 11-12. When playing turnaround figures use alternate picking: strike the lower note of a triplet with a down-stroke and the upper note with an upstroke. In **exercise 8** the note moves down the 3rd string alone. **Exercise 9** displays a third moving down the 2nd and 3rd strings.

Exercise 10 is an equally effective turnaround, and is much like Ex.8 but with an ascending movement. **Exercise 11** is also like Ex.8 except notes are coming down in sixths on the 1st and 3rd strings. At this point, you should begin to see the subtle variation with which this seemingly simple figure can be played.

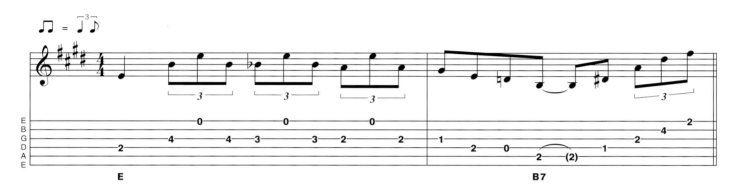

Exercise 8

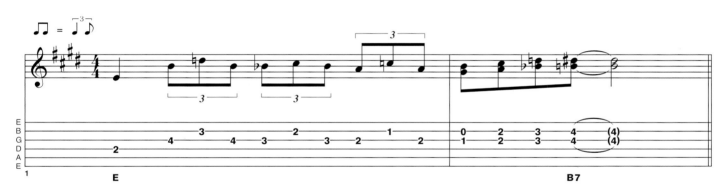

Exercise 9

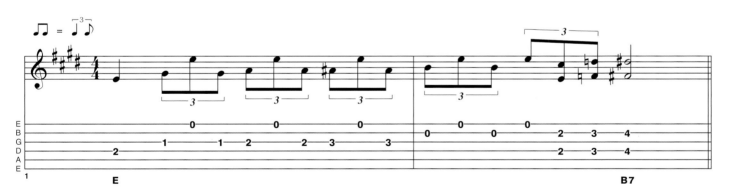

Exercise 10

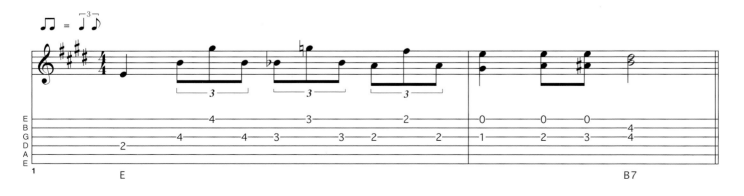

Exercise 11

Exercise 12 continues our exploration of turnarounds with a pattern higher up the neck, which takes advantage of the open top E string.

Here are two patterns in descending sixths, one high, one low, grouped together in **exercise 13**. Use one or the other and then move to the expected B chord in the last bar. The example in **exercise 14**, moving upwards, is in the key of A major.

Turnarounds can also be made of a fast single-note run. **Exercise 15** is a typical one, with pull-offs, going down the E pentatonic minor scale in first position. It is similar to those heard throughout Stevie Ray Vaughan's *Rude Mood*, and is getting you into some fancier playing of this generally simple form. Check out more of Vaughan's playing for further examples of hot-rodded turnarounds.

blues turnarounds

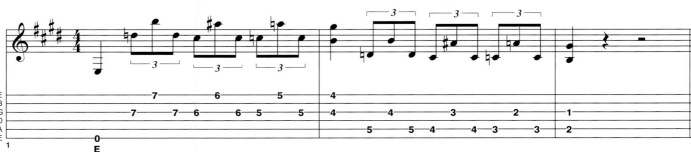

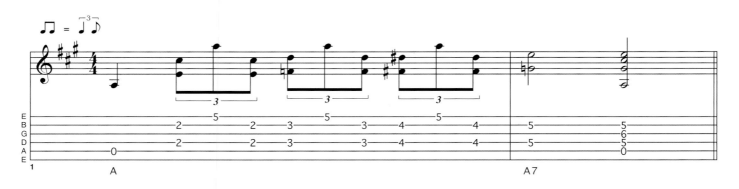

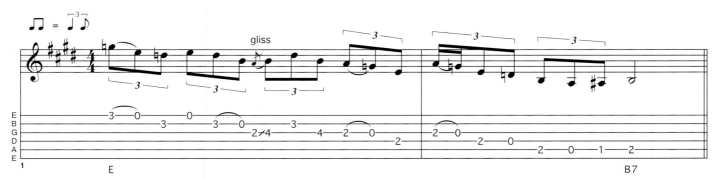

BLUES LEAD GUITAR SCALES

Playing blues lead guitar competently is a matter of learning a small number of scales and scale patterns; mastering the art of bending and fretting-hand techniques like vibrato, hammering-on, pulling-off, and slides; and gradually finding out which notes sound stronger over any given 12-bar sequence.

THE PENTATONIC MINOR

This is the most important scale for blues (and rock). The pentatonic minor on E is E G A B D. Compare this with E major: E F# G# A B C# D#. Three notes – E A and B – are the same. Two – F# and C# – have been omitted, and two – G and D – are a semi-tone lower. When the pentatonic minor is played over a 12-bar in E major the ear picks up the G and D "blue" notes but accepts this clash as the blues sound. Here are two open string patterns for this scale. The second has a small extension to it. Instead of playing the open B string, the same note is found at the fourth fret. This establishes the hand in third position. The pattern that follows for the last six notes of the bar is very important to blues.

THE E BLUES SCALE

The next two scale patterns repeat the previous two but add an extra note: Bb. Although this is not on the pentatonic minor, it is another blues note – the b5. This results in what is known as the blues scale. In a solo this b5 can be approached either by fretting it or by bending a note up to it; the effect is slightly different with each approach.

E pentatonic minor

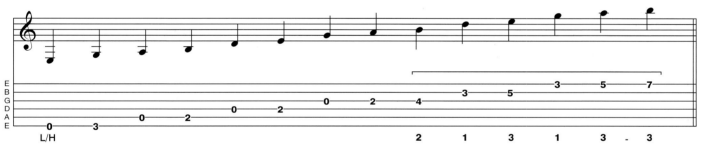

E pentatonic minor with extension

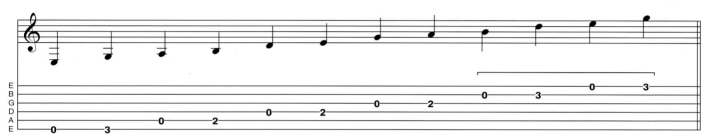

E blues scale

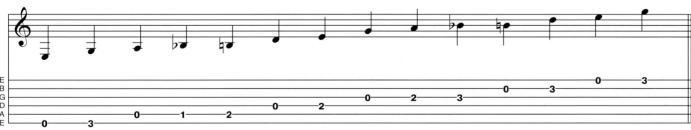

E blues scale with extension

Exercise 16 puts some of what we just learned into action, using the scale notes in first position. Notice that the open strings of the guitar – E A D G B E – have all the notes for E pentatonic minor. This is one reason why E is the most popular key for blues music on guitar. Each bar starts with a bass note. Let this ring throughout the bar, as it will give a "context" for the lead notes. Notice that bar 7 has the added flat note Bb, which you will begin to find familiar as another typical blues element.

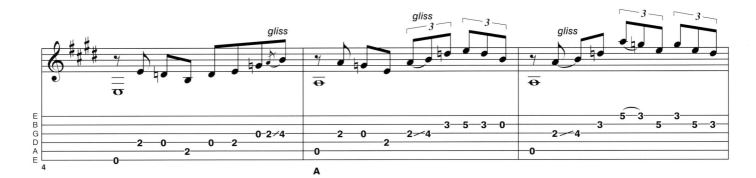

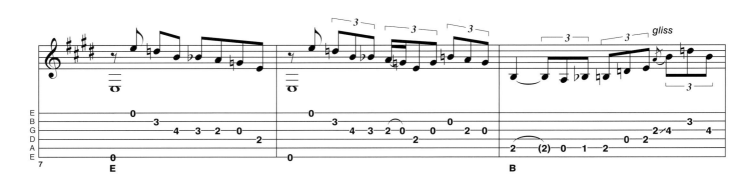

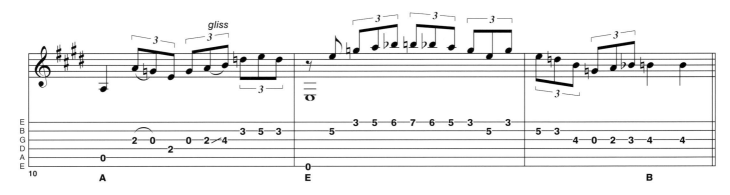

188

blues lead scales

Exercise 16

blues lead scales

Blues scales

Albert Collins, left, squeezes icepick-sharp licks from his Tele.

THE PENTATONIC MAJOR

There is also a pentatonic scale drawn directly from the major scale. E pentatonic major is E F# G# B C#. Compare this with E major: E F# G# A B C# D#. Two notes – A and D# – have been omitted, but otherwise the scales use the same notes. When the pentatonic major is played over a 12-bar in E major there are no clashing "blue" notes; the notes fit harmoniously with the chords. An important part of playing good blues lead is contrasting the

pentatonic's minor and major forms to add greater interest to your solos. Here are two open string patterns for this scale. The second has a slight extension to it. Instead of playing the open B string, the same note is found at the fourth fret. This establishes the hand in third position.

THE E MAJOR BLUES SCALE

The third of these scale patterns adds an extra note: G. This is the b3 note we have already encountered. This results in what is known as the E major blues scale.

E pentatonic major

E pentatonic major with extension

E major blues scale with extension

There are countless derivatives and descendents of the blues – and many are worth checking out – but going straight to the source will provide inspiration every time. From left to right: Buddy Guy's *Feels Like Rain*, John Lee Hooker's *Mister Lucky*, and Albert King's *Born Under A Bad Sign*.

To further practise these scales, **exercise 17** is a 12-bar solo in E that uses the pentatonic major and major blues scales. The b3 is easy to see in the music because of the "natural" accidental added to G. Sometimes this G is fretted; sometimes, as in bar 10, it is reached with a bend. This break employs a "call-and-answer" technique, whereby the first five notes of bars 1-3, 5 and 6 make a phrase that is "answered" by whatever follows.

RULE OF THUMB FOR USING THE PENTATONICS
1. In a minor key 12-bar you can play the pentatonic minor but not the major. Note that the pentatonic minor will not sound as bluesy as it does in a major key because the notes are no longer flattened versions of notes on the key scale. Compare E natural minor – E F# G A B C D – with E pentatonic minor – E G A B D. All the latter's notes are in the former.

2. In a major key 12-bar you can play the pentatonic minor *and* the major. However, if the piece you are soloing over uses any of the three minor chords of the major key (in E = F#m G#m C#m) the pentatonic minor will clash with them in an undesirable manner. The easiest solution is to use the pentatonic major

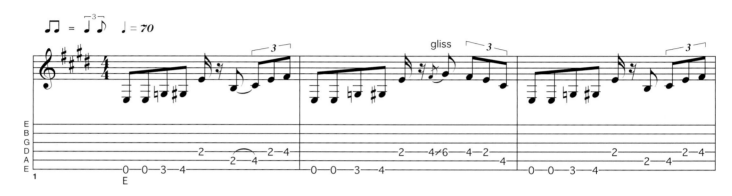

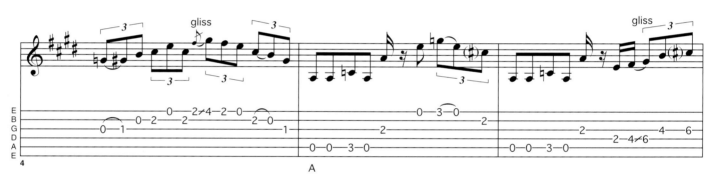

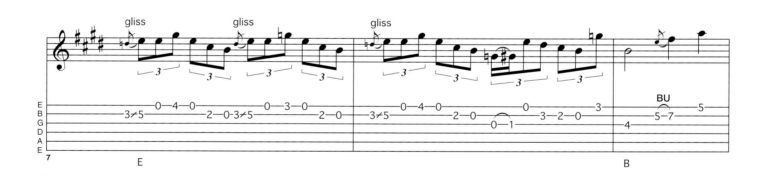

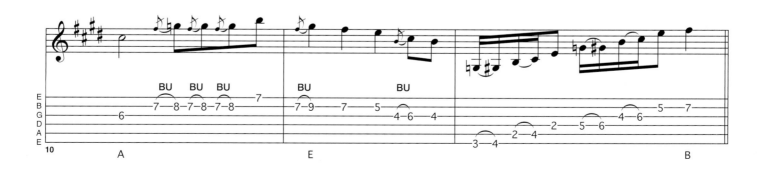

190

wherever those minor chords occur.

3. Any pentatonic minor scale pattern moved down three frets will automatically "convert" to a pentatonic major on the same root note. Remember this and you will find it very easy to switch scales in a solo.

THE "EXTENSION" BOX

Let's just concentrate for a moment on the pattern found at the top of the previous set of scales. It is good discipline to restrict yourself to playing a 12-bar solo using only these five notes and

nothing else, as in **exercise 18**. It will make you think more carefully about the way each note sounds against the harmony. By this method you get an appreciation of "chord-tones." (A similar approach to basic soloing will be taken in the *Jazz* chapter.) These are the notes on the scale that belong to each of the three chords in the 12-bar. Whenever you strike one of these over a chord to which it belongs, that note seems a strong fit. Notice in particular here in bars 1-4 the stress placed on E, the timing of the run that leads up to an A in bar 5 just as the chord changes to A, and in bar 9 the emphasised B.

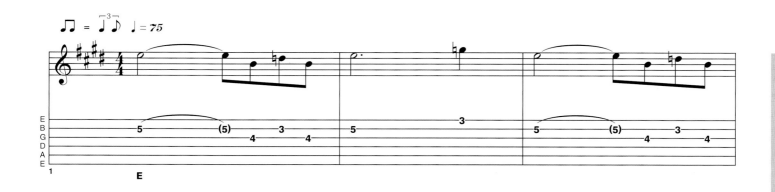

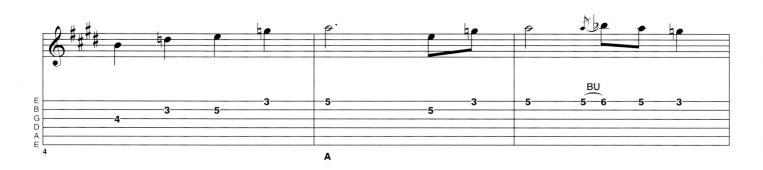

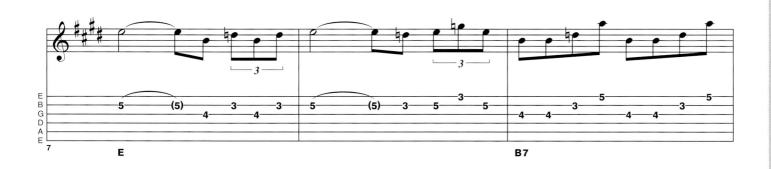

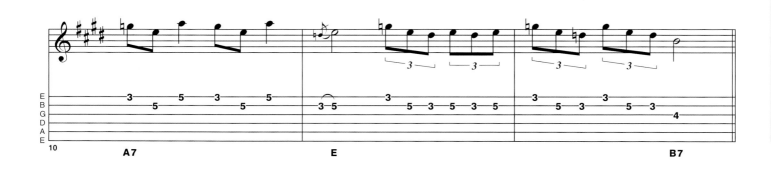

Exercise 19 presents the same extension box but with a few notes added – either by fretting or by bending – that lie within the box. We are still working with a small area of the fretboard to get the maximum musical possibilities out of it. This solo is full of blue notes.

Another important rule to remember is that every pentatonic minor scale shares its notes with the pentatonic major of the note a minor third above it (1½ tones). Thus E G A B D is the same notes as G pentatonic major: G A B D E. This means that over the chords of G, C and D we can put the extension box to a

Like Muddy Waters, Otis Rush (playing live and on record, opposite page) was born in Mississippi but moved to Chicago as a young man, where he became an authentic proponent of northern-style electric blues. A lefty, Rush plays his guitars "reverse-strung" – that is, strung as for a right-hander but flipped upside-down.

different harmonic use, as **exercise 20** shows. Notice the solo moves the patterns up for the C and D chords. (Also note here melodic elements which the pentatonic major blues shares with country guitar styles – from which it is mainly differentiated by the radically different rhythmic feel.)

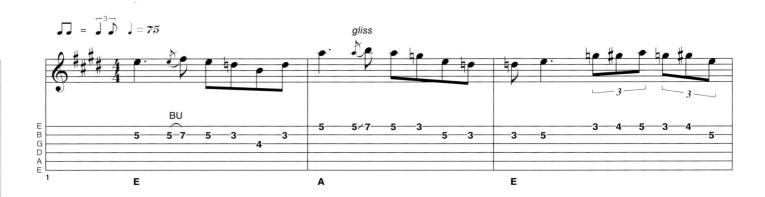

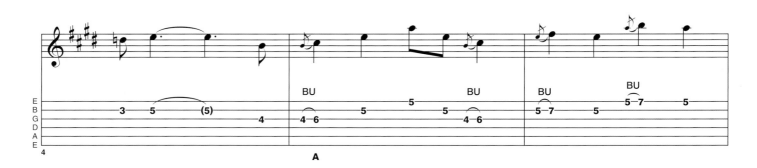

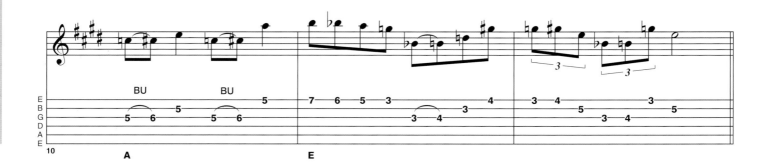

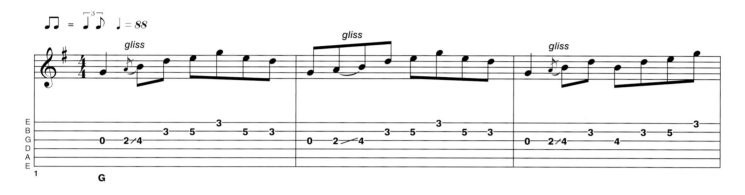

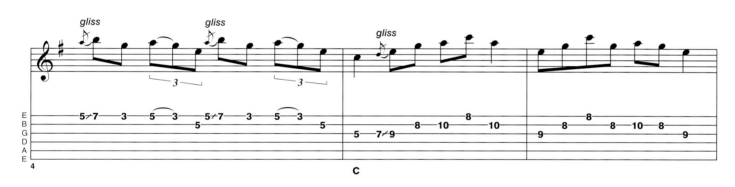

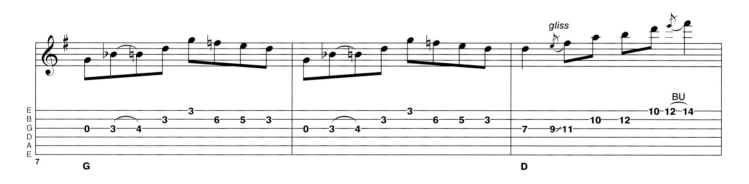

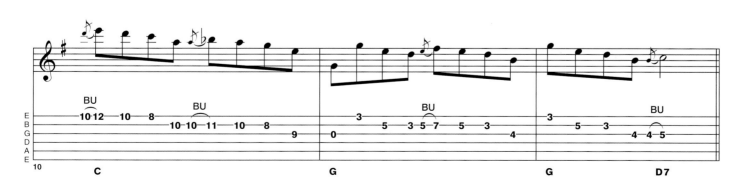

Exercise 21 shows you how the pentatonic minor and major scales in G can be put in a sequence of answering phrases.
Exercise 22 is another "chord-tone" example, this time in G. The starting position is the extension box that lies at the top of a pentatonic minor scale that would start at the third fret – the scale pattern for which is given first. A variant has been added to this scale: instead of moving to D at the 7th fret, the D is played at the 3rd on the B string. This is the most common pentatonic pattern. With no open strings it is movable and gives the pentatonic minor of any key from G upwards. Move this up 12 frets to create a pentatonic minor one octave higher; or start it on the second note for a pentatonic major from that note. Here the second note is Bb, so starting there gives Bb pentatonic major.

B.B. King's style has remained distinctive over a 50-year career.

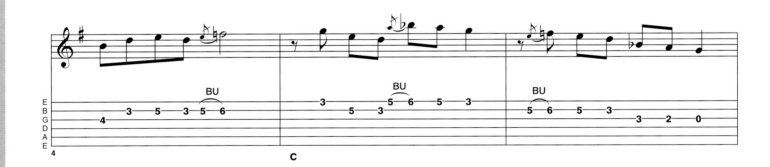
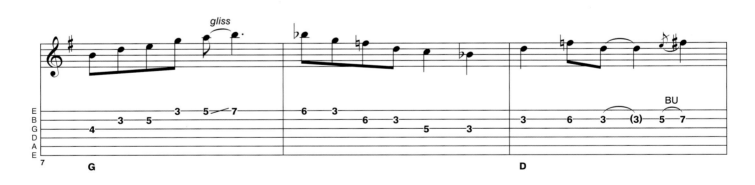
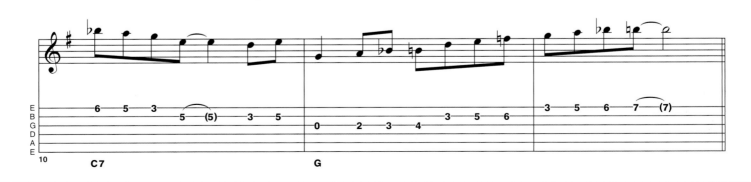

blues pentatonic scales

G pentatonic minor

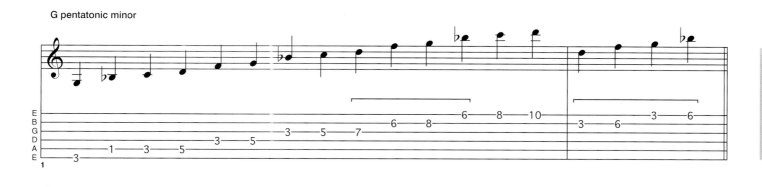

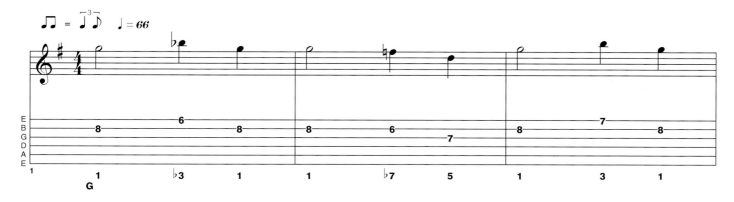

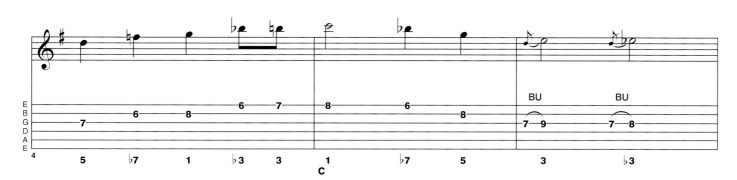

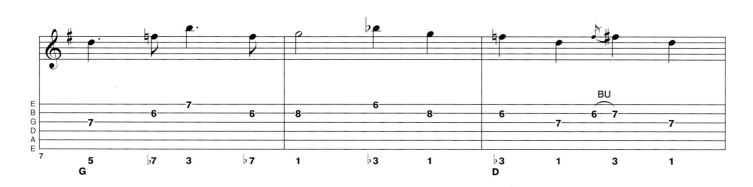

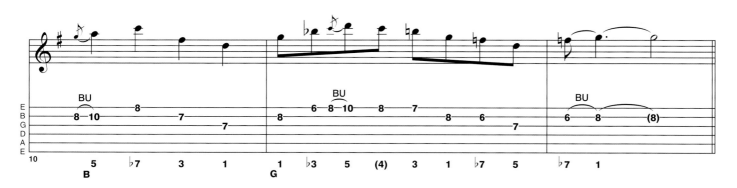

Robert Cray, left, helped to revive mainstream electric blues in the mid-'80s with his blend of hot, stinging guitar lines and vocal performances that incorporated elements of soul and R&B with the traditional blues that lay at their core. Cray's skill as a songwriter has also helped to lift his recorded work well beyond that of the run-of-the-mill blueser, and he's an artist worth seeking out and studying on many fronts.

WHEN CHORDS CHANGE: BARS 2, 5 AND 9

Your lead playing will sound more confident if you are able to reflect in your choice of notes the moments in the 12-bar when there is a chord change. The first of these will be the change from chord I to chord IV in bar 5, or bar 2 if it is a "quick-change" blues. The five examples in **exercise 23** show how to navigate the I-IV change (here the change is from A to D).

A similar moment occurs in most 12-bars at bar 9 where chord V appears. In the key of A this is an E chord. Many players find that continuing to solo over the pentatonic minor at this point does not sound as effective as elsewhere in the 12-bar. **Exercise 24** shows eight ways of making the transition. Play bar 1 in each case, followed by any one of the E bars.

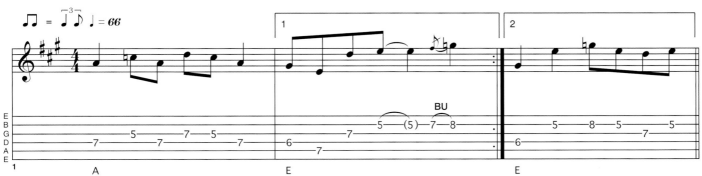

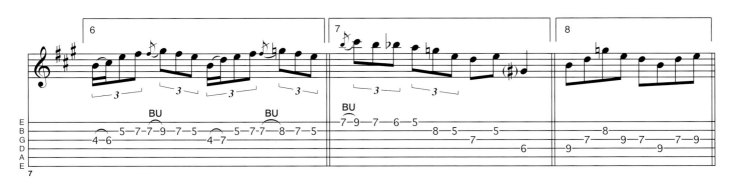

197

INTERVALS AND QUARTER BENDS

String bending is a significant part of blues lead playing. The usual bends are up a half or a whole tone, though some players go higher. It is important to be able to accurately bend either a semitone or tone because in practice this can mean the difference between playing a C against an A chord (the b3) or a C# (the normal third in A). Remember the golden rule of bending: always support the finger that is bending by putting the other fingers down, where possible, on the same string and pushing with two or three. Bends are almost never done with the fourth finger. **Exercise 25** is good for practising your bends. Play the fretted note first, then try to bend to the same pitch. Use your third finger to do the bend, with fingers one and two behind it on the same string. Pushing with all three gives more control. Be careful with the two-tone bend – strings can break!

Blues guitar also employs a bend actually smaller than a semitone: the quarter-tone bend. It amounts to little more than a "smudging" of pitch but it can be effective. Try it on the thirds that crop up throughout **exercise 26**. Another example of some typical blues double-stops is shown in **exercise 27**. They are mostly thirds, but there are sixths in bar 4.

MINOR KEY BLUES

Blues music is also found in the minor key. The first of two minor blues examples, **exercise 28** is in an elongated form and 6/8 time, where there are two beats in each bar and each beat divides into three. Notice that the half bend in bar 1 becomes a full bend in bar 5. Although some of the phrases are pentatonic minor (A C D E G), there are also bars like 8 where the A natural minor scale (A B C D E F G) is used.

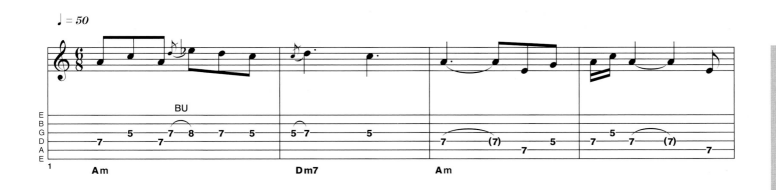

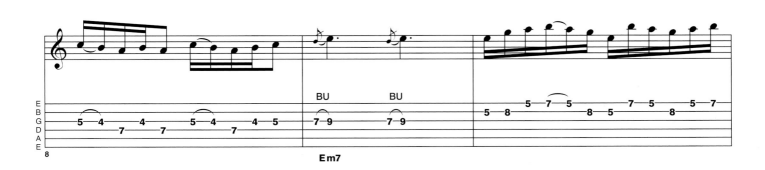
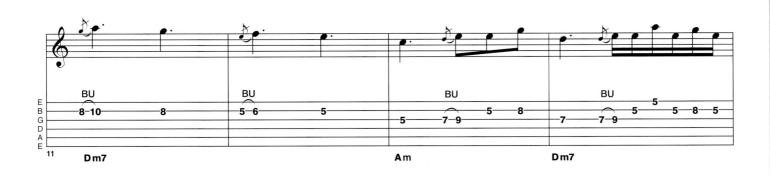

minor key blues

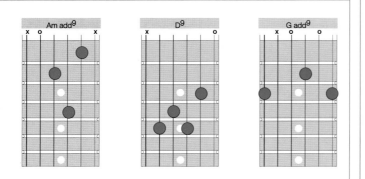

Exercise 29 is an example of a minor key blues progression that has more advanced harmony. For the first four bars you play chord tones that give the full flavour of the chords. Bars 5-8 repeat the progression but shift to a lead solo. As with the previous exercise, both the pentatonic and the natural minor scales are used. The chords backing this example are somewhat more complex than we have seen so far, so some suggestions are given, left.

MORE BLUES RHYTHM

A traditional rhythm, **exercise 30** is in the style of an acoustic blues and is best played with fingers or fingers and a pick.

minor key blues

Exercise 29

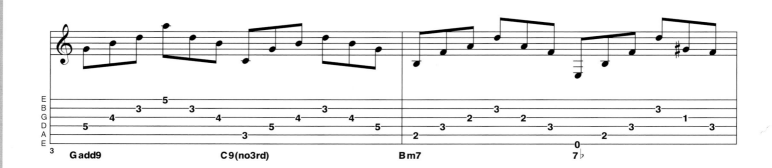

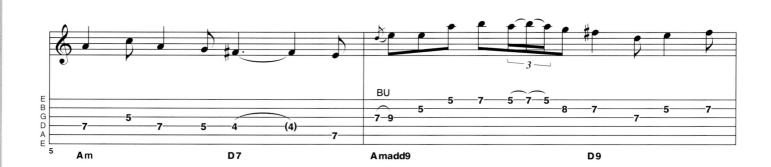

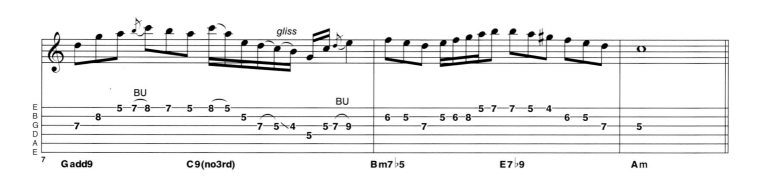

More appropriate as an electric blues, **exercise 31** is a funky blues style with rhythm chord and single note fills. Many of the chord shapes require you to damp the 5th string with your fretting hand thumb. It's a different sort of rhythmic feel than we have yet encountered: now that you've developed a good blues vocabulary, record a few bars to practise soloing over it.

CHORD BOXES

Here are a number of movable chord types that are useful in blues playing. Learn them in different positions relative to the root note (the I) given and, when you play a 12-bar, try occasionally substituting these for the straight majors you would otherwise play.

When playing with a band or a bass guitar it is not always necessary to play full chords. The **dominant 7** triads are useful for this purpose and for putting into solos for a rhythmic effect. Notice that some of them are missing a root note, which will often be played by the bassist anyway.

The **diminished 7** chord is an oddity – because any of its notes can be treated as the root! The **minor 7b5** is a colorful variation on the usual minor 7. The b5 is the same note you would be playing on the blues scale for that key.

The **7#9** (now popularly known as the "Hendrix chord") gives real edge; the **7b9** is more gloomy and resigned.

Ninths and **thirteenths** become increasingly difficult to finger on the guitar so they are often found in incomplete forms. They will substitute for the dominant 7.

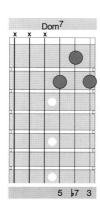
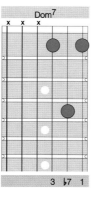
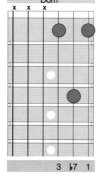

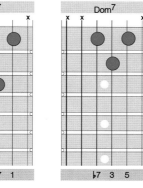
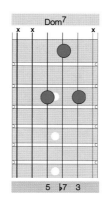
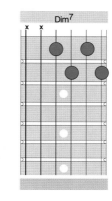
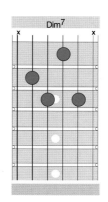

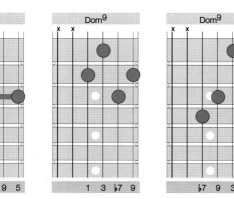
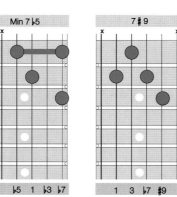
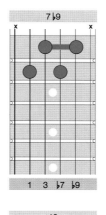
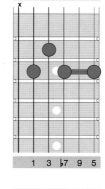
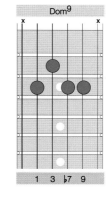

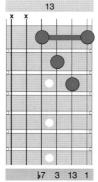
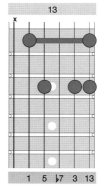

203

4

PLAYING
COUNTRY

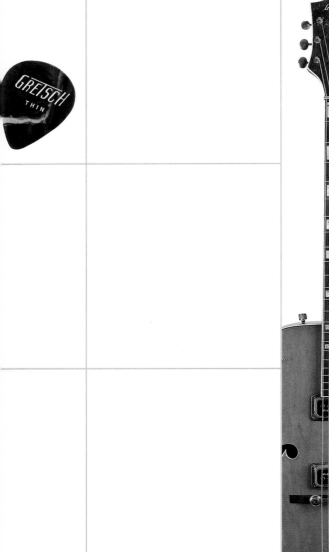

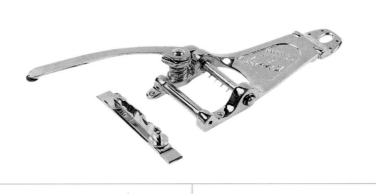

Nashville, Tennessee, is one of the world's most respected centers of excellence when it comes to making records, and country music today has come a long way from its roots as a form that was disparagingly called "hillbilly" by its detractors. The teams of session players who work in the studios of "Music City" are second to none and the guitarists, especially, are considered by discerning fans and fellow musicians alike to be among the hottest pickers on the planet. Yet most good country guitar still contains a healthy dose of rootsy twang, and the current genre – for the player – combines feel, attitude and vibe with technical demands that can rival those of the highest forms of guitar music. ● **LEE HODGSON**

Country lead guitar playing has its roots in Hawaiian (steel) guitar music, which co-existed alongside equally influential early blues and, to an extent perhaps, jazz (the incredible Belgian Gypsy guitarist Django Reinhardt's work throughout the late '30s and early '40s was clearly an influence on players as diverse as Chet Atkins, Les Paul and one of today's hottest guitarists, ex-Desert Rose Band member and current Hellecaster, John Jorgenson). But back to the lap steel guitar for a moment... It's significant that the instrument had legs fitted and ultimately pedals too – evolving into the pedal steel guitar – and, come the late '60s, its intriguing, passion-filled sounds would be mimicked by guitar virtuoso Clarence White and countless followers, bringing and essential new element of string bending into country guitar. Meanwhile, Chet Atkins and/or Jerry Reed (who both favoured a thumbpick, by the way) undoubtedly influenced modern day guitarists such as Steuart Smith and Brent Mason, whilst James Burton – who worked with, amongst others, Ricky Nelson, Elvis Presley, Merle Haggard and Emmylou Harris – was, along with country-jazzer Jimmy Bryant, a big influence on the phenomenal Albert Lee.

The development of country rhythm guitar, on the other hand, can be traced back to '20s hillbilly music and, in particular, the acoustic guitar playing of Maybelle Carter, whose thumb-plucked bass lines and to-and-fro finger strumming style was somewhat akin to the frailing of banjo players – which, interestingly, would be adopted in essence some forty or so years later by Beatle Paul McCartney (witness his technique on *Blackbird*). Consider too, if you will, the blues players of Maybelle Carter's era, such as the legendary Robert Johnson, Charley Patton and Blind Lemon Jefferson, and you might well ask yourself the question: where does rhythm

guitar end and lead guitar begin? Whatever, country guitar progressed when Kentucky guitarists, Mose Rager and Ike Everly pioneered that alternating bass and melody style, which Merle Travis continued and popularised so much in the '50s that a trademark style was born: Travis Picking. And, of course, in the '60s and beyond, the technique would be taken to unimagined heights by Chet Atkins (a name that keeps popping up!).

Finally, it's important to realise that the rock sounds of the '70s and the pop sounds of the '60s through the '90s have jointly impacted on modern country music. Meanwhile, pure country is alive and well.

This chapter aims to demystify the idiosyncrasies of country guitar playing by looking at the various approaches to both lead and rhythm guitar. Regarding solo and fill ideas, you'll be shown various classic and modern examples in the styles of some of the greats, including James Burton, Albert Lee, Jerry Donahue, Brent Mason and Dann Huff. And rhythm guitar-wise, you'll be guided through some relatively easy strumming in classic country style – including bluegrass and ballads – before tackling the alternating-bass style of Merle Travis, as well as the amazing finger style techniques of Chet Atkins and Jerry Reed.

Material-wise, after beginning with a few useful scale patterns (which will include the major pentatonic scale and the complete major scale – brief theory lesson on the mixolydian mode included!), you'll progress through practical exercises which introduce double stops (thirds and sixths) and essential vocabulary in the form of licks and runs. Plus, there are some tasty chords to learn along the way. And to improve your playing ability there are various technical exercises involving hybrid picking patterns, cross-picking, finger style/fingerpicking and so-called chicken pickin'.

COUNTRY LEAD SCALES

The A scale pentatonic pattern outlined in **diagram 1** on the opposite page might look familiar. Indeed, the five "shape boxes" (as labeled alongside the fingerboard diagram) are essentially similar, if not identical, to what rock and blues guitarists may know as minor pentatonic scale patterns. Briefly, the root note for the "minor thing" would be a minor third – three frets – below that of the "major thing." Put another way, our A major pentatonic scale here has the same notes as F#m pentatonic. Country tunes, however, often work in the major side of things, so emphasise and resolve on the brown root notes.

After learning the five individual patterns you should ultimately try to see things in terms of the whole area of the fingerboard. Accordingly, practise weaving back and forth and across, through the complete pattern – which is essentially how Albert Lee works (many of his lines are based on major pentatonic scale patterns).

Next, against a slow, repeating A-D-A-D chord progression, practise shifting licks between the scale pattern boxes. Hint: D and A are a 4th (five semitones) apart so in order to match D major, simply shift any of the material seen here up five frets (or down seven frets). Hey, even professionals often negotiate chord changes by merely regurgitating a pre-learned lick, phrase or pattern elsewhere on the fingerboard. Hey – if it works, use it!

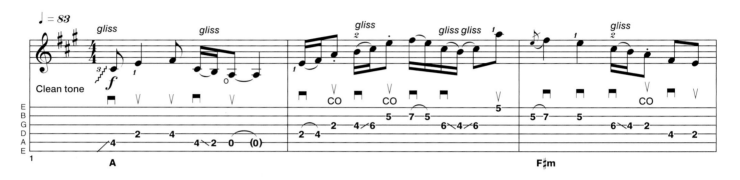

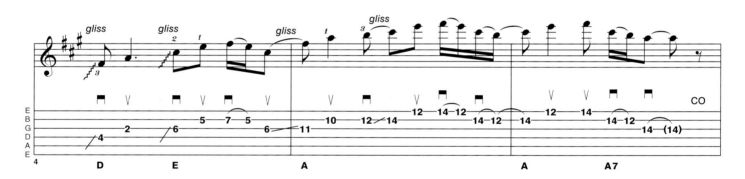

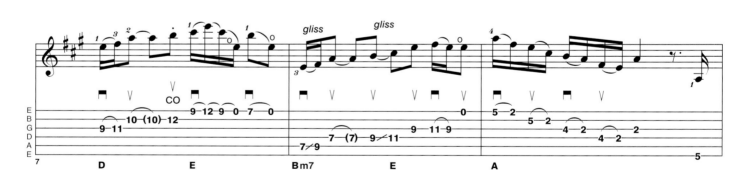

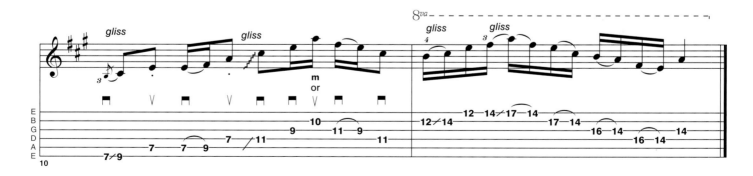

Exercise 1

lead scales

DIAGRAM 1: THE A MAJOR PENTATONIC SCALE

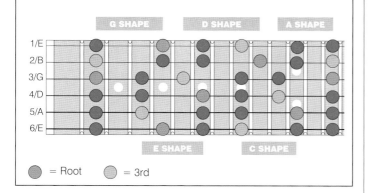

	G SHAPE	D SHAPE	A SHAPE
1/E			
2/B			
3/G			
4/D			
5/A			
6/E	E SHAPE	C SHAPE	

● = Root   ○ = 3rd

Notes in the A major pentatonic scale				
A	B	C#	E	F#
1	2	3	5	6

MAJOR PENTATONIC SCALE LICKS AND RUNS

You might wish to learn the individual licks in **exercise 1** at your leisure before seeing how the various fragments all fit together. Realise that only the notes of the A major Pentatonic scale are used throughout, despite there being chord changes. Analysis will reveal, for example, that what is the sixth of A is also the third of D. Remember though, country players often match the scale to the chord, e.g. A major pentatonic scale for A, D major pentatonic scale for D, and maybe E mixolydian mode for E – more on which later!

Picking-wise, you check out the picking suggestions shown in between the notation and TAB – it's pretty much strict alternate picking throughout, but notice that sometimes the up/off beat is a down stroke (in accordance with 1/16th note picking) while occasionally it's an up stroke, which feels natural for 1/8th note grooves. Also observe the liberal use of slides plus a few hammer ons and pull offs, which serve to keep it all flowing.

Exercise 2 introduces some basic stringbending licks. Note the following moves performed as bends: 2nd-3rd scale step (B-C#), 3rd-4th (C#-D), 5th-6th (E-F#) and 7th-Octave (G#-A) – which all relates to the I chord (A), although the notes' function may alter once the accompaniment changes e.g. C#-D becomes 6th-b7th when played against E. Observe the suggested fingerings, too.

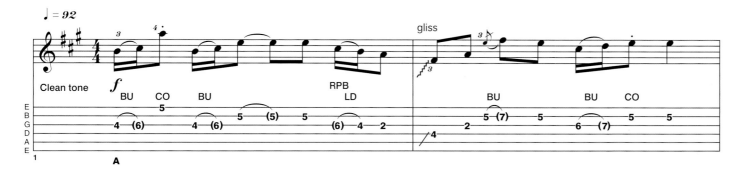

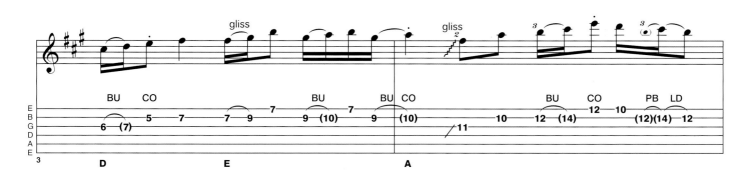

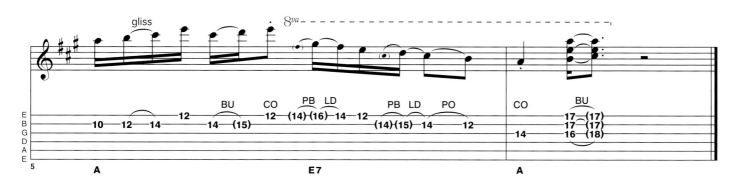

lead scales

Exercise 2

Exercise 2a will help develop your advanced bending skills. Fingerings are important here, so follow the suggestions given.

From the '50s on the sound of the pedal-steel guitar became ever more predominant in country music, so much so that standard 6-string guitarists were hankering to emulate it, but were struggling with the heavy string gauges in use at the time. It was teenage whiz James Burton who sparked a guitar-playing revolution when he fitted some light gauge banjo strings to his old red Fender Telecaster; soon easy string bending was within every guitarist's grasp.

In the '60s, Clarence White took things further when he and fellow Byrds bandmate, drummer Gene Parsons, had the insight to develop a retrofit system which "bends" (pulls, actually) the second or B string – usually on a Tele – up by a tone via a system of springs and levers activated by tugging on the strap button: *voila*, the Parsons-White "B-bender."

By the early '70s, The Eagles were featuring pseudo-pedal steel licks too, courtesy of the same B-bender, on tracks like *Peaceful, Easy Feeling*, while even Jimmy Page joined in the fun with future rock legends Led Zeppelin. It was perhaps Arlen Roth who, in the '80s especially, harnessed that raw, edgy Tele sound and style and brought it to the attention of more players. More recently, the legendary James Burton has offered praise to the undisputed stringbending king nowadays, Jerry Donahue.

Exercise 2b

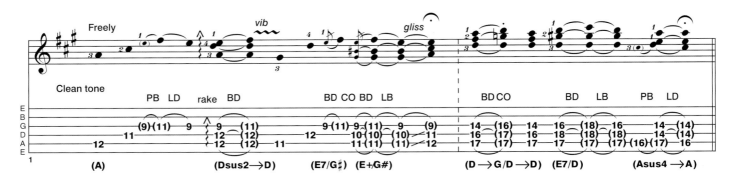

Exercise 3

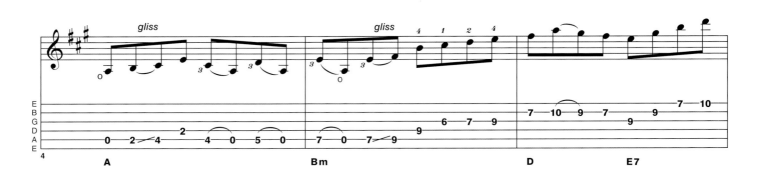

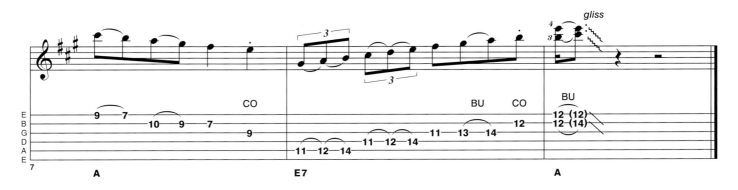

string bending

DIAGRAM 2: THE A MAJOR SCALE

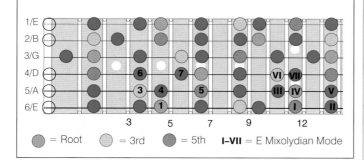

● = Root　◐ = 3rd　● = 5th　**I–VII** = E Mixolydian Mode

THE A MAJOR SCALE

There may seem to be a lot of dots on **diagram 2** above – and there are, because it offers the full A major scale, from open strings at the nut right up to the 14th fret.

Examine at the area of the fingerboard where the scale steps are shown as arabic numbers (1-7), which correspond to the seven degrees of the major scale and hence, chords built from those degrees (I, II, III, IV, V, VI, and VII). This is the basis of the so-called "Nashville Numbers System." So, in the key of A major you might expect to find some or all of the following chords: A (I), Bm (IIm), C#m (IIIm), D (IV), E (V), F#m(VI), while the VII chord, which is rarely heard in country music, would be diminished. Some or all of these chords may appear as seventh extensions: Imaj7, IIm7, IIIm7, IVmaj7, Vdom7, VIm7 (... and VIIm7b5 aka "half diminished"). See if you can pick out some shapes of chords from within the overall scale pattern – they're all there!

Now take a look at the "Dominant Chord Tones" box (above-right). The line below the first portion of the scale highlights the relationship between the "one" (root), third and fifth of the scale as the dominant chord tones. As you will have learned elsewhere

The Dominant Chord Tones Plus Extension

				1	2	3	4	5	6	b7
A	B	C	D	E	F#	G#	A	B	C#	D
1	2	3	4	5	6	7	8	9	10	11

(the *Jazz*, *Blues* and *Metal* chapters in particular highlight this), there's more within each major scale than simply that scale itself.

While the A major scale runs from A to A (and so-on from octave to octave right up the neck) on the neck diagram and as outlined in the explanatory box, we can also construct other modes by playing the notes of A major but starting from different degrees of the scale. One mode that is occasionally useful in country playing is E Mixolydian, found by playing from E to E in the A major scale (highlighted by the roman numerals in Diag.1). E Mixolydian provides a useful alternative for soloing over the V – that is, the E chord – of songs in A major. **Exercise 3** offers some A major licks and phrases to further test your new skills.

String-bender's central: The Byrds with Clarence White (left) and sometime-Hellecaster Jerry Donahue... with a few Teles.

CHORD VOCABULARY

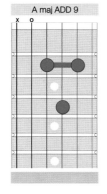
A maj ADD 9

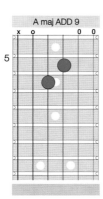
A maj ADD 9

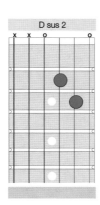
D sus 2

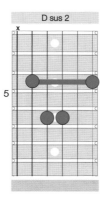
D sus 2

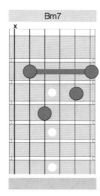
Bm7

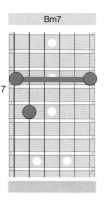
Bm7

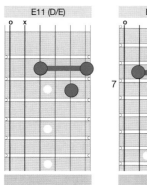
E11 (D/E)

E11 (D/E)

These chords would most likely be heard in a song in the key of A major, e.g. Aadd9 equals the I chord ("one"), Dsus2 is the IV, Bm7 is the IIm ("minor two"), E11 is the V11. Try playing them in various orders: I, IV, II, V; IV, II, V, I; II, V, I, IV... Keep rearranging them, sometimes omitting one or two chords, until you discover a progression that you like – hey, you're a composer!

LICKS IN THIRDS AND SIXTHS

In addition to single-note soloing and some complex bending, a great deal of country lead playing is executed in double-stops, two notes played together. This is done primarily in scales made up of pairs of thirds or pairs of sixths ascending and descending the major scale – that is, one note ascending from root to octave, paired by a second ascending the same scale, but starting from a third or a sixth away. The sound of this is likely to be instantly familiar to you: thirds have a slightly south-of-the-border flavor to them, while sixths ring of classic twang. Both are essential to your mastery of country lead playing.

The neck diagrams on the opposite page give you these scales in thirds and sixths respectively, all in the A major scale. Before moving on to Ex.4 below, spend some time with these diagrams, playing them up and down the neck on all suggested string groupings (five groups of adjacent strings for thirds, four groups of next-but-one pairs for sixths). It takes some practise to memorize them on all string pairings (and, beyond that, in all keys), but familiarize yourself with a couple different groupings before moving on, and you'll soon get the feel for them and learn to recognize their sound.

You should constantly monitor what sounds "resolved" and what doesn't; try to remember – in physical and sonic terms – the juxtaposition of where you are at any given point relative to either the "home base" for the root note or secondary points of resolution, as well as the "homes" for the third and fifth chords of your scale. As for memorizing the physical aspects of these scales, you'll soon note there are only three "shapes" for your fingers to make as you move up and down the neck: "straight" (both strings fingered at the same fret), "diagonal" (the lower string fingered a fret higher), and "stretch" (lower string fingered two frets higher). Simpler still, some pairings require only two shapes. In time, both sound and feel should become intuitive.

Exercise 4 lays out an extended run in thirds, keeping the double-stops to the highest two pairs of strings, with single-note licks linking them. Follow the recommended bends and glisses (slides) to start with, and use the chord accompaniment to check how the lead runs sound against the changes. Be aware of the two-string pre-bend toward the end of bar 2, and notice the brief yet effective use of pull-offs to the open high E string in bar 7.

Like all exercises in this chapter, this sequence merely represents one particular permutation and the possibilities are almost endless! It might be a good idea, therefore, to noodle around further for a while, stretch out the raw material that this exercise and the neck diagrams provide, and take the opportunity to develop your improvising skills.

THIRDS IN A MAJOR

SIXTHS IN A MAJOR

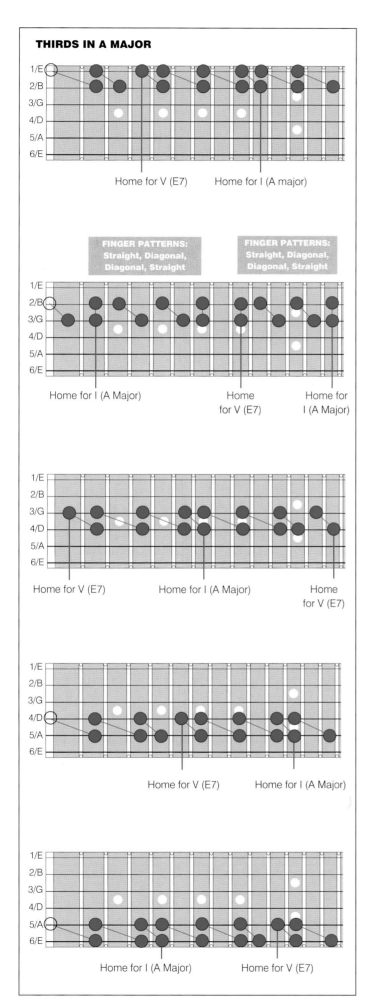

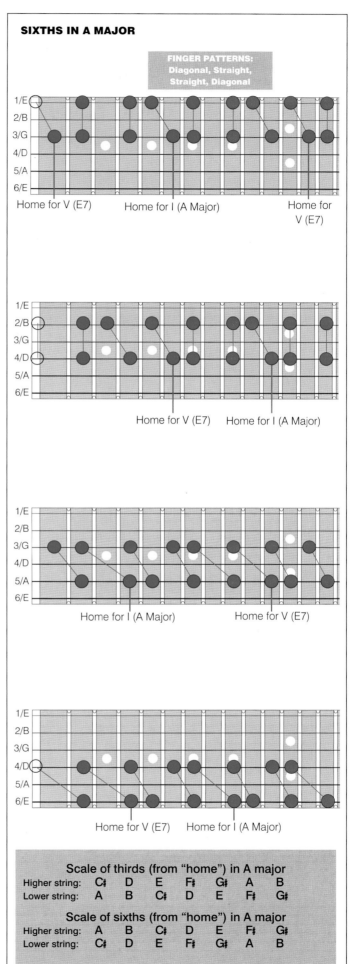

Scale of thirds (from "home") in A major

Higher string:	C♯	D	E	F♯	G♯	A	B
Lower string:	A	B	C♯	D	E	F♯	G♯

Scale of sixths (from "home") in A major

Higher string:	A	B	C♯	D	E	F♯	G♯
Lower string:	C♯	D	E	F♯	G♯	A	B

George Strait, above, offers pure country while banging out rhythm on the frontman's weapon of choice: the acoustic guitar.

Taking us into a full-length run in sixths, **exercise 5** comprises chords that are not all from the key of A major. There are three non-diatonic chords – A7 (I7), Dm (IVm) and B7 (II7) – along with the more unusual Dmadd9, A/C# and E7/G# (the diagrams for the latter three are given opposite to help ease the way). See if you can find ways of matching these chords using the sixths shapes already outlined. Incidentally, you might find of particular interest the fact that all this A stuff sounds great for E7 (V7), too; as you play bars 9 through 12 you'll be playing Mixolydian sixths, whether you know it or not!

Note that although two of the chords shown opposite appear to be "slash chords," they are in fact just first inversions (that is, the third is in the bass). A true slash chord would be a triad over a note that isn't a chord tone, such as a Bb/E (as used for the dramatic penultimate chord in Garth Brooks' live version of *Friends In Low Places* – play such a chord only if you can afford to bribe the jazz police!).

Once you've got the hang of Ex.5 as written, try improvising to the same chord changes using sixths in A major in different positions taken from the neck diagrams on the previous page. Your ear should guide you toward certain sounds and away from others. You'll hit some sticking points with the non-diatonic chords mentioned above, but try it out and see how you do.

sixths

Exercise 5

212

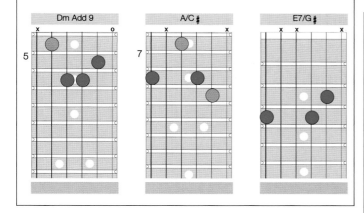

RHYTHM GUITAR

Turning our attention to rhythm guitar for a change, let's begin with the classic bluegrass-style strumming pattern in **exercise 6** (preferably played on an acoustic guitar). You could strum the full chord, but here it's a "bass-chord, bass-chord" approach. Observe the occasional fills – which shouldn't be overdone.

Exercise 7 ditches the pick for a while; try fingerpicking throughout the piece, being aware of the few "anticipated" moments where all or some of the upcoming chord appears early, adding momentum – which is effectively syncopation.

Brooks & Dunn (above-left) lean decidedly toward the pop-rock side of Nashville country, while Dann Huff's playing covers everything from crunchy rhythm to lightening-fast twangy riffs, much of which is heard in his work on Clint Black's *No Time To Kill*.

Steel String Acoustic Guitar

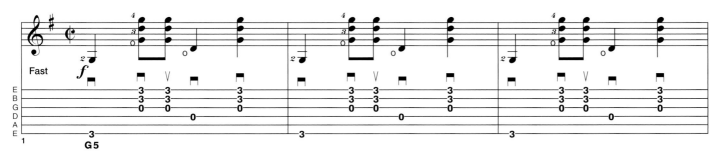

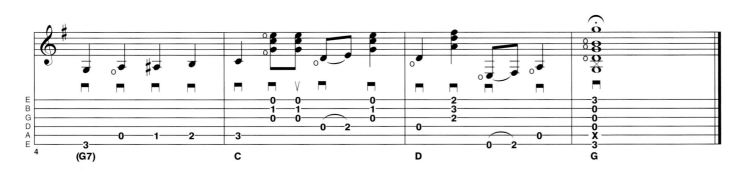

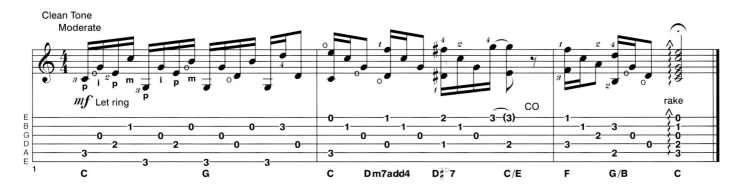

213

For **exercise 8** use a pick again, and aim to cleanly articulate the notes of the chords. It's a slow ballad that will give you some cross-picking practise. This isn't quite arpeggiating *per se*. Notice the sophisticated sounds which are on offer. The "rakes" aren't rock-style sweeping like you encounter in the *Metal* chapter; rather, they're controlled glide strokes (most often in a downward direction). Top session guitarist Dann Huff would probably add vibrato to certain chords (especially sus 2 types).

Speaking of Dann Huff, he would probably dial up a mildly dirty tone on his amp and chug away on something like **exercise 9**, which takes us to the key of D major. If you think the rakes are too gratuitous, stab at the chords more accurately. Ah, there's a real slash chord in bar 4: G/A, which is a "chord synonym" of

A11 – they're similar or identical sounds but spelled differently. (Note: the root note often tends to be perceived as being the bass note, as shown to the right of the slash.)

SOLOING

It's about time we put all the lessons into practise in the form of a complete solo, for which **exercise 10** should do nicely. Try to acknowledge the following ingredients: the A major pentatonic or A major scale (be especially on the lookout for E Mixolydian sounds over E7), stringbending, thirds and sixths, while checking out a little "chicken picking" plus the odd pinched harmonic. If you're unfamiliar with the latter, skip ahead a page for some clues. Otherwise, see how you get along with it for now.

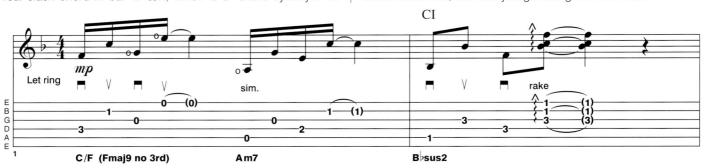

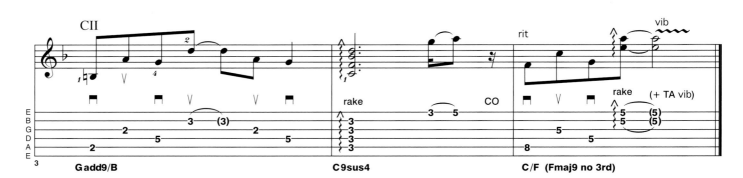

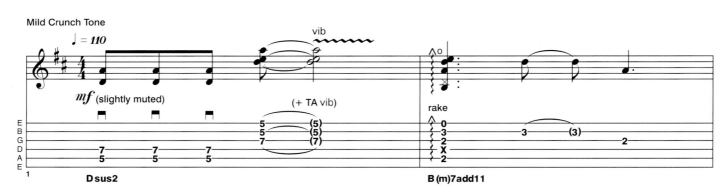

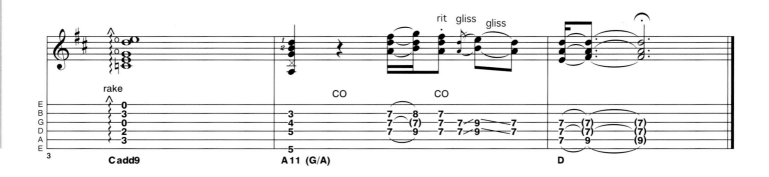

214

rhythm

CHICKEN PICKING AND PINCHED HARMONICS

"Chicken picking" derives its name from the sounds produced when you pluck percussively with your index finger ("popping" the string, some would call it) whilst damping quite a lot as you go. Furthermore, digging in aggressively and with just the tip of the plectrum should yield a so-called "pinched harmonic." Technically speaking, the flesh at the side of your thumb or the edge of a fingertip makes contact with the string fractionally after the pick strikes, and in doing so a harmonic is produced. Chicken picking and pinched harmonics may appear individually or one after the other, but they're often combined – and together or individually they provide another texture of country playing. The wild Telecaster squeals of Roy Buchanan (left) are a prime example of the style, and no doubt influenced many guitarists, including Jeff Beck, Danny Gatton and Arlen Roth.

Exercise 11 gets us into "Travis picking." Merle Travis was highly influential in the '50s – he even influenced Chet Atkins. Incredibly, he used a thumbpick plus index finger only! (Most thumbpickers, including Chet Atkins, Steuart Smith, Brent Mason, and Jerry Donahue, use at least the middle finger and commonly the third finger as well for plucking duties.)

If this style is totally new to you then take it slowly – and don't think about this kind of playing too much, just develop your motor skills while keeping that alternating bass pattern steady. Speaking of which, the bass notes should be palm damped (muted) for an authentic sound; just lean gently but firmly on the wound strings near the bridge/saddles. It can take some work to get into the swing of Travis picking, but once you've got it it's an effective and impressive tool, and can sound great in the right circumstances.

It's also important to get to grips with closed positions for your Travis picking – that is, barre chords. **Exercise 12** is in the key of E major but starts on the V chord of E, B7. Check out the rest

picking styles

Exercise 11

Exercise 12

of the chord shapes carefully because the fingerings and voicings may be unfamiliar to you, or at least unexpected. It should get your thumb and fingers working well together after a couple passes.

Exercise 13 introduces "hybrid picking," which involves using a pick plus fingers to grab chords or articulate patterns cleanly and relatively easily. Travis picking is itself a form of hybrid picking. Interestingly, Albert Lee and Danny Gatton have both featured the use of their pinky whilst plucking, which is very uncommon (see the explanation of right-hand finger use for Ex.11, too).

Turning our attention to the fretting fingerings, these may be atypical as well. It's a good idea to take it slower than suggested at first, and break down the individual sections to work out any tougher licks before linking them all together. Once you've got it all together you'll be into some pretty accomplished country guitar playing.

This workout should remind you of several great pickers: Chet, Albert, Danny Gatton, Brent Mason and maybe a hint of Dann Huff at the very end. Good luck – and remember: if you don't pick it, it won't get better!

From the frenetic picking of Roy Buchanan to the classy, refined fingerstyle of Chet Atkins, there's a lot to soak up in your quest to become a well-rounded country player – and all of it makes great listening.

picking styles

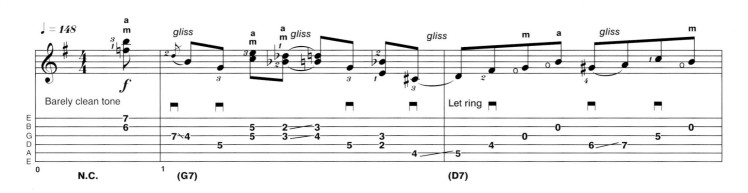

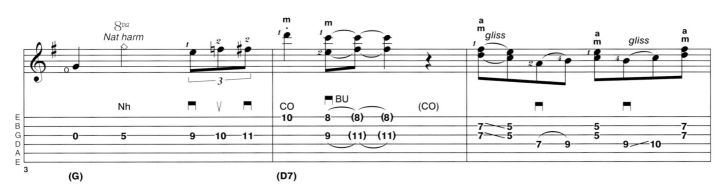

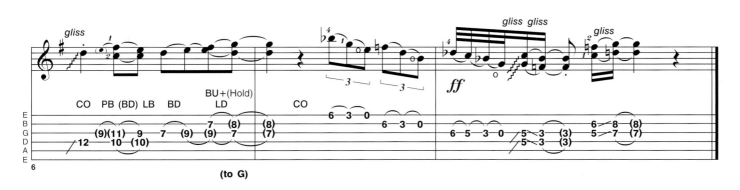

Exercise 13

217

One of the most revered guitarists of all time, Chet Atkins (above) has long been respected by musicians of all genres. A performer of superlative taste and technique, his work is an abiding influence on country players.

Exercise 14 is entitled *Chetude*, and is a piece by the author respectfully dedicated to Chet Atkins. Chet always acknowledged the influence of the incredible Lenny Breau, especially when it comes to what Chet used to call "false" harmonics. Technically speaking, an artificial harmonic is the result of fretting a note – so it's not "natural," as is a harmonic produced by damping a string lightly over the twelfth, fifth or seventh frets, for example.

Here's how you play artificial harmonics: fret a note, then touch your index finger gently onto the point an octave (twelve frets) beyond it, and pluck it using your thumb(pick) (many people, including the author, just use a flat pick) whilst possibly also plucking a normally fretted/plucked string – which is typically two or three strings away – using your third finger. This gentle damping of a note an octave away from where it is fretted will produce a soft harmonic, through the same process that gives you open-string harmonics at the twelfth fret. The designations "T" and "Ah" in Ex.14 tell you where to perform these – with a number in parentheses telling you where to damp the string.

One of Chet's friends and collaborators, Tommy Emmanuel, can perform this technique at lightning speed, and it's amazing to hear! There's quite a lot of technically challenging stuff on offer here, so practise slowly and carefully, then work up to speed.

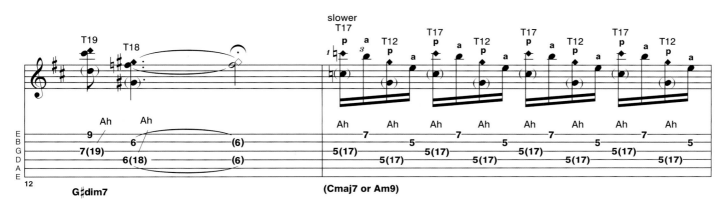

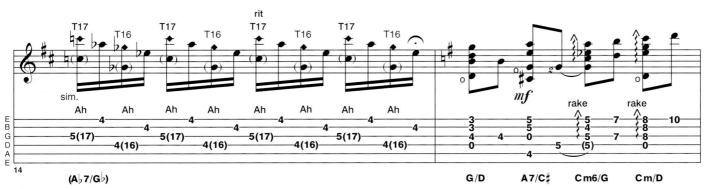

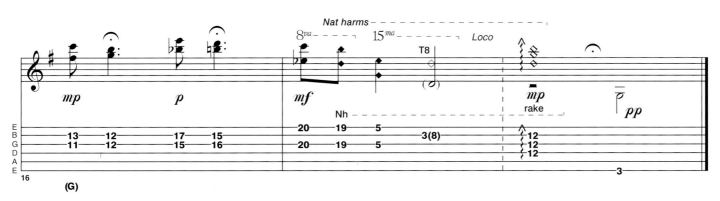

5

PLAYING
ROCK 'N' ROLL

THE CAPITOL TOWER,
HOLLYWOOD

Like a glorious laboratory accident, in the 1950s musical styles fused to form some of the greatest popular music of the 20th century. Rock'n'roll was an amalgam of country swing, big band jive and short crafted songs played with the energy of the Blues and R&B, and the early stars of rock'n'roll came from both country music and rhythm and blues. Though it was played in various related forms before it had a name, the style emerged as a recognisable genre around 1954; the term "Rock and Roll" was said to have come from the U.S. disc jockey Alan Freed, who risked his career to broadcast the music to the youth of America, though the term can also be heard in the sexual innuendoes of some early blues lyrics. ● **MAX MILLIGAN**

Rock'n'roll was enjoyed by both black and white audiences and gained popularity and notoriety as a rather aggressive form of music, disliked by parents and loved by the kids. It was the ultimate symbol of youthful rebellion, the sound of a new "teenage" generation, the embodiment of a cultural revolution in music and fashion. From the opening bars of *Hound Dog* by Elvis Presley or *Rock Around The Clock* by Bill Haley and His Comets, you can't fail to hear the energy captured from a unique period of American musical history.

We have already covered rock'n'roll guitar playing to some extent in the comprehensive *Rock And Pop* section, but as this '50s genre continues to be played today as a style unto itself, it's worth another brief but concentrated look. For many guitarists this style of playing is something from a long-gone era, but the legacy of this revolutionary age can be heard in popular music today. For those who remember the excitement of those early recordings the songs of that time have become the classics of the golden era. As with all forms of music, just knowing the chords and scales is not the whole story. To recreate the sound and feel of rock'n'roll it's important to listen to some of the-all time great players in action and check out their trademark sounds. You are what you listen to… and practice. Rock'n'roll is another musical language and we need to travel to that country to hear its cadence.

One name in particular stands out as the godfather of rock and roll guitar, Chuck Berry. Brandishing all the right ingredients – a Gibson ES-350T, slick suits, the duck walk, and stories of teenage love and hot cars – he almost single-handedly wrote the book on rock'n'roll guitar.

Born October 18th, 1926 in a cottage at 2520 Goode Avenue in St Louis, Missouri, Chuck Berry rose through the dance halls and bars to become one of the most prolific songwriters and innovators of rock'n'roll guitar, his driving double-stop lead intros being a particularly recognisable trademark. After years of being "ripped off" in publishing deals he studied the business and became his own boss. Berry's essential

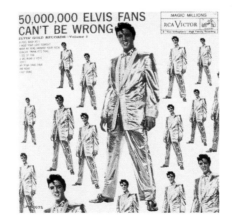

listening includes *Maybellene, Johnny B. Goode, Roll Over Beethoven, Memphis, Sweet Little Sixteen* and *No Particular Place To Go*.

Having started out playing country music, Eddie Cochran ventured into rock'n'roll in 1956. In the next three years he was to record some of the great rock'n'roll classics – playing a Gretsch 6120 with a Gibson single coil P90 in the neck position. Listen particularly to *Sittin' In The Balcony* for its cool tape echo frenzy and tasty solo, the groovy thirds riff in *Jeenie, Jeenie*, and the sheer energy of *Somethin' Else, Summertime Blues* and *C'mon Everybody*. Cochran died far too young in an automobile accident in Chippenham, England, in 1960.

Buddy Holly was another great rock'n'roller to move over to the new music after early adventures in country and western, and the string of hits achieved in his tragically short career made him one of the most important influences in popular music. He was also the first major star to brandish the hotrod styling of the beautiful Fender Stratocaster. For many guitar players the world over it became the must-have instrument. Between 1957 and his death in a plane crash in 1959 (which also took stars Ritchie Valens and The Big Bopper) Holly racked up chart hits with *That'll Be The Day, Not Fade Away, Peggy Sue* and many more classic singles.

Worth singling out for his frenetic energy, melodic soloing and sheer speed, Cliff Gallup is another of rock'n'roll's truly great guitarists. After joining Gene Vincent's Blue Caps in 1956 Gallup contributed stunning lead work to songs such as *Be-Bop-A-Lula, Blue Jean Bop, Race With The Devil, Crazy Legs* and many others. Check him out. Other must-hears include Duane Eddy, Bo Diddley, Bill Haley and His Comets, and of course Elvis Presley guitarist Scotty Moore.

The chord forms used in rock'n'roll are not as complex in their harmony as those a jazz musician would use but some voicings have crept in from that genre. The main thing to remember when tackling the exercises is to create the vibe of this raw exciting music.

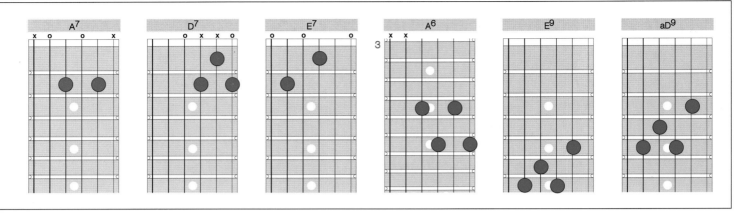

ROCK'N'ROLL RHYTHMS

Exercise 1 is based on the important chord tones in rock'n'roll. The basic structure here is a standard 12-bar pattern in the key of A. We are using the I, IV and V chords in that key – A being I, D the IV chord and E the V chord. These are often extended to add color to the sound of the chords (see Ex.2). Here we can see some of the common single-note riffs often played in unison with the bass guitar.

Looking at the A7 pattern we can see that we are playing the following chord tones: the root (A), major 3rd (C#), 5th (E), 6th (F#) and b7 (G). These patterns are then transposed to any key required.

The target speeds here for your metronome would be between 140 and 160 bpm (one quarter note per click). Adding slapback delay really brings the sound alive and is the staple diet of the rockabilly sound. The delay should be set to repeat once at about 75 per cent of the volume of the original note at a delay setting of about 100 milliseconds. If you have a tape echo handy, great – otherwise any delay will give you the right feel.

Exercise 2 offers some favorite chord voicings for rhythm sections, again in a 12 bar format in A. You will notice that the top four strings are being used to add the bright, bouncy vibe to the sound. Bars one and two could be repeated at bars three and four to give 4 bars of A7 but the A6 is a cool sound too, so mix and match.

This is played with a fast shuffle feel in the style of Bill Haley's *Rock Around The Clock*. You'll notice already how simple these parts can be, but it's the energy, "attitude" and attention to rhythm that will give them an authentic feel. Play it like you mean it and get that rhythm down, and you can't go far wrong.

Rock'n'roll rhythm guitar often borrows from the blues shuffle. In **exercise 3** each chord has its own pattern in the 12-bar sequence; the second fret notes would normally be played by finger 1, the index, and the 4th fret notes by finger 3. (Further related ideas along these lines are found in the *Blues* chapter.)

We also have the barre chord position shown so that we can later play in any key. For instance, finger 1 would play the barre chord position at the 5th fret on the E string for the A chord, finger 2 would play the A string 7th fret and finger 4 the 9th fret note. Okay, now we've got the rhythm section working well and playing tight – so let's move on to put the icing on the cake with some licks and fills.

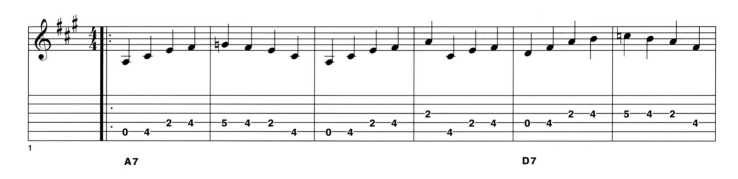

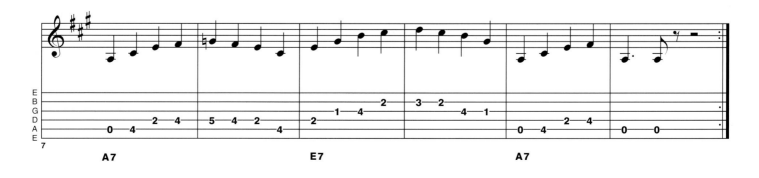

rhythm

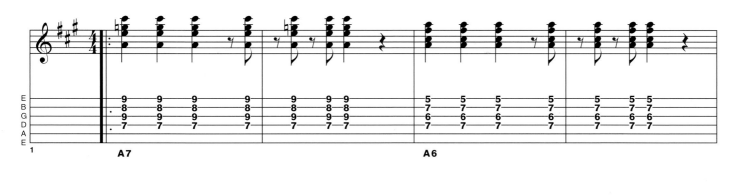

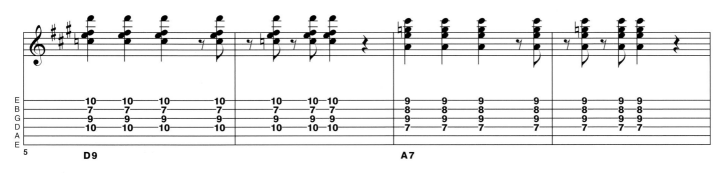

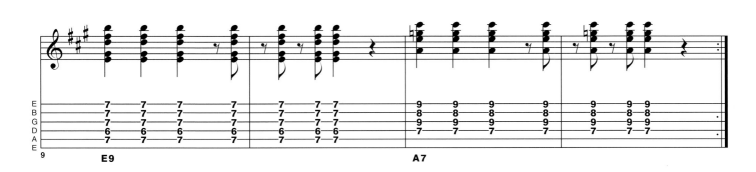

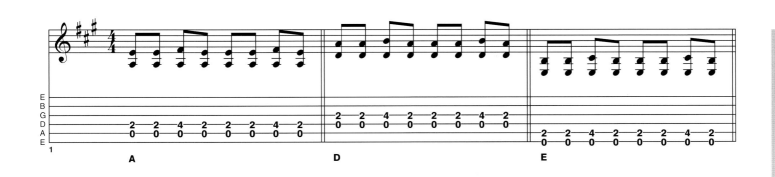

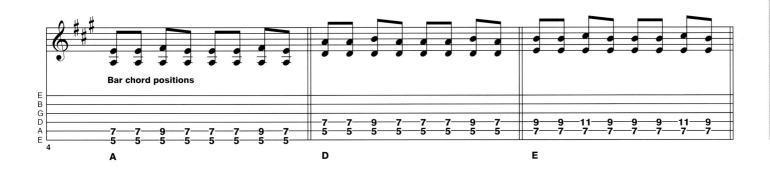

223

One of the most common sounds in rock'n'roll is the ear-ripping double stop. Although these sounds can be polished and honed for various styles of music the vibe needs to be raw to create the right effect. The first two bars of **exercise 4** is a movable pattern that can follow the I,IV,V sequences in the progression, for instance on the D (IV) chord play the line at the 10th position. The remainder of the lick should be played with a separate finger for each double stop. Remember the vibe. Check out Chuck Berry – including his classic intro to *Johnny B. Goode* – for a trademark approach to this style that defined the genre.

Exercise 5 features the technique common in Berry's playing of bending the double stop a semi-tone, or the pitch of one fret. The second bar works best starting with a release bend. That means the strings are bent on beat one then released on the off beat so the the double-stop sounds like it has fallen out the sky. Play these licks quite hard to give them an authentic, aggressive edge. These were considered raw, rebellious sounds in the '50s, and that's the way we want to approach them today.

For **exercise 6**, hold that pinky finger on the top E and don't let it bend on the first double stop. Use finger 3 assisted by the second finger to squeeze that B string up a semi-tone then descend the line using one finger for each double stop. The final slide fill to finish this lick should be played by fingers 1 and 2. Keep these nice and short – staccato. This line can be moved to the IV and V chord positions to give a full 12-bar solo: i.e. 10th

fret for D chord, 12th fret for the E.

There were many techniques from country music that influenced rock'n'roll guitar players. Merle Travis and Chet Atkins' picking styles were incorporated in many classic tracks. The line in **exercise 7** is played in the fifth position for our A7 chord, using the plectrum or thumb pick for the bass notes. Check Scotty Moore's work on the early Elvis Presley recordings. This type of lick would then be moved to the 10th position for the D7 chord but here we have an option of playing a similar style lick at the same fret. This line should be practised straight, and alternatively with swinging jazz eighths.

Many '50s guitarists were eager to build their chops and play jazz style lines. The solo in *Rock Around The Clock* features a lot of swing phrasing just like a sax break; it's a great example of the crossover playing often heard at the time. The solo in **exercise 8** follows an arpeggiated motif around the chord structure. All the eighth notes are swung, but try to nail those quarter notes right on the beat. When we reach the IV chord D, a Cliff Gallup style triplet pull-off run is played, giving the tonality of the D mixolydian scale, but it can also be played over the A chord. We return to A7 with a Chet Atkins style double-stop line. For the V chord the E augmented arpeggio gives a nice twist to the bluesy run before a Texas Playboy-style ending. Slide that final double stop away if you want, or even try an octave higher. This solo would fit nicely over a *Shake, Rattle And Roll* type of groove.

Exercise 4

Exercise 5

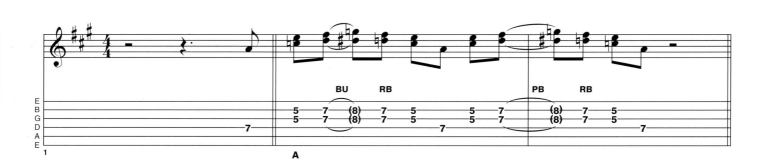

Exercise 6

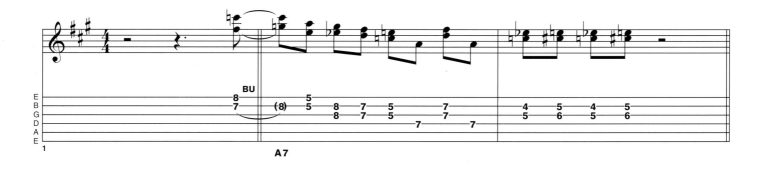

picking techniques

Exercise 7

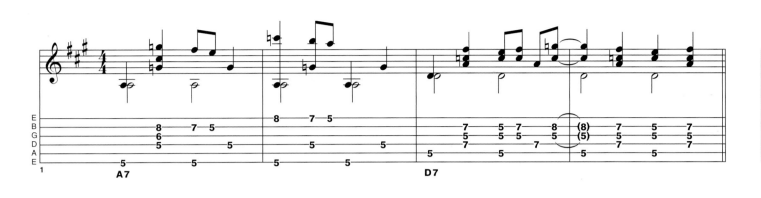

Exercise 8

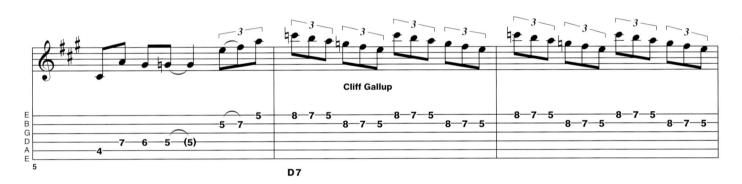

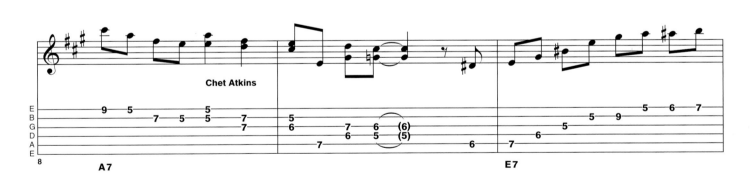

The augmented chord features in several classic rock'n'roll intros, such as Chuck Berry's *School Days* and *No Particular Place To Go*. In **exercise 9** the introduction is played with rapid-fire triplets and in this example the E+ (E augmented) would be used for a song in A. Two voicing options have been shown, one toward the middle of the fretboard and another high up.

The choked bend is a feature of many rock and roll solos. In **exercise 10** the bend on the 7th fret G string is played by finger 3 supported by finger 2. The double stop on the top two strings are played by finger 1. The bend should be choked as it reaches the pitch of the whole tone bend.

Exercise 11 is a great idea for a bouncy intro or can be incorporated in a solo. Check out the playing on The Beachboys' *Surfin U.S.A.*

Now let's try a couple of stock endings for your rock'n'roll tunes. In **exercise 12** the first one is a swinging scale run descending the major scale then finishing off with the A major arpeggio and an A13 chord. These runs would normally start on bar 11 of the twelve bar sequence. **Exercise 13** is another useful variation on the theme; just make sure the quarter notes on the first bar are not rushed and finish off with the swinging eighth notes and an A6 chord. This would then return to the tonic

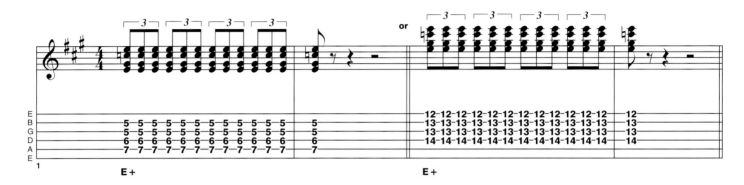

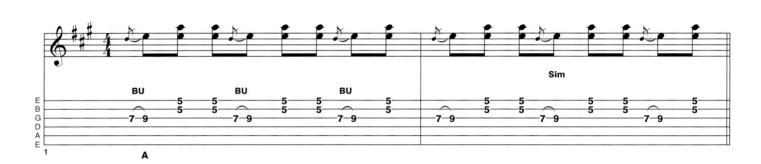

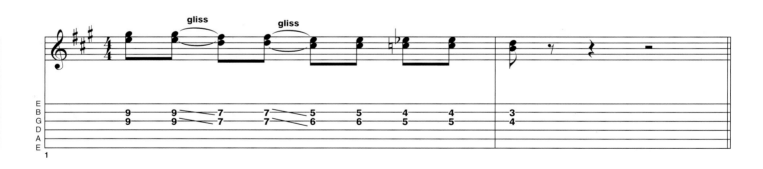

rock'n'roll lead

Exercise 9

Exercise 10

Exercise 11

Exercise 12

or I chord A.

The final example, **exercise 14**, fuses some classic riffs and rhythms together and also features some triad licks that work really well over the dominant chords used in rock'n'roll. For example, an A7 chord is the V (five) chord in the key of D. The three major chords in this key are D, G and A. We can make up licks using the notes of these chords. The favorites are to use the IV and V chord tones, so over A7 the notes of A and G triads sound really cool.

The solo starts with a line usually played in unison with the bass; start with finger 2 to get on the right track then spread the fingers for bar two: finger 1 at the 5th fret E string and finger 2 at

the 7th fret A string to create the A5 tonality. Fingers 3 and 4 play the run on the E string then it's power chord boogie. From now on it's triad licks, except for the little arpeggio run on bar 8. This uses a tri-tone substitution idea. Any dominant chord like A7 can be substituted by its flattened fifth, i.e. Eb7.

To really get the lead ideas covered in this section down right, try recording some of the rhythm parts given toward the front over a number of bars (you don't even need any fancy multitrack – any tape recorder will do) and try out your newly-learned intros, riffs and solos over the top. Then transpose the parts into different keys to broaden your vocabulary, and even try making up some new riffs and leadlines of your own. Have fun.

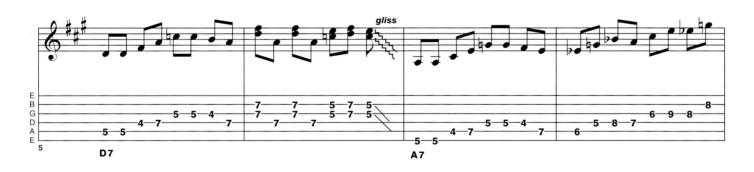

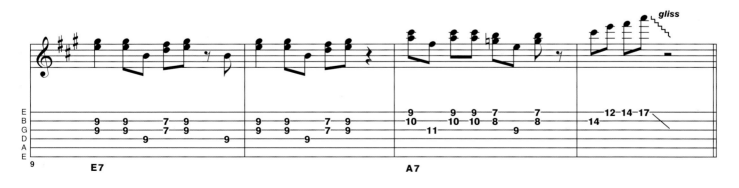

227

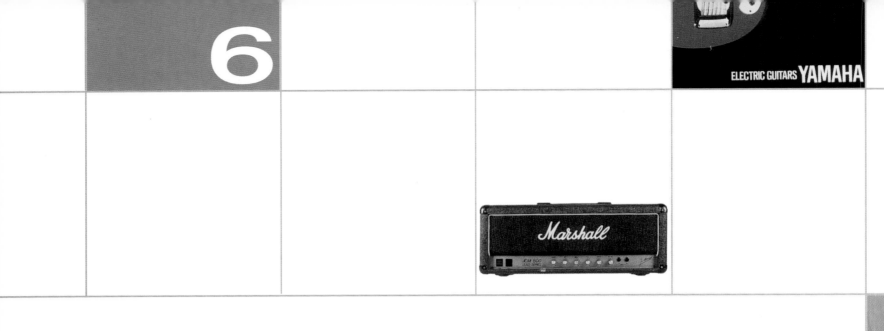

6

ELECTRIC GUITARS YAMAHA

PLAYING
M E T A L

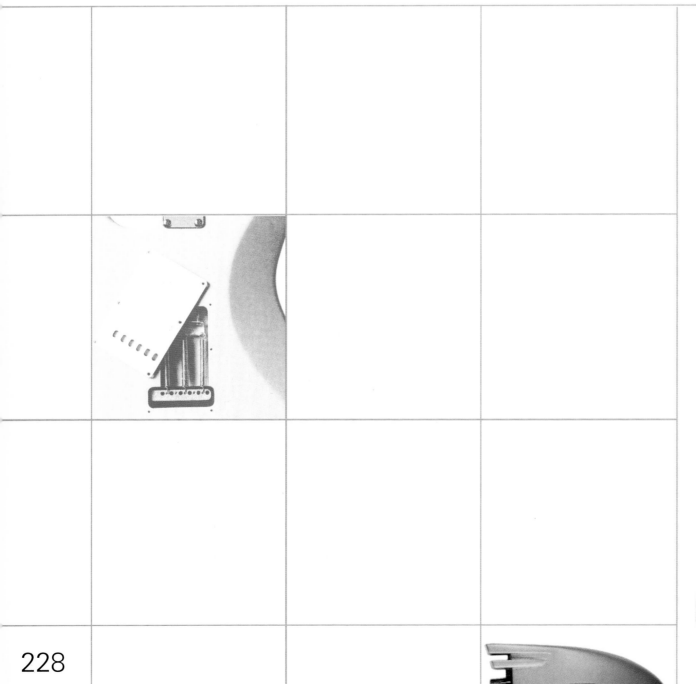

The psychedelic era of the late '60s, fuelled by the power trios such as Cream and the Jimi Hendrix Experience, crossed into a heavier age with the onset of the '70s. Hard rock and heavy metal styles were emerging, founded on energy and innovation. Led Zeppelin and The Who gave rise to Black Sabbath and Deep Purple, who would go on to influence the direction of modern heavy music. Blues licks and distorted riffs became a trademark of the genre. ● MARTIN GOULDING

By the late '70s, the nuances of rock and metal guitar playing were evolving into a more modern sound. With the wheels already set rolling by players such as Tony Iommi, Ritchie Blackmore, Uli Jon Roth and Michael Schenker, it was Dutchman Eddie Van Halen who would revolutionize the way modern electric guitar is played. Right from the arrival of his band's debut album *Van Halen* in 1978, it was clear he was an innovator who would influence a generation of guitar players.

With more interest in the exciting new styles, players were drawn to legato techniques and sought to extend their improvisation over the entire neck. Another contributing factor to the modern sound was the fact that the instrument itself was suggesting a new approach. With players modifying their necks, the advance of locking tremolo systems, a preference for light gauge strings, low actions and hotter pick ups the machine was advancing as rapidly as the person who played it. Meanwhile, advances in amplifier technology saw increased levels of gain which inspired a more vocal approach thanks to the drive and sustain now attainable.

These new characteristics were used to their maximum potential by mid-'80s Van Halen-influenced virtuosos Steve Vai and Joe Satriani, who launched full investigations into every possible nuance of the style, and highlighted the results with a series of guitar instrumental albums, which remain as "must-haves" for any serious student.

Swedish maestro Yngwie Malmsteen also made a massive impact when he released his instrumental debut *Rising Force* in 1984 as he blended his love for classical music into a heavy metal format, and influenced a legion of neo-classical players.

There was innovation on the band front, too. From the legacy of Black Sabbath came Metallica, Megadeth, Anthrax and Slayer, pioneers of the thrash metal movement which gained momentum throughout the decade. The later part of the '80s saw bands like Queensrÿche and Savatage introducing a more compositional approach, and as the '80s turned to the '90s there came more and more diversity. On one hand progressive metal was taking off, influenced by the legendary Rush, while Dream Theater was to provide a massive impact on intelligent rock playing. On another, the growing intricacies of death

metal and black metal – as played by bands such as Death, Sepultura, Emperor and Mayhem – showcased the most intense and certainly the most technical rhythm playing you can find. Grunge, a punk/metal hybrid, was also in full swing with bands like Pearl Jam, Soundgarden and Nirvana, as was the technological sound of industrial metal from bands like Ministry and Nine Inch Nails.

Today the rock/metal scene and its exponents are not so much moving forwards or backwards, but outwards in every possible direction. The world's most proficient masters of the genre – players like Greg Howe and Tony MacAlpine – are continually pushing their playing to the edge of the instrument's capabilities with their fusion-metal hybridization, as is top UK virtuoso Shaun Baxter, with his unique bebop-metal style. Likewise, Rage Against the Machine guitarist Tom Morello could be described as a "virtuoso of sound" who is pushing the guitar in yet another direction. Korn have blended west coast hip-hop with death riffs and framed them in a commercial accessibility. And with bands like Deftones and Slipknot also on the scene, we – as conscientious listeners – still find ourselves very much in a rock/metal dominated musical age.

In the following pages, I will introduce you to the four main areas of modern rock and metal technique: picking, legato, sweeping and tapping. There will also feature heavy rock rhythm techniques, an introduction to rock and metal playing through some traditional blues-based ideas, and we will cover some popular soloing scales and modes – with a section at the end on combining your techniques. All of these will be divided into sub-sections with specific numbered exercises relating to each. Practise using a heavy, distorted sound as this will serve to highlight the effectiveness of your muting technique as well as providing an appropriate tone for these styles.

All of the exercises should be played with a metronome to keep your timing tight, and attempted very slowly at first. Speed is the result of perfected technique and is something which will happen with consistent practice sessions over time. Stay focused. Set short-term and long-term goals with your playing and always believe that you have the capability to succeed, whatever it is you are doing.

ROCK AND METAL RHYTHM PLAYING

Let's start by looking at some ideas used in the rock/metal rhythm style. Due to the heavy nature of the preferred tone, you'll find the big barre chords used in the pop styles sound muddy. By whittling down the intervals to the root and fifth we are left with a much more focused sound and an easier shape to move around. These diads are known as "power chords" and form the basis of many rock riffs. Play each of the individual rhythm exercises as constantly-repeating bars to build up stamina and drive in your rhythm work.

The first bar, **exercise 1**, shows the basic power chord shape voiced root and 5th on the sixth, fifth and fourth string. Make sure

you mute all other strings with the left hand index. **Exercise 2** shows the power chord voiced fifth and root. **Exercise 3** will develop the palm mute technique. The positioning of the palm mute should be back where the strings come out of the bridge. When done correctly, the result should be heavy and percussive. Use down strokes and set the right hand in lead playing position.

Exercise 4 shows a moving harmony over a static bass. Get your attack and rhythm right, and this is a simple yet ominous riff. **Exercise 5** reverses this for a moving bass over a static harmony, while **exercise 6** sees some variation on our basic power chord. Used by players such as George Lynch, raising and lowering the fifth can be an effective way of creating tension.

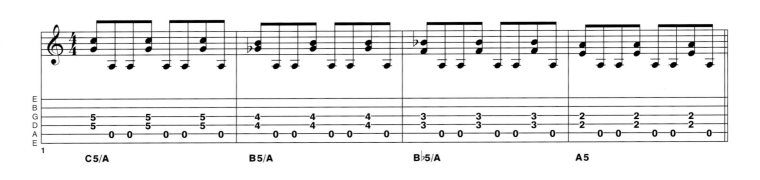

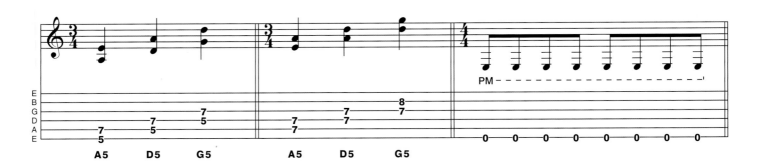

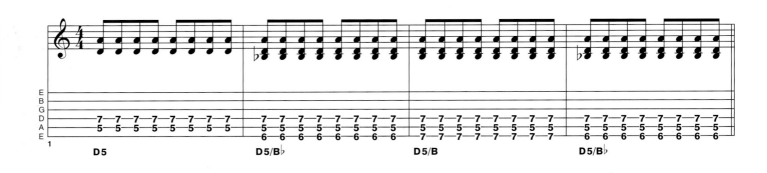

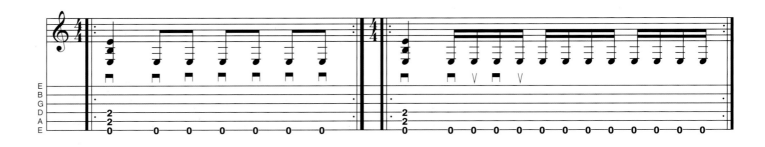

Exercises 7 to **10** are geared towards developing speed and stamina. When executing the bass rhythm, use the left hand to mute the remaining strings. Make sure you pick at the back near the bridge. You should use the palm mute technique on the bass and let the chord sustain for its duration and no more. These techniques should be executed with your right hand positioned similar to the lead playing position: rest your forearm on the front of the guitar and pivot from the wrist. Build the speed slowly and over time, trying to keep the arm relaxed. These exercises are in the style of the thrash metal movement of the mid '80s, led by bands like Metallica, Megadeth, Anthrax and Slayer. **Exercise 11** is a combination of some of the ideas that have come before.

The use of single-line ideas is very common in the rock/metal style. **Exercise 12** is an idea in the style of Randy Rhoads. Keep it as all down strokes and make sure that there is clear note separation. **Exercise 13** is a triplet-based idea in the style of Michael Schenker. Use alternate picking throughout, hitting every other note on the up and down stroke.

Single line riffing at its extreme can merge the boundaries of rhythm and lead playing, especially in the heavier, more progressive metal styles. I would recommend listening to *Awake* by Dream Theater and *The Politics of Ecstasy* by Seattle-based progressive metal band Nevermore.

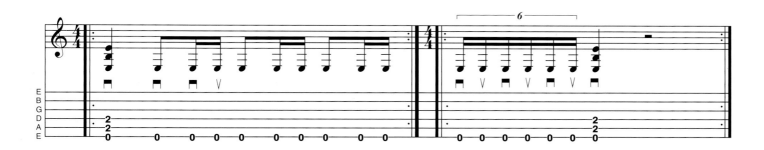

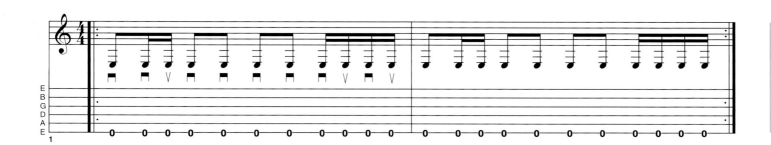

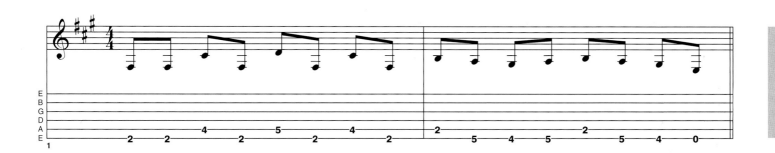

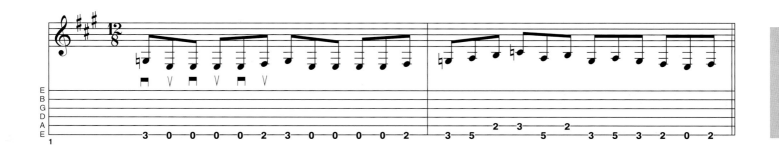

rhythm techniques

Exercises 14

Exercise 15

Exercise 16-19

Exercises 20

Exercises 21

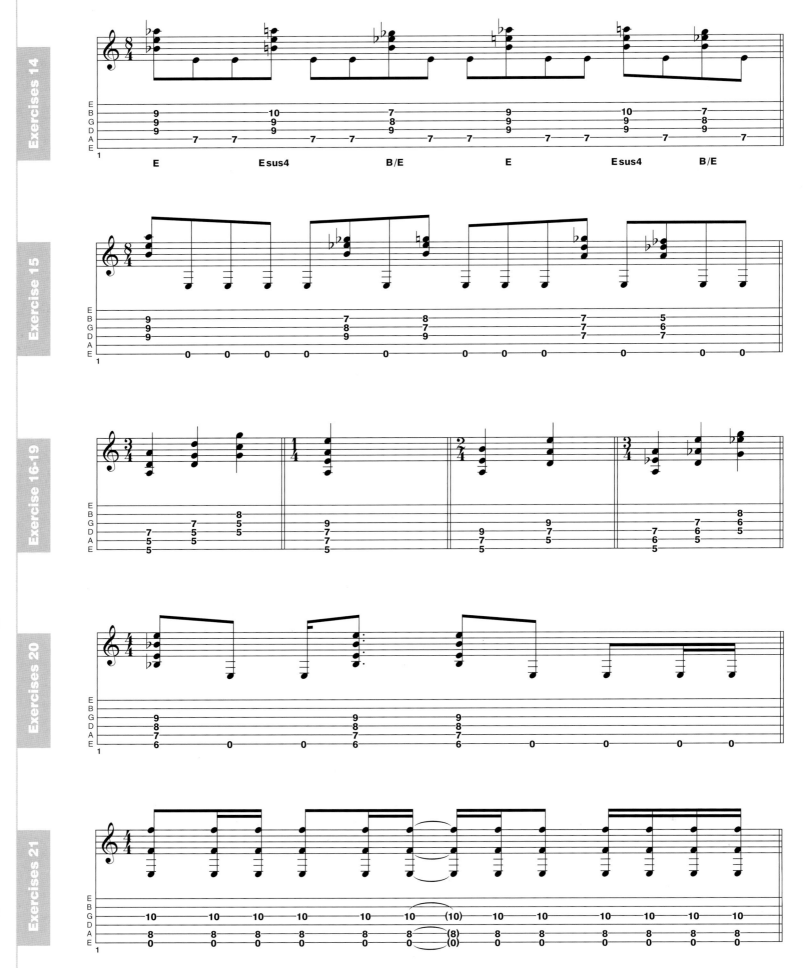

Exercises **14** and **15** are examples of the ways triads are used. By superimposing different triads over a static bass, you can come up with more sophisticated harmonies. Ex.14 is in the style of Edward Van Halen, Ex.15 John Petrucci. These triads will sound relative to the tonal centre of E, therefore the notes of the B minor triad, viewed from E, would make an E major 9 chord. Try working out what the G and D triads would be from an E root.

Next are some variations on the basic power chord. **Exercise 16** shows three versions of power chords voiced with the fifth on bass – a darker sound associated more with doom and death metal styles. Try these repeatedly, and transpose to different positions. The next couple will really start to stretch the reach of your pinkie! **Exercise 17** is a stacked power chord for a fuller sound, widely used by Swedish progressive death metal band, Meshuggah. **Exercise 18** is the add 9 power chord, also commonly used in progressive metal styles.

Exercise 19 is the flat 5 diad, which has a more demonic quality, while **exercise 20** is a modern sounding groove incorporating a stacked flat 5 diad in the style of Korn.

For **exercise 21**, drop your low E a whole tone down to D. The exercise uses the octave technique as a riff idea. Be careful with the muting, especially between the octave. This is in the style of the Deftones, and also serves as an introduction to dropped D tuning, which is popular among heavier bands.

TRADITIONAL ROOTS

The pentatonic scale is a fundamental template for hard rock and heavy metal improvisation. Digest **diagrams 1–5** until you are comfortable with the A minor pentatonic scale and its blues variation in all five positions – a skill essential to master in order to then "weld on" other concepts (many readers will already be familiar with the pentatonic scale from lessons in *Rock & Pop*, *Blues* and other genres, but refreshing your knowledge with these diagrams will help prepare you for exercises that follow).

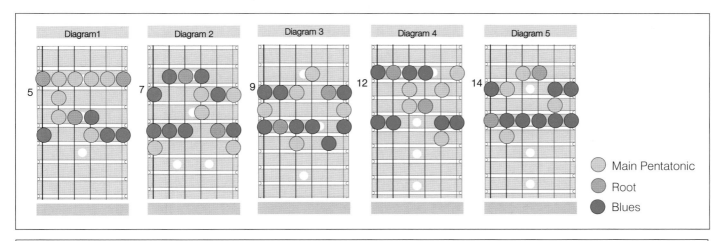

Diagram1 Diagram 2 Diagram 3 Diagram 4 Diagram 5

5   7   9   12   14

○ Main Pentatonic
● Root
● Blues

Edward Van Halen (left) forever changed the way rock lead guitar would be played with the fluid solo work and astounding two-handed tapping heard right from his band's eponymous debut album released in 1978. Ozzy Osbourne's *Blizzard Of Ozz* album (above-left) carries some stunning guitar work from the late – though perpetually influential – Randy Rhoads, including the instantly familiar riff on the hit track *Crazy Train*. From the other side of the metal tracks, John Petrucci's eclectic-progressive virtuosity, as heard with his band Dream Theater, proves equally inspirational.

German metal maestro Michael Schenker (left) remains a seminal force in heavy rock guitar. His instrumental power is heard to great effect on the solo album *Adventures Of The Imagination* (above-left), along with any of his work with UFO. An equally powerful, dynamic player on all fronts, George Lynch shines on Dokken's *Tooth And Nail* (above-right).

Exercises 22 through **28** are some traditional blues licks in first position A minor pentatonic. Since the '50s, these licks have stood the test of time and still form the basis of the rock and metal sounds.

Exercises 29 through **32** are double stop riffs, with Ex.30 and Ex.31 going on to incorporate the 6th to add colour. Ex.32 shows the short step from rock'n'roll to heavy rock, with a riff in the style of early rock pioneer Michael Schenker. Notice that the flat 5 gives it a bluesy slant. With Ex.31 we are also back into bending. Before taking this on, digest these pointers on executing the bend:

1. The thumb should be situated over the 6th fret, forming a pivot point with the index finger.

2. The actual bend comes from a rotation of the wrist, so keep the fingers rigid.

3. You should notice the thumb squeezing towards the second

finger with each bend.

4. When bending with the third finger, also use the second finger for support.

In order to eliminate string noise, make sure that the left hand index finger always mutes the string above and all strings below the note being played. With the right hand, use the heel as a pivot point to rest on any idle bass strings. As with all exercises move from the wrist and keep the arm relaxed.

Exercises 33 through **36** are a batch of "hammer on" and "pull off" techniques. With their legato tone they make excellent rapid-fire licks, and have been a characteristic of the post-Van Halen rock players like George Lynch and Randy Rhoads. Again, play each repeatedly to build up speed and stamina. Ex.35 and Ex.36 use the bluesy flat 5. Strive to make the notes equal in volume by pulling downwards and away from the string. With the hammer on, try to be as powerful and accurate as possible.

traditional licks

Exercises 22-25

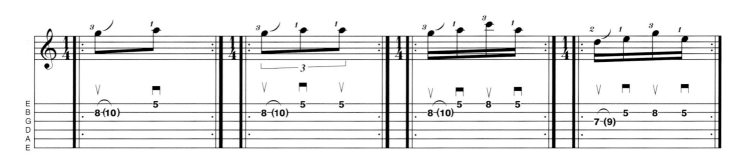

Exercises 26-29

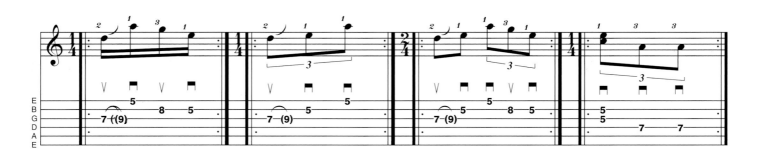

bends

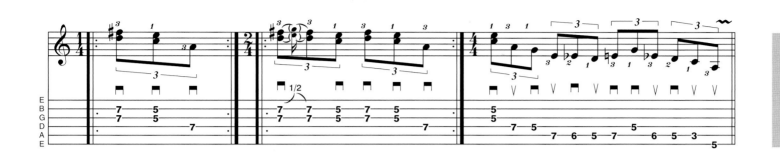

Exercises 30-32

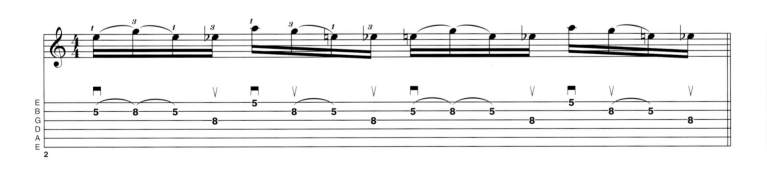

Exercise 33

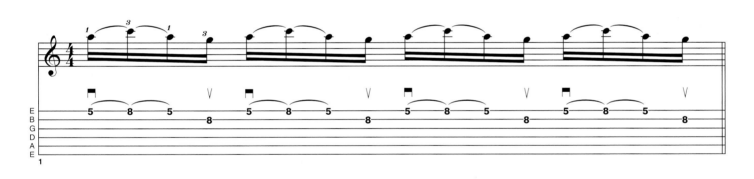

Exercise 34

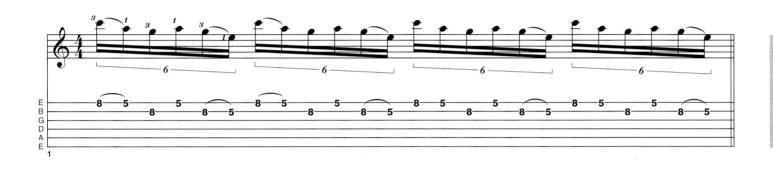

Exercise 35

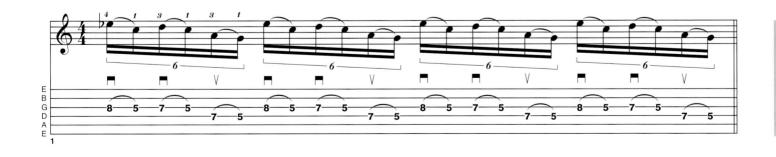

Exercise 36

Exercise 37 is a run in the style of Zakk Wylde. It provides a great example of taking a motif and moving it up the neck horizontally using five positions. Try this approach to any other static licks you may know.

The series of ideas in **exercises 38** through **41** expands the range to cover two pentatonic positions. Rooted in the style of Steve Vai, they demonstrate how players were starting to stretch out technically. When attempting these exercises, try to avoid any jerky movements. Keep your thumb at the back of the neck and stretch out your fingers to reach for the notes. Even for many experienced players, this will be a serious workout for that little finger! Remember to practise these ideas slowly and with a metronome. Once the techniques have been mastered slowly, gradually start to increase the tempo.

Slides (as in finger slides up or down th neck, *not* bottleneck slides) are an essential element of metal technique as they help you navigate through positions and free up the neck. **Exercise 42** demonstrates how you can cover three octaves by using a 3rd finger slide. Notice that the move starts in fifth position, travels through first and second, and ends in third. **Exercise 43** shows a sliding technique which can be useful in moving horizontally. Once you've mastered it, try to apply this technique throughout the five positions. Also experiment on different string groupings and in different keys.

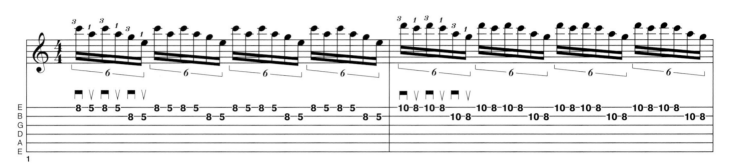

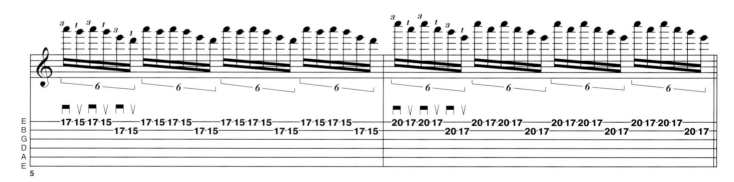

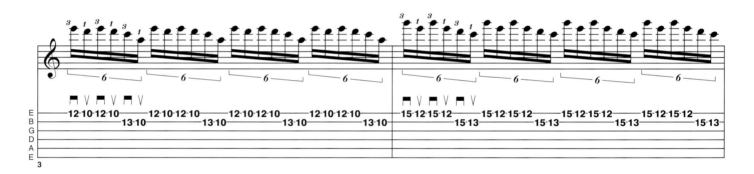

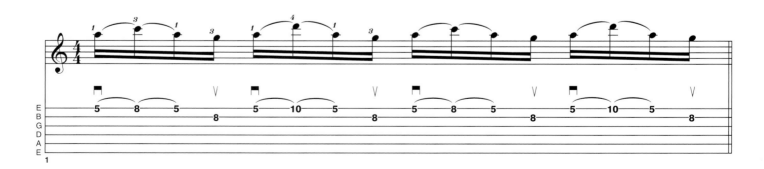

up the neck

Exercises 37

Exercise 38

slides

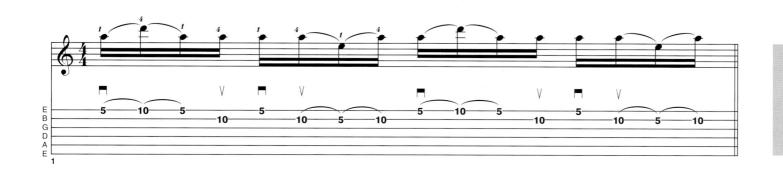

Exercise 39

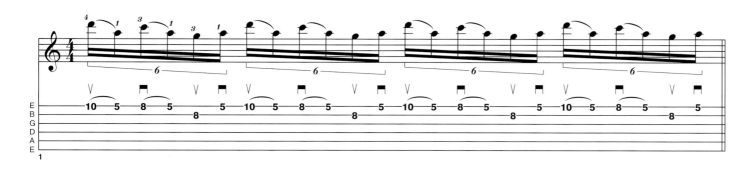

Exercise 40

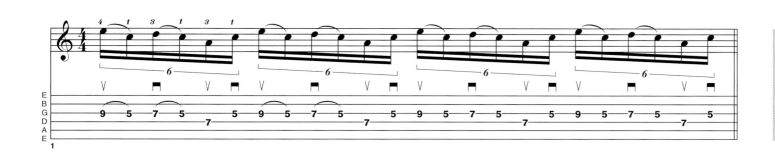

Exercise 41

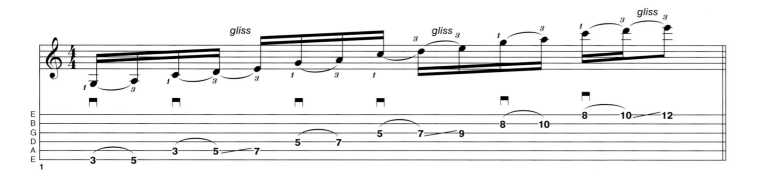

Exercise 42

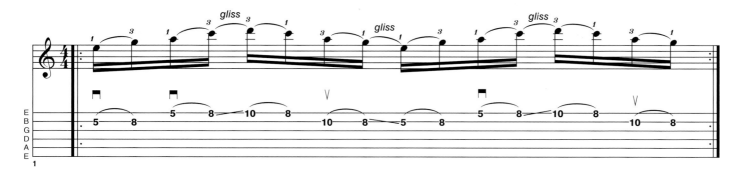

Exercise 43

PICKING TECHNIQUE

One of the most fundamental techniques in the heavy rock style is the picking technique. Initially inspired by players outside the genre such as Al Di Meola and Steve Morse, it is widely used to add tension to solos and provide a more aggressive feel. Pushing things further, the integration of fast picking, blues phrasing and a strong melodic angle towards classical music gave birth to the neo-classical style consolidated by Yngwie Malmsteen. The following exercises will tighten synchronization between both hands and serve as examples of linear playing.

Before digging in, however, check out the *Scale Overview* below, which serves as a primer for what follows. **Exercise 44** uses A Aeolian to ascend the high E string. The exercise moves up the neck in beats by each consecutive note and then works back to create a cycle. **Exercises 45** and **46** are fragments to be practised statically at first and then applied to the framework shown in Ex. 46. **Exercise 47** is a picking piece in the style of Yngwie Malmsteen. Always tap your foot on the beat and accent the downstroke. With the right hand, move from the wrist and mute by resting on the bass strings.

DIAGRAM 1:
A AEOLIAN MODE

 = Root

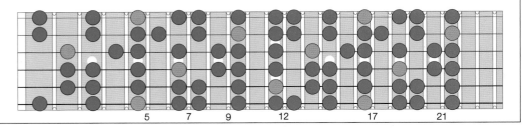

SCALE OVERVIEW

Diagram 1 (above) is a neck diagram showing the A Aeolian mode. A Aeolian is the sixth mode in the key of C major and is a commonly used sound in rock and metal improvisation. Looking at the notes of C major from the perspective of A yields the intervallic formula **R 2 b3 4 5 b6 b7**. **Diagrams 2** through **6** show the traditional scale shapes. Notice that within each shape can be found the minor pentatonic template, thus it may be more helpful to view the Aeolian mode as a pentatonic scale with the addition of the 9th (shown in green) and the b6 (shown in gray).

This is one of the minor modes within the scale. To construct the Dorian mode, which is built on the second degree of the scale, simply raise the b6 to a 6. To construct the Phrygian mode, built on the 3rd degree, simply flatten the 9.

Nowadays it is common to see two shapes "welded" together to form a three-note-per-string scale shape, which lends itself to fast execution. To help you with the *Picking Technique* exercises above and following, I have combined the fifth and first traditional positions in **diagram 7**. For the *Legato* study which follows from page 239, **diagram 8** combines shapes two and three.

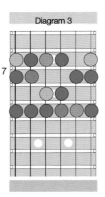
Diagram 2

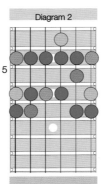
Diagram 3

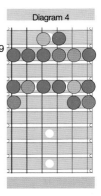
Diagram 4

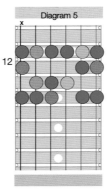
Diagram 5

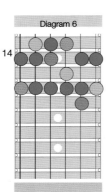
Diagram 6

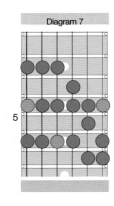
Diagram 7

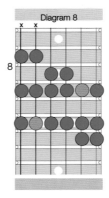
Diagram 8

Lesser-known but highly respected British metal guitarist Shaun Baxter virtually invented the "jazz metal" genre with his 1994 album of the same name, left.

= Root
= 9th
= b6

a aeolian mode

picking

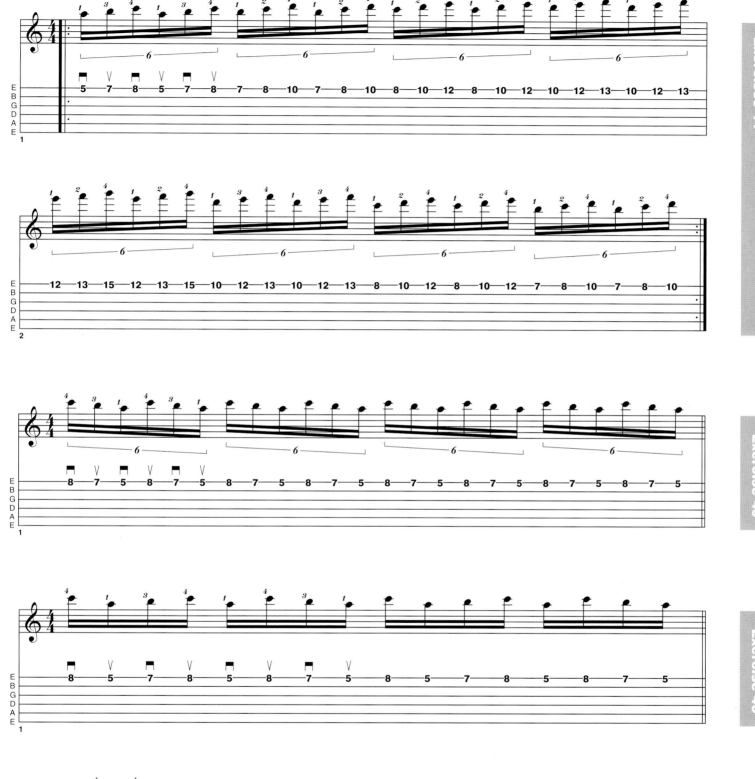

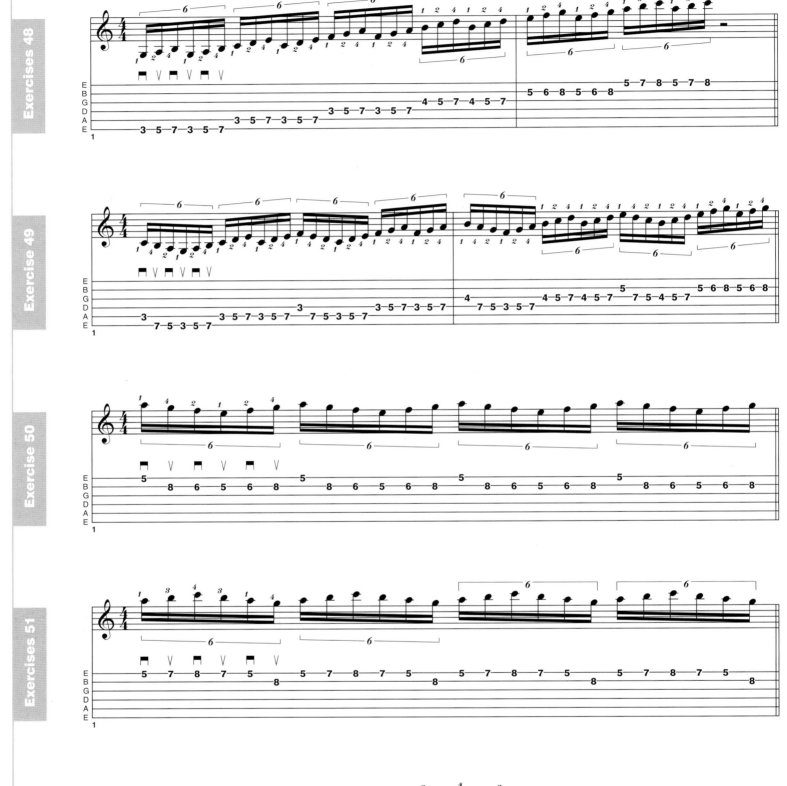

Exercises 48

Exercise 49

Exercise 50

Exercises 51

Exercises 52

Exercises **48** and **49** are a couple of ideas that run vertically up the scale using our three-note-per-string scale. You should also work out the descending ideas by simply reversing the notes, and practice them both ways. To make the runs sound more aggressive, try palm muting the bass strings for a chunkier sound. Once you have established control in this position, start exploring all the others. Use your technique to learn the neck.

Exercises 50 through **52** are excellent technique builders in the style of Paul Gilbert (Racer X). Practise them slowly, try to keep your fingers close to the strings on all the exercises, and realise that speed is a result of good technique, which itself is a result of focus and patience. Build the tempo up slowly over time, and always use a metronome to chart your progress. One of the best pickers at the moment is John Petrucci from U.S. progressive metal act Dream Theater, and he's definitely worth a listen for his excellent execution of these techniques. Check him out on their albums *Images And Words* and *Awake*.

LEGATO TECHNIQUE

The next major technical area to focus on is legato playing. Smooth and fluid sounding, it serves as a contrast to the more aggressive picking style. As picking came into metal from the jazz-rock virtuosos of the '70s, likewise players such as Edward Van Halen were being influenced by the legato-dominated style of fusion maestro Alan Holdsworth, a player who has influenced the direction of many rock and metal soloists.

One of the most outstanding players of the '80s and '90s is Joe Satriani, whose fluid, lyrical style has won him success with the non-playing audience as well as respect among the top players in the world. Note that when playing legato styles, a smooth high-gain amp setting with plenty of sustain and natural compression is often helpful in getting the sound and feel right.

Exercise 53 through **56** are fragments in A Aeolian. Follow the rule that the first note on a string is picked and all subsequent notes on the same string are hammered or pulled.

Highly respected by players and non-players alike, Joe Satriani remains at the top of the tree of legato-style metal virtuosi. Having come to prominence in the '80s and '90s, he is still a major influence on budding rock guitarists.

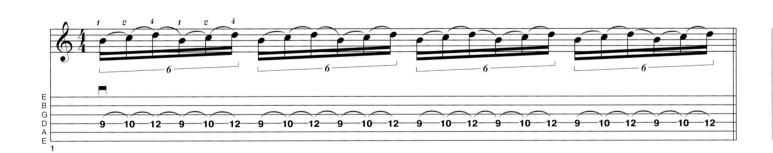

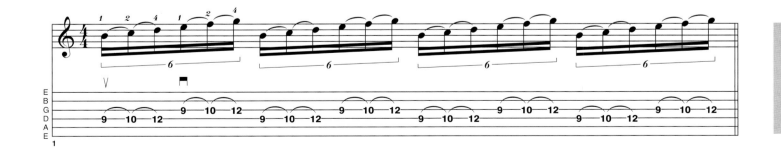

legato

Exercise 55

Exercise 56

Exercise 57

Exercise 58

Exercises 59

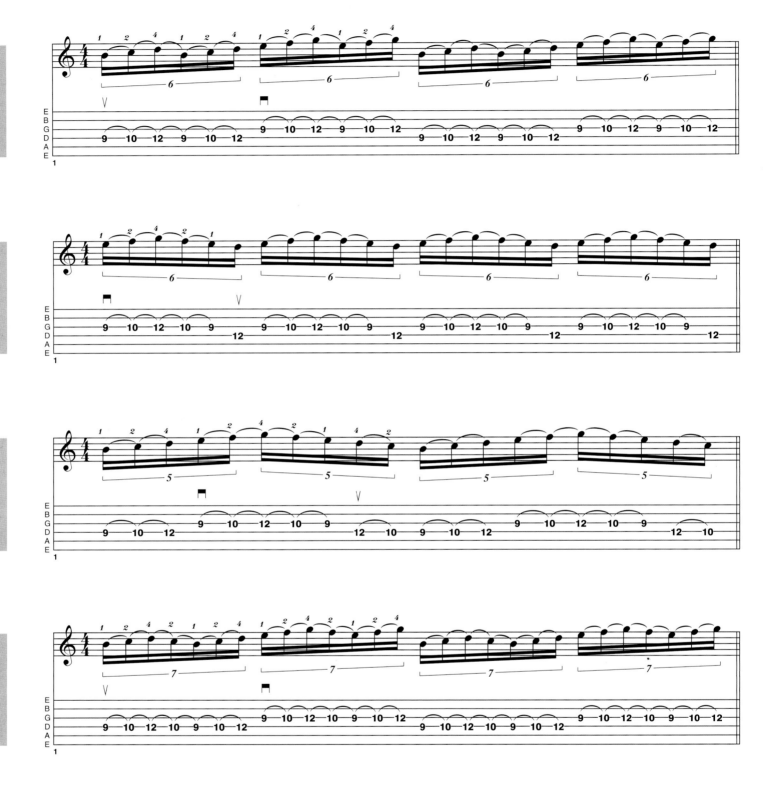

Long the dynamic duo of flamboyant shred, Steve Vai and Joe Satriani are both "must hears" for any student of metal guitar. Satriani's *Surfing With The Alien* (far left) and Vai's *Passion And Warfare* remain absolute classics of the genre.

Exercises 57 and **58** are two more fragments in A Aeolian. Through practise you will develop speed, stamina and accuracy which will also benefit your picking technique. Watch the timing as the fingers will try to go down like a reflex action. Control them by practising slowly, and keep the index finger down unless changing string.

Now let's try crossing the neck some. **Exercises 59** and **60** are simply fragments connected together, but they work as smooth runs once you begin to build up speed and fluidity over

time. Try expanding this idea with other fragments from Exs.57–62 to get yourself moving between different positions on the neck.

Exercises 61 and **62** demonstrate sliding ideas that will help you traverse the neck even more swiftly. Once you have mastered these, try applying the ideas to other string sets and start to learn the surrounding positions. It is a good idea to use the pentatonic scale as a pointer to where you are in relationship to the chord, so you don't get lost when meandering around the scale.

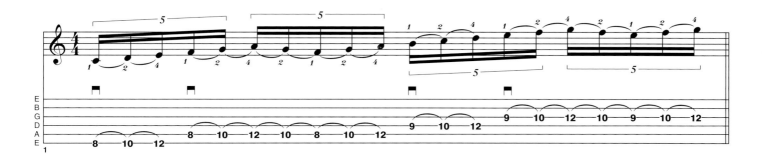

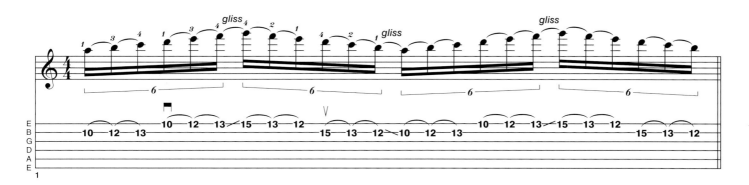

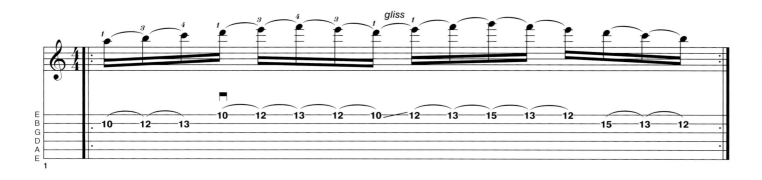

243

Sweedish maestro Yngwie Malmsteen is the long-time supremo of neo-classical metal playing. His technique makes great use of impressive arpeggio-based runs which traverse the neck with astounding agility.

Exercise 63 is an example of Satriani's method for rolling around the scale using slides to create greater range. Try extending this idea all the way through the scale.

Exercise 64 is an octave block. The first six notes are then repeated in the next two octaves. This is a great way to expand the basic scale shape to create a longer line. Technically they are more straightforward as the shape of the first six notes is exactly the same in the second and third octaves. When you get to the top, try running back down again. **Exercise 65** shows how you can arrange two fragments symmetrically and then move the combination up the three octave pathway. Remember: these ideas are also excellent picking patterns. Again, try to keep an eye on your muting technique and keep your fingers as close to the strings as possible.

ARPEGGIO TECHNIQUE

Although earlier heavy metal players like Ritchie Blackmore used arpeggio-based ideas, it wasn't until the post-Van Halen era that arpeggio-oriented playing gained a major foothold in metal. This was a fast melodic style, heavily influenced by classical virtuosi like Paganini and Bach. It was a perfect complement to the scale-based ideas, and allowed great distance to be covered on the neck. Try these exercises in the style of Yngwie Malmsteen.

Exercise 66 is an E minor arpeggio idea on one string. Try to stabilise the hand with the thumb at the back of the neck and stretch out the fingers. The index hammer on will need to be as powerful and accurate as possible. **Exercises 67** and **68** are minor and diminished arpeggios respectively. Notice the diminished chord sets up tension which resolves to the minor.

Along with **exercise 69**, which serves as an example over three strings, these three lines employ the use of sweep picking, a technique allowing fast execution of one-note-per-string ideas. With these exercises, it is crucial that the notes do not ring into each other, so lift off when the note has been played. Follow the picking directions and allow the pick to "fall" on to the next string wherever indicated.

further slides

Exercises 63

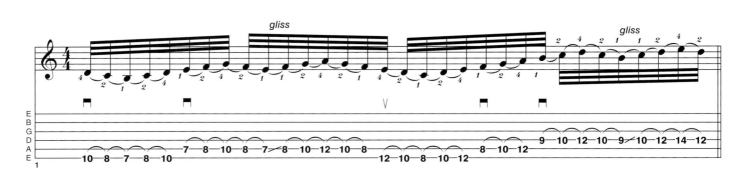

Exercises 64

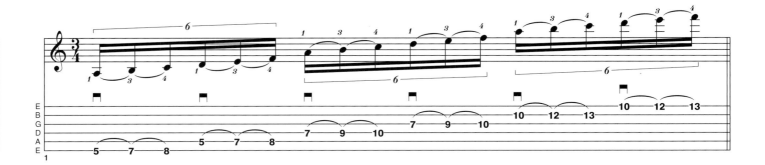

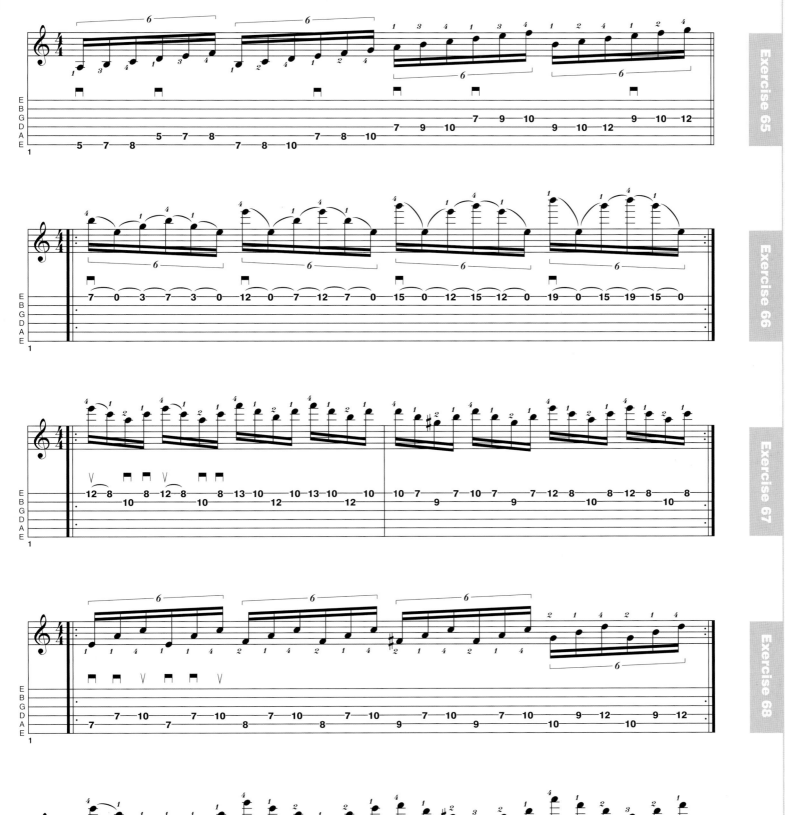

Exercise 70 is an arpeggio exercise based on a typical minor progression. Concentrate on clean execution, the pick dropping to the next note in one smooth glide. This has a different feel to articulating individual strokes. On the way up, drag the pick through the strings. Keep your hand relaxed, and don't hold the pick too tight: it should be flush to the string and slightly sympathetic to the direction in which you are moving.

Exercises 71 and **72** are A minor shapes commonly played in rock and metal. Play them repeatedly until your picking is clean and rhythmic, and the notes well defined. Ex.72 has a mini barre with the third finger on the 14th fret. Make sure you roll over the string to ensure note separation.

Exercise 73 is the colourful A minor add 9 arpeggio.
Exercise 74 is an A minor to G sharp diminished string skipping exercise. This was seen as an alternative way of playing arpeggios by players such as Paul Gilbert and Nuno Bettencourt. As the shapes are different they can provide ideas that would be difficult to sweep, so learning both techniques will inspire a different vocabulary of ideas. Make sure you mute the string above as you hit the note and keep your right hand pivoting on the bass strings to mute.

Exercise 75 is a sequenced run. Keep the down strokes even and accent the upstrokes on beats three and four to stabilise your timing.

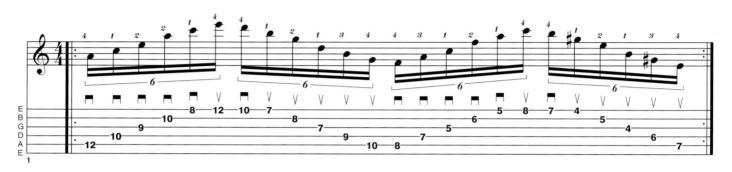

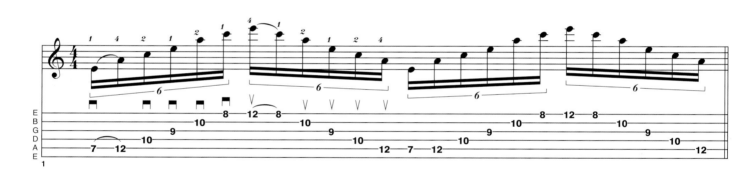

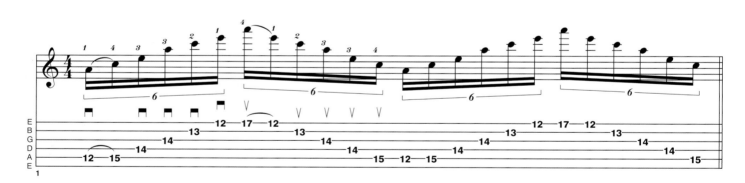

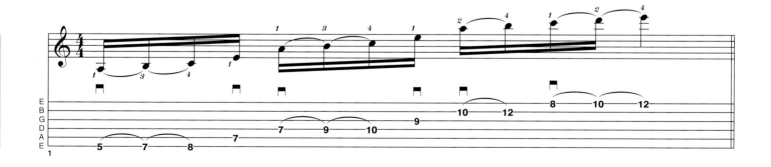

arpeggios

As with the work of many guitarists "let loose" from the confines of their usual band, Nuno Bettencourt's *Schizophonic* strives to exhibit the full – and rather eclectic – range of his skill.

Nuno Bettencourt, left, is a player respected for his great technical ability – including stunning alternative arpeggio technique – who has also crossed over to mainstream success with his band Extreme.

arpeggios

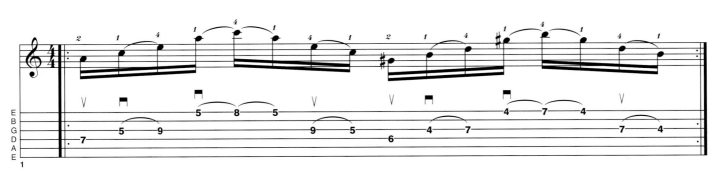

Exercise 74

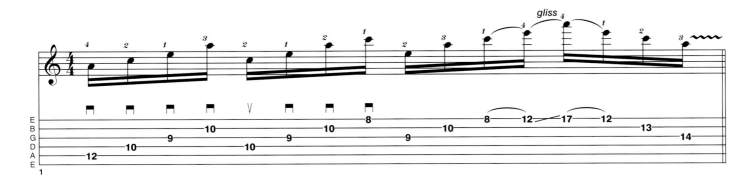

Exercise 75

247

two-handed tapping

Paul Gilbert of Racer X is a gifted all-rounder, with plenty of lessons to teach the metal student – from speed picking to blinding arpeggios.

TWO-HANDED TAPPING

The last of the four main categories of rock and metal technique used to generate notes is "two-handed tapping." This was introduced by revolutionary guitarist Edward Van Halen on his band's debut album in 1978. Fairly straightforward after initial practise, it's an accessible way of playing very fast licks.

Exercises 76 through **78** are in the style of E.V.H. and feature A minor arpeggios. Although E.V.H. used his right hand index finger to execute the tap, I strongly advise you to learn this technique using your second right hand finger and hold your pick

normally in order to seamlessly integrate tapping into the other components of your style. When tapping, rest the heel of your hand on the unplayed strings and tap from the wrist. Make the tap powerful and accurate – do not dab at the string. Also ensure all pull offs are of a down and outwards direction.

Exercise 79 is in the style E.V.H.'s guitar extravaganza, *Eruption*. Play each segment a number of times, then try to link the fragments up bit by bit until you memorize the exercise. Once memorized, you can develop your speed. **Exercise 80** is a method used by E.V.H. to cross strings. The tap (indicated by the arrow) leads the way on to the next string. Elements similar to this are employed in his solo on Michael Jackson's hit *Beat It*.

Tapping gives players the technical facility to play lines at incredible speed; it has brought the guitar as an instrument in line with keyboard virtuosi, and many players use its almost un-guitaristic sound to broaden their style. The next six exercises are in the style of instrumental virtuoso Greg Howe. **Exercise 81** is a pentatonic sequence that enables an execution that would be impossible for the left hand alone. **Exercise 82** is the technique applied to an A minor arpeggio. Isolate the taps and you will recognise that the left hand is simply playing one shape and the taps are outlining the next position. (Hammer the left hand where indicated by the symbol.)

Exercise 76

Exercises 77

Exercises 78

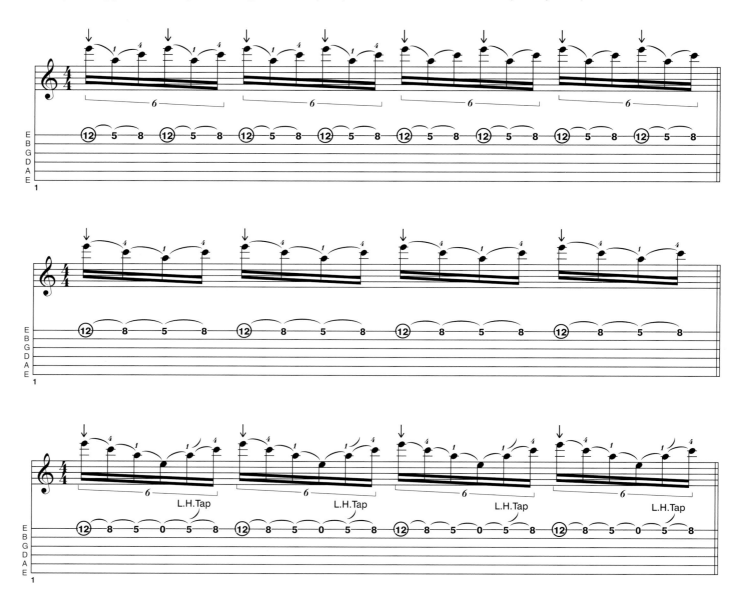

two-handed tapping

Continuing in the style of Greg Howe, **exercise 83** is a scalar sequence. Practise slowly and concentrate on the timing. **Exercise 84** is a two-handed approach to a blues scale fragment; **exercise 85** is an adaptation from conventional playing whereby the tap replaces the note normally played by the left hand pinkie, and **exercise 86** is a Cmaj7 arpeggio which uses a tap and slide. Try applying these last three ideas to the next two octaves to create fast lines over the whole neck.

COMBINING TECHNIQUES

Our final section looks at some of the ways you can combine the components of your technique to create musical concepts. In order to flow, you'll need to find "exit points" to lead you from one technique to another. This will help prevent you from getting caught up in a shape.

Exercises 87 and **88** are a rapid-fire pentatonic lick and a development adding the 9, respectively. This is a simple way to hotrod blues licks. Notice the "exit" point being the 8th fret bend. As this is a very popular blues-lick-oriented bend, you should have no problem in following up from here with some other related ideas.

Exercise 89 is a legato run up to its exit bend; **exercise 90** displays alternate picking; and **exercise 91** is a legato lick with a blues phrase providing us with another useful "exit" point.

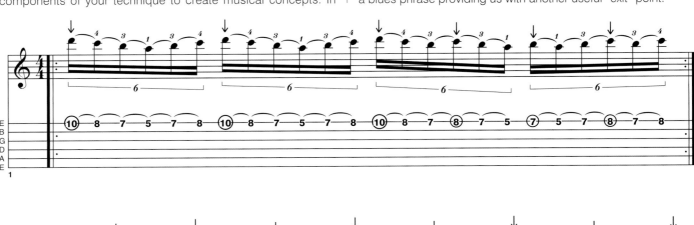

Exercise 83

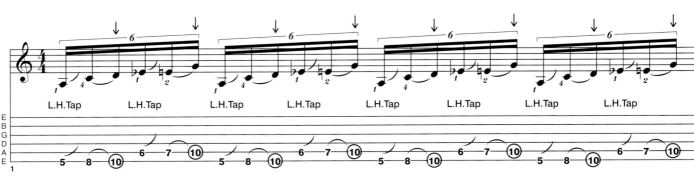

Exercise 84

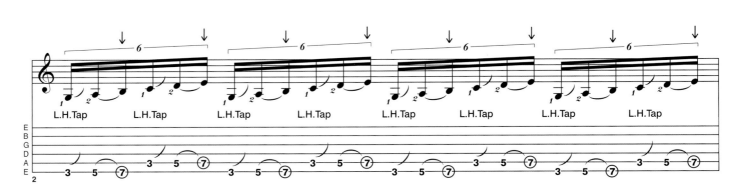

Exercises 85

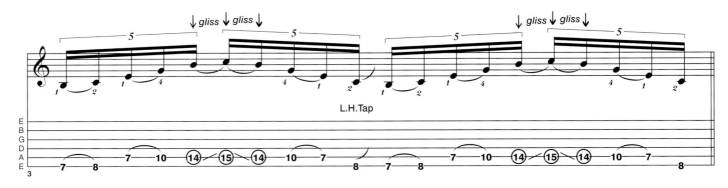

Exercises 86

two-handed tapping

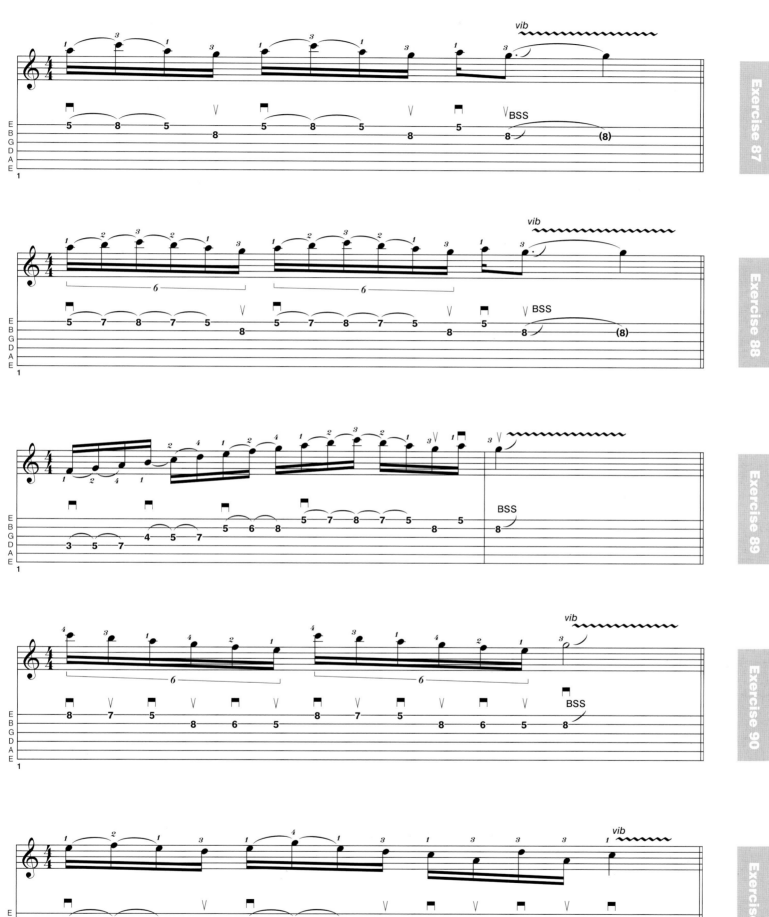

Exercise 87

Exercise 88

Exercise 89

Exercise 90

Exercise 91

combining techniques

combining techniques

Exercises 92

Exercise 93

Exercise 94

Exercise 95

Exercise 96

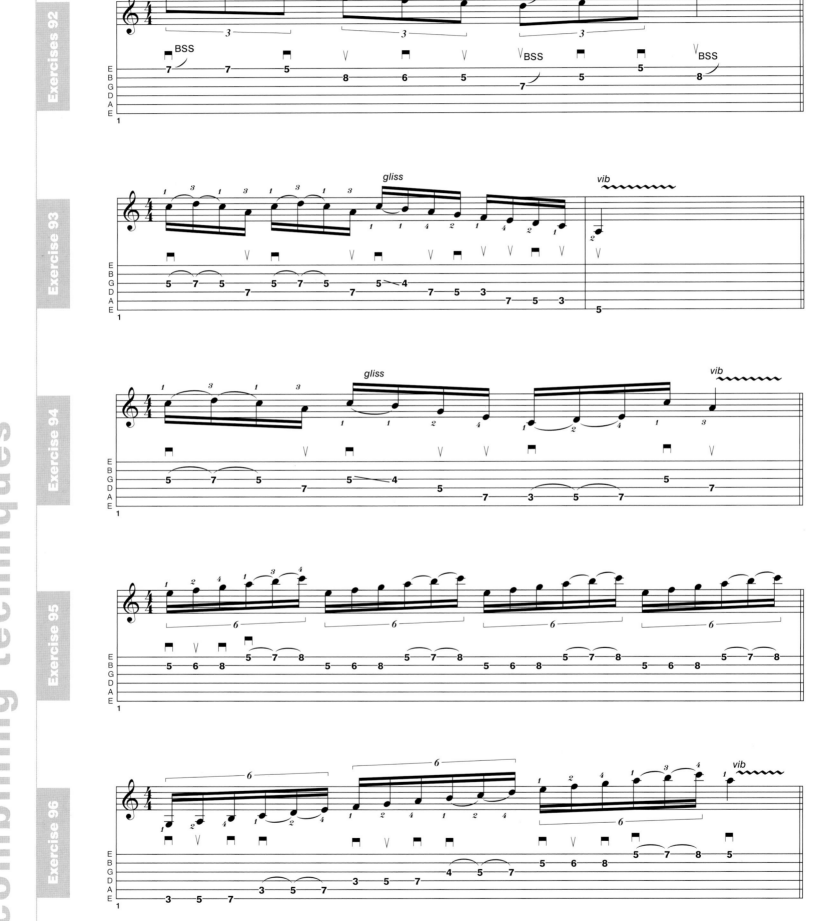

Exercise 92 is a triplet lick combining A Aeolian and pentatonic ideas. Be careful with the intonation on the semitone bend. Exercise 93 is a riff that uses a slide to make the transition from blues phrase to scalar run, while exercise 94 is a similar idea, but uses an arpeggio fragment. Both examples exit on the root note. Exercise 95 demonstrates the combination of picking and legato, which gives a different sound to using one or the other exclusively. Make sure you practice slowly first as the changeover can often throw off the timing. Exercise 96 is an extension of this idea.

Now let's combine an arpeggio and a scale fragment in exercise 97. Follow the picking directions and check your muting technique. Exercise 98 ascends a two octave arpeggio into a legato-based run, exiting on a slide.

Exercise 99 is an arpeggio lick which is extended by a right hand tap. The descending form is executed with a series of left hand hammers before ending with a scalar idea. Finally, Exercise 100 has an extended legato run climaxing with a tap before descending. Again, concentrate on timing and accuracy.

All of the "exit" points should be played with wide vibrato. On the top two strings, push upwards and on the remaining four, pull downwards. Like the bending technique, the motion comes from the rotation of the wrist, not the fingers. Concentrate on returning to pitch as you vibrato, and tail off by sliding down the neck.

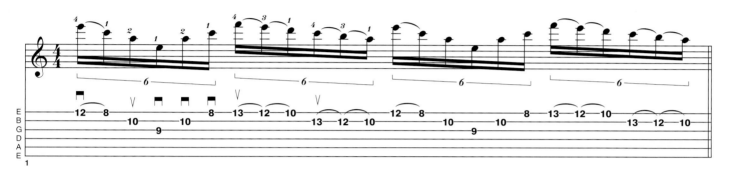
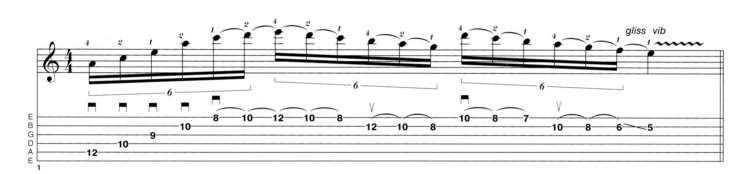
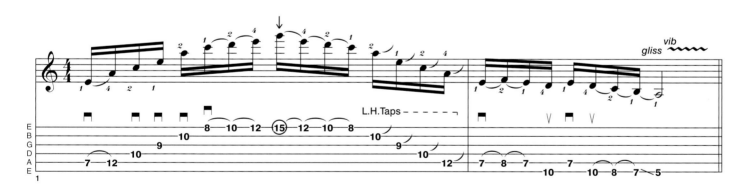
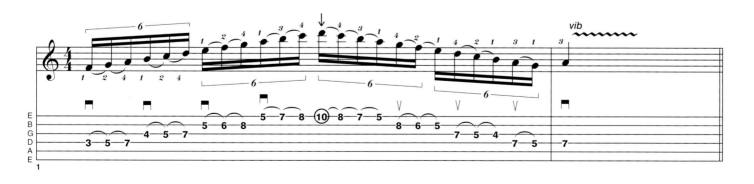

7

PLAYING
LATIN

latin rhythms

Latin music has long had a following at the pop and rock fringes, and has occasionally found its way to superstardom in the hands of a Carlos Santana, for example. The recent proliferation of Latin rhythms in pop and dance hits, however – along with the close focus on Latin styles in Ry Cooder's popular and influential *Buena Vista Social Club* – has breathed new life into the genre, and turned new listeners on to the infectious rhythms and melodies of this compelling music. ● NESTOR GARCIA

To avoid some common misconceptions and misuses of this style of music, let's start by learning the original patterns so you can identify the source of these traditional tunes; then you can transform them, if you like, into something more original or blend them into whatever other styles you play.

We're going to look at some basic riffs from the Afro-Cuban tradition: son montuno, mambo and cha-cha-cha. These are three of the most common styles in a *descarga* – a Latin jam session – and we're going to examine some of the basic ingredients to help you cook up some hot salsa. This music is all about rhythm, but even a whole heap of rhythm is useless without feel. Latin music is designed to make you move your hips, so if they're stationary you haven't quite got it yet!

The guitar, like the piano, is used as a percussion instrument; think drums, cowbells, anything. The way to take control of the groove is to use repetitive patterns, just like a percussionist would. In this context, most of the guitar patterns are based on piano and Cuban *tres* patterns.

Rhythm patterns are centered around the *clave*. A clave is one of a pair of short wooden sticks used as a percussion instrument in Latin music. They usually play the clave rhythm, which is considered to be the centerpoint of Afro-Cuban music. Sometimes they are referred to as 3:2 or 2:3 This merely refers to the amount of rhythmic hits in the bar. The 3:2 has three in the first bar, and two in the second. In a tune, all the other instruments will play rhythms that are related to this basic rhythm.

Exercise 1 is the two basic types of clave: Son clave and Rumba clave. Away from your guitar and in any possible situation, tap a clave rhythm with your right hand while keeping time, in quarter notes, with your left hand. Then reverse hands. (I've written the son clave in 2:3 as this is the most common form used for cha-cha-cha and mambo, though you find them in 3:2 as well – just reverse the bars.) In 2:3 clave the guitar starts on a downbeat; the upbeats are in the 3 side of the clave.

Exercise 2 is the pattern played by the timbale player on the side of the timbales, here transposed with a 2:3 Son clave. It is called *cáscara*. Use this as a warm up exercise, playing it purely as a rhythm pattern, and then try to use it in the scale in **exercise 3** and play it with your own scales and arpeggios, just to get the idea firmly seated in your body.

Exercise 4 is a line based on the pattern played by the *tres cubano*, an acoustic guitar with three pairs of strings, tuned G, C and E, outlining a second inversion C major triad. Sometimes you can find it in D. This is used primarily to play *son montuno*, the oldest form of what we today know as salsa. This line is played in the 2:3 son clave. All the salsa and mambo patterns are based on *son montuno* patterns.

Hundreds of tunes and styles are based on the I-IV-V chord progression. Faster, slower, in major or a minor flavor… Three

chords, three inversions and twelve keys equals 108 possible varieties of finger entertainment for a Sunday morning, and you can transpose the line in **exercise 5** over many variations of them. Then add some of these rhythms and you are done. What about a bit of tapping at the same time? Perhaps a 2:3 son clave? Sunday afternoon is starting to look busy too? It's easy to change into a minor feel, if you ignore the trickier fingering. Just take the thirds of the I and IV chords and flatten them, taking them from major thirds to minor thirds, as in **exercise 6**. Try transposing the major riff from Ex.5 to other keys, then transpose it into the minor as has been done here for you. If you also slow the tempo down to something around 70-100 bpm, it becomes a *guajira* tempo. Pronounced "gwa-hear-ah," this is a traditional music of the peasants of Cuba, usually accompanied by *tres cubano*.

Exercise 7 is another typical chord progression, similar to those found in the *Buena Vista Social Club* (check out this CD for some pure Afro-Cuban grooves). It outlines the I-V-V-1 in A minor key in 2:3 clave. Transpose it to different keys.

Exercise 8 is a *montuno* line. This is one of the most common patterns found in salsa and Latin jazz. You may find you'll get a better feel if you follow the pulse in "cut-time." It outlines a Dm7 type of vamp but you can use it also over Dm7-G9 progression.

Rumba Clave

Son Clave

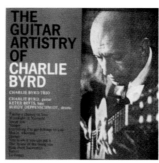

From trad Latin to salsa-spiced jazz. Influential Brazilian guitarist Baden Powell shaped the form of the bossa nova (far left), while Charlie Byrd adapts such textures for his *The Guitar Artistry Of...* album (center). Saxophonist Bud Shank and guitarist Laurindo Almeida travel south of the border for *Brazilliance*.

Latin

Exercise 5

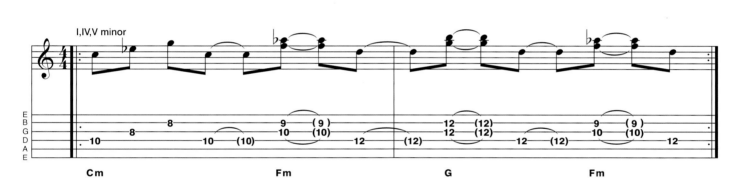

Exercise 6

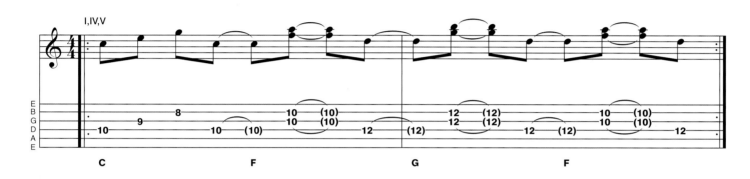

Exercise 7

Exercise 8

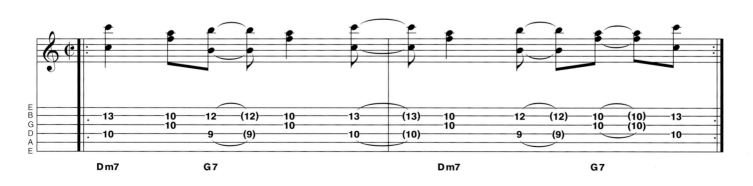

Exercise 9 is a typical *son montuno* line in 2:3 clave. Notice that the downbeat of the montuno falls on the "two-side" of the clave (the bar with two notes in it), and the syncopated bar of the *montuno* falls on the "three side" of the clave. How you use the clave direction depends on whether the melody of the tune is in either direction (2:3 or 3:2). For the moment just try to get this line together. Concentrate on tempo and the ability to hold it for a long time. Record the clave and then play the line over it.

Exercise 10 is a pattern in the 3:2 clave. This is a very basic pattern to describe the concept of playing with the clave, but remember that there are many variations to this pattern. It is just a starting point. It maintains the same chord progression as the previous example in 2:3 and begins with an eight-note rest.

The basic rhythm for the cha-cha-cha is found in **exercise 11**. We all know this pattern from the organ riff in Santana's version of *Oye Como Va*. Try to play this line while tapping the 2:3 son clave with your foot. Concentrate on the note lengths, don't rush!

Exercise 12 is going to add some variation to the cha-cha-cha. It would originally have been played on a piano, and this has been adapted for guitar. It is important to have some co-ordination between thumb and fingers here, so don't worry if it takes a bit of time to get going. Remember, this is only a

variation, so don't overdo it unless you want a really busy feel. Hold it tight.

Playing during a percussion solo, like congas or timbale, requires lots of concentration and good sense of rhythm. Close your eyes if necessary to improve your concentration and be relaxed at the same time. **Exercise 13** is a common *montuno* line, often used over a percussion solo. This is just another exercise to reinforce your rhythm. This time it outlines a C7 mambo in 2:3 clave (remember?). Transpose it. You would use the same pattern over, for example, D7 to C7, for two bars each. Try taking it through the A blues progression.

Exercise 14 is the sort of thing you might find in a Mongo Santamaria tune. It's just two triads with a nicely syncopated rhythm. If you're playing this over a conga solo, be prepared to play this groove, and only this groove, for five to ten minutes, and maybe even longer. You think it sounds easy, but you'll need to really focus on your playing, because the soloist will be playing patterns and fills that will throw you off in no time.

Exercise 15 and **16** are examples of lines used in mambo and cha-cha-cha. Take note of the use of octaves, with fingers 1 and 4 of your left hand, and double stops. Start playing them slowly (90 bpm cut time) up to 120 bpm. The first example can be played over Am7- D7 or over just a D7. Hips starting to move?

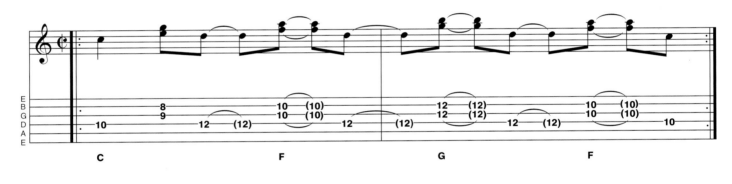

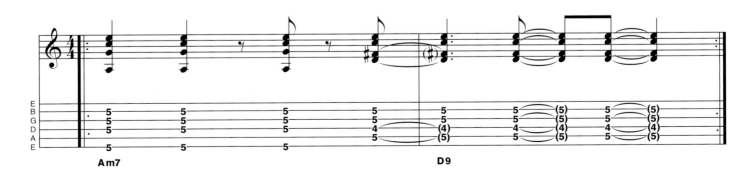

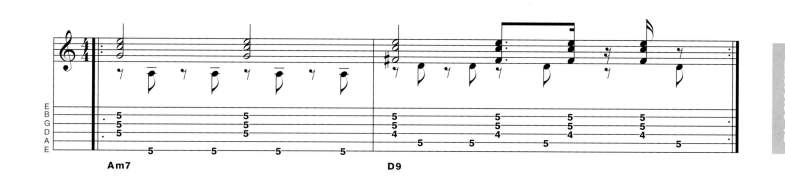

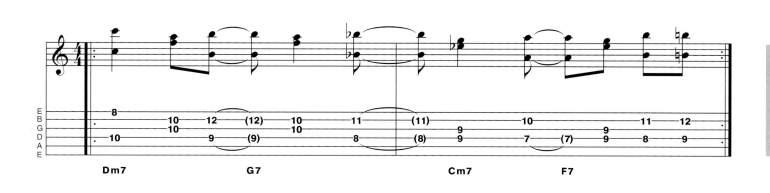

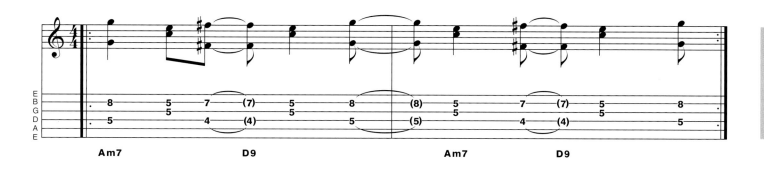

8

PLAYING
AFRICAN

Infectiously rhythmic, explosively joyous, delightfully melodic – African guitar is a style that works its way quickly into your blood, and stays there for good. It's as much fun to play as it is irresistible to listen to, and the fundamentals aren't particularly difficult to tackle with a little practise and special attention to the rhythmic essentials. Once mastered, it can be pursued as a style unto itself, or blended into countless other genres of music to give your usual playing some extra life and sparkle. ● **KARI BANNERMAN**

It is hardly surprising that the list of stars influenced yearly by their collaborations with African musicians is growing. Take Ry Cooder's work with Ali Farka Toure, Taj Mahal and Fouday Musa, or Paul Simon's work with Ladysmith Black Mambazo. Africa possesses the largest menu of both traditional and urban grooves in the world, a potential source of inspiration for anyone needing to resuscitate their depleting creative energy.

In this brief look at African guitar styles we're going to explore two "Palm Wine" guitar grooves: the *Sikyi* (pronounced see-chi), and the *Amponsah* (arm-pawn-sa), then move on to explore the broader "highlife" style of music. There was a time when no palm wine drinking session was complete without acoustic guitar music; hence the label. It is a characteristically happy sounding music, a music of celebration. It's influences can also be heard on albums like Jean-Luc Ponty's *Tchokola*, Koo Nimo's *Osabarifa*, and Peter Gabriel's *Passion*.

Highlife is a generic name for various types of dance music from west Africa. Essentially, though, it is the music created when west African musicians used the instruments provided by their colonial bosses to play indigenous music, instead of the European waltzes, foxtrots and other expatriate music.

Amponsah-style guitar – created by the itinerant seamen of Liberia – is central to highlife music. Even the intricate guitar melodies that characterise the Congolese "*soukous*" style of African popular music contain at least one guitarist playing Amponsah groups – as does Paul Simon on his *Rhythm Of The Saints* album. Other fine examples of these sounds on Eric Agyeman/Ab Crentsil/T Frimpong's *Classic Highlife* and Bessa's *Bessa Live*.

Be aware that much of this style of playing has been adapted for guitar down the years, and would originally have been played on a more traditional stringed instrument, such as a kora. The kora is a traditional Senegambian instrument which resembles a balalaika in shape, using a large gourd as a body. It does, however, have considerably more strings, which are played in a harp-like fashion, without fretting them at all. Some of the exercises to following will contain suggestions for approximating this sound and feel on the guitar.

SIKYI RHYTHMS

The heartbeat of Sikyi and most African music is to be found in the drum section. For practical reasons, we will use a drum machine to recreate that feel.

Exercise 1 is a simple, three-part rhythm you can set up to accompany yourself with. Otherwise, if you don't have a drum machine, you could play the bell rhythm with a coin on an empty bottle, as is done in west Africa. Once you have programmed it in (a cabasa is a shaker, incidentally) try to feel the rhythm so that

you hear the pattern of the bell, and not the four-beat pulse of the time signature. It's a pattern that is similar to the "chop" rhythm of reggae but without the first beat of the eighth-note.

Rhythmical independence is crucial to all African music. Some forms have no time signature at all, being made up of a polyrhythmic structure whereby, for example, signatures of 2/4, 4/4 and 6/8 will coexist in a staggered bar system. This makes them completely unintelligible to the uninitiated. In any case, it's a music you have to develop a *feel* for to play right.

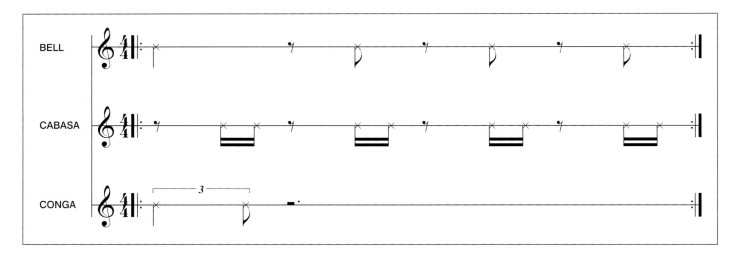

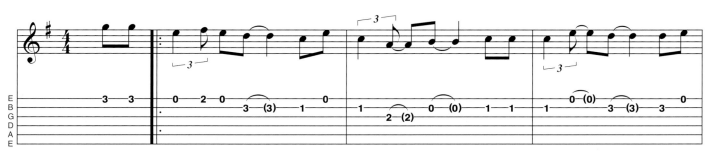

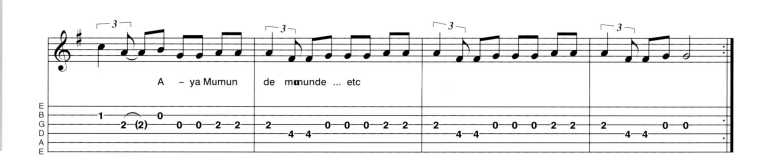

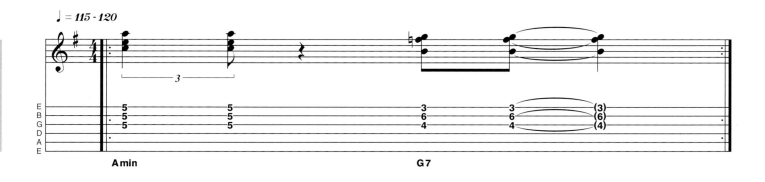

african rhythm

Exercise 1

Exercise 2

Exercise 3

TRADITIONAL TUNES

The most direct translation that I can manage of the folk tune *Mumunde* that we're going to look at now (pronounced "Mommoo-dey") is "Happy Magical Dwarf." **Exercise 2** gives us the melody, the chorus repeating three times from bar four onwards. Play it with a happy feeling and record it, along with the drum pattern you have programmed, four or five times. We'll use this as the backing to practise our other exercises to. Listen to it over and over again until you really feel it.

Exercise 3 is a simple rhythmic strum. Even though it is based on two chords, the note and inversion choice is important to retain the flavor of Sikyi. Play the A minor with a crisp and tight plectrum action, and the G7 a little looser. If you're using a 4-track, record this onto your tape as well.

You may find that when you play exercise 4, you will start to feel the African vibe coming through, what Osibisa used to call "criss-cross rhythms that explode with happiness." Practise it with your ever-expanding backing track. Whether you are playing this with a plectrum or fingerstyle, practise it until there's a flow, or dance, to your right-hand action. Left-hand fingerings are suggestions only (t: thumb, i: index, m: middle), so check them out and then make up your mind.

Play the groove in **exercise 5** smoothly and in time to the backing tape and you will be merrily adopted by every Ghanian family in town, for you are now playing Sikyi music. If you add a "head" with a slur starting on the fourth beat of the intro, and a pulled-off tail on the next fourth beat, you will be playing the style as an Ashanti would really play it. We are using the mixolydian mode here, as the F is being kept natural, and this can be used as a tool for soloing.

Try playing Ex.5 an octave higher than written to get an ethnic Kora feel. use your index finger as a capo at the 12th fret – or even try it in open position on a Nashville-tuned guitar (a standard six-string guitar strung with the high-octave strings from a 12-string, or similar gauges).

Exercise 6 is a typical Palm Wine guitar solo intro, which you could join up to Ex.5 (as the start Ex.5 and end of Ex.6 imply). The phrase is in thirds from 12th position and moves down to third position. This downward movement is characteristic of most African melodies (see Ex.1). Note also how breaking away from the diad on the fourth beat adds more character to the line you're playing. The line also echoes the cyclical, non-resolving nature of Sikyi, which is typical of the vast majority of African music forms. Use your whammy bar to slide into the notes to get a Sunny Ade "Juju" feel. Again, a happy feel is vital before you can join it up with Ex.5.

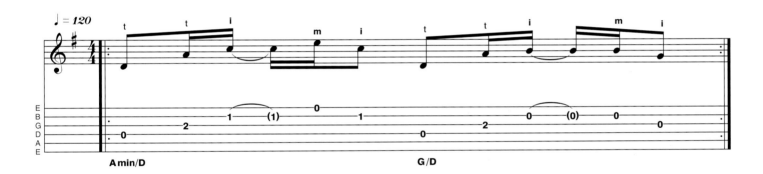

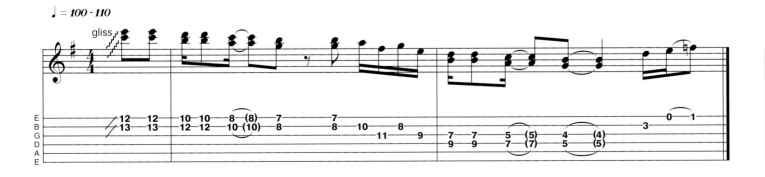

263

HIGHLIFE RHYTHMS

Our basic rhythm for this style is found in **exercise 7**. It cannot be overemphasized just how crucial rhythm is to this kind of music, so make sure you get it under your skin: dance to it. Make sure the tempo is comfortable; anything from 100bpm to 120bpm will be fine.

Exercise 8 is the melody from the song *Yaa Amponsah*, which is the story about a young, newly married bride. As before, record the melody and rhythm track to play along to.

Exercise 9 is a typical Amponsah guitar groove. Practise it with your rhythm section slowly at first, gradually building up the tempo until you can reach 120bpm comfortably. Essentially, it is a fingerstyle or two-fingers-and-plectrum groove, because some of the voicings are unplayable with a plectrum alone. In Africa, because of the dominant influence of the kora and the *nyatiti* (another lute-style instrument), the right-hand two-finger picking style is predominant, but use whatever is comfortable.

The chord symbols are just a guide; to get the flavor use my exact inversions. Numerous variations of this progression have spawned a thousand songs all over west Africa and beyond – just ask Brian Eno or Mick Fleetwood. It is related to calypso and I know that it plays a crucial part in the ongoing cross-fertalization of grooves between Africa, Europe and the Caribbean.

HIGHLIFE JAZZ

Exercise 10 is a rhythm lick using the 7sus and 7 chords. Here we are moving into the area of highlife big bands and highlife jazz. Try the more complex chords written underneath as a jazzier variation. This is more big band highlife, as it utilizes these crossover chords. The essence of Amponsah is retained in the melody lines, the rhythm and the bassline. Use a right hand semi-muted, snappy plectrum style to make the rhythms come alive. When you have mastered it, practise it alternately with Ex.3.

Exercise 11 is a typical Amponsah phrase used by local guitarists – the sound of the diminished chord is very reminiscent of the tonality of several indigenous harmonies and that's why it's used. This exercise is really quite simple. Start with the diminished triad and just move the shape down the fretboard, retaining the fingering until you hit the F6 chord and C. The following phrases are sixth diads, much as you'd find at the beginning of *Soul Man* by Sam and Dave.

Finally, **exercise 12** gives you an impression an Amponsah bassline. Note the syncopation and polyrhythms against the guitar. Practise until you really feel it, when you don't need to think of the notes, the bars, or the phrases. This is called the *"adakamu"* style, as it is traditionally adapted from the phrasing of the square box bass drum, and adakamu means "box."

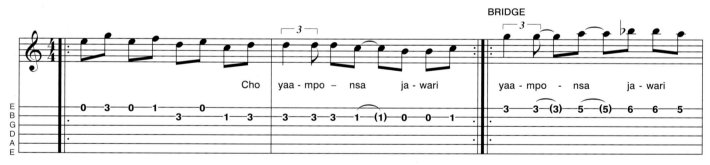

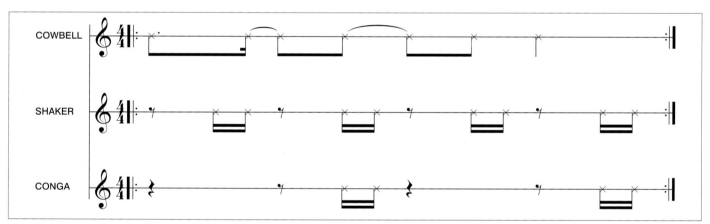

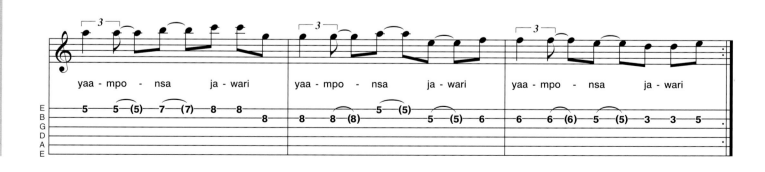

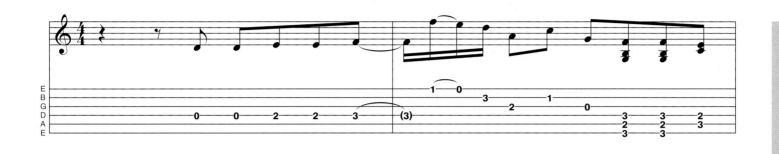

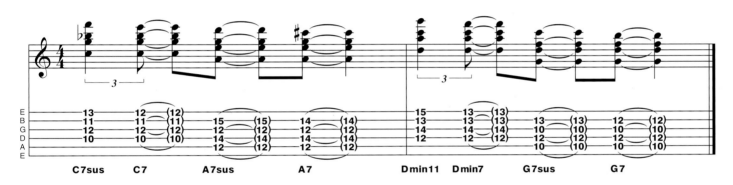

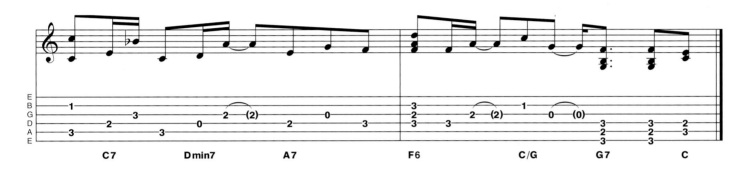

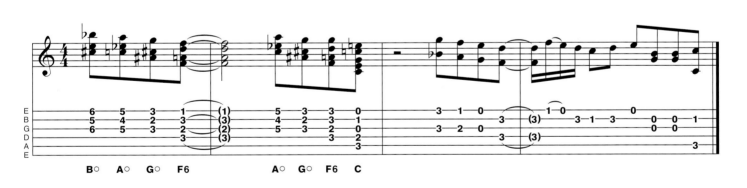

highlife jazz

Exercise 9

Exercise 10

Exercise 11

Exercise 12

9

PLAYING
CLASSICAL

Like the study of any classical instrument, the serious pursuit of proficiency in classical guitar is a major discipline. That said, any competent guitarist willing to put in some time and effort can learn enough of the basics of classical guitar technique, sound and style to add an exciting new element to his or her repertoire. As genre distinctions fall further by the wayside in contemporary guitar-based music, achieving a basic grasp of classical technique can add diversity to your own style, and perhaps turn you on to a whole new direction in your playing. ● **DAVID BRAID**

The 10 exercises in this section are designed to give an overview of classical guitar technique and types of music played in this style. Most of the pieces are specially composed studies, each highlighting particular playing techniques and/or musical devices. Before getting into the exercises, however, it's important for us to take a quick look at classical playing technique.

PLAYING POSITION
The classical playing position stems directly from the practicality of keeping the instrument steady while being free to play. The position not only allows the player to move easily around the fingerboard with the left hand, but also enables them to make sudden right hand position changes, for example, from an arpeggio to a chord strum. The left leg should be raised by the use of a small foot stool which raises the guitar neck so all parts of the fingerboard can be reached easily. Without using the hands at all the guitar is held in four places:
1. Resting on the left thigh
2. Leaning against the right inner thigh
3. Underneath the right forearm (before the elbow)
4. The back leaning on the left side of the chest.

POINTS TO NOTE
1. The force of gravity ensures the right hand falls naturally into place over the sound hole
2. The shoulders and arms should be completely relaxed
3. The guitar neck should be angled sufficiently so that the left hand is quite close to the eye. As most music is played from memory, the left hand is guided by looking at the frets you are about to go to. (The hand follows the eye, not vice-versa.)
4. Both thumbs should be in a natural, straight position and all fingers should be curved in (on both hands).

BASIC TECHNIQUE
One of the fundamental aspects of classical guitar music is counterpoint: two or more lines played simultaneously. It is because of this musical requirement that the independence and collaboration of fingers and thumb in the right hand is so essential. Although other styles of guitar playing use right hand finger style, the demands of accuracy and speed in the classical repertoire have given rise to special exercises designed to bring these points to great refinement. It can take some work to get to this point, but it will pay dividends in your performance ability.

ARPEGGIO TECHNIQUE

The photo above is from the player's point of view. Points to notice are, 1: that you are positioned over the middle of the instrument; 2: the right-hand (RH) thumb is straight and well in front of the fingers; 3: the left-hand (LH) thumb is approximately opposite the second finger and well behind the neck.

It is important that the RH does note move between individual strokes of the fingers and thumb, both because one's spatial relation to the string can be lost and also because time (one of the most important aspects of music) is lost moving the hand back to a position where the string can be reached.

ARPEGGIOS

The basis of the right hand technique is the arpeggio. This is shown below in four stages. In classical guitar notation the fingers on both hands are given special letters and numbers (numbers for the left and letters for the right in order to make a clear distinction between them).

The right hand fingers and their notation symbols are: Thumb: **p**; Index: **i**; Middle: **m**; Ring: **a**. The little finger is not used. The left hand fingers are numbered 1–4 from the index to the little finger.

HALF-ARPEGGIO

The half-arpeggio is when strings four (or five or six) to one are played with the thumb and three fingers of the right hand, with a particular finger assigned to each string. Before playing it is important to prepare the fingers on the strings (as in the photo top-left) in order to ensure the correct angle of playing stroke. As you can also see in this photograph, the thumb is far in front of the fingers in order for both to move freely without colliding with each other. This is especially important, as to make a strong tone it is essential that the fingers and thumb follow through after playing the string.

Of the five individual photos seen left, the top-left photograph shows the same stage of preparation from the front. Note the slight angle in the wrist, which produces enough height for the fingers to move into the hand. The remaining photos show the progression of movement of the thumb and three fingers as they play strings four to one.

Note that the fingers which are yet to play remain on the string until it is their turn to move. This is necessary to ensure that no time is lost looking for the string. Ideally the exercise should be repeated a number of times in succession without a break between each cycle. When playing in this way it is important not to replace the fingers on the strings for preparation each time until the moment they are required to play the string again, as it would stop the previous notes from sounding, resulting in an unpleasant sudden break in the sustained note.

FULL-ARPEGGIO

The full-arpeggio is an extension of the half-arpeggio where two extra notes are played, making it a cycle of six instead of four. This is done by playing the second string (with **m**) and then the third string (with **i**) again immediately after the **a** finger has played the first string.

LEARNING NOTATION

Musical notation is written on a grid of five horizontal lines called a "stave" (or staff). Each line and each space on the stave represents a note of a different pitch, named after the first seven letters of the alphabet: A, B, C, D, E, F, G. After this the notes start repeating in a higher or lower "octave" – so-called because there are eight main steps from one note to its equivalent note, above or below.

The symbol at the beginning of the stave is called a clef. There are several types of clef, but this one, a treble clef, is really the only one you will come across as a guitarist (other clefs, such as the bass clef, show different parts of the musical range).

The notes on the lines of the treble clef stave are, from the bottom: E, G, B, D, F (it may help you remember this order if you make up a mnemonic using these letters – a common one is *Every Good Boy Deserves Fun*). The notes in the spaces, going

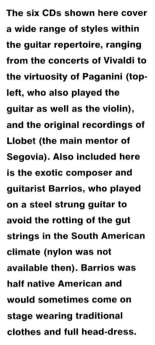

The six CDs shown here cover a wide range of styles within the guitar repertoire, ranging from the concerts of Vivaldi to the virtuosity of Paganini (top-left, who also played the guitar as well as the violin), and the original recordings of Llobet (the main mentor of Segovia). Also included here is the exotic composer and guitarist Barrios, who played on a steel strung guitar to avoid the rotting of the gut strings in the South American climate (nylon was not available then). Barrios was half native American and would sometimes come on stage wearing traditional clothes and full head-dress.

up, are: F, A, C, E (as illustrated on the sample stave below). When notes are used that go outside the range of the stave, either above or below, short lines called "ledger lines" – long enough for just one note – are added to extend the stave.

Most music is divided into bars, as shown in the second diagram above, by vertical "barlines" which group the music into equal sections to make it easier to read. Although the bars divide the music evenly according to the time signature they are not to be heard as such – you must not pause or stop at each barline. A double barline indicates the end of the piece of music.

The notes themselves can last different lengths of time, as indicated by symbols called "note values" (illustrated below). A whole note is called a *semibreve*, a half note is called a *minim*, a quarter note is called a *crotchet*, an eighth note is called a *quaver*, and a sixteenth note is called a *semiquaver*.

TIME SIGNATURES

The type and amount of note values in each bar is indicated at the beginning of the music by the "time signature." This consists of two small numbers arranged vertically. The top digit indicates the number of beats per bar and the lower number indicates the value of each, which is represented by its fraction of a semibreve (whole note). So, for example, the crotchet (quarter note) is indicated by the lower number 4; the minim (half note) is indicated by a 2; and the semiquaver (sixteenth note) is indicated by a 16.

The most frequently used time signature is 4 4 – four crotchets in a bar – often called "common time," and therefore sometimes indicated by just a capital C at the start of the passage instead of the two fours. Other frequently used time signatures are 2/4 and 3/4 and 6/8. The latter has the note value of a quaver and divides the bar into two halves of 3/8.

GUITAR NOTATION

As well as the standard musical notation, there are some additional signs specific to written guitar music:

A number from 1–4, written above or under a note on the stave, indicates which left-hand finger is to be used to hold down that note on the fingerboard. (If the number 0 appears, the open string is to be played.)

A number in a circle indicates which string is to be played.

Roman numerals (I, II, III, IV, V etc) indicate the fret position at which to hold down the notes.

The letters p, i, m and a (as already mentioned in the introduction) above or below the stave refer to the right-hand fingering.

To ease the way for non-music readers, all exercises will also be represented in TAB, but you can use this chapter to brush up on your music-reading skills – which will be essential for any further pursuit of classical guitar study.

ACCIDENTALS

On the following pages, our first two exercises deal with two main points: accidentals (sharps in exercise 1 and flats in exercise 2) and music in two parts. Accidentals are sharp, flat or natural signs placed in the music next to particular notes in order to raise or lower them by a semitone (one fret on the guitar). The note affected remains sharpened or flattened until the next bar line or until it is returned to its original pitch by a natural sign. The lower part in both exercises is played with p and the top part with alternating i and m.

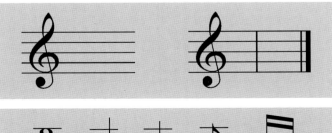

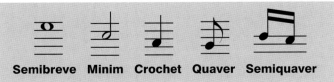

Semibreve   Minim   Crochet   Quaver   Semiquaver

The great Andrés Segovia, who throughout the twentieth century single-handedly raised the status of the guitar from a humble salon instrument to a full classical instrument capable of high art music.

In **exercise 1**, Note the marking *f* at the start: this stands for "forte" – strong/loud. The piece gradually drops in volume to *p* "piano" – soft/quiet – in bar five. These symbols are called "dynamics" and are indications to alter the volume of the piece. In bars seven and eight the piece picks up in volume again to *mf* – "mezzo forte" (medium loud).

The word "rit" is short for "ritardo" which means to hold back, or slow down. This is to be done throughout the section indicated by the dotted line. The curved line between the two Ds in bar eight is a "tie." The tie tells us that the second of these notes is not to be played, but that the first-played note is merely sustained through this beat.

The tie should not to be confused with a "slur," which is between two notes of different pitch and means that the second one is only played with the left hand (by executing a pull off or hammer on).

Exercise 2 is another piece in 2/4 with further accidentals to keep an eye out for. Also, notice that the notes in bar eight have two stems, going up and down. This is because both parts have the exact same notes at this point, playing in unison, even though they are still considered two parts.

The G in bar nine should be left to ring on so it makes a passing harmony with the E-flat which you will play at the start of the next bar.

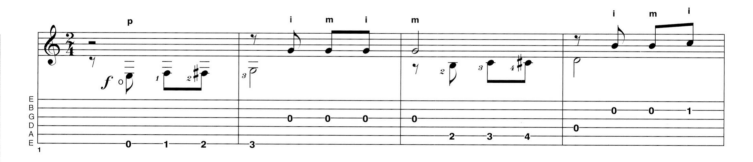

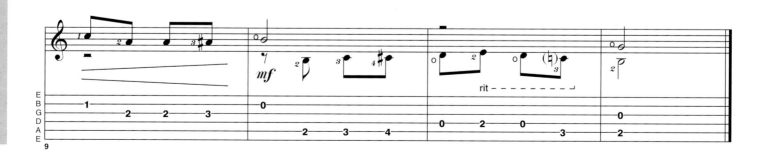

Exercise 1

accidentals

accidentals

British guitarist Julian Bream is in many ways an heir to Segovia, even though he is self-taught and developed independently. His exciting, fiery playing and devotion to authenticity of repertoire quickly established him as the leading guitarist of the second half of the twentieth century.

Exercise 2

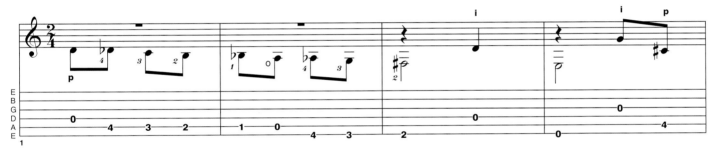

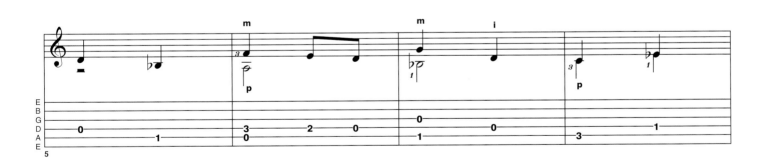

Exercise 3 is the theme from *The Surprise Symphony* by Joseph Haydn (1732-1809). This piece has a "key signature" of A. This is a set of sharps or flats written at the start of the music which indicates that those particular notes are to be raised or lowered by a semitone throughout the entire work (unless canceled out by a natural accidental). The key signature indicates a "key," which is a hierarchy of chords based around one main chord called the "tonic triad." The sharps and flats always appear in the same order so that it is not necessary to actually check which line or space the sharp or flat sign appears on. The order of Sharps is: F#,C#,G#,D#,A#,E#,B#. A simple way of remembering this order is by using the mnemonic: *Father*

Charles Goes Down And Eats Breakfast. The order of flats is simply the reverse: Bb,Eb,Ab,Db,Gb,Cb,Fb. In exercise 3 there are three sharps: F#,C#,G#.

There is a loud chord right at the end of the piece which in the original version for orchestra was put in by the composer to stop the audience talking during the performance. The word "*sempre*" before the dynamic marking of *pp* means "always" so the entire piece is to be played at *pp: pianissimo* (very quiet) until a different dynamic is encountered. This happens at the final chord which is marked *sfz*. This stands for "*sforzando*," meaning forced – an indication to accent the chord heavily and suddenly (strummed very quickly across with p).

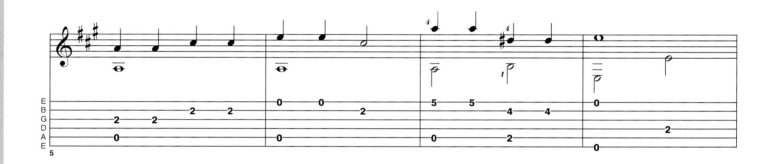

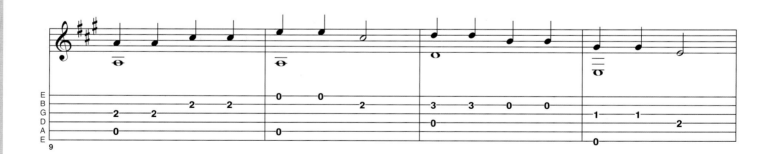

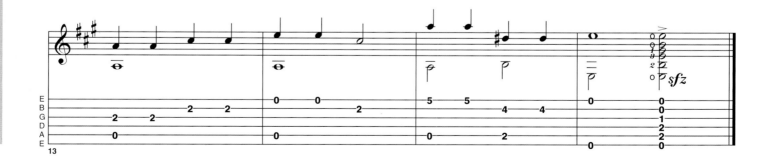

dynamics

Exercise 3

This piece in **exercise 4** is based entirely on the half-arpeggio technique discussed in the introduction. These change direction now and then, for example in bar four and from the section marked *p* (piano).

There is an *f* (forte) marking right at the start, and the piece returns to this dynamic three bars from the end. Note, however, the hairpin marking before the *f*. This means that the music gets gradually louder during this section. The indication "rall" on the third to last bar means "rallentando" which means to slow down. This is to be done gradually during section marked by the dotted line. Getting such dynamics right – or indeed wrong – makes an enormous difference in the feel of a classical piece.

One of many female guitarists who rose to prominence in the third generation following Segovia, Sharon Isbin has also collaborated with jazz guitarist Larry Coryell.

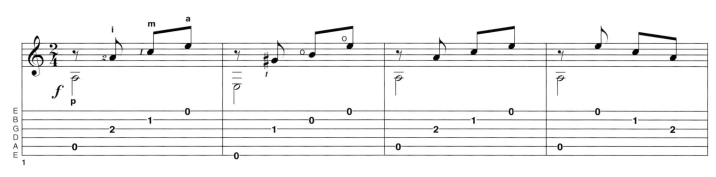

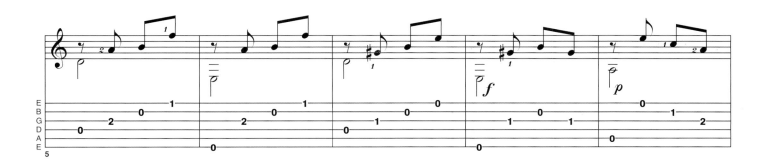

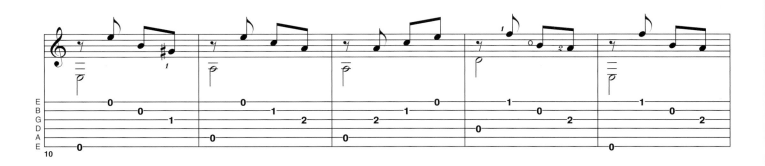

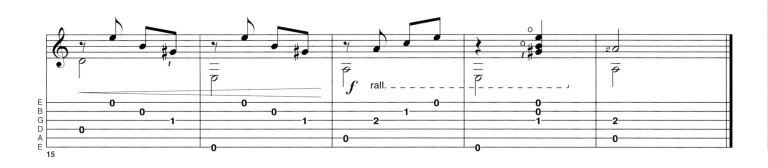

Exercise 5 brings in four new points. The first is playing in higher positions. When playing at first position the first finger plays all the notes at the first fret, the second at the second fret and so on. When playing at a different position the first finger determines which number that position is called. For instance, if playing in second position, the first finger now plays the notes at the second fret, the second finger those at the third and so on. This piece is played entirely in the second position.

The second technique is the half-barre. This is when the first finger is used to hold down three or four strings simultaneously.

This is done by holding it straight across the strings just behind, and in line with, the fret. The notation for this is as written above the first note: a fraction 1/2 followed by a capital C and a Roman numeral indicating the position at which the half-barre is to be held, in this case second position.

The third point in this piece is the dotted note. This is simply a way of increasing the length of a note by half. So when, for instance, a minim is dotted, it is worth three crochets instead of the usual two. This is done in the lower part in bar one, two and later in the piece.

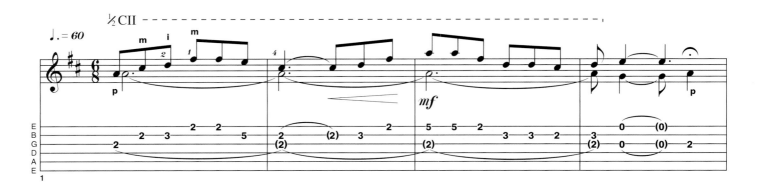

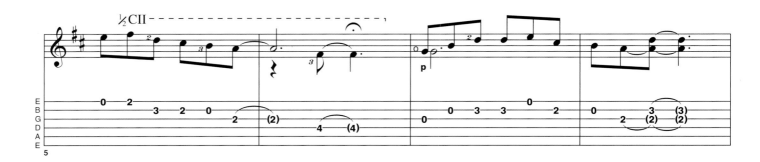

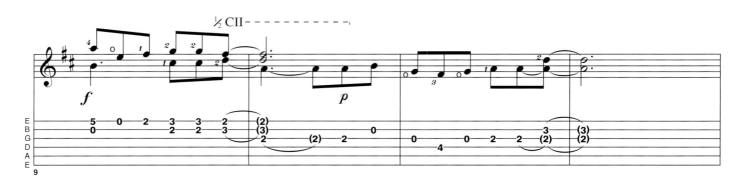

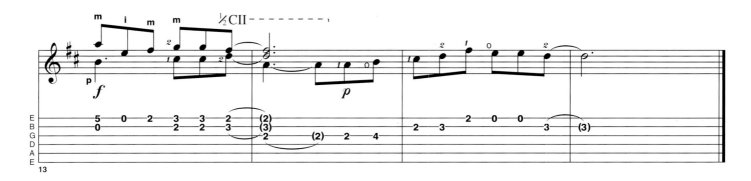

The fourth point in this piece is the metronome marking. This is an exact way of determining the speed or "tempo" of a piece. It is written as a note equaling a number, which means that that particular number of the written note value should occur in one minute. In this piece there are 60 dotted crochets per minute. The work begins *mp* (*mezzo piano* – medium quiet). There are two sharps in the key signature, F# and C#, making it the key of D (when the key is not specified as either major or minor, it is always major).

Exercise 6 is arpeggio-based, as was exercise 4, but this time the full-arpeggio is used, with the added difference that the a finger plays together with p at the start of most bars. The "3" and the square bracket above the first three notes indicates a "triplet," which is a type of "irrational rhythm." This means that there are three notes in the time of two. In this case three quavers (in the time of one crochet – ordinarily two quavers). The triplet is used continuously throughout the piece but is only written in at the start in order not to clutter up the score.

This piece makes use of the full-barre, which is similar to the half-barre except that it covers all six strings. This is used at the third position throughout lines one and three.

Regarded by many as one of the truly great living guitarists, David Russell's astounding technical ability has allowed him total musical freedom to transcribe and perform such major works as Handel's harpsichord pieces.

275

276

Exercise 7 uses an irrational rhythm, this time a sextuplet, with six semiquavers in the time of the usual four (in one crochet). Additionally, there is a tune in the top part indicated by the stems going upwards. This use of melody with an arpeggio is very idiomatic for the guitar. Ideally, this top part is played using a right hand technique called "apoyando" or "rest stroke." This is achieved by the finger coming to rest on the adjacent (lower) string after the string is played. This makes for a particularly strong and warm tone. Due to its opposing movement, the thumb, however, comes to rest on the next higher string. Apoyando is usually used for a part with little accompaniment. Combining it in an arpeggio, as here, requires careful practice.

At the last bar there is the marking *D.C. al X*. This means that you are to return to the beginning ("Da Capo," meaning from the start) and stop when you reach the first symbol (at the end of line two) then jump from there and play the as-yet unplayed last bar. This piece has a key signature of one sharp (F#) which indicates the key of E minor. Note also the accidentals of B-flat and D# in bars two and five.

Exercise 8 uses "slurs," known as *ligado* on the classical guitar. Ligado going up, as in bar one, is played by hammering the left hand finger onto the string so that it sounds and produces the note found at the fret where the finger lands. It is

Exercise 7

apoyando

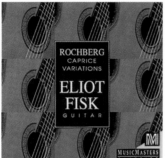

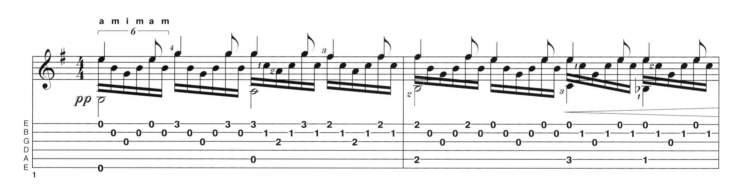

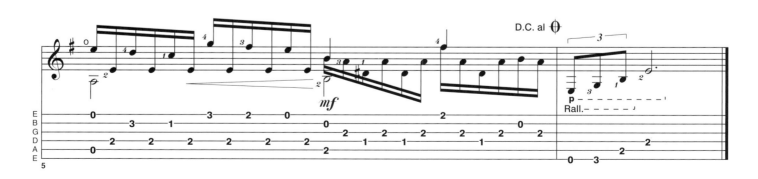

important for the hammer-on finger to hit the string on the beat, rather than anticipate the note and push it ahead of the beat. In bar five there is an example of ligado going down. This is done by removing the finger quickly (downwards) so that the note beneath (either an open string, or one held by another finger as in this piece) is sounded. This is more difficult than slurring up as the left hand finger must pluck the string slightly as it comes off to produce some movement in the string.

Several types of ligado can be produced, ranging from a smooth connection between notes to a percussive attack. Ligado

going up is varied by the speed of the finger landing on the string. The sound of slurring down depends on how much sideways movement (in relation to the string) is applied. A very smooth type is produced by very little plucking (sideways movement) with the finger, but with more of a quick lifting up of the finger off the string.

Also in this exercise there are several changes of position. These are marked throughout the score by Roman numerals. Notes: "*Con brio*" means "*with life;*" "*Acc*" is short for "*accelerando,*" which means to speed up throughout the section.

Kazuhito Yamashita, an extremely gifted player – though one who sometimes appears to be vying with Eliot Fisk for the title of "world's fastest guitarist" – is a great artists and interpreter of the main repertoire and much new music. Seemingly more lighthearted but no less serious in its pursuit of the art, Leo and Ichiro's CD *Penny Lane* (below left) takes a stroll through the Lennon and McCartney composition by way of framing classical guitar in a pop context.

Exercise 9 has a key signature of three sharps, making the key of A. In the major keys, the key note can be easily found from the amount of sharps as it is always one semitone higher than the last one. For example, in this piece there are three sharps: F#, C#, G#, (*Father Charles Goes...*), so the key note is A, a semitone above G#. Triplets are used throughout this piece (again, only marked at the start to keep the score clear).

There are also repeated sections such as bars three and four which appear later as bars seven and eight. Repetition is a device found in most styles of music as it helps to re-establish important compositional themes and also has the added bonus that, because of the new context in which the repeat appears, it sounds slightly different due to its new function, being altered somewhat by what is going on around it at that point.

In bars five and six there are two notes playing together in the top part. These are to be played with i and m and must sound exactly together. The best way to achieve this is to actually keep the fingers together while playing as if they were one large finger. The marking "*Molto Rall*" in the last bar means to slow down considerably, i.e. rather quickly. *Molto* means "much" or "a lot," and can be annexed to various words in music such as "*molto accelerando*" – speed up a lot.

repetition

Cuban guitarist Manuel Barrueco, two whose albums are pictured far left, is considered by many to be the "players' favorite." His is a balanced approach somewhat akin to the pianist Dinu Lipatti's school, where the composition itself takes precedence over the performer. Near left: a moment of deep concentration from Sharon Isbin in concert.

There is a metronome marking at the start of this piece in **exercise 10** which indicates 72 crochets to the minute. This is rather quick, and is designed to give the piece a lively character. The word "*Allegro*" means quick and imparts a particular brisk quality required by the composer with the more exact tempo given by the metronome marking.

There are two new types of dynamic marking in this piece: "*cresc*," short for *crescendo* – meaning to get louder, as many players may already know – and "*dim*," short for "*diminuendo*," meaning the reverse, to get quieter. These are gradual indications and are to be realised throughout the passage marked by the dotted line.

This piece is written in the Baroque style and is highly linear or "contrapuntal," that is, it makes much use of the play between two lines (known as counterpoint, as discussed in the introduction). A device particular to this style is "imitation." This is done by the lines copying one another, as in a canon or round, so the piece gives the impression of chasing itself. Imitation can be clearly seen between bars one and three where the initial figure on C is repeated on the lower pitch of E. Imitation is used later in the piece between bars 14 and 15, where the tune starting on the low G (bar 14, marked *ff*) is repeated exactly at the end of the next bar, but an octave higher.

Note that the first bar has only one crochet beat in it. This is called an "*anacrusis*" or "up beat" and is used to give an animated start to the music.

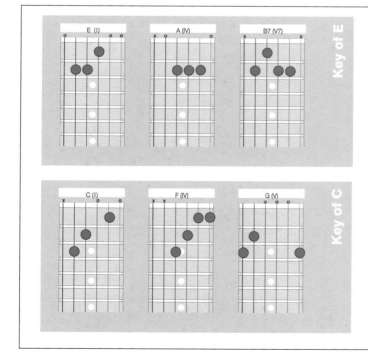

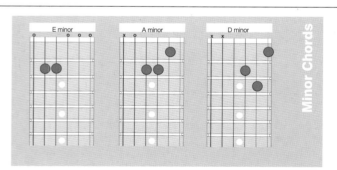

Though exercises in this chapter apply techniques for single-line playing primarily – if occasionally in two parts – a look at some basic chords on the classical guitar (namely the I, IV and V in two popular keys and some basic minor chords) is also worth a brief detour. The width of the classical guitar neck and the flatness of its fingerboard can actually make it a more difficult instrument to chord than many other types of guitar, and full barre chords are not easily achieved by the beginner.

baroque style

280

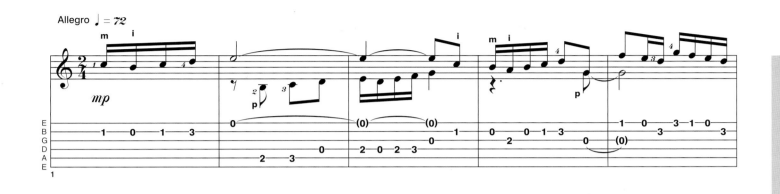

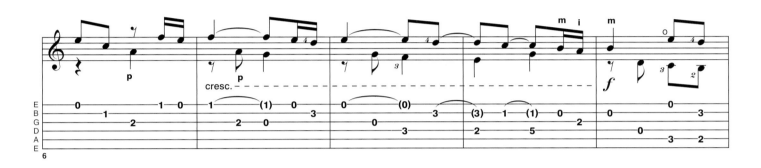

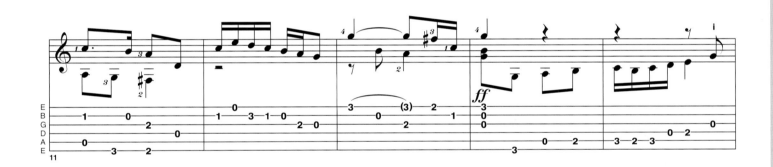

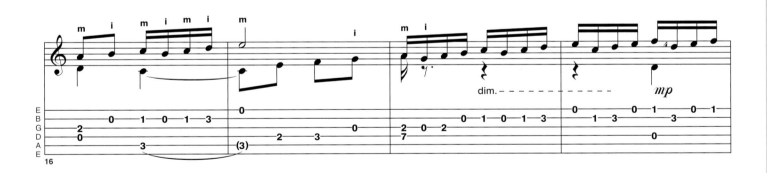

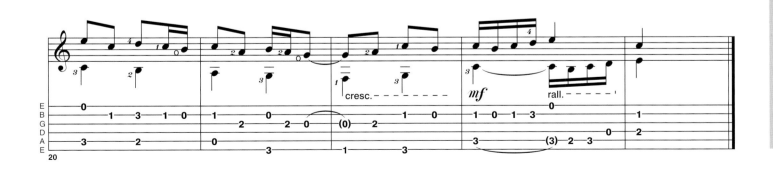

baroque style

PLAYING
JAZZ

evolution of jazz

From the early days of jazz to the present, guitarists have constantly challenged the limitations of their instrument – not only with their sound but also with their technique. Charlie Christian, the father of electric jazz guitar, and Pat Metheny, one of today's modern jazz innovators, both play jazz on an electric guitar but the difference in their sound and approach is quite apparent. ● CARL FILIPIAK

They each have a distinct tone, technique, and uniqueness to their soloing, yet both are parallel players in the evolution of jazz guitar. From Charlie to Pat – and everything in between and beyond – there's a world of great guitar styles to learn and enjoy.

Let's take a quick look at a few things that shaped Charlie Christian's sound and ideas. Using a hollowbody guitar plugged into an amp, his swing-influenced lines were amazingly fluid, executed by his technique of using all down strokes. Pat Metheny's sound incorporates a variety of guitars, stereo amplification and effects to create his ambient signature sound. His post-bop lines are played amazingly fluidly by the heavy use of left hand hammer ons and pull offs. You can see how a change in any of those four parameters – guitar, amplification, technique and style – can create such a diverse sound.

A look at how the guitar evolved from Charlie Christian to Pat Metheny will help us get started. Charlie Christian made a tremendous impact on jazz guitar in the late 1930s, and some of his greatest work can be heard on recordings with Benny Goodman. Christian joined Goodman's band in 1939 and died just a few years later in March of 1942. Let's examine some things that shaped the aural landscape of guitar during his era.

Electricity+Amplifier+Guitar=MUCH LOUDER!

With more volume than the acoustic guitar and banjo, the new wave of electric guitarists could now compete with the horn sections. Feel the power! This monumental change now elevated the guitarist's position from an accompanist in the band to one of the soloists. It wasn't long before the sounds of amplified guitars were heard on more and more recordings and not just in jazz. The electric guitar became a defining sound of rock'n'roll and the blues. Many jazz guitarists were influenced by these sounds and by the mid to late '60s would be part of the new movement to be known as jazz-fusion. More about this a little later.

Wes Montgomery came into prominence in the late 1960s and many consider him to be the father of modern jazz guitar. Wes was a modern bop player who displayed a sophisticated melodic and harmonic sense. The keys to his style were the use of his thumb, which produced a very warm sound, and his ability to play octaves faster than most guitarists could play single lines. At that time this made him instantly recognizable and created a new standard in modern jazz guitar.

Also carrying on in the tradition of Wes were two incredible guitarists, George Benson and Pat Martino. Both had amazing technique and used a pick for most of their

single note lines. These two virtuosos became the new standard and elevated the sound of jazz guitar once again. Just check out their solos on George Benson's *Cookbook* CD and Pat Martino's *Footprints* and you'll see what I mean.

Electricity+Louder Amp+Guitar+Effects=Jimi Hendrix

What's Jimi Hendrix got to do with Jazz? A Lot! He influenced the sound of jazz guitarists that were entering the next movement, which was called fusion. Jazz was now beginning to borrow heavily from the sounds of rock music. Using a solid body guitar, massive amplification and effects in an innovative way, Hendrix created sounds that fit in perfectly with the new direction of jazz. These concepts would be incorporated in a jazz context by guitarist John McLaughlin. Using a solid body guitar with increased sustain was a radical departure from the sound of an archtop guitar and a relatively small amp. Considered the first fusion record, Miles Davis's album *Bitches Brew* was a landmark recording during this era, and featured John McLaughlin turning up the volume.

With the increased volume the guitar entered the realm of the wind instrument. Unlimited sustain meant one could now play lines by using hammer ons and pull offs alone. That sort of sound was developed and perfected by Allan Holdsworth, who uses legato technique with an overdriven and compressed tone that sounds remarkably "horn like" in nature. It's what jazz guitarists have wanted to do all along!

Jim Hall, an incredible guitarist, has probably influenced and changed the sound of contemporary jazz guitar more than anyone else. A jazz player with some serious history, he was one of the early guitarists to employ hammer ons and pull offs to achieve a more fluid sound. This was quite a departure from the more percussive technique of picking every note. He helped inspire the next generation of great players that includes Mick Goodrick, Pat Metheny, John Scofield, Mike Stern, Bill Frisell and John Abercrombie. Jim Hall is the bridge that connects the traditional elements of jazz and points them to the future. It now becomes easier to hear how contemporary guitarists fit into all this, their unique styles arising from the infinite possibilities of combining jazz with the elements of rock and beyond. Contemporary guitar is capable of incredible sounds and has come a long way musically since the early days of Charlie Christian. No longer on the sidelines, guitarists are now much more harmonically advanced, technically proficient and have a much higher profile in the jazz world than ever before. I can't wait to hear where it takes us to next.

SEVEN BASIC SOUNDS

Now that we've seen the direction jazz guitar is headed, let's take a look at some of the things we have to learn in order to get there. Knowing how to recognize the seven basic sounds in all keys is very important. They are the major, minor, dominant, diminished, minor 7 flat 5, augmented and suspended sounds.

The first three (major, minor and dominant) sounds are especially important. Use the sixth and the fifth string to locate the nearest root, match the appropriate sound and you will be able to play just about any chord progression (we'll get to them soon). For now, try these examples in the keys of G (sixth string root) and C (fifth string root), then see if you can transpose them elsewhere.

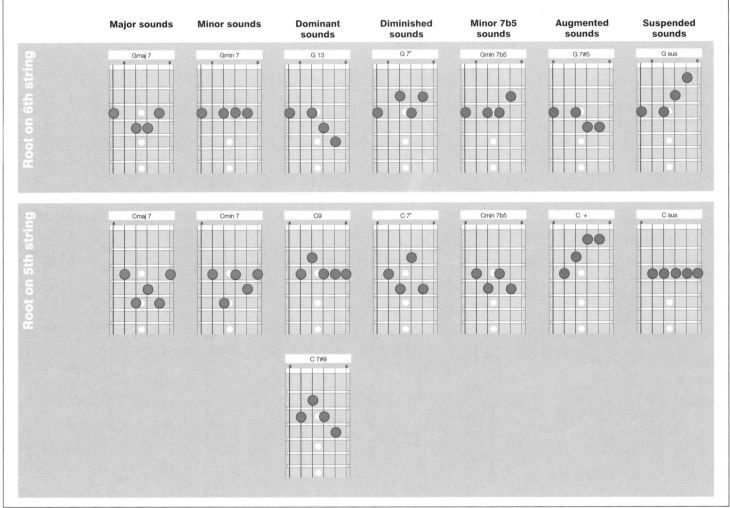

| Major sounds | Minor sounds | Dominant sounds | Diminished sounds | Minor 7b5 sounds | Augmented sounds | Suspended sounds |

Root on 6th string: Gmaj 7, Gmin 7, G 13, G 7°, Gmin 7b5, G 7#5, G sus

Root on 5th string: Cmaj 7, Cmin 7, C9, C 7°, Cmin 7b5, C +, C sus

C 7#9

TWO NOTE DIADS

Don't be deceived by the simplicity of these two note diads. In many musical settings they sound great! They are the guide tones of chords, which are the 3rds and 7ths and imply the quality of the chord (major, minor or dominant). They work great played alongside a bass player who fills in the root of the chord.

Even before Charlie Christian took the amplified guitar to new heights, Eddie Lang was on the scene as the first real jazz guitar virtuoso. In his short career (his tragic, premature death was caused by a poorly performed tonsillectomy), Lang performed with early jazz greats such as Bix Beiderbecke, Frankie Trumbauer, Paul Whiteman, King Oliver, Red Nichols and Bing Crosby.

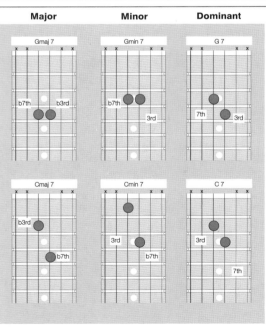

| Major | Minor | Dominant |

Gmaj 7 (b7th, b3rd) | Gmin 7 (b7th, 3rd) | G 7 (7th, 3rd)

Cmaj 7 (b3rd, b7th) | Cmin 7 (3rd, b7th) | C 7 (3rd, 7th)

basic chords and diads

progressions

	II	V	I

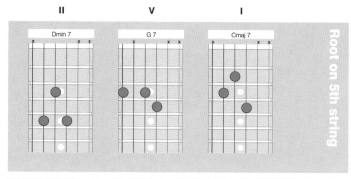

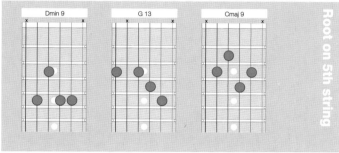

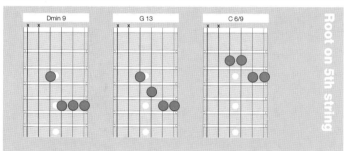

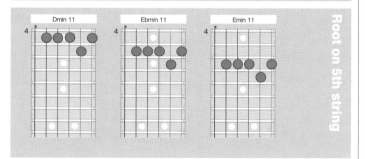

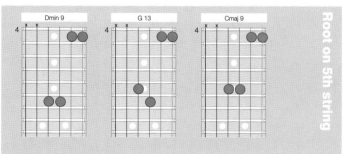

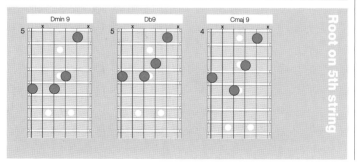

Root on 5th string

2–5–1 PROGRESSIONS

The 2–5–1 is one of the most widely used sequences in jazz. When you take a C major scale and build chords in thirds on each note of that scale, the seven chords will be:

C major 7,
D minor 7,
E minor 7,
F major 7,
G7,
A minor 7,
B minor 7 flat 5.

The 2nd chord is D Minor 7, the chord that starts on the fifth degree of the scale is G7 and the "one" chord is C Major 7. A 2–5–1 in the key of C is: D Minor 7, G7, and C Major 7. Here is a page of assorted 2–5–1 patterns. I would suggest starting out by mastering the first two examples, then proceed to each of the remaining progressions.

Charlie Christian is the original star of electric jazz guitar, and was enormously influential in the early days of the instrument. Some of his best work was recorded with the Benny Goodman orchestra from 1939 to 1942.

285

MINOR 2-5-1 PROGRESSIONS

The 2-5-1 in a minor key is a minor 7 flat 5 chord, followed by a dominant 7 flat 9 chord, then a minor 7 or minor 9 chord. In C minor the sequence would be Dmin7b5, G7, and Cmin7. The first two examples are extremely useful but try all of them for different settings (which we will explore later).

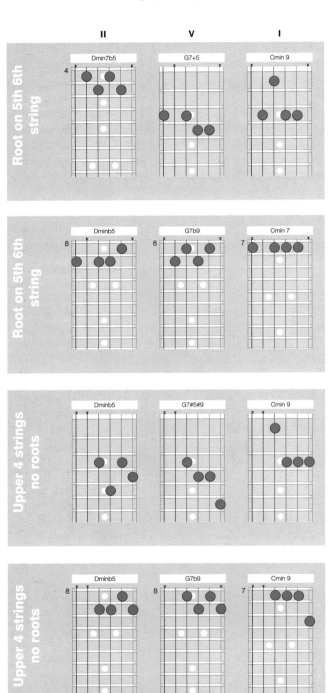

UPPER VOICINGS

Master this page and you will see how you can move chords around and resolve to the next sound with great voice leading. Practise by transposing to different keys and work out some 2-5-1 sequences. Resolve to the nearest form when the sounds change from minor to dominant to major.

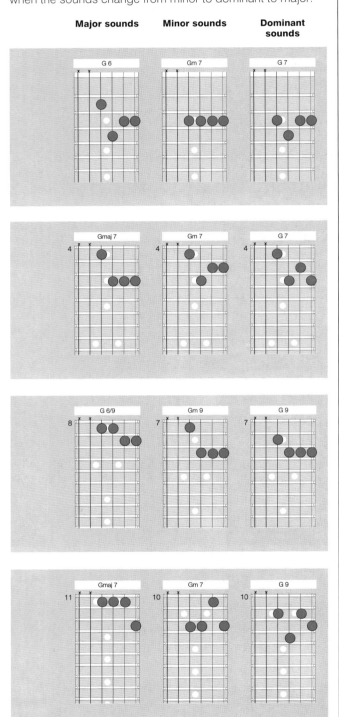

chord progressions

1–6–2–5 PROGRESSIONS

This is another pattern of equal importance. A quick look at the seven chords in the key of C (diatonic harmony) shows that the chord that occupies the sixth scale degree is an A minor 7th chord. A 1–6–2–5 in the key of C Major would be: Cmaj7, Amin7, Dmin7, G7. You may notice there is only one dominant chord in a key, built on the 5th scale degree. This chord, the G7 in the key of C, creates tension that resolves to the on chord, Cmaj7. Any chord in the key can have its arrival preceded by a dominant chord. This is called a secondary dominant and that's how the A7 chord will be explained in the following sequence:

1	6	2	5
Cmaj7	**A7**	**Dmin7**	**G7**

The secondary dominant A7 is the dominant of 2, or the "5" of 2. Many tunes feature this sequence so try to learn it in as many keys as possible. Some "standards" employing the 1–6–2–5 include *Oleo, Rhythm-a-ning, The Theme, Moose The Mooch, Ready And Able* and *Tipping* (all in the rhythm changes "A" section) and *Have You Met Miss Jones, Turnaround In Blues* (last two bars) and *St. Thomas*. Try these three four-chord 1–6–2–5 patterns to hear the sound of A7 resolving to Dmin7, as well as G7 resolving to Cmaj7. The first sequence is made up of roots and guide tones, the second features added tensions, and the third uses upper-four-string voicings.

The Complete Atomic Basie
E = MC² · COUNT BASIE ORCHESTRA + NEAL HEFTI ARRANGEMENTS

It's a rhythm thing: when the roots of jazz were being formulated, the guitarist's role was first an foremost as a member of the rhythm section. The album *Pioneers of the Jazz Guitar* contains more solid work from early greats than you can shake a swing-time stick at – with some sweet soloing besides. From a later era, Freddie Green's rock-steady chops on The Count Basie Band's 1957 recording *The Complete Atomic Basie* remains a stunning example of how to play the changes with major groove.

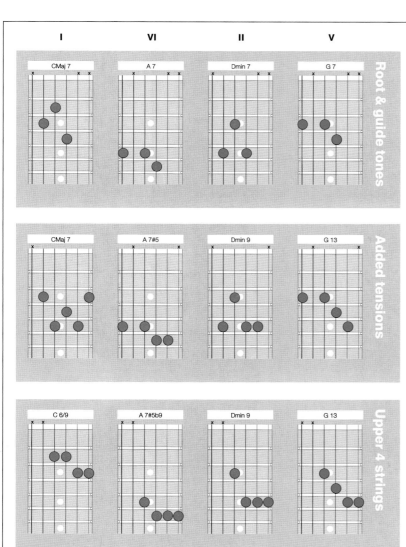

MOVING FURTHER

Understanding just a few concepts like diatonic harmony, related 2s and 5s, subflat 5s, and chord families can help you produce some harmonically complex chord sequences. This may take a while to understand thoroughly, but don't let this discourage you from trying out some new and interesting patterns.

Diatonic harmony produces tonic, sub dominant and dominant chords built on the root, 4th and 5th degree of the major scale. Since they share common tones 3 and 6 they are said to have "diatonic" harmony. The 2 chord has sub-dominant harmony and the 7 chord has dominant harmony. A 2–5 pattern is important because it implies a key. A dominant chord can be preceded by its related 2 chord, a 5th above the root. Since the 3 and 7 of a dominant chord are shared by another dominant chord a tri-tone away, they are considered substitutes for on another: G7=Dflat7. Chords with upper tensions 9, 11 and 13 don't effect the basic quality of sound. Cmin7, Cmin9 and Cmin11 are all minor family chords and are interchangeable. The major family includes C6, Cmaj7, Cmaj9, C6/9. The dominant family includes C7, C9 and C13.

Root & guide tones — I: CMaj 7, VI: A 7, II: Dmin 7, V: G 7

Added tensions — CMaj 7, A 7#5, Dmin 9, G 13

Upper 4 strings — C 6/9, A 7#5b9, Dmin 9, G 13

SONG FORMS

Finally, let's play some tunes! There are three basic forms you should master: jazz blues, minor blues and rhythm changes – illustrated in turn in **exercises 1–3**. These will help you learn tunes from *The Real Book* (a "fake book" owned by every jazz player, containing hundreds of popular jazz standards). For example, the jazz blues form is used in many tunes by Charlie

Parker, Wes Montgomery, Sonny Rollins, Thelonius Monk and many others. Learn these in a few more keys and you'll get a lot of mileage out of this section with a little practise and perseverance. Notice that no rhythms are given here. For now, use basic chord forms or chords you've just learned and strum through each of these exercises in your own style. Next, we'll put some rhythms to them to start playing some more familiar songs.

ESSENTIAL RHYTHMS

Let's talk about how to play the five essential rhythms that will not only help you with the three basic forms, but with many others as well. These will allow you to function in a variety of musical styles.

Exercise 4 is a rhythm called "four to the bar." This perfectly exemplifies the 4/4 time signature, and is a rhythm you'll hear in plenty of classic jazz. Four to the bar is traditionally played with all downstrokes on the quarter notes, sometimes with the occasional upstroke on an eighth note for emphasis, to suggest a solid rhythm, with chord changes according to the tune. It often works best when you are supplying the time (no bass player or drummer) or for playing rhythm guitar charts in a big band – think Freddie Green. Sometimes chords change as fast as one per beat, which takes some fancy finger work, but here we'll strum two bars against muted strings to get the rhythm down, then play two bars with a chord change every two beats. As in the previous exercise, use basic chord forms or those you have already learned elsewhere. After you've got the feel of it, try playing four to the bar against the jazz blues in Ex.1.

Exercise 5 is a "jazz waltz." As you might guess it's in 3/4, but a jazz waltz also works great in 6/8, just double it up. Also, note the importance of the rests for the feel of the rhythm. Repeat

the two bars until you get a feel for it. After you've got this down, try it on the standard tunes *Alice In Wonderland, Bluesette, Someday My Prince Will Come* and *Windows*.

The "bossa nova" rhythm in **exercise 6** works great for sambas as well as bossas – a samba being faster. While there are many variations of Latin and Brazilian rhythms used in jazz, this is a great one to start out with and is multi-functional. Listen out for these rhythms in the standard tunes *Blue Bossa, One Note Samba, Wave* and *Triste*, all of which you can learn yourself. (Get deeper into these rhythms in the *Latin* chapter.)

The easy way to approach a "ballad" is to play the root on beats 1 and 3 and on beats 2 and 4 play the notes of the chord that are left on the D, G and B strings, as exemplified in **exercise 7**. Simple, but effective.

Exercise 8 gives an example in "odd time," in this case 5/4, probably the most-used odd time signature in jazz. Think of it as a jazz waltz in 3/4 plus two extra quarter notes: 3+2=5. Many odd time signatures can be played using this concept. *Take Five* is a classic jazz tune in 5/4 which most of you will recognize, and a good one to learn on your own once you get this rhythm down. Again, note the major contribution of the rests to the rhythmic feel of this exercise.

IMPROVISATION

Finally it's time to move on to what many guitarists think of as the essence of jazz: soloing and improvisation. We'll start by talking about soloing "over" and "through" the chord changes.

Learn the C major scale in all positions and you've also learned the location of it's related modes. They are: D Dorian, E Phrygian, F Lydian, G Mixolydian, A Aeolian, B Locrian. We'll learn more about modes a little later in the chapter, but for now let's use it as a C major scale. Since a 2–5–1 in C major is built from the notes of the 2nd, 5th and root of the scale, simply play notes of the C Major scale over all three changes. The scale generates the harmony and the chords imply the scale. Chords are scales and scales are chords – simple.

While playing a C major scale may not make you sound like Pat Martino (or insert your favorite jazz player here!) it will be a fairly easy and melodic way to start playing "through" changes – improvising in the scale of the key of the tune, while the changes go on behind your solo.

Another way that jazz players solo to chords is to use a different scale for each chord. Chord-scale relationships is a way to start playing "over" the changes instead of through them. One is not better than the other, just different.

Playing over the changes reflects the sound of each chord in a 2–5–1 progression. For the 2 chord, Dmin7, play in the D dorian scale – simply a C major scale starting on the 2nd scale degree: D, E, F, G, A, B, C, D. Over the 5 chord, G7, play G mixolydian, which starts on the 5th degree of the C major scale. Its scale spelling is: G, A, B, C, D, E, F, G. Over the 1 chord, Cmaj7, you're back to the notes of the C major scale. That's a basic look at modes as applied to the theory of improvisation used in jazz guitar soloing. We'll explore some ways to use each mode a little better in the next section.

Right now, however, let's break down some more elements essential in jazz soloing. We have already talked about guide tones – the 3rds and 7ths which define the quality of the chord – and chord scales – which reveal the melodic relationships between scale, chord and harmony. So let's move on to arpeggios and how to use melodic embellishments.

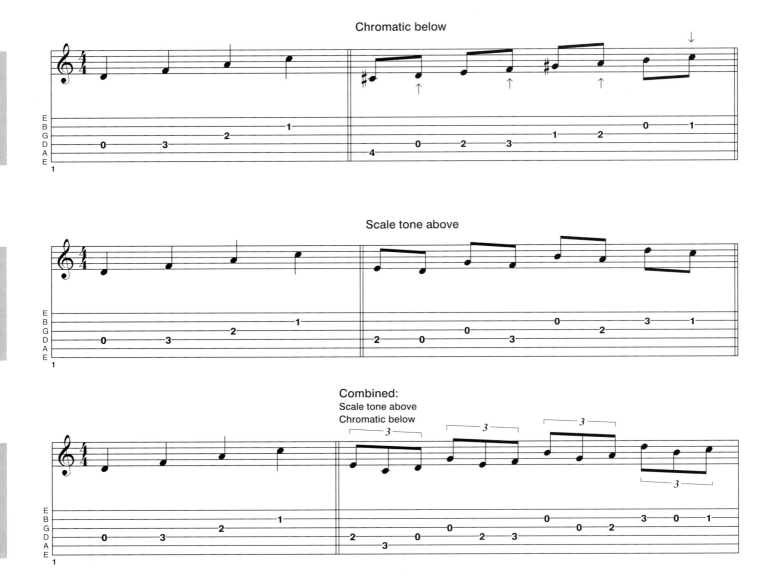

soloing

Exercise 9

Exercise 10

Exercise 11

soloing

MELODIC EMBELLISHMENT

Arpeggios outline the targeted chord tones (root, 3rd, 5th, 7th and above) and melodic embellishment approaches the chord tones chromatically, scale-wise, from above and below. In the following exercises I've used a Dmin7 arpeggio and have shown several ways to approach each chord tone to produce a more melodic effect. By combining notes that are chromatically above and below the targeted chord tones, our playing becomes more melodic and still defines the harmonic sound of the chord, in this case Dmin7. **Exercise 9** takes a "chromatic below" approach to the chord tone (guide tones are indicated by arrows in the exercise). **Exercise 10** uses a scale tone above approach, while **exercise 11** combines the two in one approach, and **exercise 12** combines them in another. **Exercise 13** uses a double chromatic below, and **exercise 14** a double chromatic above.

Now do the same for G7 and Cmaj7 and you'll hear what we're getting at. When combined with other concepts (guide tones, chords, scales and arpeggios) melodic embellishments will get us closer to some of the ways jazz lines are created.

As a young musician, Pat Martino was influenced by John Coltrane, Wes Montgomery, Stan Getz and Johnny Smith, then earned gigs as a rock and jazz sideman before taking his own fluid, virtuoso solo work into the realms of fusion and beyond.

Combined:
Chromatic below
Scale tone above

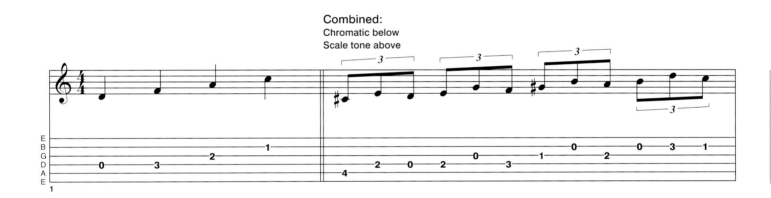

Exercise 12

Double chromatic below

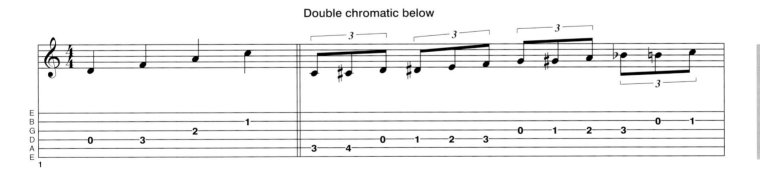

Exercise 13

Double chromatic above

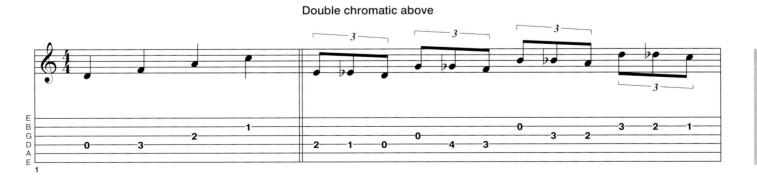

Exercise 14

DEVELOPING A JAZZ LINE

You now have a handle on many of the essential building blocks of jazz soloing, so let's examine a series of different ways of combining these melodic approaches to chords and scales in order to develop a variety of solo lines with different moods and feels, starting with the extremely simple and building to some more complex approaches. Still in our familiar key of C major, we'll use our four-bar 2–5–1 progression of Dmin7, G7 and Cmaj7 over eleven great ways of building your solo lines.

Play them individually to hear how each approach works, then try stringing selected examples together – or even all of them – for a long solo that shifts between techniques. When you get the hang of it, record the chord progression for as many bars as you like and try playing along.

There isn't a whole lot to say about each exercise; you just need to play through them to hear and feel how each approach works. **Exercise 15** starts us off simply hitting the guide tones; **exercise 16** takes it a step further, linking 3rds and 7ths. **Exercise 17** uses "octave displacement" to run down from the 2 toward the 5, then jumping to the octave and running down to the 1, while **exercise 18** uses an example of "altered tension" in the flatted 9th.

Exercise 19 picks up the pace with eighth notes (squeezing three into a triplet for starters, to boot), while **exercise 20** keeps it breezy to outline minor 7th arpeggios over the changes. **Exercise 21** gets your fingers stretching a little further with "interval leaps," and **exercise 22** outlines some short hops in lines made up of jumps between 5ths.

There are few better places to turn for great improvisational work than Joe Pass and Jim Hall, two of jazz's all-time great all-arounders. Above left, Pass goes it solo for *Virtuoso*, while Hall joins pianist Bill Evans on the impressive *Undercurrent*, right.

Exercise 15

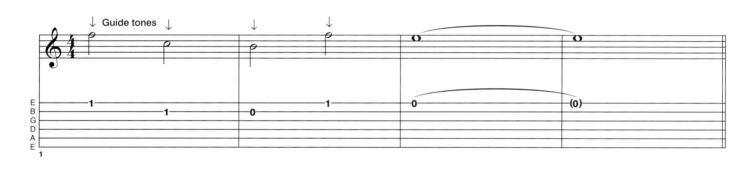

Exercise 16

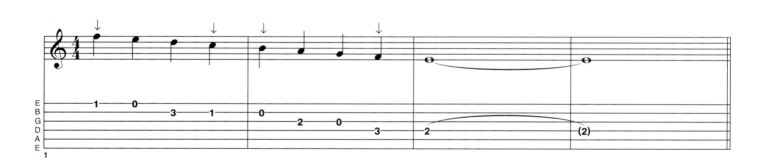

Exercise 17

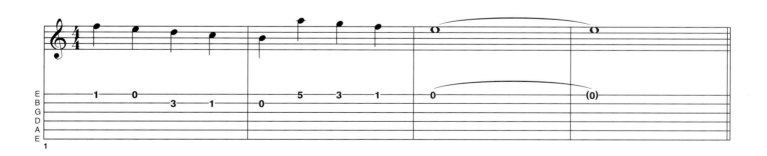

soloing

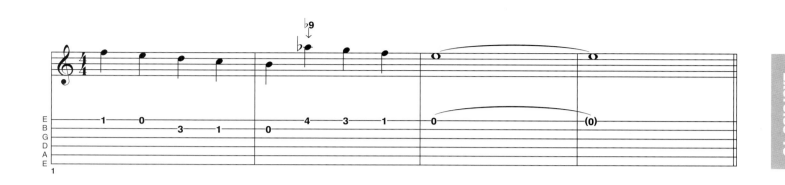

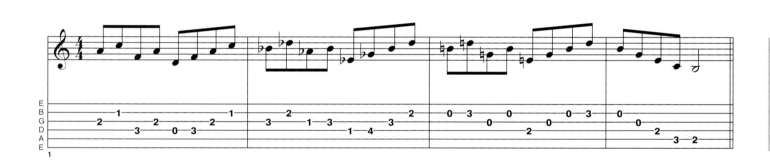

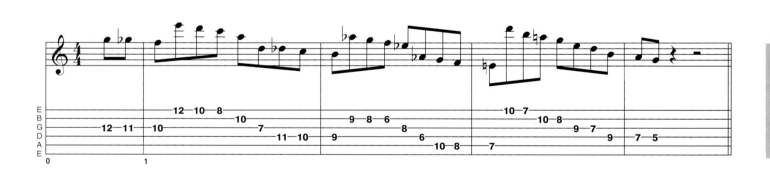

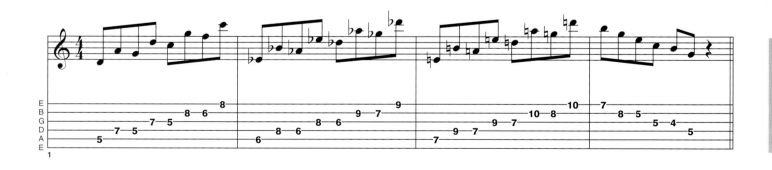

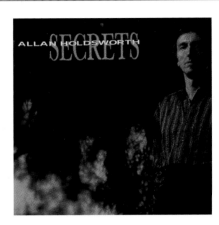

Wrapping bop influences and stunning technique in thoroughly modern sounds with atmosphere to spare, Pat Metheny remains at the forefront of the modern jazz pack. Residing further toward the heart of fusion, British guitarist Allan Holdsworth runs the gamut from rock to jazz, hitting all stops in between and certainly sounding like no one else on earth along the way.

We'll wrap up our eleven techniques for developing jazz lines with three more effective approaches, still using our 2–5–1 progression in C major (Dmin7, G7, Cmaj7). **Exercise 23** shows you a "chord over chord" technique, which layers chords on top of each other. **Exercise 24** uses "motifs," melodic riffs similar in shape and feel, which move with the changes.

Finally, **exercise 25** uses "chromatic" lines – runs that move short intervals for a tight, occasionally off-key sound that still falls in at all the right reference points and makes a great change from sweet, strictly melodic runs.

Although these are "only" eighth notes, these lines move pretty swiftly at faster tempos, especially with some of the unfamiliar tonal leaps required, so take your time and go at them slowly at first, building speed with practise.

Exercise 23

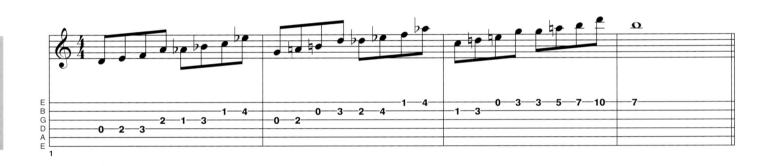

Exercise 24

Exercise 25

soloing

ESSENTIAL SCALES AND MODES

Before concluding our exploration of jazz guitar with an extended exercise of Bebop lines, let's look at a few techniques which we don't have room to cover here in any great depth, but which will help you extend your playing beyond the obvious clichés and simple melody lines. If this chapter has whet your appetite to explore jazz guitar further, you can expand on these concepts on your own, or seek out more in-depth instruction.

The four essential scales to know are the major scale,, melodic minor, diminished scale and the whole tone scale. Knowing their spelling and scale formulae will aid you greatly in knowing how to use them. We'll look at them in our old friend C major, but once learned they can be transposed to any key to give you a full arsenal of improvisational tools.

Here are the chords built from a C major (Ionian) scale and their corresponding modes. As we briefly discussed earlier in this section, you find these modes in any particular key by playing the major scale in that key, but starting on each subsequent note rather than on the root (or "one"), thus:

Cmaj7	C Ionian
Dmin7	D Dorian
Emin7	E Phrygian
Fmaj7	F Lydian
G7	G Mixolydian
Amin7	A Aeolian
Bmin7b5	B Locrian

So the following relationship would give you a modal approach to soloing over our familiar 2–5–1 changes in C major.

| Dmin7 | G7 | Cmaj7 |
| *use:* **D Dorian** | **G Mixolydian** | **C Major Scale** |

C melodic minor is an easy variation to learn, simply: C, D, Eb, F, G, A, B, C.

Two modes that are extremely useful are built from the 4th and 7th degrees of the scale. They are: F Lydian b7 and B altered dominant. Play F Lydian b7 over F9#4 chord types; play B altered dominant over B7#9, B7flat9, B7flat5, B7#5

The C diminished scale runs C, D, Eb, F, Gb, Ab, A, B, C. Play the B diminished half step, whole step scale over these chord types: B7flat9, B7#9, B7flat5, B13.

The C whole tone scale is: C, D, E, F#, G#, Bb, C. Play it over C+, C7+5, C9#11 and chords of that type.

Remember chords are scales and scales are chords. One implies the other. For example, look at D Dorian – the notes of the scale reveal the chord qualities:

| D | E | F | G | A | B | C | D | E | F | G | A | B | C | D |
| R | | -3 | | 5 | | b7 | 9 | | | 11 | | 13 | | |

D Dorian sounds great over a Dmin7, Dmin9, Dmin11 and even Dmin13 chord (sometimes the 13th will appear an octave lower as the sixth). Now look at a G altered dominant scale over a G7 chord:

| G | Ab | Bb | Cb | Db | Eb | F |
| Root | b9 | #9 | M3 | b5 | #5 | b7 |

Play this scale over G7, G7flat9, G7#9, G7flat5, G7#5, or any combination of these.

Wes Montgomery (performing live, left, and on record, below left) is considered by many to be the true father of modern jazz guitar, executing octave runs faster than most guitarists can play single lines. George Benson (seen on the album *It's Uptown*, below right) set new standards of bop guitar virtuosity before moving on to even broader fame as a jazz and soul vocalist.

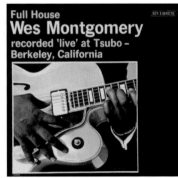

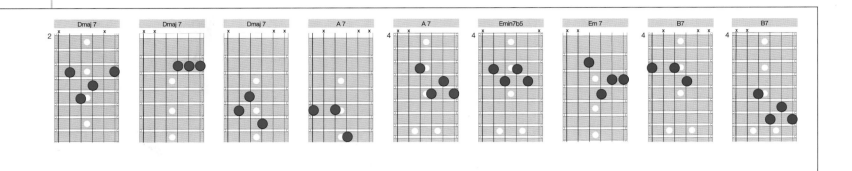

Exercise 26

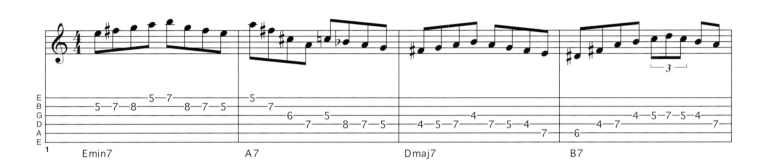

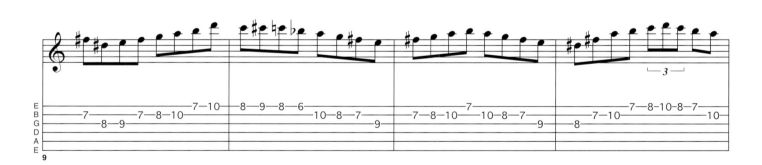

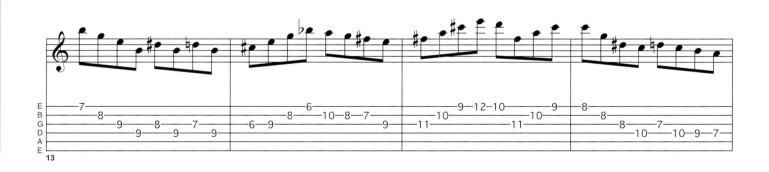

bop solo lines

2–5–1–6 BOP LINES

Exercise 26 offers eight Bop lines over a 2–5–1–6 progression in a new key, D major (the chords from the first four bars repeat throughout each four-bar line, though you can try your own variations). Have someone play the chords or tape them to hear the sound of the line and its various degrees of tension.

Not only are they eight useful lines to study, but they can also be played in one continuous etude. As always, start off slowly at first then build speed as you get the hang of it – though speed in itself isn't the objective; we're looking to build melodic and harmonic awareness and compile a handy bag of lines (derived from scales and modes) to use as improvisational building blocks to apply to your other playing.

The chords shown in the nine diagrams to the left are variations on chords you will have encountered already in this chapter, transposed to appropriate positions for this exercise. They will help you with some useful voices to get started, but try working out others for yourself to use in your own backing track.

As an added challenge, refer back to the Essential Scales And Modes page to help you analyze some of these licks. I hope you have fun with this exercise and it helps you to master some of those great lines that you've heard your favorite artists play.

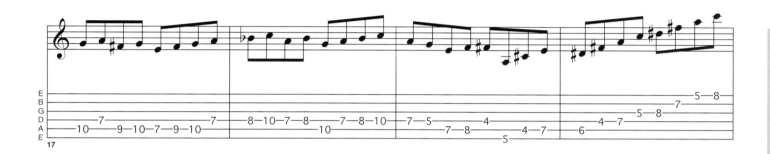

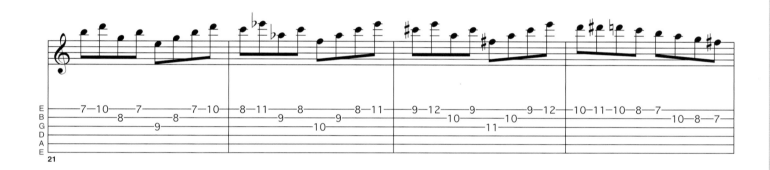

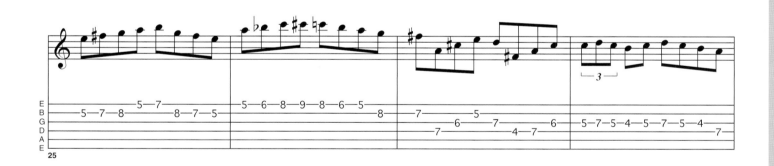

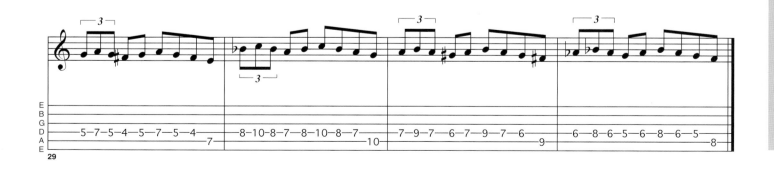

Abalam Trade name for abalone laminated to thin plastic sheet, the result of a new cutting technique which yields more of the useable shell and less waste.

abalone Shellfish used for inlay material on guitars. Comes in many iridescent hues, most prized being the green heart. Becoming rare.

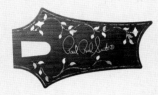

AC Short for "alternating current," an electric current that can change the direction in which it flows. This is the type of electricity that flows from common domestic wall outlets (commonly 120V in the US, 230-240V in the UK). See also *DC*.

acoustic General term for any hollowbody acoustic guitar. An acoustic musical instrument is one that generates sound without electrical amplification. Also, a term related to sound and hearing.

acrylic Paint containing acrylic resin, widely used in guitar finishes as a more eco-friendly substitute for cellulose lacquers.

action Often used to describe only the height of the strings above the tops of the frets; thus "high action," "low action," "buzz-free action" etc. In fact, the term can refer to the entire playing feel of a given instrument; thus "good action," "easy action" etc.

active (active electronics, active circuit) Circuitry in some guitars that boosts signal and/or widens tonal range with necessary additional (usually battery) powering. Refers to a pickup or circuit that incorporates a preamp. See also *preamp*.

active crossover See *crossover*.

active powered Not necessarily amplified, but using (active) electronics to assist or improve functioning.

ADAT Type of multi-track digital audio tape.

ADT Artificial (or automatic) double tracking. Used to reinforce

an existing signal, for instance making one singer sound like two.

alder Medium weight hardwood commonly used for solid guitar bodies, for example some of those made by Fender.

alerce South American tree related to the larch.

alnico Magnet material used for pickups and speakers (generally of more "vintage" design). It is an alloy of aluminum, nickel, and cobalt. Also, a nickname for a single-coil Gibson pickup with flat-sided polepieces.

alphabeto 17th century Italian notation system using an alphabet of chord symbols.

alternating current See *AC*.

amp(lifier) Electrical circuit designed to increase the level of a signal; but more usually, an audio system for boosting sound before transmission to a loudspeaker. The system could be a power amp, or backline instrument amplifier, or line amp.

amp rack Sturdy frame or rack designed for mounting power amps. It is usually deeper than regular instrument racks, and often very heavy.

amplification Making a signal bigger (may refer to voltage, analogous to signal level and loudness, or current). General term for amps, speakers and associated gear.

analog (UK: analogue) System which reproduces a signal by copying its original amplitude waveform. Examples include the groove of an old vinyl recording, the electrical signal on a magnetic tape recording, or the voltage levels of an analog synthesizer. As opposed to digital, where the signal is recorded as a series of numbers.

anode (plate) Part within a vacuum tube (UK: valve) which collects current.

anodized (UK: anodised) Finish given to metal by electrolysis. Often refers, erroneously, to Fender's gold-tinted aluminum pickguards of the 1950s (which are alodined).

anti-surge "Delayed" fuse (body marked "T") that withstands brief current surges without breaking. Note that it doesn't prevent current surges.

apoyando In classical performance, a right-hand technique (also known as the rest stroke) in which the playing finger passes "through" the string, coming to rest on the adjacent string.

archtop Guitar with arched body top formed by carving or pressing. Usually refers to hollowbody or semi-acoustic instruments; thus "archtop jazz guitar". As opposed to the other principal type of acoustic guitar, the flat-top.

arpeggio Broken chord in which the notes are played sequentially rather than together.

arrangement Music that emerges after allocating different parts of a composition to various instruments and/or voices. Also, the adaptation to guitar of music originally intended for instruments other than guitar. See also *transcription*.

ash Medium to heavy hardwood commonly used for solid guitar bodies, for example by Fender.

ashtray Nickname for the bridge cover originally supplied but often missing from vintage-style Fender Telecaster guitars.

atonal Type of composition, usually of the 20th century, which has no allegiance to a tonal center.

attack Speed at which a sound (or filter, or envelope) reaches its maximum level. For instance, percussive sounds usually have fast attacks, while smooth, liquid sounds have slow attacks.

attenuate Reduce in strength.

attenuator Electronic circuitry that reduces level, usually in fixed steps of useful round-figure amounts, such as -10dB, -20dB. Also the knob or switch that controls such a setting.

aux return Abbreviation of auxiliary return. Inputs on a mixer used for adding back the signal from/with the FX.

aux send Abbreviation of auxiliary send. Output typically from a mixer to FX and other locations.

B+ Symbol used to indicate high voltage supply in an amplifier circuit schematic. Also "HT" (for High Tension), the latter particularly used in the UK.

baby blue Popular (unofficial) name for Fender's early Sonic Blue Custom Color.

backlash Any "give" in a tuner's operation where the string-post does not immediately move when the tuner button is turned.

backline Musical instrument amps (usually for guitars) placed in a line across the back of the stage, or stacked up in a wall or crescent for visual effect. In modern stage sets, can also include racks of sampler channels and their sub-mixers, or indeed anything on the stage.

backplate Panel fitted over a cavity in the rear of a guitar body, allowing access to pots and wiring or vibrato springs.

baffle Front panel or baseboard of a speaker cabinet onto which direct-radiating drivers and smaller horn flares are mounted.

Bakelite First plastic, invented 1909. Used for some guitars, parts and components from the '30s to the '50s.

balanced Signals or in/out connections where a pair of

ac to bullet

conductors (hot and cold) are separate from the ground (earth) shield, carrying opposing versions of the same signal at exactly the same level, and also having near identical impedances compared to ground (earth). Greatly helps to avoid noise problems in compatible circuitry and equipment, and longer cable lengths can be used than with unbalanced leads.

ball-end Metal retainer wound onto the end of a guitar string and used to secure it to the anchor point at the bridge.

bandurría Spanish folk instrument with a pear-shaped body and steel strings.

banjo tuners Rear-facing tuners found on some guitars, notably on some early Martin OM and Gibson reverse-body Firebird models.

bass pickup See *neck pickup*.

B-bender String-pulling device giving a pedal-steel effect on regular electric guitar. The best known models are by Parsons-White, and Joe Glaser.

bias For a tube (valve) guitar amp, a critical "tune-up" setting (and also of a tape machine or other piece of equipment), generally involving some auxiliary voltage or current that helps the circuitry to work properly.

biasing Setting the bias of the tubes (valves) within an amp for optimum performance. See *bias*.

Bigsby Simple single-spring non-recessed vibrato device developed by Paul Bigsby. Now sometimes

used as a generic term for similar designs by other makers.

binding Protective and decorative strip(s) added to edges of the body and/or fingerboard and/or headstock of some guitars.

birdseye Type of maple with small circular figure.

blackface Used to denote "vintage" Fender amps manufactured between approximately 1963 and 1967, so-called because of their black control panels. Also used to describe the sound produced by these amps. (Black control panels were occasionally returned to in later years, but any post-'67 Fender amps would not accurately be termed blackface.) See also *brownface*, *silverface*.

blade pickup (bar pickup) Pickup (humbucker or single-coil) that uses a long single blade polepiece for each coil, rather than the more usual individual polepieces for each string.

block markers Square-shape or rectangular-shape position markers in the fingerboard.

blond (blonde) Natural finish, usually enhancing plain wood color; or (on some Fenders) a slightly yellowed finish.

blue-bell Describes the blue painted bell-shaped magnet cover on original Celestion-manufactured Vox 12-inch speakers.

Bluesbreaker Nickname for the Marshall 2x12 combo used by Eric Clapton on the John Mayall album of the same name. Originals are highly sought after, and the model was re-issued by Marshall in the late 1980s.

board (UK: desk) Mixer, mixing console, mixdown unit.

boat neck Alternative name for V-neck (describes shape). See *V-neck*.

bobbin Frame around which pickup coils are wound.

body Main portion of the guitar, onto which are (usually) mounted the bridge, pickups, controls etc. Can be solid, hollow, or a combination of the two.

bolt-on neck Describes a (usually solidbody) guitar with neck bolted rather than glued to the body. Typified by most Fender electric guitars. In fact, such a neck is most often secured by screws.

bookmatched Wood split into two thin sheets and joined together to present symmetrically matching grain/figure patterns.

bossa nova Means "new trend" in Portuguese. Musical style derived from the influence of Brazilian samba rhythms on West Coast jazz in the early 1960s.

bottleneck Style of guitar playing using a metal or glass object to slide up and down the guitar strings instead of fretting individual notes. The broken-off neck of a bottle was originally used, hence the name.

bound See *binding*.

bout Looking at a guitar standing upright, the bouts are the outward curves of the body above (upper bout) and below (lower bout) the instrument's "waist."

boutique amp High-end, generally hand-built and hand-wired guitar amplifier produced usually in limited numbers by an independent craftsman.

box Slang term for (usually hollowbody "jazz") guitar.

BPM Beats per minute – the tempo of the music.

braces (bracing) Wood structures beneath a hollowbody guitar's front and back intended to enhance strength and tonal response.

Brazilian rosewood Hardwood derived from the tropical evergreen Dalbergia nigra and used in the making of some guitar bodies, necks and fingerboards. Now a protected species, meaning further exportation from Brazil is banned.

bridge Unit on guitar body that holds the saddle(s). Sometimes also incorporates the anchor point for the strings.

bridge block On acoustic guitars, this refers to the drilled section of a bridge through which the strings are threaded.

bridge pickup Pickup placed nearest the bridge. At one time known as the lead or treble pickup.

bridgeplate On electric guitars, this is the baseplate on to which bridge components are mounted; on acoustic guitars, the reinforcing hardwood plate under the bridge.

bronze Metal used as outer wrap on modern flat-top acoustic strings. As a material for this purpose it has replaced the less durable brass.

brown (brown sound) Soft distortion produced by a guitar amp when run at slightly lower mains voltages than its specs require. (Derived from the term "brown-out," the partial loss of power to a city's supply grid — itself a contrast to "blackout," a total loss of power.)

brownface Used to denote Fender amps manufactured between approximately 1960 and 1963, so-called because of their brown control panels. See also *blackface*, *silverface*.

bullet Describes the appearance of the truss-rod adjustment nut visible at the headstock on some Fender and Fender-style guitars.

burst Abbreviation of sunburst (finish), but often used specifically to refer to one of the original sunburst-finish Gibson Les Paul Standard models made between 1958 and 1960.

button Knob used to turn tuners (machine heads).

cab Abbreviation of (speaker) cabinet, commonly used for enclosure containing drivers for one or more frequency ranges.

cable Another name for a cord (lead) to supply mains power, or to connect amps and speakers, or to connect instruments and amplifiers. Can also be used generally for the sheathed connecting wires, with or without connectors.

camber See *radius*.

cans Slang term for headphones.

cante Means folk-singing in Spanish; one of the components of flamenco.

capacitor (cap) Frequency-dependent electrical component. Within an electric guitar tone control, for example, it's used to filter high frequencies to ground (earth) making the sound progressively darker as the control is turned down. Used similarly in guitar amplifiers, as well as for filtering noise from power supplies by passing AC signal to ground.

capo (from capo tasto or capo dastro) Movable device which can be fitted over the fingerboard behind any fret. It shortens the strings' length and therefore raises their pitch. Used to play in different keys but with familiar chord shapes.

carbon graphite Strong, stable, man-made material used by some modern electric guitar makers. Has a very high resonant frequency.

cathode biased In a tube amp, an output stage which is biased according to the voltage drop across a resistor connected to the cathode of the power tube(s). Often considered a source of "vintage" tone, it is a feature of the tweed Fender Deluxe, the Vox AC-30 and others. See also *fixed bias*.

cavity Hollowed-out area in solidbody guitar for controls and switches: thus "control cavity."

CE Mark applied to equipment sold in EU (European Union) countries, theoretically indicating that the equipment meets (largely unspecified) Euro regulations.

cedar Evergreen conifer of the Mediterranean; the timber is used particularly in the making of classical guitar necks. In flat-top and other building the term often refers to "western red cedar," which is not a cedar at all but a North American thuya or arbor vitae.

cellulose See *nitro-cellulose*.

center block Solid wooden block running through the inside of a semi-acoustic guitar's body.

ch Abbreviation of channel. Can be used of a splitter, mixer, crossover, power amp, and so on.

chamfer Bevel or slope to the edges of a guitar's body.

changer Unit at the bridge end of a pedal steel guitar neck with "fingers" to which strings are attached and that connect to the player's choice of pedals and levers.

Charlie Christian Pioneering electric guitarist whose name was popularly applied to one of Gibson's first pickups, since reissued on the ES-175 Charlie Christian model.

chassis Steel or aluminum casing that houses the electronics of an

amp or an effects unit.

checkerboard binding Binding made up of small alternate black and white blocks running around the circumference of a guitar body. Normally associated with high-end Rickenbacker guitars.

cherry Shade of red stain used in translucent guitar finishes and most commonly associated with Gibson who used it extensively from the '50s onwards. Hence often referred to as Gibson Cherry Red.

choke Small transformer within some guitar amps which helps to filter AC noise from the circuit.

choking String colliding with a higher fret as the string is played and/or bent.

chops Slang for player's technical proficiency.

class A Amplifier with output tubes set to operate throughout the full 360-degree cycle of the signal. Class A is sometimes considered "sweeter" sounding harmonically, but is less efficient power-wise than class AB. (The term is often incorrectly used to describe guitar amps which are in fact cathode-biased class AB circuits with no negative feedback, and therefore share some sonic characteristics with class A amps.) See *class AB*.

class AB Amplifier with output tubes set to cut off alternately for a portion of the signal's 360-degree cycle, thereby sharing the load and increasing output efficiency. (In reality, this is the operating class of the majority of guitar amps, and certainly of many classics by Marshall, Fender, Mesa/Boogie and others.) See *class A*.

clay dot Refers to the material used for the dot inlays on Fender guitars from circa 1959 to 1963.

coil(s) Insulated wire wound around bobbin(s) in a pickup.

coil-split Usually describes a method to cut out one coil of a humbucking pickup, giving a slightly lower output and cleaner, more single-coil-like sound. Also known, incorrectly, as coil-tap.

coil-tap (tapped pickup) Pickup coil which has two or more live leads exiting at different

percentages of the total wind, in order to provide multiple output levels and tones. Not to be confused with coil-split.

combo Abbreviation of combination, meaning a combination in one cabinet of an instrument amplifier and speaker system. Also, old-fashioned/obsolete term for a band or group of musicians.

compensation Small distance added to each string's speaking length to make the guitar play in-tune. This additional string length compensates for the sharpening effect of pressing the strings down onto the fingerboard.

comping Playing style, usually associated with jazz, which sustains the tempo and rhythm of a piece while simultaneously stating its chord changes.

compound radius See *radius*.

compressor Sound processor that can be set to smooth dynamic range and thus minimize sudden leaps in volume. Overall perceived loudness is in this way increased without "clipping."

concert Name originated by Martin to designate a specific style of large-bodied flat-top acoustic guitar. Also, in classical guitar terminology a concert guitar is one intended for the public performance of "serious" music.

concert pitch Standardized instrument tuning used in most Western music (at least since 1960) where the A above middle C has a fundamental frequency of 440Hz. This can be measured using an electronic tuner or checked against a tuning fork.

concerto Extended work for a solo instrument and an orchestra.

conductor wires Wires attached to the start and finish of a pickup coil which take the output signal to the controls. A four-conductor humbucker, for example, actually has five output wires: four conductor wires and a fifth (bare) wire which comes from the pickup's grounding plate and/or cover and must always be connected to ground (earth).

conical radius See *radius*.

contoured body Gentle curving of the front and/or back of a solid guitar body, and usually designed to aid player comfort.

control(s) Knobs and switch levers on outside of guitar activating the function of electric components that are usually mounted below the pickguard or in back of the body.

control cavity See *cavity*.

cord (cable, UK: lead) Cable to supply unit with power, or to connect amplifiers and speakers, or to connect instruments and amplifiers.

counterpoint Music that consists of two or more independent melody lines.

coupling Exchange of mechanical energy between an instrument's string(s) and soundboard.

course Usually means a pair of strings running together but tuned apart, usually in unison or an octave apart, as on a 12-string guitar, mandolin, or baroque guitar. Technically, the term can also refer to a single string (or, rarely, a group of three strings).

cross-head screw Screw that has two slots in a "cross" shape in its head.

cross-head screwdriver Screwdriver with a cross-shaped point to fit a cross-head screw. Sometimes known as a Phillips (head) screwdriver.

crossover Circuit, sometimes built into amps and/or speakers, that splits a signal into two or more complementary frequency ranges.

current Flow of electrons in an electrical circuit, measured in amps.

custom color Selected color finish for a guitar, as opposed to natural or sunburst. Term originated by Fender in the late '50s, now widely used.

cutaway Curve into body near neck joint, aiding player's access to high frets. A guitar can have two ("double," "equal," "offset," "twin") cutaways or one ("single") cutaway. Sharp ("florentine") or round ("venetian") describe the shape of the horn formed by the cutaway.

cypress Conifer native to southern Europe, east Asia and North America and widely planted for decorative purposes and for wood. Used in the 19th century for the bodies of cheaper guitars taken up by the flamencos.

damping Deadening of a sound, especially by stopping the vibration of a string with, for example, the palm of the hand.

DC Short for "direct current." Electric current flowing only in one direction. Tube (valve) amps utilize DC voltages for the vast portion of their internal operation.

DC resistance "Direct current" resistance: a measurement (in ohms) that is often quoted in pickup specs to give an indication of relative output.

dead string length Portion of the string beyond the nut and behind the saddle.

decal (UK: transfer, sticker) Small sheet with logo, brandname or trademark, usually on headstock. Licked by the good Captain, baby.

desk See *board*.

DI Abbreviation of direct injection. Means of isolating, adjusting and balancing a line-level instrument signal (from keyboards, guitars etc) so it can be connected to the PA's stagebox or to a recording mixer at a suitable level and without creating buzzes.

digital System of recording or processing which stores and processes analog information by converting it into a series of numbers (binary 1s and 0s).

digital modeling See *modeling amp*.

dings Small knocks, dents or other signs of normal wear in a guitar's surface. A true indicator of aged beauty if you're selling; a cause for mirth and money-saving if you're buying.

diode Electronic component used within some guitar amps as a solid-state rectifier to convert AC current to DC. Also occasionally used in solid-state overdrive circuits. See also *rectifier*.

dissonance Perceived sonic clash between two or more notes that are sounded together.

distortion Signal degradation caused by the overloading or intentional manipulation of audio systems (such as guitar amplifier). Often used deliberately to create a harsher and grittier or sweeter and more compressed sound.

dive-bomb See *down-bend*.

Dobro Product of the Dopyera Brothers or the successors to their brandname, subsequently adopted as a generic term for a guitar with metal resonator(s) inside.

dog-ear Nickname for some P-90 pickups, derived from the shape of the mounting lugs on the cover. See also *soap-bar*.

dot markers Dot-shape position markers in fingerboard.

dot-neck Fingerboard with dot-shape position markers; nickname for Gibson ES-335 of 1958-62 (and reissues) with such markers.

double-locking vibrato See *locking vibrato*.

double-neck (twin-neck) Large guitar specially made with two necks, usually combining six-string and 12-string, or six-string and bass.

down-bend Downward shift in the strings' pitch using a vibrato. In extreme cases this is known as dive-bombing.

down-market See *low-end*.

DPDT switch Double-pole double-throw switch, usually miniature or sub-miniature variety used for guitar coil-tap or other such switching.

Dreadnought Large flat-top acoustic guitar designed by Frank H. Martin and Harry Hunt and named for a type of large British battleship. Now used to describe any acoustic of this body style.

dropped headstock (pointed headstock, droopy headstock) Long, down-pointing headstock popularized on 1980s superstrats.

dynamics Expression in music using a range of volume (intensity) shifts.

ears Jazz slang for player's speed and ability to learn and interpret new tunes.

earth (UK term; also known as ground, especially in US) Connection between an electrical circuit or device and the ground. A common neutral reference point in an electrical circuit. All electrical components (and shielding) within a guitar (and amplifiers, signal processors, etc) must be linked to earth as the guitar's pickups and electrics are susceptible to noise interference. See also *shielding*.

ebonized Wood darkened to look like ebony.

ebonol Synthetic material made of compressed paper and resin, used as fingerboard material by some manufacturers, notably Steinberger.

ebony Dense, black hardwood used for fingerboards and bridges.

effects (effects units, FX) Generic term for audio processing devices such as distortions, delays, reverbs, flangers, phasers, harmonizers and so on.

effects loop Patch between the preamp and power amp (or sometimes within preamp stages) of guitar amp, processing unit or mixer for inserting effects that will operate on selected sound signals.

electric Term simply applied to any electric guitar; in other words, a guitar intended to be used in conjunction with an amplifier.

electro-acoustic (electro) Acoustic guitar with built-in pickup, usually of piezo-electric type. The guitar usually has a preamp and includes volume and tone controls.

electro-acoustics Academic name for key parts of PA where electronics and acoustics come together, meaning inter-disciplinary work with mikes, mike amps, power amps, speakers, cables, cans and acoustics.

electron tube See *tube*.

electronic tuner Typically battery-powered unit that displays and enables accurate tuning to standard concert pitch.

end-block Thick wooden block used to join sides of guitar at the lower bout.

EQ See *equalization*.

equalization (EQ) Active tone control that works by emphasizing or de-emphasizing specific frequency bands. General term for tone control.

étude Means "study" in French. Classical piece intended to help develop technical skills, and sometimes also of musical value.

European spruce Sometimes called German spruce, picea abies tends to come from the Balkans. Spruce originally meant "from Prussia." Used for soundboards.

face See *plate*, *soundboard*.

fan-strutting Wooden struts beneath lower soundboard of guitar, arranged approximately in the shape of an open fan.

Farad Measure of electrical capacitance, and usually (for electric guitar capacitors) quoted in microfarads (mF or µF) or picofarads (pF).

feedback Howling noise produced by leakage of the output of an amplification system back into its input, typically a guitar's pickup(s).

f-hole Soundhole of approximately "f" shape on some hollowbody and semi-acoustic guitars.

figure Natural pattern on surface of wood; thus "figured maple".

fine-tuners Set of tuners that tune strings to very fine degrees, usually as fitted to a locking vibrato or a specialized bridge.

finger String holder actuated by footpedal or knee lever to alter the pitch of a pedal steel guitar.

fingerboard (fretboard, board) Playing surface of the guitar that holds the frets. It can be simply the front of the neck itself, or a separate thin board glued to the neck.

finish Protective and decorative covering on wood parts, typically the guitar's body, back of neck, and headstock.

five-position switch See *five-way switch*.

five-way switch (five-position switch) Selector switch that offers five options, for example the five pickup combinations on a Strat-style guitar.

fixed bias In guitar amps, a technique for biasing output tubes using a pot to adjust negative voltage on the tube's grid as compared to its cathode. (Note that the name is somewhat misleading as "fixed-bias" amps generally have a bias which is adjustable, whereas cathode-biased amps are set and non-adjustable.) See *cathode biased*.

fixed bridge Non-vibrato bridge.

fixed neck See *glued neck*.

flame Dramatic figure, usually on maple.

flame-top Guitar, often specifically a Gibson Les Paul Standard, with sunburst maple top.

flat-blade screwdriver See *slot-head screwdriver*.

flat-top Acoustic guitar with flat top (as opposed to arched) and usually with a round soundhole.

floating bridge Bridge not fixed permanently to the guitar's top, but held in place by string tension (usually on older or old-style hollowbody guitars).

floating pickup Pickup not fixed permanently to the guitar's top, but mounted on a separate pickguard or to the end of the fingerboard (on some hollowbody electric guitars).

floating vibrato Vibrato unit (such as the Floyd Rose or Wilkinson type) that "floats" above the surface of the body.

flowerpot inlay Describes an inlay depicting a stylized vase and foliage used by Gibson on, notably,

its L-5 model.

14-fret/12-fret Refers to the point at which a flat-top acoustic guitar's neck joins the body.

French polishing Traditional varnishing technique that uses a small fabric pad to rub shellac dissolved in alcohol into the wood of a guitar body.

frequency Number of cycles of a vibration occurring per unit of time; the perceived pitch of a sound. See also *Hertz*.

fretboard See *fingerboard*.

fretless Guitar fingerboard without frets; usually bass, but sometimes (very rarely) guitar.

frets Metal strips positioned on the fingerboard of a guitar (or sometimes directly into the face of a solid neck) to enable the player to stop the strings and produce specific notes.

fretwire Wire from which individual frets are cut.

friction peg Traditional tuning peg held in position by the friction of the wooden peg in its hole. Now only on flamenco guitars, though still commonly seen on other stringed instruments such as violins and cellos.

frontline Arrangement of amplifiers and speakers when placed at the front of the stage, in front of musicians, as was sometimes done in the '50s and early '60s. See also *backline*.

FX Abbreviation for effects. Also known more formally as signal processors – boxes that can be used to alter sound in a creative and/or artistic manner.

gain Amount of increase or change in signal level. When dBs are used, increased gain is shown as +dB; reduction is shown -dB; and no change as 0dB.

gauge Outer diameter of a string, always measured in thousandths of an inch (.009", .042" etc). Strings are supplied in particular gauges and/or in sets of matched gauges. Fretwire is also offered in different gauges, or sizes.

gig Live musical event.

glued neck (glued-in neck, set neck, fixed neck) Type of neck/body joint popularized by Gibson which permanently glues the two main components together.

golpeador (golpe) Thin protective plate used to protect the top of a flamenco guitar from the player's finger-tapping.

greenback Describes a particularly desirable Celestion 12" guitar speaker that had a green magnet-cover.

ground (also known as earth, particularly in the UK) Connection between an electrical circuit or device and the ground. A common neutral reference point in an electrical circuit. All electrical components (and shielding) within a guitar (and amplifiers, signal processors, etc) must be linked to earth as the guitar's pickups and electrics are susceptible to noise interference.

ground wire Wire connected from vibrato, bridge, tailpiece, switch, pickup cover, grounding plate etc to ground (earth).

grounding plate Metal baseplate of pickup that is connected to ground (earth).

grunge tuning Tuning all strings down one half step (one semitone) for a fatter sound.

gut Cured animal intestines used for classical strings before development of nylon.

hang-tags Small cards and other documents hung on a guitar in the showroom, and prized when still available with vintage instruments.

hardtail Guitar with non-vibrato bridge (originally used primarily to distinguish non-vibrato Fender Stratocasters from the more common vibrato-loaded models).

hardware Separate components (non-electrical) fitted to the guitar: the bridge, tuners, strap buttons, and so on.

harmonic Usually refers to a ringing, high-pitched note produced by touching (rather than fretting) strategic points on the string while it is plucked, most noticeably at the fifth, seventh and 12th fret. In fact, "harmonics" also occur naturally during the playing of the acoustic or electric guitar (or any stringed instrument) and are part of any guitar's overall voice.

harmonic bar Fitted inside an acoustic guitar, usually one above the soundhole and one below.

harmonic distortion "Ordinary" distortion occurring in analog (audio) electronics, speakers and mikes, involving the generation of harmonics.

headless Design with no headstock, popularized by Ned Steinberger in the early 1980s.

headstock Portion at the end of the neck where the strings attach to the tuners. "Six-a-side" type (Fender-style) has all six tuners on one side of the headstock. "Three-a-side" type (Gibson-style) has three tuners on one side, three the other.

heel Curved deepening of the neck for strength near body joint.

herringbone Describes a black-and-white decorative inlay for acoustic guitars, as popularized by the Martin company.

Hertz (Hz) Unit of frequency measurement. One Hertz equals one cycle per second. See *frequency*.

hex pickup Provides suitable signal for an external synthesizer.

high-end (up-market, upscale) High- or higher-cost instrument, usually aimed at those seeking the best materials and workmanship.

hockey stick Refers to the shape of the headstock on Fender's Electric XII 12-string guitar.

hook-up wire Connecting wire (live or ground) from pickup to pots, switches etc.

horn Pointed body shape formed by cutaway: thus "left horn," "sharp horn," etc. See also *cutaway*.

hot In electrical connections, means live. Also used generally to mean powerful, as in "hot pickup."

hot-rodding Making modifications to a guitar, usually its pickups and/or electronics.

HT Symbol denoting high voltage in amplifier circuits (short for High Tension) and particularly used in the UK. See *B+*.

humbucker (humbucking) Noise-canceling twin-coil pickup. Typically the two coils have opposite magnetic polarity and are wired together electrically out-of-phase to produce a sound that we call in-phase. See also *phase*.

hybrid Technically, any instrument that combines two or more systems of any kind. But now most often indicates a guitar that combines original-style magnetic "electric" pickups with "acoustic"-sounding piezo-electric pickups.

iced-tea Description of the color of a Les Paul Standard which has faded with time and UV exposure.

impedance Electrical resistance to the flow of alternating current, measured in Ohms (Ω). A few electric guitars have low-impedance circuits or pickups to match the inputs of recording equipment; the vast majority are high impedance. Impedance matching is important to avoid loss of signal and tone. Also commonly encountered with speakers, where it is important to match a speaker's (or speaker cab's) impedance to that of the amplifier's speaker output (commonly 4Ω, 8Ω or 16Ω).

in-between sound Legendary tone achieved on older Fender Strats fitted with three-way Centralab switch by jamming the switch between settings so that pairs of pickups operate at once. Made easier from early '80s when Fender fitted a five-way version of the switch, a quarter of a century after the model was launched.

Indian rosewood Hardwood from tropical evergreen tree, known as East Indian rosewood or Dalbergia latifolia. Used for acoustic guitar bodies, fingerboards or necks, especially now that Brazilian rosewood is not freely available.

inertia block See *sustain block*.

inlay Decorative material cut and fitted into body, fingerboard, headstock etc.

insulation Plastic, cloth or tape wrap, or sheath (non-conductive), around an electrical wire, designed to prevent wire(s) coming into contact with other components and thus shorting the circuit.

intonation State of a guitar so that it is as in-tune with itself as physically possible. This is usually dependent on setting each string's speaking length by adjusting the point at which the strings cross the bridge saddle, known as intonation adjustment. Some bridges allow more adjustment, and therefore greater possibilities for accurate intonation, than others.

jack (UK: jack socket) Mono or stereo connecting socket, usually ¼" (6.5mm), used to feed guitar's output signal to amplification.

jackplate Mounting plate for output jack (jack socket), usually screwed on to body.

jack socket See *jack*.

jewel light Fender-style pilot light with faceted cut-glass "jewel" screwed on over a small bulb.

juerga Spontaneous flamenco event.

jumbo Large-bodied flat-top acoustic guitar. Also used as a name for extra wide and high frets on a guitar fingerboard.

kerfed lining Lining that has been partly cut through at intervals to make it flexible enough to follow the shape of a hollowbody guitar's sides.

Kluson Brand of tuner, originally used on old Fender, Gibson and other guitars, and now reissued.

knurled Serrated or cross-hatched patterning to provide grip on metal (or plastic) components; thus "knurled control knobs" (as fitted to a Telecaster-style guitar).

lacquer See *nitro-cellulose*.

laminated Joined together in layers; usually wood (bodies, necks) or plastic (pickguards).

lead Shorthand for lead guitar: the main guitar within a group; the one that plays most of the solos and/or riffs. Also (UK) term for cord; see also *cable*, *cord*.

lead pickup See *bridge pickup*.

leaf switch See *toggle switch*.

LED Abbreviation of light emitting diode, a small light often used as an "on" indicator in footswitches, effects and amplifier control panels. Sometimes also used as a component within circuits.

legato Term used in musical notation to instruct the musician to play smoothly.

lever switch Type of pickup selector switch historically used by Fender – for example the five-way lever switch. A single, pivoted lever moves between contacts to direct the input-to-output path. See *pickup switch*, *selector*, *toggle switch*.

ligado Left-hand technique involving hammering-on and pulling-off. Especially important in flamenco playing.

linear taper See *taper*.

lining Continuous strip of wood used to join sides of hollowbody guitar to top and back. See also *kerfed lining*.

locking nut Unit that locks strings in place at the nut, usually with three locking bolts.

locking trem See *locking vibrato*.

locking tuner Special tuner that locks the string to the string-post and thus aids string-loading.

locking vibrato Type of vibrato system that locks strings at nut and bridge saddles (hence also called "double-locking") in an effort to stabilize tuning.

logarithmic taper See *taper*.

logo Brandname and/or trademark, usually on the headstock.

low-end (down-market, bargain, budget) Low- or lower-cost instrument, often aimed at beginners or other players on a restricted budget.

lower bout See *bout*.

lug Protruding part or surface. On electrical components, a lug (sometimes called a tag) allows a connection to be made.

lute Medieval and Renaissance

stringed musical instrument.

luthier Old word for maker of violins and/or guitars.

machine head See *tuner*.

magnetic pickup Transducer using coils of wire wound around a magnet. It converts string vibrations into electrical signals.

mahogany Very stable, medium weight hardwood favored by most guitar makers for necks, and by many for solid bodies.

mains Term for high AC voltage (particularly in the UK) as supplied by domestic wall socket – that is, the "main" domestic supply.

maple Hard, heavy wood, often displaying extreme figure patterns prized by guitar makers. Varying kinds of figure give rise to visual nicknames such as quilted, tigerstripe, curly, flame.

master volume/tone Control that affects all pickups equally. In amplification, a master volume control governs the output level – or operating level of the power section – when partnered with a gain, drive or volume control that governs the level of the individual preamp(s).

microfarad See *Farad*.

microphonic Used of a pickup, this means one that is inclined to squeal unpleasantly, usually due to incomplete wax saturation, to loose coil windings, or to insecure mountings that create so-called microphonic feedback.

MIDI Abbreviation of Musical Instrument Digital Interface. The industry-standard control system for electronic instruments. Data for notes, performance effects, patch changes, voice and sample data, tempo and other information can be transmitted and received.

mint Entirely as new, perfect

condition; as used to describe vintage or collectable guitars.

mint green (snot green) Descriptive term for the color of a type of Fender pickguard material used from late 1959 to 1963 (and reproduced on some vintage-style reissues). Originally white, the celluloid nitrate material can age to a dirty pale green.

mod Abbreviation for modification. Any change or after-market customization made to a guitar, amplifier or effects pedal.

modeling amp Guitar amplifier using digital technology (though occasionally analog solid-state circuitry) to emulate, or model, the sounds of classic tube amps.

mother-of-pearl Shell of some molluscs, for example abalone, used for inlays in decoration of rosettes, fingerboards, headstocks, tuning pegs etc.

mother-of-toilet-seat Slang for plastic mother-of-pearl-like material used for inlays in place of the real thing.

mounting ring Usually plastic unit within which Gibson-style pickups are fitted to the guitar body.

mustache bridge Describes the shape of a flat-top acoustic guitar bridge plate, typically found on the Gibson J-200 model.

Nashville tuning Replacing the lowest three strings with strings tuned an octave higher in order to fill out recorded rhythm parts.

neck Part of the guitar supporting the fingerboard and strings; glued or bolted to the body, or on "though-neck" types forming a support spine on to which "wings" are usually glued to form the body.

neck block In acoustic guitars, the end of the neck inside the body where it is built up to meet the top and back of the guitar.

neck pickup Pickup placed nearest the neck. At one time known as the rhythm or bass pickup.

neck pitch Angle of a guitar's neck relative to the body face.

neckplate Single metal plate

through which screws pass to achieve a bolt-on neck fixing (Fender-style). Some bolt-on neck-to-body joints use separate washers for each screw.

neck pocket Rout, or recess, into which the neck fits on the body of a bolt-on-neck guitar.

neck relief Small amount of concave bow in a neck (dipping in the middle) that can help to create a relatively buzz-free action.

neck-tilt Device on some Fender (and other) neck-to-body joints that allows easier adjustment of the neck pitch.

nickel Major component of most metal guitar strings.

nitro-cellulose (US: lacquer) Type of finish used commonly in the '50s and '60s but now rarely seen on production guitars.

Nocaster Collector's term to describe Fender guitars made during the transition from the Broadcaster model name, contested by Gretsch, to Telecaster. These guitars had the part of the decal (transfer) bearing the model name clipped from the headstock.

nodal bar In some classical guitars by David Rubio, a strut extending from beneath the bridge on the treble side of the soundboard. Intended to modify treble response. (From "node," a stationary part of a vibrating body.)

noise Any undesirable sound, such as mains hum or interference.

noise-canceling Type of pickup with two coils wired together to cancel noise, often called humbucking. Any arrangement of pickups or pickup coils that achieves this.

nut Bone, metal or (now usually) synthetic slotted guide bar over which the strings pass to reach the tuners and which determines string height and spacing at the headstock end of neck.

nut lock See *locking nut*.

Offset Contour Body Fender trademark used to describe the distortion of a conventional solidbody shape to aid the player's

comfort and present the neck at a more comfortable angle. Fender's Jazzmaster and Jaguar models were the first with this design.

offshore Made overseas; more specifically and often used to mean outside the US.

ohm Unit of electrical resistance.

open tuning Tuning the guitar to a chord or altered chord, often for slide playing.

out of phase Audible result of the electrical linking of two coils or two pickups in either series or parallel in such a way as to provide at least partial cancellation of the signal. Usually the low frequencies are cancelled so that the resulting sound is thin, lacking in warmth, and often quite brittle. To create an audible result that is in-phase (for example of two coils within a humbucker) the coils must be linked electrically out-of-phase. Phase relationship also depends on polarity of magnets. See also *humbucker*.

oxblood Describes the color of the woven grille cloth used on Fender amps in the early '60s.

PAF Gibson pickup with Patent Applied For decal (sticker) on base – as was the first, vintage version of the Gibson humbucker.

parallel Electrical circuit that has all the positive points joined together and all the negative points joined together. If we consider that a single-coil pickup has a positive (live, hot) and negative (ground, earth) output, when two single-coil pickups on a Stratocaster (position two and four on a five-way switch), for example, are selected together, they are linked in parallel. Can also apply to the parallel linking of resistors or capacitors in a circuit, etc. See also *series*.

passive Normal, unboosted circuit.

P Bass Commonly used abbreviation for Fender's Precision Bass and similar models.

PCB Abbreviation for printed circuit board, a mass-produced fiber board with copper "tracks" making connections between components. It is now the most common circuit board in modern consumer electronics, and is employed in the majority of guitar amplifiers, other than those that use expensive hand-wired designs.

pearl See *mother-of-pearl*.

pearloid Fake pearl, made of plastic and pearl dust.

pentode Tube (valve) containing five functional elements. Most output tubes in guitar amplifiers are pentodes. Also see *triode*.

phase Relationship of two waveforms with respect to time. See also *out of phase*.

Phillips screwdriver See *cross-head screwdriver*.

pick (plectrum, flat pick) Small piece of (usually) plastic or metal – and in olden times tortoiseshell – that is used to pluck or strum a guitar's strings.

pickguard (UK: scratchplate) Protective panel raised above body or fitted flush on to guitar body.

pickup Any unit mounted on a guitar (or other stringed instrument) which transforms string vibration to an electrical signal to be passed along to an amplifier. See *magnetic pickup, piezo pickup, transducer*.

pickup switch Selector switch

that specifically selects pickups individually or in combination.

piezo pickup (piezo-electric pickup) Transducer with piezo-electric crystals that generate electricity under mechanical strain. In a guitar, it senses string and body movement. "Piezo-loaded saddles" are bridge saddles with an integral piezo element.

pin bridge Acoustic guitar bridge that secures the strings by pins rather than by tying.

pitch Frequency of a note: the perceived "lowness" or "highness" of a sound. See also *neck pitch*.

P-J Bass Describes a Fender Precision Bass with an additional Jazz Bass pickup added at the bridge position. A popular mod with bass players, and subsequently adopted by Fender on a number of its basses.

plain strings Plain steel guitar strings with no outer windings. See *wound strings*.

plantilla In classical terminology, the outline of a guitar body.

plate Scientific term for the vibrating soundboard (also known as top plate, where back plate is used for the back of the guitar). See *soundboard, top;* and also *anode*.

plectrum See *pick*.

plexi Nickname for Marshall amplifiers of the mid to late-'60s that used gold-painted "plexiglas" plastic control panels. Also used to refer to the sound produced by Marshall amps of this era, or the reproduction of such a tone.

P-90 Model name for early Gibson single-coil pickup.

point-to-point Method of constructing hand-wired amplifier circuits where individual components are connected directly to each other, without the use of a circuit board.

pointed headstock See *dropped headstock.*

pointy Type of body design generally used by rock players – prevalent in the 1980s and since – with a jagged, pointed, angular outline. Also used of headstock: see *dropped headstock.*

polarity Relationship of positive and negative electrical currents (or north and south magnetic poles) to each other. The magnetic polarity of a pickup refers to the north or south orientation of the magnetic field as presented to the strings.

pole Simultaneously-switched circuit within an electrical switch; thus "two-pole."

polepieces Non-magnetic (but magnetically conductive) polepieces are used to control, concentrate and/or shape a pickup's magnetic field. Can be either adjustable (screw) or non-adjustable (slug) as in an original Gibson humbucker. Magnetic polepieces are those where the magnet itself is aimed directly at the strings, as in an original Stratocaster single-coil.

polyester Type of modern plastic finish used on some guitars.

polyphonic Music made up of several independent lines, each of which is known as a voice.

polyurethane (urethane) Type of modern plastic finish that is used on some guitars.

position markers Fingerboard inlays of various designs; visual clues to the player of fret positions.

pot (potentiometer) Variable electrical resistor that alters voltage by a spindle turning on an electrically resistive track. Used for volume and tone controls, etc.

power amp Output stage of a guitar amplifier that converts the preamp signal to the signal capable of driving a speaker. In a tube (valve) amp, this is where the big tubes live.

preamp (pre-amplifier) Circuit designed to boost low-level signals to a standard level and EQ them before they're sent toward the power amp (hence "pre-amplifier") for full amplification. Guitar circuit usually powered by battery that converts the pickup's output from high to low impedance (preamp/buffer) and can increase the output signal and boost or cut specific frequencies for tonal effect. Also, the first gain stage in a guitar amp, which generally also includes the EQ circuitry and any overdrive-generating stages.

pre-CBS Fender guitars and amps made before CBS takeover in 1965.

prelude Originally the opening piece of a set. But since the 19th century, preludes no longer have to precede. Put it where you want it.

pressed top Arched top (usually laminated) of hollowbody guitar made by machine-pressing rather than hand-carving.

pull/push pot Combination component offering the functions of both a volume/tone potentiometer and a mini-toggle (usually of DPDT type) switch. See also *push-pull.*

purfling Usually synonymous with binding, but more accurately refers to the decorative inlays around the perimeter of a guitar alongside the binding.

push-pull Power amplifier in which output tubes (valves) operate on alternate cycles of the signal. (This is the most common power amp format in guitar amps that contain more than one output tube.) See also *pull/push pot.*

pyramid bridge Flat-top acoustic guitar bridge having pyramid shaped "bumps" at each side. Common to early Martins.

quarter-sawn Wood cut on radius of tree so that "rings" are perpendicular to the surface of the plank. Structurally preferable to flat-sawn wood for guitar building.

quilted Undulating figure seen on surface of wood, usually maple.

radius Slight curve, or camber, of a fingerboard surface, of the strings, or of the bridge saddles. The term comes from the way that this curve is measured, where the fingerboard, for example, is considered as the top part of a wedge cut from a cylinder of a certain radius. Conical (or compound) radius is where the fingerboard radius increases from the nut to the top fret.

rectifier Component within a guitar amplifier which converts electrical current from AC to DC; can comprise solid-state diodes or a tube (valve) rectifier.

refinish (refin) New finish on a guitar, replacing or added to the original. Usually considered detrimental to a collectable guitar.

reissue Instrument or amp based on an earlier and usually classic model, reintroduced at a later date.

relief See *neck relief.*

resistor Electrical component which introduces a known value of resistance (measured in ohms) to the electrical flow in a circuit.

resonant frequency Frequency at which any object vibrates most

with the least stimulation.

resonator Generic term for guitar with metal resonator(s) in its body to increase volume.

retro Past style reintroduced, often with some changes, as a "new" design, usually with deliberate references. Thus retro guitars use flavors of mainly '50s and '60s designs to inform new concoctions.

retrofit Any component added to a guitar after it leaves the place where it was made (retrofit pickup, vibrato, tuner etc) and one that fits directly onto the intended guitar with no alteration to the instrument.

reverb (reverberation) Ambience effect combining many short echoes; can be imitated electronically, generally by the installation of a spring unit in guitar amps, or digitally in pedals and studio effects units.

rhythm pickup See *neck pickup.*

ribs Classical term for the sides of a guitar.

Ricky Common abbreviation of Rickenbacker; do not allow it ever to lose that number.

rosette Intricate decoration around soundhole, usually in marquetry, abalone inlay or wooden mosaic, often on classical guitars.

rosewood Variegated hardwood traditionally used for acoustic guitar backs, sides and fingerboards. Brazilian or Rio is the most highly prized; Indian is more common.

rout Hole or cavity cut into a guitar, usually into the body. Cavities of this kind are thus said to be routed (rhymes with "shouted") into the body.

saddle(s) Part(s) of a bridge

where the strings make contact; the start of the speaking length of the string; effectively the opposite of the (top) nut.

sag Slight drop in power supply of a guitar amplifier (particularly noticeable in designs comprising tube rectifiers) when a powerful note or chord is played, producing a compression-like softening and squeezing of the signal.

salmon pink Popular (unofficial) name for Fiesta Red, an early Fender Custom Color. Paint is likely to fade depending on its exposure to ultra-violet light, and faded Fiesta Red can look pink. Often confused with Shell Pink, a rare Fender color introduced in the '50s.

samba Portuguese word for a Brazilian dance with African origins.

scale length (string length) Theoretical length of the vibrating string from nut to saddle; actually twice the distance from nut to 12th fret. The actual scale length (the distance from the nut to saddle after intonation adjustment) is slightly longer. See *intonation*, *compensation*.

scallop Gentle sloping of sides of bracing for lightness and tonal modification. Also describes mid-'80s fad for scooping out the fingerboard between frets, allegedly to assist speedy playing.

scratchplate See *pickguard*.

scratch test To verify if a pickup on a guitar plugged into an amp is working by gently rubbing ("scratching") the tip of a screwdriver on the pickup's polepieces and listening for sound.

selector Control that selects from options, usually of pickups.

semi See *semi-acoustic*.

semi-acoustic (semi-solid, semi) Electric guitar with wholly or partly hollow thin body. Originally referred specifically to an electric guitar with a solid wooden block running down the center of thinline body, such as Gibson's ES-335.

semi-solid See *semi-acoustic*.

serial number Added by maker for own purposes; sometimes useful for determining the period of the

instrument's construction.

series Electrical linkage of positive and negative points within an electrical circuit with additive effect – for example, the two pickup coils within a series-wired humbucker. In this instance, the total resistance of a series-wired humbucker is the sum of the resistance of each coil. Parallel linkage of the same two coils results in the resistance being one quarter of the sum total. Generally, the higher the resistance the "darker" the resulting tone. Also applies to method of linkage of capacitors or resistors within an amplifier or other electrical circuit. See *parallel*.

set neck (glued neck, glued-in neck, fixed neck) Type of neck/body joint popularized by Gibson which permanently "sets" the two main components together, usually by gluing.

set-up General term including but not restricted to a broad and complex combination of factors (string height, saddle height, intonation adjustments, fret condition, neck relief, etc) required to get the guitar playing to its optimum level.

shellac Natural thermoplastic resin made from secretions of lac insect, which lives on trees in India and Thailand. Dissolved in alcohol, it creates a finish that is applied to guitars by French polishing.

shielding (screening) Barrier to any outside electrical interference. Special paint or conductive foil in the control or pickup cavity to reduce electrical interference. See also *ground*.

signal Transmitted electrical information – for example between control circuits, or guitar and amplifier, etc – usually by means of a connecting wire or cord (lead).

silverface Fender guitar amps with silver control panels, generally produced between 1968 and the late '70s and considered somewhat

inferior tonally to earlier "blackface" versions, though often still very good amps by today's standards. See also *blackface*, *brownface*.

single-coil Original pickup type with a single coil of wire wrapped around (a) magnet(s).

single-ended Amplifier in which the power tube (valve) – usually just one – operates through the entire cycle of the signal. Such amps are necessarily, therefore, class A. Classic examples include the Fender Champ and Vox AC-4.

sitka spruce (picea sitchensis) Large conifer, originally from North America. Popularly used for soundboards on acoustic guitars, especially by US makers.

skunk-stripe Walnut strip inserted in back of one-piece Fender maple necks after truss-rod is inserted.

slab board (slab fingerboard) Fender type (circa 1959-62) in which the joint between the top of the neck and the base of the fingerboard is flat. Later this joint was curved.

slash soundhole Scimitar-shaped soundhole, used primarily by Rickenbacker, but seen on some Gretsch Electromatics and other guitars.

slide Metal or glass tube worn over a guitarist's finger to produce glissando effects. Also, the style of playing using these effects; thus "Did Lowell like to play slide?" See also *bottleneck*.

slot-head screw Type with a single slot in its head.

slot-head screwdriver Type with a flat, single blade, also known as a flat-blade screwdriver.

slot-head tuner Tuner with a slot cut into the top of its string-post with a hole running down the center of its string post.

slotted headstock One with cut-outs that allow access to the tuning-peg posts.

slush lever See *vibrato*.

snakehead Headstock shape that is narrower at the top than the bottom. Usually refers to early Gibson type.

snot green See *mint green*.

soapbar Nickname for P-90 pickup with a cover that has no mounting "ears". See *dog-ear*.

solid General term for any solidbody guitar.

solid-state Circuitry using transistorized components rather than tubes (valves).

soundboard Vibrating top of a guitar body. See *top*, *plate*.

soundhole Aperture in the top of an acoustic guitar's body that increases sound projection. Similar function to f-holes on hollowbody and semi-acoustic guitars.

spaghetti logo Early Fender logo with thin, stringy letters resembling spaghetti, prominent in the '50s and early '60s and on reissues of those designs.

SPDT switch Single-pole double-throw miniature switch.

speaker (loudspeaker, driver) Component consisting of a ceramic or alnico magnet, voice coil, and paper cone, driven by an amplified signal to reproduce sound waves in moving air.

speaking length Sounding length of a guitar's string: the part running from the nut down to the bridge saddle.

splice-joint One method of fixing a guitar head to its neck when each has been carved from a different section of wood.

splined Grooved surface of potentiometer shaft that assists tight fitting of a control knob.

spring claw Anchor point for vibrato springs in body-rear vibrato cavity. Adjusting the spring claw's two screws will affect the position and potential travel of the vibrato.

spruce Soft, light hardwood used for the soundboard on many acoustic guitars.

stock State of a guitar, irrespective of condition, where everything is exactly as supplied when new. Individual items on a guitar exactly as supplied when new (thus "stock pickup," for example).

stop-tail Slang for the style of wrapover bridge fitted to low and mid-priced Gibson solidbodies. See *wrapover bridge*.

stop tailpiece See *stud tailpiece*.

strap button Fixing point on body to attach a guitar-strap; usually two, on sides (or side and back) of guitar body.

straplock Safety device for preventing a guitar from falling off the guitar strap during wild and uninhibited performance. Most common are those made by Jim Dunlop and Schaller.

Strat Abbreviation of Fender Stratocaster, so universally used that Fender have trademarked it and use it themselves.

string block In classical-guitar terminology, this is the drilled section of a bridge through which the strings are threaded.

string length Sounding length of string, measured from nut to bridge saddle (see also *scale length*).

string post Metal shaft on tuner with a hole or slot to receive the string and around which the string is wound.

string-retainer bar Metal bar typically placed behind locking nut to seat strings over curved surface of locking nut prior to locking. Also occasionally used like a string tree to increase behind-the-nut string angle on guitars without nut locks.

string tree Small unit fitted to headstock that maintains downward string-tension at nut.

string winder Device to assist in the speedy winding of a string onto the tuner's string-post.

struts (strutting) Classical-guitar term for braces. See *braces*.

stud tailpiece (stop tailpiece) Type of tailpiece fixed to solid or semi-acoustic guitar top, either as a single combined bridge/tailpiece unit, or else as a unit separate from the bridge.

sunburst Decorative paint finish in which (usually) pale-colored center graduates to darker edges.

superstrat Updated, hot-rodded Fender Stratocaster-inspired design popularized in the '80s with more frets, deeper cutaways, more powerful pickups in a revised layout, and a high-performance (locking) vibrato system.

sustain Length of time a string vibrates. Purposeful elongation of a musical sound, either by playing technique or electronic processing.

sustain block (inertia block) Metal block under the bridgeplate of a floating vibrato (vintage-style Fender, for example) which, because the vibrato is not permanently fixed to the body,

replaces the body mass necessary for sufficient string sustain.

sympathetic resonances Sounds produced by open strings that are not struck.

syncopation Displacement of the normal beat.

synth access Guitar type with a built-in pickup to enable connection to an external synthesizer unit.

synthesizer Electronic instrument for sound creation, using analog techniques (oscillators, filters, amplifiers) or digital techniques (FM or harmonic synthesis, sample-plus-synthesis etc). Preset synthesizers offer a selection of pre-programmed sounds which cannot be varied; programmable types allow the user to vary and store new sounds. Guitar synthesizers at first attempted to build much of the required circuitry into the guitar itself, but the trend now is to synth-access systems. See *synth access*.

system vibrato See *vibrato system*.

tab (tablature) System of musical notation indicating the position of the fingers on frets and strings.

table See *plate, soundboard, top*.

tag See *lug*.

tags See *hang-tags*.

tailpiece Unit on body separate from bridge that anchors strings. See also *trapeze tailpiece, stud tailpiece*.

taper Of a potentiometer: determines how smoothly the resistance is applied as the control is turned down. Most modern pots use a logarithmic taper as opposed to a linear taper.

tapped pickup See *coil-tap*.

Tele Abbreviation of Fender Telecaster, so universally used that Fender have trademarked the name and use it themselves.

thinline Hollowbody electric guitar with especially narrow body depth; term coined originally by Gibson for its Byrdland model introduced in 1955.

three-position switch See *three-way switch*.

three-way switch (three-position switch) Selector switch that offers three options.

through-neck (thru-neck) Neck that travels the complete length of a guitar, "through" the body, and usually with "wings" added to complete the body shape.

tigerstripe Dramatic figure, usually on maple. See *flame*.

timbre Tone quality or "color" or "flavor" of a sound.

tin To apply solder to a wire before making the soldered joint.

tobacco burst Dark red-to-brown sunburst finish originally popularized by Gibson.

toggle switch Type of selector switch that "toggles" between a small number of options. It is sometimes called a leaf switch.

Tolex Trade name of vinyl covering manufactured by DuPont corporation and commonly used by Fender (and some others) on guitar amps and hardshell cases. (Often generically – if incorrectly – used to refer to any vinyl amp covering.)

tone wood Fancy name for wood used in making musical instruments; wood purported to have superior tonal qualities.

top Vibrating face of the guitar. See *soundboard, plate*.

top nut See *nut*.

tranny Short for "transistorized."

Nickname given to solid-state circuitry or equipment.

transcription Adaptation of music originally written/intended for instruments other than guitar; the piece of music that emerges from such an adaptation.

transducer Unit that converts one form of energy to another; the term is sometimes used generically for piezo-electric pickups, but technically applies to any type of pickup or loudspeaker, etc. See *magnetic pickup, piezo pickup*.

transverse bar Bar glued across back of guitar, especially in classical guitar building.

trapeze tailpiece Simple tailpiece of trapezoidal shape.

treble-bleed cap Simple circuit where capacitor (sometimes with an additional resistor) is attached to volume control potentiometer and thus retains high frequencies when the volume control is turned down.

treble pickup See *bridge pickup*.

tree-of-life inlay Very decorative inlay on guitar fingerboard depicting vine-like foliage. Interpreted by a number of manufacturers over the years on high-end models, for example the PRS Rosewood Limited.

tremolo (tremolo arm, tremolo system, trem) Erroneous but much-used term for vibrato device/system. The musical definition of tremolo is the rapid repetition of a note or notes. Perhaps this is why Fender applied the name to its amplifier effect, which is a regular variation in the sound's volume.

triode Tube (valve) containing three functional elements, and most common in the preamp circuits of guitar amplifiers in the form of "dual triodes" – tubes which contain two triodes in a single glass bottle.

truss-rod Metal rod fitted inside the neck, almost always adjustable and which can be used to control neck relief.

truss-rod cover Decorative plate covering truss-rod access hole, usually on headstock.

tube US term for the electrical component that the British call a

valve; an abbreviation of electron(ic) vacuum tube. In a guitar amp, a tube amplifies the input signal by regulating the flow of electrons.

Tune-o-matic Gibson-originated bridge adjustable for overall string height as well as for individual string intonation.

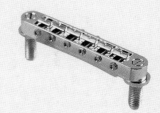

tuner Device almost always fitted to the headstock, one per string, that alters a string's tension and pitch. Also called machine head or (archaically) tuning peg. See also *electronic tuner*.

tuner button Knob that the player moves to turn the tuner mechanism in order to raise or lower a string's pitch.

TV finish Translucent off-white or "limed mahogany" finish used by Gibson on low and medium-priced solidbodys in the '50s, especially certain Les Paul models.

twang Essential element of early rock'n'roll guitar tone, achieved by using bridge pickup on Fender Strat, Gretsch 6120 or similar, and popularized by players such as Duane Eddy.

tweed Linen material used primarily by Fender – but by some other makers as well – to cover guitar cases and amplifier cabinets, originally in the '50s. The term is now generally used to define an amp from that period (such as a '59 Bassman), or the sonic characteristics produced by such amps, or the emulation of such characteristics in modern amps.

12-fret/14-fret Refers to the point at which a flat-top acoustic guitar's neck joins the body.

twin-neck See *double-neck*.

two-pole See *pole*.

'ud Arabic stringed instrument introduced into Spain by the Moors, with important consequences for lute making.

unwound string See *wound string*.

up-bend Upward shift in the strings' pitch brought about by using a vibrato.

up-market See *high-end*.

upper bout See *bout*.

upscale See *high-end*.

valve Short for "thermionic valve;" the British term for electron tube. See *tube*.

Variac Trademarked variable AC transformer. Not a safety transformer.

Varitone Six-way switch fitted to some Gibson semi-solid guitars, typically the ES-345 and ES-355. Linked to network of chokes and capacitors, makes guitar sound like it's played down a telephone line.

varnish Protective and decorative surface applied to guitar bodies. Includes shellac, applied by French polishing, to man-made urethane, applied by spray.

vibrato (slush lever, trem, tremolo, tremolo arm, vibrato bridge, vibrato system, wang bar, whammy) Bridge and/or tailpiece which alters the pitch of the strings when the attached arm is moved. Vibrato is the technically correct term because it means a regular variation in pitch. Also used to define this effect when contained within a guitar amp.

vibrato system System comprising locking vibrato bridge

unit, friction-reducing nut, and locking tuners.

virtuoso Instrumental performer with excellent technical abilities.

V-joint One method of fixing head to neck, or neck to body. More complex than normal splice-joint.

V-neck Describes shape of cross-section of neck on, typically, some older Strats, Teles, and Martins.

waist In-curved shape near the middle of the guitar body, usually its narrowest point.

wang bar See *vibrato*.

Watt Unit of electrical power, commonly used to define the output of guitar amps, the power-handling capabilities of speakers, etc. Technically, the rate that energy is transferred (or work is done) over time, equal to a certain amount of horse-power, or joules per second. Named for James Watt, British pioneer of steam power.

western red cedar Not a cedar at all, but Thuya plicata, the North American arbor vitae, a conifer. First used as a soundboard material by classical guitar maker José Ramírez III and now used by many classical (and some flat-top) builders.

whammy See *vibrato*.

wolf note (wolf tone, dead note) Note with a sound unpleasantly different from or less resonant than those around it. The phenomenon is much affected by the instrument construction, and can be indicative of a minor flaw in a guitar.

wrapover bridge Unit where strings are secured by wrapping them around a curved bar.

X-brace Pattern of bracing in an "X" shape, popularized by Martin.

zero fret Extra fret placed in front of the nut. It provides the start of the string's speaking length and creates the string height at the headstock end of the fingerboard. In this instance the nut is simply used to determine string spacing. Used by some manufacturers to make the tone of the open string and the fretted string more similar.

INDEX
ACKNOWLEDGEMENTS

index

index

Qq

quarter sawn 21
Queen 144
Queensrÿche 226

Rr

Rager, Mose 205
Raitt, Bonnie 179
Ramîrez II **11**, 13
Reed, Jerry **205**,
Reinhardt, Django 23, 205
Renbourn, John **126**
Rhoads, Randy 231
rhythm(s)
    African 260, 262
    blues 180–183, 201–203
    country 214–215
    jazz 287
    Latin 254
    metal 228–229
    rock-pop 142–155
Rice, Tim 19
Richards, Keith **129**, 137, 149
Rickenbacker guitars
    360 **32**, 33
    360/12 **36**
    381V69 36, **37**
    460 **32**, 33
    pickups **38**
riffs 156–159, 210–213,
Rio Grande (pickups) 94
Rivera **43**, **47**
Rocco Company 54
Rodriguez, Manuel **13**
Roland
    JC-120 Jazz Chorus **50**
    Space Echo **55**, 57
Rolling Stones 141, 147
Rolph (pickups) 94
Romero, Pepe **13**
Ross Compressor **54**
Roth, Uli Jon 226
Rush, Otis **179**, 192–**193**
Roth, Arlen 208, 216
Russell, David **273**

Ss

Santa Cruz **19**
Santana, Carlos **33**, 47, 141,
    253, 256
Satriani, Joe **28**, **239**, **241**,
    242
Schaller (tuners) 22, **67**
Schenker, Michael 226
Scofield, John 281
Segovia, Andrés 10, **268**
Selmer Tremolo **56**
Sepultura 226
set-neck guitars 30–31
Seymour Duncan (pickups)
    38, 94–**95**, 97, 103
Shinei Siren/Hurricane **56**
shipping guitars 115
shuffle (rhythm) 182–183
Simon, Paul 259
Skaggs, Ricky **17**
Sky (pickups) 103
Slayer 226
Slipknot 226
slot-head acoustics 68
Smallman, Greg **11**, 13
Smith, Johnny **20**
Smith, Randall 46-47
Smith, Steuart 205
Smiths, The 162, 164
Sola Sound 55
Soldano **47**
soldering techniques 104–105
solid state amps 50–51
soloing (see lead guitar)
Soundgarden 226, **149**
speakers **47**–49
speaker cabinets 48-49
Sperzel (tuners) **64**, **67**
Spin Doctors 154
Squier Stratocaster 44
Standel (amps) 50
Status Quo 144
Stradivari, Antonio 10
Strait, George **212**
Straits, Dire 168, **173**
Stern, Mike 281
Stern, Stephen 23
Steinberger 40

string gauges 66–67
string height 78
string types 17, 62, 66, 69
Stromberg 20, **21**
Sumlin, Hubert 179
strumming patterns 128–129
Summers, Andy 152, 164
Sunn (amps) 49
Super Furry Animals 144
Supro 46, 52
Sutton, Bryan 17
switches (types and
    replacement) 100–103
SWR **53**

Tt

Takamine **18**
Taylor guitars 18, **19**
Taylor, James 14
Television **157**
THD (amps) 47
Thin Lizzy 157
Thompson, Richard **15**
through-neck guitars 32–33
tone woods **10**, 15, **16**, 20–22,
    27, **29**,
tools 112–**113**
Torres, Antonio de **10**-11, 13
Toure, Ali Farke 259
Townshend, Pete 32, 49
Trace Acoustic **53**
Trainwreck (amps) 47
Travis, Merle 205, 216
Travis picking 216–217
T.Rex 144, 145
tremolo effect 56
tremolo tailpiece (see vibrato
    tailpiece)
Trout, Walter, 179
Trower, Robin 56
truss rod 16, 70–71
tubes **44**
tuners (machine heads) 64, 65
    67
turnarounds 185–186
tweed 44–46
two-handed tapping 246–248

Uu

U2 **150**
Uni-Vox Uni-Vibe 56, **57**

Conversion Chart

FRACTIONS OF INCHES	DECIMALS OF INCHES	DECIMALS OF MILLIMETRES
1/64"	0.015625"	0.39687mm
1/32"	0.031250"	0.79375mm
3/64"	0.046875"	1.19061mm
1/16"	0.062500"	1.58750mm
5/64"	0.078125"	1.98435mm
3/32"	0.093750"	2.38125mm
7/64"	0.109375"	2.77809mm
1/8"	0.125000"	3.17500mm
9/64"	0.140625"	3.57183mm
5/32"	0.156250"	3.96875mm
3/16"	0.187500"	4.76250mm
7/32"	0.218750"	5.55625mm
1/4"	0.250000"	6.35000mm
9/32"	0.281250"	7.14375mm
5/16"	0.312500"	7.93750mm
11/32"	0.343750"	8.73125mm
3/8"	0.375000"	9.52500mm
13/32"	0.406250"	10.31875mm
7/16"	0.437500"	11.11250mm
15/32"	0.468750"	11.90625mm
1/2"	0.500000"	12.70000mm
17/32"	0.531250"	13.49375mm
9/16"	0.562500"	14.28750mm
19/32"	0.593750"	15.08125mm
5/8"	0.625000"	15.87500mm
21/32"	0.656250"	16.66875mm
11/16"	0.687500"	17.46250mm
23/32"	0.718750"	18.25625mm
3/4"	0.750000"	19.05000mm
25/32"	0.781250"	19.84375mm
13/16"	0.812500"	20.63750mm
27/32"	0.843750"	21.43125mm
7/8"	0.875000"	22.22500mm
29/32"	0.906250"	23.01875mm
15/16"	0.937500"	23.81250mm
31/32"	0.968750"	24.60625mm
1"	1.000000"	25.40000mm

COMMON FINGERBOARD RADIUSES

7 2/5"	7.400000"	184.00000mm
9 1/5"	9.200000"	241.00000mm
10"	10.000000"	254.00000mm
12"	12.000000"	304.00000mm

COMMON SCALE LENGTHS

22 1/5"	22.200000"	571.00000mm
22 7/10"	22.700000"	577.00000mm
24"	24.000000"	610.00000mm
24 3/5"	24.600000"	625.00000mm
24 3/4"	24.750000"	629.00000mm
25"	25.000000"	635.00000mm
25 1/10"	25.100000"	638.00000mm
25 1/2"	25.500000"	648.00000mm

This comprehensive listing includes the books that were useful to us during the research for this volume, as well as some others that are generally recommended.

Charles Alexander (ed) *Masters Of Jazz Guitar* (Balafon/Miller Freeman 1999)

Tony Bacon *The History Of The American Guitar* (Friedman Fairfax/Balafon 2001); *50 Years Of Fender* (Backbeat 2000); *50 Years Of The Gibson Les Paul* (Backbeat 2002)

Tony Bacon (ed) *Echo & Twang: Classic Guitar Music Of The 50s* (Backbeat 2001); *Electric Guitars: The Illustrated Encyclopedia* (Thunder Bay/Balafon 2000); *Fuzz & Feeback: Classic Guitar Music Of The 60s* (Miller Freeman 2000)

Tony Bacon & Paul Day *The Fender Book* (Miller Freeman/Balafon 2nd edition 1998); *The Gibson Les Paul Book* (Miller Freeman/Balafon 1993); *The Gretsch Book* (Miller Freeman/Balafon 1996); *The Guru's Guitar Guide* (Making Music 2nd edition 1992); *The Rickenbacker Book* (Miller Freeman/Balafon 1994); *The Ultimate Guitar Book* (DK/Knopf 1991)

Tony Bacon & Barry Moorhouse *The Bass Book* (Miller Freeman/Balafon 1995)

Paul Bechtholdt & Doug Tulloch *Guitars From Neptune – Danelectro* (Backporch 1995)

Robert Benedetto *Making An Archtop Guitar* (Centerstream 1994)

David Braid *Play Classical Guitar* (Backbeat 2001)

Dave Burrluck *The Players Guide To Guitar Maintenance* (Miller Freeman/Balafon 1998); *The PRS Guitar Book* (Backbeat 2002)

Walter Carter *Epiphone: The Complete History* (Hal Leonard 1995); *Gibson: 100 Years Of An American Icon* (General Publishing 1994); *History Of The Ovation Guitar* (Hal Leonard 1996); *The Martin Book* (Balafon/Miller Freeman 1995)

Paul Day *The Burns Book* (PP 1979)

A.R. Duchossoir *The Fender Stratocaster* (Mediapresse 1988); *The Fender Telecaster* (Hal Leonard 1991); *Gibson Electrics – The Classic Years* (Hal Leonard 1994)

Tom & Mary Anne Evans *Guitars: Music, History, Construction And Players* (Oxford University Press 1977)

Jim Fisch & L.B. Fred *Epiphone: The House Of Stathopoulo* (Amsco 1996)

S.P. Fjestad *Blue Book Of Guitar Values* (Blue Book 1994)

Ritchie Fliegler *The Complete Guide To Guitar And Amp Maintenance* (Hal Leonard 1994)

Chris Gill *Guitar Legends: The Definitive Guide To The World's Greatest Guitar Players* (Studio Editions 1995)

Alan Greenwood *Vintage Guitar Magazine Price Guide* (VG Books 1998)

Hugh Gregory *1000 Great Guitarists* (Balafon/Miller Freeman 1994)

George Gruhn & Walter Carter *Electric Guitars And Basses* (Miller Freeman 1994); *Acoustic Guitars & Other Fretted Instruments* (Miller Freeman 1993); *Gruhn's Guide To Vintage Guitars* (Miller Freeman 2nd edition 1999)

Phil Hardy & Dave Laing *The Faber Companion To 20th-Century Popular Music* (Faber 1990)

Steve Howe & Tony Bacon *The Steve Howe Guitar Collection* (Miller Freeman/Balafon 1994)

Adrian Ingram *The Gibson ES-175* (Music Maker 1994)

JTG Gibson *Shipping Totals 1946-1979* (JTG 1992)

Colin Larkin (ed) The *Guinness Encyclopedia Of Popular Music* (Guinness 1992)

John Morrish (ed) *The Classical Guitar: A Complete History* (Backbeat 2002); *The Fender Amp Book* (Balafon/Miller Freeman 1995)

Hans Moust *The Guild Guitar Book 1952-1977* (GuitArchives 1995)

Michael Naglav *Höfner Guitars – Made In Germany* (Musikkeller undated c1996)

Kevin O'Connor *Principles Of Power* (Power Press 1999); *Ready Set Go!* (Power Press 1996); *The Ultimate Tone* (Power Press 1995); *Tonnes Of Tone* (Power Press 1996)

David Petersen & Dick Denney *The Vox Story* (Bold Strummer 1993)

Aspen Pittman *The Tube Amp Book* (Groove Tubes 1995)

Norbert Schnepel & Helmuth Lemme *Elektro-Gitarren Made In Germany* English translation J P Klink (Musik-Verlag Schnepel-Lemme 1988)

Pete Prown & H.P. Newquist *Legends Of Rock Guitar* (Hal Leonard 1997)

Rittor *60s Bizarre Guitars* (Rittor 1993)

Rikky Rooksby *How to Write Songs On Guitar* (Miller Freeman/Balafon 2000)

Jay Scott *Gretsch: The*

Guitars Of The Fred Gretsch Company (Centerstream 1992); *50s Cool: Kay Guitars* (Seventh String Press 1992)

Harry Shapiro & Caesar Glebbeek *Jimi Hendrix: Electric Gypsy* (Heinemann 1990)

Mary Alice Shaughnessy *Les Paul: An American Original* (Morrow 1993)

Robert Shaw *Great Guitars* (Hugh Lauter Levin 1997)

Richard R. Smith *Complete History Of Rickenbacker Guitars* (Centerstream 1987); *Fender: The Sound Heard 'Round The World* (Garfish 1995)

John Teagle *Washburn: Over 100 Years Of Fine Stringed Instruments* (Amsco 1996)

Paul Trynka (ed) *The Electric Guitar* (Virgin 1993); *Rock Hardware – 40 Years Of Rock Instrumentation* (Balafon/Miller Freeman 1996)

James Tyler *The Early Guitar: A History & Handbook* (Oxford University Press 1980)

Thomas A Van Hoose *The Gibson Super 400* (GPI 1991)

Tom Wheeler *American Guitars* (HarperPerennial 1990)

Michael Wright *Guitar Stories Volume 1: The Histories Of Cool Guitars* (Vintage Guitar Books 1995)

YMM Player *History Of Electric Guitars* (Player Corporation 1988)

Principal guitar, amp and effects photography was by Miki Slingsby. Most of the reproductions are from the Balafon Image Bank. Other images were supplied by *The Guitar Magazine*, *Guitarist*, C.F. Martin, Pignose, Randall, and Roland. All music notation files were produced by Cambridge Notation.

Special thanks to Tom Anderson; Martin Hartwell at Akai UK; Danny Jones at Arbiter; Rick Batey; Robert and Cindy Benedetto; Chris Francis at Cambridge Notation; Celestion; Charlie Chandler, Paula Chandler, and all at Chandler Guitars; Paul Day; FCN Music; Robbie Gladwell; Jess Hunter; Simon Weir and the team at *The Guitar Magazine*; Neville Martin and all at *Guitarist*; Gibson Keddy at John Hornby Skewes & Co.; Nico Dupas at Line 6 Europe; Dick Boak at C.F. Martin; Ken Parker; Ben Allen at Rosetti.

Trademarks
Throughout this book many trademarked names are used. Rather than put a trademark symbol next to every occurrence of a trademarked name, we state here that we are using the names only in an editorial fashion, primarily as references to standard industry designs, and that we do not intend to infringe any trademarks.

Owners credits
Guitars photographed were owned at the time of photography by the following individuals and organizations, and we are most grateful for their help.

The Acoustic Centre; Akai UK; Terry Anthony; Arbiter Group; Scot Arch; Aria UK; Chet Atkins; Tony Bacon; Robin Baird; Colin Barker; Barnes & Mullins; The Bass Centre; Jeff Beck; Steve Boyer; Dave Brewis; Brian Moore Custom Guitars; Clive Brown; Ron Brown; Burns London; Dave Burrluck; Simon Carlton; Julian Carter; Carvin Guitars; Doug Chandler; Chandler Guitars; Chinery Collection; Eric Clapton; Don Clayton; Russell Cleveland; Brian Cohen; Country Music Hall Of Fame; Neville Crozier; Paul Day; Chris DiPinto; Jerry Donahue; Mark Duncan; Dynamic Audio Industries; Duane Eddy; Edinburgh University Collection; EMD International; John Entwistle; FCN Music; Fender Japan; Fender Musical Instruments; Fred Gretsch Enterprises; Lou Gatanas; Debbie German; David Gilmour; Dave Gregory; Gruhn Guitars; Robin Guthrie; Horniman Museum; Alan Hardtke; George Harrison; Head Stock; Keith Henderson; Tony Hicks; Rick Hogue; Adrian Hornbrook; Steve Howe; Adrian Ingram; James Tyler Guitars; Jim Jannard; Scott Jennings; Gerard Johnson; Joe Johnson; Clive Kay; Korg UK; Andrew Large; Jay Levin; Adrian Lovegrove; Garry Malone; Mandolin Brothers; Phil Manzanera; Martin Guitars; Bill Marsh; Graeme Matheson; Paul McCartney; Charles Measures; Paul Midgeley; Modulus Guitars; Albert Molinaro; Gary Moore; Lars Mullen; Music & Audio Distribution; Music Ground; John Nelson; Carl Nielsen; David Noble; Marc Noel-Johnson; Steve Ostromogilsky; Jimmy Page; Peavey Electronics; Nick Peraticos; PRS Guitars; Bill Puplett; Pat Quilter; Patrick Eggle Guitars; Buzz Peters; Tim Philips; Arthur Ramm; John Reynolds; Rickenbacker International; Alan Rogan; Rosetti; Todd Rundgren; Carlos Santana; Schecter Guitars; Floyd Scholz; Selectron; Sensible Music; John Sheridan; John Hornby Skewes; Nicky Skopelitis; John Smith; Sotheby's; Robert Spencer; Strings & Things; TE.D; Teuffel Guitars; Tom Anderson Guitarworks; Paul Unkert; Valley Arts Guitars; Veillette Guitars; Arthur Vitale; Washburn UK; Mick Watts; Bert Weedon; Bruce Welch; Paul Westlake; Lew Weston; Robert Witte; Michael Wright; Yamaha-Kemble Music; Bryan Zajchowski